# Indian Battles, Captivities, and Adventures, from the Earliest Period to the Present Time

## John Frost

Frost

7-HBC

INDIANS TORTURING A PRISONER.   Page 67

# INDIAN BATTLES

## CAPTIVITIES AND ADVENTURES

NEW YORK
J. C. DERBY

1 _____ ' — Wars
2 ____ "        "  — Caghuston,

# INDIAN BATTLES,

# CAPTIVITIES,

## AND

# ADVENTURES.

### FROM THE EARLIEST PERIOD TO THE PRESENT TIME.

### EDITED BY JOHN FROST, LL.D.

**WITH MANY ILLUSTRATIONS.**

### NEW YORK:

DERBY & JACKSON, 119 NASSAU STREET.

CINCINNATI:—H. W. DERBY & CO.

1857.

# CONTENTS.

|  | PAGE |
|---|---|
| DISCOVERY OF AMERICA BY CHRISTOPHER COLUMBUS,......... | 5 |
| LANDING OF OUR FOREFATHERS AT PLYMOUTH,.... ..... ..... | 13 |
| COMMENCEMENT OF HOSTILITIES WITH THE NATIVES,.... ...... | 24 |
| WASHINGTON'S EXPEDITION IN 1758, AND DEFEAT OF GENERAL BRADDOCK BY THE INDIANS IN 1755,.... ... ..... ..... .... | 88 |
| EXPEDITION AND DEFEAT OF GENERAL HARMER BY THE INDIANS, 1790.. ..... .... .... ....... .... .... .... ..... ...... | 89 |
| EXPEDITIONS OF GENERALS SCOTT AND WILKINSON IN MAY AND AUGUST, 1791,.... .... ... .... .... .... ... .... .... .... | 94 |
| DEFEAT OF GENERAL ST. CLAIR BY THE INDIANS, 1791,........ | 109 |
| DEPREDATIONS OF THE INDIANS ON THE FRONTIERS IN 1791, 1792, AND 1793,.... .... .... .... ... .... .... .... .... .... | 118 |
| DEFEAT OF THE INDIANS BY GEN. WAYNE, AUGUST 20, 1794,..... | 122 |
| A NARRATIVE OF THE CAPTIVITY OF MRS. JOHNSON, ......... | 128 |
| BURNING OF ROYALTON,..... ..... ..... ..... ..... .... | 183 |
| CAPTIVITY OF ZADOCK STEELE,.... .... .... ..... ..... .... | 209 |
| EVENTS ON THE NORTH WESTERN FRONTIER FROM 1794 TO 1811, | 277 |
| TIPPECANOE WAR,..... .... .... .... .... .... .... .... | 284 |
| SURRENDER OF DETROIT,.... ..... ..... .... ...... ..... | 290 |
| DEFENCE OF FORT HARRISON,.... ..... ..... ..... ..... .... | 297 |
| EVENTS OF NORTH WESTERN FRONTIER DURING 1813, ......... | 303 |
| THE CREEK WAR,..... ..... ..... ..... ..... ..... ..... | 315 |
| THE BLACK HAWK WAR,.... ..... ..... ..... ..... ..... | 359 |
| THE FLORIDA WAR,..... ..... ..... ..... ..... ..... ..... | 365 |
| INCIDENTS IN THE BORDER WARS OF THE MEXICAN INDIANS,..... | 378 |
| RECENT INCIDENTS IN THE TEXAS AND MEXICAN BORDER WARS,.. | 392 |

# INDIAN NARRATIVES.

---

## DISCOVERY OF AMERICA BY CHRISTOPHER COLUMBUS.

MANKIND owe the discovery of the western world to the gold, the silver, the precious stones, the spices, silks, and costly manufactures of the East; and even those incentives were for a considerable time insufficient to prompt to the undertaking, although the most skilful navigator of the age proffered to risk his life in the attempt.

Christopher Columbus, who was destined to the high honor of revealing a new hemisphere to Europeans, was by birth a Genoese, who had been early trained to a seafaring life, and, having acquired every branch of knowledge connected with that profession, was no less distinguished by his skill and abilities than for his intrepid and persevering spirit. This man, when about forty years of age, had formed the great idea of reaching the East Indies by sailing westward; but as his fortune was very small, and the attempt required very effectual patronage, desirous that his native country should profit by his success, he laid his plan before the senate of Genoa; but the scheme appearing chimerical, it was rejected. He then repaired to the court of Portugal; and although the Portuguese were at that time distinguished for their commercial spirit, and John II., who then reigned, was a discerning and enterprising prince, yet the prepossessions of the great men in his court, to whom the matter was referred, caused Columbus finally to fail in his attempt there also.   He next applied to Ferdinand and Isabella, King and Queen of Arragon and Castile, and at the same time sent his brother Bartholomew (who followed the same profession, and who was well qualified to fill the immediate place under such a leader) to England, to lay the proposal before Henry VII., which likewise, very fortunately for the future well being of the country, met with no success.   Many were the years which Christopher Columbus spent in ineffectual attendance at the Castilian court; the impoverished state into which the finances of the united kingdoms were reduced, the war with Grenada, repressing every disposition to attempt to great designs; but the war being at length terminated, the powerful mind of Isabella broke through all obstacles : she declared herself the patroness of Columbus; whilst her husband, Ferdinand, declining to partake as an adventurer in the voyage, only gave it the sanction of his name. Thus did the superior genius of a *woman* effect the discovery of one half of the globe.

The ships sent on this important search were only three in number, two of them very small; they had ninety men on board.   Although the expense of the expedition had long remained the sole obstacle to its being undertaken, yet, when every thing was provided, the cost did not amount to more than seventeen thousand seven hundred and sixty dollars, and there were twelve months' provision put on board.

Columbus set sail from Port Palos, in the Province of Andalusia, on the 2d of August, 1492: he proceeded to the Canary Islands, and from thence directed his course due west, in the latitude of about 28 north.   In this course he continued for two months without falling in with any land, which caused such a spirit of discontent and mutiny to arise as the superior address and management of the commander became unequal to suppress, although for these qualities he was eminently distinguished.   He was at length reduced to the necessity of entering into a solemn engagement to abandon the enterprise and return home if land did not appear in three days. Probably he would not have been able to retain his people so long from acts of violence and outrage, in pursuing so untried and dreary a course, had they not been sensible that their safety in returning home depended very much on his skill as a navigator in conducting the vessel.

At length the appearance of land changed their despondency to the most exulting rapture. It was an island abounding with inhabitants, both sexes of which were quite naked, their manners kind, gentle, and unsuspecting. Columbus named it San Salvador; it is one of the cluster which bears the general name of Bahama; it was only 3° 30' latitude to the south of the Island of Gomora, one of the Canaries, from whence he took his departure. This navigator was still so confirmed in the opinion which he had formed before he undertook the voyage that he believed himself then to be on an island which was situated adjacent to the Indies. Proceeding to the south, he saw three other islands, which he named St. Mary of the Conception, Ferdinand, and Isabella. At length he arrived at a very large island; and as he had taken seven of the natives of San Salvador on board, he learned from them it was called Cuba; but he gave it the name of Juanna. He next proceeded to an island which he called Espagniola, in honor of the kingdom by which he was employed; and it still bears the name of Hispaniola. Here he built a fort and formed a small settlement; he then returned home, having on board some of the natives whom he had taken from the different islands. Steering a more southern course, he fell in with some of the Caribbee Islands, and arrived at the port of Palos on the 15th of March, 1493, having been seven months and eleven days on this most important voyage.

On his arrival letters patent were issued by the king and queen, confirming to Columbus and to his heirs all the privileges contained in a capitulation which had been executed before his departure, and his family was ennobled.

Not only the Spaniards, but the other nations of Europe, seem to have adopted the opinion of Columbus, in considering the countries which he had discovered as a part of India — whence Ferdinand and Isabella gave them the name " Indies," in the ratification of their former agreement with Columbus. Even after the error was detected the name was retained; and the appellation of " West Indies " is now given by all Europe to this country, and that of Indians to the inhabitants.

Nothing could possibly tend more effectually to rouse every active principle of human nature than the discoveries which Columbus had made; no time was therefore lost, no expense spared, in preparing a fleet of ships with which this great man should revisit the countries he had made known. Seventeen ships were got ready in six months, and fifteen hundred persons embarked on board them, among whom were many of noble families and who had filled honorable stations. These engaged in the enterprise from the expectation that the new-discovered country was either the Cipango of Marco Paulo, or the Ophir from which Solomon obtained his gold and precious merchandise. Ferdinand, now desirous of securing what he had before been unwilling to venture for the obtaining, applied to the pope to be invested with a right in these new-discovered countries, as well as to all future discoveries in that direction; but as it was necessary that there should be some favor of religion in the business, he founded his plea on a desire of converting the savage natives to the Romish faith, which plan had its desired effect.

Alexander VI., who then filled the Papal chair, it ought to be mentioned, was the most profligate and abandoned of men. Being a native of Arragon, and desirous of conciliating the favor of Ferdinand for the purpose of aggrandizing his family, he readily granted a request which, at no expense or risk, tended to extend the consequence and authority of the Papacy; he therefore bestowed on Ferdinand and Isabella " all the countries inhabited by infidels which they had discovered." But as it was necessary to prevent this grant from interfering with one not long before made to the crown of Portugal, he appointed that a line, supposed to be drawn from pole to pole, one hundred leagues to the westward of the Azores, should serve as a limit between them; and in the plenitude of his power conferred all to the east of this imaginary line upon the Portuguese, and all to the west of it upon the Spaniards.

Columbus set sail on his voyage from the Port of Cadiz on the 25th of September, 1493: when he arrived at St. Espagniola, he had the affliction to find that all the Spaniards whom he had left there, amounting to thirty-six in number, had been put to death, by the natives, in revenge for the insults and outrages which they had committed. After having traced out the plan of a town in a large plain near a spacious bay, and given it the name of Isabella in honor of his patroness the Queen of Castile, and appointed his brother Don Diego to preside as deputy governor in his absence, Columbus, on the 24th of April, 1494, sailed with one ship and two small barks to make further discoveries in those seas. In this voyage he was employed five months, and fell in with many small islands on the coast of Cuba, but with none of any importance except the Island of Jamaica.

Soon after his return to Hispaniola he resolved to make war with the Indians, who, according to the Spanish historians, amounted to one hundred thousand men; these, having experienced every lawless act of violence from their invaders, were rendered extremely inveterate, and thirsted for revenge, a disposition which appears to have been foreign from their natures. Having collected his full force, he attacked them by night whilst they were assembled on a wide plain, and obtained a most decisive victory, without the loss of one man on his part. Besides the effect of cannon and firearms, the noise of which was appalling, and their effect against a numerous body of Indians, closely drawn together, in the highest degree destructive, Columbus had brought over with him a small body of cavalry. The Indians, who had never before seen such a creature, imagined the Spanish horses to be rational beings, and that each, with its rider, formed but one animal: they were astonished at their speed, and considered their impetuosity and strength as irresistible. In this onset they had, beside, another formidable enemy to terrify and destroy them: a great number of the largest and fiercest species of dogs which were then bred in Europe had been brought hither, which, set on by their weapons, without attempting resistance, they fled with all the speed which terror could excite. Numbers were slain, and more made prisoners, who were immediately consigned to slavery.

The character of Columbus stands very high in the estimation of mankind; he is venerated not only as a man possessing superior fortitude, and such a steady perseverance as no impediment, dangers, or sufferings could shake, but as equally distinguished for piety and virtue. His second son, Ferdinand, who wrote the Life of his father, apologizes for this severity towards the natives on account of the distressed state into which the colony was brought: the change of climate, and the indispensable labors which were required of men unaccustomed to any exertions, had swept away great numbers of the new settlers, and the survivors were declining daily; whilst such was the irreconcilable enmity of the natives, that the most kind and circumspect conduct on the part of the Spaniards would not have been effectual to regain their good will. This apology seems to have been generally admitted; for all modern writers have bestowed upon the discoverer of the new world the warmest commendations unmixed with censure. It is an unpleasant task to derogate from exalted merit, and to impute a deliberate plan of cruelty and extirpation to a man revered for moral worth; but although a pert affectation of novel opinions could only originate in weak minds, and can be countenanced only by such, yet a free and unreserved scrutiny of facts can alone separate truth from error, and apportion the just and intrinsic degree of merit belonging to any character. That Columbus had forméd the design of waging offensive war against the Indians, and reducing them to slavery, before he entered upon his second voyage, and, consequently, before he was apprised of the destruction of the people which he had left upon the Island of Hispaniola, may be inferred from his proceeding himself with such a number of fierce and powerful dogs.

Having found the natives peaceable and well disposed, he had no reason to apprehend that they would commence unprovoked hostilities : the cavalry which he took over, whilst it tended to impress those people with the deepest awe and veneration, was fully sufficient for the security of the new colony, if the friendship of the natives had been sincerely meant to be cultivated by a kind and equitable deportment; but to treat them as a free people was inconsistent with the views which led to planting a colony; for as the grand incentive to undertake the distant voyages was the hope of acquiring gold, so, as Columbus had seen some worn as ornaments by the natives, and had been informed that the mountainous parts of the country yielded that precious metal, he had excited expectations in his employers, and in the nation at large, which both his interest and ambition compelled him as far as possible to realize. The Spaniards could not obtain gold without the assistance of the natives, and those were so constitutionally indolent that no allurements of presents or gratifications could excite them to labor. To rescue himself therefore from disgrace, and to secure further support, he seems deliberately to have devoted a harmless race of men to slaughter and slavery. Such as survived the massacre of that dreadful day and preserved their freedom fled into the mountains and inaccessible parts of the island, which not yielding them sufficient means of resistance, they were compelled to obtain a portion of food from their cruel pursuers by obtaining gold dust in order to support life; a tribute being imposed upon them which was rigorously exacted. These wretched remains of a free people, thus driven from fruitfulness and amenity, compelled to labor for the support of life, a prey to despondency, which the recollection of their former happiness sharpened, and which their hopeless situation rendered insupportable, died in great numbers, the innocent but unrevenged victims of European avarice. Such are the facts which have ever been admitted; yet, strange contradiction! Columbus is celebrated for his humanity and goodness. But should he not rather be considered as a most consummate dissembler, professing moderation while he meditated subversion, and, like most of the heroes and conquerors whom history records, renouncing every principle of justice and humanity when they stopped the career of his ambition? Ferdinand Columbus, his son and biographer, has with great address covered the shame of his father; whilst the admiring world has been little disposed to censure a man the splendor of whose actions so powerfully fascinates and dazzles.

# LANDING OF OUR FOREFATHERS AT PLYMOUTH.

THE English, conducted by John Cabot, in the year 1497, found the way to North America soon after Columbus had successfully crossed the Atlantic; but as the torrents in that country brought down no gold, and the Indians were not bedecked with any costly ornaments, no attempts were made to explore the country for near a century after its discovery. Sir Francis Drake, who traversed the whole circumference of the globe in one voyage and in one ship, which had never been achieved before, when afterwards annoying the Spaniards in the West Indies and on the main, gained some knowledge of the eastern shore of the northern continent, as he had before of the western parts about the same parallel. Sir Walter Raleigh, however, was the first navigator who explored the coast, bestowed on it a name, and attempted to settle a colony.

At that time colonization made no part of the system of government, so that there were few stimulants to abandon a native soil for the purpose of seeking possession in another hemisphere. At length a powerful incentive arose, stronger than the influence of kings, than the love of ease, than the dread of misery. Religion, which had long been converted into the most powerful engine which human subtlety ever made use of to subjugate the mass of mankind, no sooner ceased to be so perverted than by its own proper force it compelled large bodies of people to renounce every present enjoyment, the instinctive love of a native soil, rooted habits,

2 (13)

and dearest connections, and to settle in the dreary wilds of a far-distant continent.

When England, by a very singular concurrence of circumstances, threw off the Papal yoke, state policy so predominated in the measure that the consciences of men were still required to bend to the discipline, conform to the ceremonials, and assent to the doctrines which the governing powers established. Although a dissent from the church of Rome was considered as meritorious, yet a dissent from the church of England was held to be heretical, and an offence to be punished by the civil magistrate. The human mind, somewhat awakened from a long suspension of its powers by a Wickliffe, further enlightened by an Erasmus and Melancthon, and at length called forth into energy by the collusion of those two ardent and daring spirits, Luther and Calvin, then began to bend all its attention towards religious inquiries, and exercised all its powers in such pursuits. Hence arose a vast diversity of opinions, which gave rise to numerous sects and denominations of Christians; but as the Protestant establishment in England held it essential to preserve a unity of faith, those novel opinions obtained no more quarter there than under Papal power.

In the year 1610 a company of persecuted religionists, composing the church of a Mr. Robinson, having previously determined to remove to a country where they might be enabled to worship God agreeably to the dictates of their consciences, emigrated to Holland, and settled in the city of Leyden, where they continued to reside until the year 1620. Although the ecclesiastical laws of Holland did not at this time sanction or condemn the principles of any particular sect of Christians, yet great were the disadvantages under which the emigrants labored; for, notwithstanding the Dutch gave them a welcome reception, and manifested a disposition to treat them with great respect, they never could be prevailed upon by the former to conform to their mode of worship, or to renounce principles which the English conceived destructive to moral society; nor did the emigrants here succeed in other respects agreeable to their views. So far from increasing their little flock, they found that, in the course of ten years, they had experienced a diminution of more than one half their original number; many, in consequence of the impoverished state of the country, had spent their estates and returned to England. Hence it was that the remaining few formed the determination of attempting once more to seek a country better adapted to their pious purposes, and such as would promise a more fruitful abode to their offspring. By some the unexplored parts of America were proposed; and after a day set apart for solemn humiliation and praise to Almighty God, it was resolved that a part of the church should first emigrate to America, and, if there meeting with a favorable reception, should prepare an abode for the remainder.

They easily obtained a royal grant of a very extensive tract of land now called New England, whither they intended to repair, not to amass wealth or to exterminate the inhabitants, but to subsist by industry, to purchase security by honorable intercourse with the natives, and to acquire strength under the auspices of freedom.

They made a purchase of two small ships, and on the 5th of August, 1620, having repaired to Plymouth, England, for the purpose, were in readiness to embark; previous to which they were very affectionately addressed by their pious pastor, Dr. Robinson, who, in fervent prayer, commended them to the holy keeping of Him who rules the destinies of all men.

At 11 A. M., with a fair wind, they set sail, and bade adieu forever to their native country. Nothing material occurred to obstruct their passage until the 20th, when they experienced a tremendous gale, which threatened them with instant destruction. For three days successively they were tossed about at the mercy of the waves: the ships were, however, enabled to keep company until the storm had somewhat abated, when those on board one of them, conceiving their vessel no longer seaworthy, abandoned her, and were received on board the other.

On the 10th of November, they, to their inexpressible joy, discovered land, which proved to be that of Cape Cod, where they with much difficulty the day following succeeded in landing: as soon as on shore, they fell upon their knees and returned thanks to the Almighty for enabling them to reach in safety their place of destination. But, although they had thus far succeeded in their views, although they had been enabled to flee from persecution, to cross a wide and boisterous ocean, what was their situation now! Sojourners in a foreign land, — traversing the broken and unwrought shores of a wild and unexplored country, — they found here no friends to welcome them, or house to shelter them from the inclemency of an approaching winter. On one side they beheld nought but a hideous and desolate wilderness, the habitation of wild and ferocious animals, and probably the abode of a race of beings not less wild and unmerciful; on the other the briny ocean, foaming and with tremendous roar dashing against the huge and projecting rocks, which, as far as the eye could perceive, marked the sea-beaten shores.

After succeeding with much difficulty in discovering a harbor in which their ship could ride with safety, they made choice of ten of the most resolute of their number to explore the adjacent country, and discover, if possible, a more convenient place for their future abode; who, on the morning of the 16th, provided with a musket each, set out for this purpose. They had not penetrated the woods above three miles when they discovered five of the natives, which were the first seen by them since their arrival. They were clothed with the skins of animals, and armed with bows and arrows. The English, with signs of friendship, made towards them, but were no sooner discovered by the savages than they, with a terrible yell, fled with the greatest precipitancy. Night approaching, the English erected a small temporary encampment, and, after placing their sentinels, retired to rest. Early the ensuing morning they continued their journey, following for a considerable distance the tracks of the five Indians above mentioned, in hopes thereby to discover their habitations and obtain therefrom a fresh supply of provision, of which they were in much want; but in this they did not fully succeed. At about noon they arrived at an extensive plat of clear ground, near which they discovered a pond of fresh water, and several small hillocks of raised earth, which they conjectured to be the graves of the Indians. Proceeding a little farther west, they discovered a large quantity of stubble, which they imagined to be that of some kind of Indian grain peculiar to the country; they also discovered a spot where they suspected an Indian hut had recently stood, as they found near by some planks curiously wrought and a small earthen pot. Proceeding still farther, they discovered a number more of the little hillocks of broken ground as above described, and which they now began to suspect to be the place of deposit of something more than the dead. Curiosity leading them to examine more closely one of these what they had before supposed to be Indian sepulchres, they, to their great surprise, found it to contain a large quantity of the Indian grain (corn) above mentioned. It was still in the ear, and excited to no small degree the curiosity of the English, as they had never before seen any thing of the kind. By a few of the company the discovery was deemed of importance; but by others, who had attempted to eat of the corn in its raw state, it was pronounced indifferent food, of little value. They, however, concluded it best to return and make known the discovery to their brethren.

Having succeeded with some difficulty in reaching the place from which they started, they were met by those whom they had left behind with the most unspeakable joy and satisfaction; to whom they exhibited a specimen of the grain which they had found, and recommended the spot from which it was procured as the most convenient and suitable at which to abide during the approaching winter. The company accordingly, on the 25th, proceeded for and in safety reached the place above mentioned, with which, being so much pleased, they termed New Plymouth, in remembrance of the port at which they last embarked in Europe. Here they concluded to abide until such time as further discoveries could be made. They erected a few temporary huts, sufficient to shelter them from the weather, and soon after, by mutual consent, entered into a solemn combination as a body politic; and, on the 10th of December, assembled to form for themselves such a government and laws as they should deem the most just and equitable; previous to which the following instrument was drawn up, which, being first read and assented to by the company, received their signatures, to wit: —

"In the name of God, amen. We, whose names are underwritten, the loyal subjects of our dread sovereign King James, by the grace of God King of Great Britain, France, and Ireland, and defender of the faith, &c., having undertaken, for the glory of God, advancement of the Christian faith, and the honor of our king and country, a voyage to plant the first colony in the northern parts of America, do by these presents solemnly and mutually, in the presence of God and one another, covenant and combine ourselves together into a civil body politic for our own convenience and the preservation and support of the ends aforesaid; and by virtue hereof do enact, constitute, and frame such just and equal laws, ordinances, acts, constitution, and officers, from time to time, as shall be thought most meet and convenient for the general good of the colony, unto which we promise all due submission and obedience.   In witness whereof, we have hereunto subscribed our names, at New Plymouth, on the 10th day of December, A. D. 1620.

| | |
|---|---|
| John Carver, | John Alden, |
| William Bradford, | John Turner, |
| Edward Winslow, | Francis Eaton, |
| William Brewster, | James Chilton, |
| Isaac Allerton, | John Craxton, |
| Miles Standish, | John Billington, |
| Joseph Fletcher, | Richard Bitteridge, |
| John Goodman, | George Soule, |
| Samuel Fuller, | Edward Tilley, |
| Christopher Martin, | John Tilley, |
| William White, | Thomas Rogers, |
| Richard Warren, | Thomas Tinker, |
| John Howland, | John Ridgdale, |
| Stephen Hopkins, | Edward Fuller, |
| Didgery Priest, | Richard Clarke, |
| Thomas Williams, | Richard Gardiner, |
| Gilbert Winslow, | John Allerton, |
| Edmund Morgeson, | Thomas English, |
| Peter Brown, | Edward Liester." |

The company next proceeded by ballot to the choice of a governor; and, on counting the votes, it appeared that John Carver had the greatest number, and was declared chosen for one year.

On the 19th of December, Mrs. Susannah White, the wife of William White, was delivered of a son, which was the first born of the English in New England.

On the 21st it was agreed by the company to despatch a second exploring party by water, to make, if possible, further discoveries.  The persons selected for this purpose were Governor Carver, Messrs. Bradford, Winslow, Standish, Howland, Warren, Hopkins, Allerton, Tilley, Clarke, Tinker, Turner,

and Brown : they embarked at 10 A. M., with a view of
circumnavigating the deep bay of Cape Cod.  On the morning of the 23d they discovered a large party of the natives
on shore, who were employed in cutting up a fish resembling
a grampus.   By order of Governor Carver, the English
made immediately for the shore ; but were no sooner discovered by the Indians than they, with a yell peculiar to savages,
deserted their fish and fled with precipitancy.  The English
landed and took possession of the fish, which, having enkindled
a fire, they cooked, and found to be excellent food.  They concluded to continue encamped here through the night ; and
while employed a few rods from their boat, in which their
arms were deposited, in erecting a temporary dwelling for
the purpose, they were suddenly attacked by a large party
of the natives, who discharged a shower of arrows among
them.   The English, nearly panic-struck at so sudden and
unexpected an onset, were on the eve of retreating to their
boat, when they were reminded by their governor (a brave
and experienced man) of the importance of facing the enemy
and maintaining their ground, as a precipitate flight might
prove their total destruction : in the mean time two or three
of the company were despatched for their arms, which having
obtained, the whole were ordered to form a close body and
proceed with moderate pace for the boat, and, if hard pushed
by the natives, to face about and give them the contents of
their muskets.  The Indians, perceiving the English retiring,
rushed from their strong coverts, and were on the point of
attacking them in the rear with clubs, hatchets, stones, &c.,
when they received the fire of the latter, which brought three
or four of them to the ground.  The Indians halted, viewed
for a few moments, with marks of astonishment and surprise,
their wounded brethren, and then, with one general, united
yell, which probably might have been heard at the distance
of three miles, fled in every direction.  This was the first
engagement between the English and natives in New England,

and probably the first time that the latter had ever heard the report of a musket.

The English embarked and returned immediately to New Plymouth, having been absent four days without making any important discoveries. The company despairing of making any further discovery of importance during the winter, concluded to remain at their winter quarters until the spring ensuing. The winter proved an uncommonly tedious one, during which a great proportion of the company sickened and died: unaccustomed to hardship, and deprived of many of the necessaries of life, they fell victims to the inclemency of the season. Being thus reduced to a very small number, they would have fallen an easy prey to the savages had the latter (relying on the superiority of their strength) attacked them; but the natives having by bitter experience learned the effects of their firearms, although they were daily seen by the English at a distance, not one of them could be prevailed upon to approach them within gunshot until about the 20th of March, 1621, when, to their great surprise, an Indian came boldly up to them and addressed them in broken English. He informed them that he belonged to an eastern part of the country, and was acquainted with a number of their countrymen, who came frequently there to procure fish, and of whom he learned to speak their language.

This Indian proved very serviceable to the company, in supplying them with provision, in acquainting them with the state of the country, the number and strength of the natives, and the name of their chief sachem, to whom he said the land which they improved belonged. The Indian being dismissed with many presents and friendly assurances, he the day following returned, accompanied by the grand sachem (Massasoiet) and a number of his chief men, to whom the English gave a welcome reception, presenting them with many trinkets which the natives esteemed of great value. With Massasoiet a treaty was proposed and concluded the day following,

in which it was stipulated that the English and natives were
to live amicably together, and that the latter were to furnish
the former with provision, and to receive in pay therefor such
articles as the former were willing to part with; to which
terms both parties continued ever after faithfully to adhere.

In May, 1621, the English planted their first corn in New
England. In July following their worthy governor sickened
and died. His death was greatly lamented by those of the
company who survived him, and by whom he was interred
with all possible solemnity. His loving consort survived him
but a few weeks. In August the company made choice of
Mr. William Bradford to fill the vacancy occasioned by the
death of Governor Carver.

New England from this period began to be rapidly peopled
by the Europeans: so great was the emigration from the
mother country, that, in less than six years from the time that
the first adventurers landed at New Plymouth, there were
seven considerable towns built and settled in Massachusetts
and Plymouth colonies.

In the summer of 1627 Mr. Endicot, one of the original
planters, was sent over to begin a plantation at Naumkeag,
(now Salem.) The June following about two hundred persons, furnished with four ministers, came over and joined
Mr. Endicot's colony; and the next year they formed themselves into a regular church. This was the first church gathered in Massachusetts, and the second in New England. The
church at Plymouth had been gathered eight years before.
In 1629 a large embarkation was projected by the company in
England: at the request of a number of respectable gentlemen,
most of whom afterwards came over to New England, the general consent of the company was obtained that the government
should be transferred and settled in Massachusetts.

In 1630 seventeen ships from different ports in England
arrived in Massachusetts with more than fifteen hundred
passengers, among whom were many persons of distinction.

Incredible were the hardships they endured: reduced to a scanty pittance of provisions, and that of a kind to which they had not been accustomed, and destitute of necessary accommodations, numbers sickened and died; so that, before the end of the year, they lost two hundred of their number. About this time settlements were made at Charlestown, Boston, Dorchester, Cambridge, Roxbury, and Medford.

In the years 1632 and 1633 great additions were made to the colony. Such was the rage for emigration to New England that the king and council thought fit to issue an order, February 7, 1633, to prevent it. The order, however, was not strictly obeyed.

In 1635 the foundation of a new colony was laid in Connecticut, adjoining the river which passes through the state: of this river and the country adjacent Lord Say and Lord Brook were the proprietors: at the mouth of said river a fort by their direction was built, which, in honor to them, was called Saybrook Fort. New Haven was settled soon after the building of this fort, as was a number of other towns of considerable note in Connecticut. Some difficulty arising among those who first settled at New Plymouth, a part of the inhabitants, to prevent any serious consequences, removed to a pleasant and fertile island to the south-west of Cape Cod, now called Rhode Island, while others settled at Providence, Warwick, Taunton, &c. Thus it was that in the course of a very few years a great part of New England, which so late was an uncultivated forest resounding with the yells of savages and beasts of prey, became the place of abode of our persecuted forefathers.

But this newly-settled country was not to be acquired without bloodshed. The natives, although they at first appeared harmless and well disposed towards the new settlers, from the rapid increase and too frequent aggressions of the latter the jealousy of the former was excited, which they soon began more openly to manifest, as will appear by what follows.

# COMMENCEMENT OF HOSTILITIES WITH THE NATIVES.

THERE was a tribe of Indians which inhabited the borders of Connecticut River, from its mouth to within a few miles of Hartford, called *Pequots*, a fierce, cruel, and warlike tribe, and the inveterate enemies of the English; never failing to improve every opportunity to exercise towards them the most wanton acts of barbarity. In June, 1634, they treacherously murdered a Captain Stone and a Captain Norton, who had been long in the habit of visiting them occasionally to trade. In August, 1635, they inhumanly murdered a Mr. Weeks and his whole family, consisting of a wife and six children, and soon after murdered the wife and children of a Mr. Williams, residing near Hartford. Finding, however, that by their unprovoked acts of barbarity they had enkindled the resentment of the English, (who, aroused to a sense of their danger, were making preparation to exterminate this cruel tribe,) the Pequots despatched messengers with gifts to the governor of the new colonies — the Hon. Josiah Winslow. He being, however, inflexible in his determination to revenge the deaths of his friends, dismissed these messengers without an answer. The Pequots finding the English resolute and determined, and fearing the consequence of their resentment, the second time despatched messengers with a large quantity of wampum (Indian money) as a present to the governor and council; with whom the latter had a considerable conference, and at length concluded a peace on the following terms:—

### ARTICLES.

I. The Pequots shall deliver up to the English those of their tribe that are guilty of the deaths of their countrymen.

II. The Pequots shall relinquish to the English all their right and title to the lands lying within the colony of Connecticut.

III. The English, if disposed to trade with the Pequots, shall be treated as friends.

To these articles the Pequots readily agreed and promised faithfully to adhere, and at the same time expressed a desire to make peace with the Narraganset Indians, with whom they were then at war.

Soon after the conclusion of peace with the Pequots, the English, to put their fair promises to the test, sent a small boat into the river, on the borders of which they resided, with the pretence of trade; but so great was the treachery of the natives, that, after succeeding by fair promises in enticing the crew of said boat on shore, they were by them inhumanly murdered.

The Pequots, despairing of again deceiving the English in the manner they had late done, now threw off the mask of friendship, and, avowing themselves the natural enemies of the English, commenced open hostilities against them, barbarously murdering all that were so unfortunate as to fall into their hands. A few families were at this time settled at or near Weathersfield, Connecticut, the whole of whom were carried away captives by them. Two girls, the daughters of a Mr. Gibbons, of Hartford, were in the most brutal manner put to death : after gashing their flesh with their knives, the Indians filled their wounds with hot embers, in the mean time mimicking their dying groans.

The Pequots, encouraged by the trifling resistance made by the English to their wanton acts of barbarity, on the 20th

3

of June, 1636, besieged Fort Saybrook, in which there were about twenty men stationed: the Indians were to the number of about one hundred and fifty. They surrounded and furiously attacked the fort at midnight, horribly yelling, and mimicking the dying groans of such as had fallen victims to their barbarity; but the English, being fortunately provided with a piece of cannon or two, caused their savage enemies to groan in reality, who, after receiving two or three deadly fires from the besieged, retreated, leaving behind them dead or mortally wounded about twenty of their number: the English sustained no loss in the attack.

The governor and council of Massachusetts colony, alarmed at the bold and daring conduct of the Pequots, on the 20th of August despatched Captain Endicot, of Salem, with ninety men, to avenge the murders committed by them, unless they should consent to deliver up the murderers and make reparation for the injuries which the English had sustained. Captain Endicot was directed to proceed first to Block Island, (then inhabited by the Pequots,) put the men to the sword, and take possession of the island: the women and children were to be spared. Thence he was to proceed to the Pequot country, demand the murderers of the English, a thousand fathom of wampum, and a number of their children as hostages.

Captain Endicot sailed from Boston on the morning of the 20th. When he arrived at Block Island, about sixty Indians appeared on the shore and opposed his landing; his men soon, however, effected a landing, and after a little skirmishing drove the Indians into the woods, where they could not be found. The English continued two days on the island, in which time they destroyed one hundred wigwams and about fifty canoes, when they proceeded for the Pequot country. When they arrived in Pequot Harbor, Captain Endicot acquainted the enemy with his designs and determination to avenge the cruelties practised upon his countrymen. In a few moments nearly five hundred of the enemy collected upon the shores;

but as soon as they were made acquainted with the hostile views of the English, they hastily withdrew and secreted themselves in swamps and ledges inaccessible to the troops. Captain Endicot landed his men on both sides the harbor, burned their wigwams and destroyed their canoes, killed an Indian or two, and then returned to Boston.   Enough, indeed, had been done to exasperate, but nothing to subdue, a haughty and warlike enemy.

Sassacus (chief sachem of the Pequots) and his captains were men of great and independent spirits; they had conquered and governed the nations around them without control; they viewed the English as strangers and mere intruders, who had no right to the country, nor to control its original proprietors, independent princes and sovereigns; they had made settlements at Connecticut without their consent, and brought home the Indian kings whom they had conquered, and restored to them their authority and lands; they had built a fort, and were making a settlement, without their approbation, in their very neighborhood.   Indeed, they had now proceeded to attack and ravage the country.   The Pequots, in consequence, breathed nothing but war and revenge; they were determined to extirpate or drive all the English from New England.   For this purpose they conceived the plan of uniting the Indians generally against them.   They spared no art nor pains to make peace with the Narragansets and to engage them in the war against the English, to whom they represented that the English, who were merely foreigners, were overspreading the country, and depriving the original inhabitants of their ancient rights and possessions; that, unless effectual measures were immediately taken to prevent it, they would soon entirely dispossess the original proprietors and become the lords of the continent.   They insisted that, by a general combination, they could either destroy or drive them from the country; that there would be no necessity of coming to open battles; that by killing their cattle, firing their houses, laying ambushes on the roads, in the fields, and wherever they could surprise and destroy them, they might accomplish their wishes. They represented that, if the English should effect the destruction of the Pequots, they would also soon destroy the Narragansets. So just and politic were these representations, that nothing but that thirst for revenge which inflames the savage heart could have resisted their influence; indeed, it is said that for some time the Narragansets hesitated.

The governor of the colonies, to prevent a union between these savage nations and to strengthen the peace between the Narraganset Indians and the colonies, despatched a messenger to invite Miantinomi, their chief sachem, to Boston. The invitation was accepted by Miantinomi, and while at Boston with the governor and council he entered into a treaty, the substance of which was as follows; viz., that there should be a firm peace maintained between the English and Narragansets and their posterity; that neither party should make peace with the Pequots without its being first mutually assented to; that the Narragansets should not harbor the enemies of the English, but deliver up to them such fugitives as should resort to them for safety. The English were to give them notice when they went out against the Pequots, and the Narragansets were to furnish guides.

In February, 1637, the English in Connecticut colony represented to the governor and council their desire to prosecute more effectually the war with the Pequots, who yet continued to exercise towards them the most wanton acts of barbarity. They represented that, on the 10th of January, a boat containing three of their countrymen was attacked by the enemy as it was proceeding down the river; that the English for some time bravely defended themselves, but were at length overpowered by numbers; that the Indians, when they had succeeded in capturing the boat's crew, ripped them up from the bottom of their bellies to their throats, and in like manner split them down their backs, and, thus mangled, hung them upon trees by the river side.  They represented that the affairs of Connecticut colony at this moment wore a most gloomy aspect; that they had sustained great losses in cattle and goods the preceding years, but were still more unfortunate the present; that a most dreadful and insidious enemy were now seeking opportunity to destroy them; that they could neither hunt, fish, nor cultivate their fields, nor travel at home or abroad, but at the peril of their lives; that they were obliged to keep a constant watch by night and day; to go armed to their daily labors and to the houses of public worship.  And although desirous to prosecute the war more effectually with the common enemy, they were not in a situation to do it; and therefore humbly prayed for assistance.

The report of the horrid and unprovoked cruelties of the Pequots, practised upon the defenceless inhabitants of Connecticut colony, roused the other colonies to harmonious and spirited exertions against them.  Massachusetts determin 1 to send two hundred and Plymouth forty men to assist the r unfortunate brethren in prosecuting the war.  Captain Patri k, with forty men, was sent forward before the other troops, in order that he might be enabled seasonably to form a junction with the troops in Connecticut, who, notwithstanding their weak and distressed state, had engaged to furnish ninety men.

On Wednesday, the 10th of May, the Connecticut troops proceeded for their fort at Saybrook.  They consisted of ninety Englishmen and seventy Mohegan and river Indians — the latter commanded by Uncus, sachem of the Mohegans, and the former by Captain John Mason, who was accompanied by the Rev. Mr. Stone, of Hartford, as chaplain.  The Mohegans, being detached from the English on their way to Saybrook, fell in with a considerable body of the enemy, whom they attacked and defeated; they killed twenty-two, and took eighteen of them prisoners.

Among the prisoners there was one who was recognized as a perfidious villain: he had lived in the fort with the English some time before, and well understood their language: he remained attached to their interest until the commencement of hostilities with the Pequots, when he deserted the garrison and joined the enemy, whom he served as guide, and through whose instigation many of the English had been captured and put to death.  Uncus and his men insisted upon executing him according to the custom of their ancestors; and the English, in the circumstances in which they then were, did not judge it prudent to interfere.  The Indians enkindled a fire, near which they confined the prisoner to a stake, in which situation he remained until his skin became parched with the heat: the Mohegans then violently tore him limb from limb. Barbarously cutting his flesh in pieces, they handed it round from one to another, eating it while they sung and danced round the fire in a manner peculiar to savages. The bones and such parts of the unfortunate captive as were not consumed in this dreadful repast were committed to the flames and consumed to ashes.

On the 16th Captain Mason and his men proceeded for Narraganset Bay, at which place they safely arrived on the 21st.  Captain Mason marched immediately to the plantation of Canonicus, a Narraganset sachem, and acquainted him with his designs, and immediately after despatched a messenger to Miantinomi to inform him likewise of the expedition. The next day Miantinomi, with his chief counsellors and warriors, met the English.  Captain Mason informed him that the cause of his entering his country with an armed force was to avenge the injuries which the Pequots had done the English, and desired a free passage to their forts, which they intended to attack.  After a solemn consultation in the Indian manner, Miantinomi observed that "he highly approved of the expedition, and would send men to assist the English, but that they were too few in number to fight the enemy; that the Pequots were great warriors, and rather slighted the English."

Captain Mason landed his men and marched to the plantation of Miantinomi, which, by previous agreement, was to be the place of general rendezvous. In the evening an Indian runner arrived with information that Captain Patrick, with the men under his command, had arrived at the plantation of Roger Williams, in Providence, and was desirous that Captain Mason should postpone his march until such time as he could join him. Captain Mason, after mature deliberation, determined, however, not to wait his arrival, although a junction was considered important. His men had already been detained much longer than was agreeable to their wishes, and the Mohegans apparently were impatient for battle. The little army, therefore, (consisting of ninety Englishmen, sixty Mohegans and river Indians, and about two hundred Narragansets,) commenced their march on the 24th, and in the evening of that day reached Nihantick, which bounded on the country of the Pequots. Nihantick was the seat of a Narraganset sachem, who seemed displeased with the expedition, and would not suffer the English to enter his fort. Captain Mason, suspecting the treachery of this fellow, placed a sentinel at night at the entrance of the fort, determined that, as he could not be permitted to enter, no one should come out to advise the enemy of his approach.

On the morning of the 25th Captain Mason was joined by an additional number of the Narragansets and a few of the Nihanticks. They formed a circle, and, brandishing their scalping knives, made protestations how gallantly they would fight and what numbers they would kill, &c. Captain Mason had now under his command near five hundred Indians in addition to his former force, with whom he early resumed his march for the head quarters of the enemy. The day proved uncommonly warm, and the men, through excessive heat and want of provision, were only enabled by night to reach Paucatuck River, where the Narragansets began to manifest great fear and inquire of Captain Mason his real

designs. He assured them that "it was to attack the Pequots in their fort;" at which they appeared greatly surprised, and exhibited a disposition to quit the English and
return home.

Wequash, a Pequot sachem who had revolted from Sassacus,
was the principal guide of the English, and he proved faithful.
He gave such information respecting the distance of the forts
of the enemy from each other, and the distance they were
then from that of the chief sachem's, as induced Captain Mason to determine to attack the latter, which his guide represented as situated at the head of Mystic River. He found his
men so much fatigued in marching through a pathless wilderness, with their provision, arms, and ammunition, that this
resolution appeared to be absolutely necessary. The little
army accordingly, on the morning of the 26th, proceeded
directly for Mystic, and at about sundown penetrated a thick
swamp, where, imagining that they could not be far distant
from the fort, they pitched their little camp between two large
rocks, now known by the name of "Porter's Rocks," situated
in Groton: the sentinels, who were considerably advanced in
front of the main body of the English, distinctly heard the
enemy singing and dancing through the night at their fort.

The important day was now approaching when the very
existence of Connecticut was to be determined by the sword
in a single action, and to be decided by the valor of less than
one hundred brave men. About two hours before day the
men were aroused from their slumbers by their officers, and,
after commending themselves and their cause to the Almighty,
proceeded with all possible despatch for the enemy's fort.
When within a few rods of the fort, Captain Mason sent for
Uncus and Waquash, and desired them in their Indian manner to harangue and prepare their men for combat. They
replied that "their men were much afraid, and could not be
prevailed upon to advance any farther." "Go, then," said
Captain Mason, "and request them not to retire, but to

surround the fort at any distance they please, and see what
courage Englishmen can display." The day was now dawn-
ing, and no time was to be lost; the fort was soon in view; the
soldiers pressed forward, animated with the reflection that it
was not for themselves alone they were about to fight, but
for their parents, wives, children, and countrymen. As they
approached the fort within a short distance, they were discovered by a Pequot sentinel, who roared out, "Owanux!
Owanux!" (Englishmen! Englishmen!) The troops pressed
on, and as the Indians were rallying poured in upon them the
contents of their muskets, and, instantly hastening to the principal entrance of the fort, rushed in, sword in hand. An important moment this; for, notwithstanding the blaze and thunder of the arms of the English, the Pequots made a manly
and desperate resistance: sheltered by their wigwams, and
rallied by their sachems and squaws, they defended themselves, and, in some instances, attacked the English with a
resolution that would have done honor to Romans. After a
bloody and desperate conflict of near two hours' continuance,
in which hundreds of the Indians were slain and many of
the English killed and wounded, victory still hung in suspense.
In this critical state of the action Captain Mason had recourse to a successful expedient: rushing into a wigwam
within the fort, he seized a brand of fire, and in the mean
time crying out to his men, "We must burn them!" communicated it to the mats with which the wigwams were covered,
by which means the whole fort was very soon inwrapped in
flames: as the fire increased, the English retired and formed
a circle around the fort: the Mohegans and Narragansets,
who had remained idle spectators to the bloody conflict, now
mustered courage sufficient to form another circle in the rear
of them. The enemy were now in a deplorable situation;
death inevitably was their portion. Sallying forth from their
burning cells, they were shot or cut in pieces by the English:
many of them, perceiving it impossible to escape the vigi-

lance of the troops, threw themselves voluntarily into the flames.

The violence of the flames, the reflection of the light, the clashing and roar of arms, the shrieks and yells of the savages in the fort, and the shoutings of the friendly Indians without, exhibited a grand and awful scene. In less than two hours from the commencement of the bloody action the English completed their work : eighty wigwams were burned, and upwards of eight hundred Indians destroyed; parents and children, the sannup and the squaw, the aged and the young, perished in promiscuous ruin : the loss of the English was comparatively trifling, not exceeding twenty-five in killed and wounded.

After the termination of this severe engagement, as the English were proceeding to embark on board their vessels, (which, fortunately for them, at this moment arrived in the harbor,) they were attacked in the rear by about three hundred of the enemy, who had been despatched from a neighboring fort to assist their brethren. The English gave them so warm a reception that they soon gave way and fell back to the field of action, where, viewing for a few moments, with apparent marks of horror and surprise, the shocking scene which it presented, they stamped, bellowed, and with savage rage tore their hair from their heads, and then, with a hideous yell, pursued the English, as if with a determination to avenge the deaths of their friends even at the expense of their lives. They pursued the English nearly six miles, sometimes shooting at a distance from behind rocks and trees, and sometimes pressing hard upon them and hazarding themselves in open field. The English killed numbers of them, but sustained no loss on their part; when a Pequot fell, the Mohegans would cry out, " Run and fetch his head !" The enemy finding at length that they discharged their arrows in vain, and that the English appeared to be well supplied with ammunition, gave over the pursuit.

In less than three weeks from the time the English embarked at Saybrook they returned, with the exception of the few killed and wounded, in safety to their respective habitations. Few enterprises were ever, perhaps, achieved with more personal bravery; in few have so great a proportion of the effective men of a whole colony, state, or nation been put to so great and immediate danger; in few have a people been so deeply and immediately interested as were the English inhabitants of Connecticut at this important crisis, — in these respects even the great armaments and battles of Europe are comparatively of little importance, — and it ought never to be forgotten, that, through the bravery and unconquerable resolution of less than one hundred men, Connecticut was once saved, and the most warlike and terrible tribe of Indians in New England completely exterminated.

The few Pequots that now remained alive, conceiving it unsafe to inhabit longer a country so exposed to invasion, removed far to the westward; among whom was Sassacus, their principal sachem. On the 25th of June the Connecticut troops under command of Captain Mason, together with a company from Massachusetts commanded by Captain Stoughton, were sent in pursuit of them. They proceeded westward, and on the 27th fell in with, attacked, and defeated a considerable body of them. They took about fifty of them prisoners, among whom were two sachems, whose lives were offered them on condition of their serving as guides to the English.

· The English on their march frequently fell in with small detached parties of the enemy, whom they captured or destroyed, but could not obtain any information relative to the main body commanded by Sassacus. Finding that the two sachem prisoners would not give them the information required, they, on the 27th, beheaded them at a place called Menunkatuck, (now Guilford,) from which circumstance the place still bears the name of "Sachems' Head." The English, on the 30th, arrived at Quinnipiak, (now New Haven,) where they were informed by a friendly Pequot that the enemy were encamped in a swamp a few miles to the westward. The troops pushed forward, and on the succeeding day arrived at the border of said swamp, which they found a thicket so extremely boggy as to render it inaccessible to any one but the natives; the English, therefore, thought it most advisable to surround the swamp and annoy the enemy as opportunity presented. The Indians, after a few skirmishes, requested a parley, which being granted them, Thomas Stanton, interpreter to the English, was sent to treat with them. He was authorized to offer life to such as had not shed the blood of Englishmen; upon which the sachem of the place, together with about three hundred of his tribe, came out, and, producing satisfactory proof of their innocence, were permitted to retire: but the Pequots boldly declared that "they had both shed and drank the blood of Englishmen, and would not upon such terms accept of life, but would fight it out." The English, unwilling to brook the threats and insulting language of the Pequots, attempted now to devise means to attack the whole body of them without further delay. The officers were, however, divided in opinion as to the mode of attack: some were for setting fire to the swamp, others for cutting their way through with hatchets, and others for surrounding it with a high fence, or palisade; neither of which plans were, however, fully adopted. As night approached the English cut through a part of the swamp, by which means its circumference was much lessened, and they enabled so completely to surround the enemy as to prevent their escape during the night. Early the ensuing morning the Indians, perceiving themselves completely hemmed in by the English, made a violent attempt to break through their lines; they were, however, driven back with great loss. They next attempted to force the line formed by the Connecticut troops; but here they met with a much warmer reception. The contest now became close and severe; the Indians, who

MISSION OF THOMAS STANTON TO THE PEQUOTS.  Page 36.

were about six hundred in number, appeared determined not to yield but at the expense of their lives. One of the most resolute of them walked boldly up to Captain Mason with an uplifted tomahawk, and when about to give the fatal stroke received a blow from the latter, who, with his cutlass, severed the head of the savage from his body. The enemy soon after made another attempt to break through the lines of the English, and in which, after a violent struggle, they finally succeeded. About sixty of their bravest warriors escaped, the remainder being either killed or taken prisoners. The loss of the English was eleven killed and about twenty wounded.

The prisoners taken were divided among the troops, some of whom were retained by them as servants, and the remainder sent to the West Indies and sold to the planters. The prisoners reported that the whole tribe of Pequots was now nearly exterminated; that in different engagements there had been upwards of two thousand of them killed, and about one thousand captured, among whom were thirteen sachems; and that six yet survived, one of whom was Sassacus, who had fled with the fragment of his tribe to the country bordering on Hudson River inhabited by the Mohawks.

After the swamp fight the Pequots became so weak and scattered that the Mohegans and Narragansets daily destroyed them and presented their scalps to the English; the few that fled with Sassacus to the westward were attacked and totally destroyed by the Mohawks. The scalp of Sassacus was, in the fall of 1638, presented to the governor and council of Massachusetts.

Soon after the extermination of the Pequots the Narragansets, the most numerous tribe in New England, being displeased with the small power with which they were vested and the respect which the English uniformly manifested for Uncus, appeared disposed to break their treaty of friendship. Miantinomi, without consulting the English according to agreement, without proclaiming war, or giving Uncus the

4

least information, raised an army of one thousand men and
marched against him.  The spies of Uncus discovered the
army at some distance and gave him intelligence.  He was
unprepared ; but, rallying about five hundred of his bravest
men, he told them they must by no means suffer Miantinomi
to enter their town, but must go and give him battle on the
way.  The Mohegans, having marched three or four miles,
met the enemy upon an extensive plain.  When the armies
had advanced within fair bowshot of each other, Uncus had
recourse to stratagem, with which he had previously acquainted his warriors.  He desired a parley, which being
granted, both armies halted in the face of each other.  Uncus,
gallantly advancing in front of his men, addressed Miantinomi to this effect: "You have a number of stout men
with you ; and so have I with me.  It is a great pity that so
many brave warriors should be killed in consequence of a
private misunderstanding between us two.  Come like a brave
man, as you profess to be, and let us decide the dispute alone:
if you kill me, my men shall be yours ; but if I kill you, your
men shall be mine."  "No," replied Miantinomi; "my men
come to fight; and they shall fight."  Upon which Uncus
falling instantly to the ground, his men discharged a shower
of arrows among the Narragansets, and without a moment's
interval, rushing upon them in the most furious manner with
a hideous yell, put them to flight.  The Mohegans pursued
the enemy with the same fury and eagerness with which they
commenced the action.  The Narragansets were driven down
rocks and precipices, and chased like a doe by the huntsmen :
many of them, to escape from their pursuers, plunged into a
river from rocks of near thirty feet in height ; among others
Miantinomi was hard pushed : some of the most forward of
the Mohegans, coming up with him, twirled him about, and
impeded his flight, that Uncus, their sachem, might alone have
the honor of taking him.  Uncus, who was a man of great
bodily strength, rushing forward like a lion greedy of his

prey, seized Miantinomi by the shoulder, and, giving the Indian whoop, called up his men who were behind to his assistance.   The victory was complete.   About fifty of the Narragansets were killed, and a much greater number wounded and taken prisoners; among the latter was a brother of Miantinomi and two of the sons of Canonicus, whom Uncus conducted in triumph to Mohegan.   Some few days after Uncus conducted Miantinomi back to the spot where he was taken, for the purpose of putting him to death.   At the instant they arrived on the ground, an Indian, who was ordered to march in the rear for the purpose, sunk a hatchet into his head and despatched him at a single stroke.   He was probably unacquainted with his fate, and knew not by what means he fell. Uncus cut out a large piece of his shoulder, which he devoured in savage triumph, declaring in the mean time that "it was the sweetest meat he ever ate; it made his heart strong!" The Mohegans buried Miantinomi at the place of his execution, and erected upon his grave a pillar of stones.   This memorable event gave the place the name of "Sachem's Plains."   They are situated in an eastern corner of Norwich.

The Narragansets became now greatly enraged at the death of their sachem, and sought means to destroy Uncus, whose country they in small parties frequently invaded, and, by laying ambushes, cut off a number of his most valuable warriors. As Uncus was the avowed friend of the English, and had in many instances signalized himself as such, they conceived it their duty to afford him all the protection possible.   They despatched messengers to acquaint the Narragansets with their determination, should they continue to molest and disturb the repose of the Mohegans.   The messengers of the English met with quite an unfavorable reception, to whom one of the Narraganset sachems declared that "he would kill every Englishman and Mohegan that came within his reach; that whoever began the war he would continue it, and that nothing should satisfy him but the head of Uncus!"

The English, irritated at the provoking language of the Narragansets, now determined not only to protect Uncus, but to invade their country with an army of three hundred men; first to propose a peace on their own terms, but, if rejected, to attack and destroy them. For this purpose Massachusetts was to furnish one hundred and ninety, and Plymouth and Connecticut colonies fifty-five, men each.

The Narragansets learning that an army was about to enter the heart of their country, and fearful of the issue, despatched several of their principal men to sue for peace on such terms as the English should be pleased to grant. The governor and council demanded that they should restore to Uncus all the captives and canoes which they had taken from him, and pledge themselves to maintain perpetual peace with the English and their allies, and to the former pay an annual tribute of two thousand fathom of white wampum. These, indeed, were hard terms, against which the Narragansets strongly remonstrated; but, aware that the English had already a considerable force collected for the express purpose of invading their country, they at length thought it most prudent to acquiesce.

During the war between the Narragansets and Uncus, the former once besieged the fort of the latter until his provisions were nearly exhausted, and he found that his men must soon perish either by famine or the tomahawk unless speedily relieved. In this crisis he found means of communicating an account of his situation to the English scouts, who had been despatched from the fort in Saybrook to reconnoitre the enemy. Uncus represented the danger to which the English would be exposed if the Narragansets should succeed in destroying the Mohegans. It was at this critical juncture that the greatest part of the English troops in Connecticut were employed on an expedition abroad. A Mr. Thomas Leffingwell, however, a bold and enterprising man, on learning the situation of Uncus, loaded a canoe with provision, and, under cover of night, paddled from Saybrook into the River Thames, and had the address to get the whole into the fort. The enemy soon after discovering that Uncus had received supplies, raised the siege: for this piece of service Uncus presented said Leffingwell with a deed of a very large tract of land, now comprising the whole town of Norwich.

The English in New England now enjoyed a peace until the year 1671, when they again took up arms to revenge the death of one of their countrymen who had been inhumanly murdered by an Indian belonging to the Nipnet tribe, of which the celebrated Philip, of Mount Hope, (now Bristol, R. I.,) was sachem. It was thought the most prudent step by the governor and council first to send for Philip and acquaint him with the cause of their resentment and the course which they were determined to pursue in case he refused to deliver into their hands the murderer. Philip being accordingly sent for, and appearing before the court, appeared much dissatisfied with the conduct of the accused, assuring them that no pains should be spared to bring him to justice; and more fully to confirm his friendship for the English, expressed a wish that the declaration which he was about publicly to make might be committed to paper, that he and his council might thereunto affix their signatures. The governor and council, in compliance with the request of Philip, drew up the following, which, after being signed by Philip and his chief men, was presented to the governor by Philip in confirmation of his friendly assurances : —

"Whereas my father, my brother, and myself have uniformly submitted to the good and wholesome laws of his majesty the King of England, and have ever respected his faithful subjects, the English, as our friends and brothers, and being still anxious to brighten the chain of friendship between us, we do now embrace this opportunity to pledge ourselves that we will spare no pains in seeking out and bringing to

4 *

justice such of our tribe as shall hereafter commit any outrage against them; and to remove all suspicion, we voluntarily agree to deliver up to them all the firearms which they have heretofore kindly presented us with until such time as they can safely repose confidence in us; and for the true performance of these our sacred promises, we have hereunto set our hands.

Chief Sachem.

PHILIP's ⋈ mark.

Chief Men.

POKANOKET's ⋈ mark.

UNCOMBO's ⋈ mark.

SAMKAMA's ⋈ mark.

WOCOKOM's ⋈ mark.

In presence of the governor and council."

Notwithstanding the fair promises of Philip, it was soon discovered by the English that he was playing a deep game; that he was artfully enticing his red brethren throughout the whole of New England to rise, *en masse*, against them, and drive them out of the country. The Narragansets for this purpose had engaged to raise four thousand fighting men. The spring of 1672 was the time agreed upon on which the grand blow was to be given. The evil intentions of Philip were first discovered and communicated to the English by a friendly Indian of the Narraganset tribe: fortunately for them, this Indian had been taken into favor by the Rev. Mr. Elliot, by whom he had been taught to read and write, and became much attached to the English. The governor, upon receiving the important information relative to the hostile views of Philip, ordered a military watch to be kept up in all the English settlements within the three colonies; by some of whom it was soon discovered that the report of their Indian friend was too well founded, as the Indians of different tribes were daily seen flocking in great numbers to the head quarters of

Philip, previously sending their wives and children to the Narraganset country, which they had ever done previous to the commencement of hostilities.

The inhabitants of Swanzey, a small settlement adjoining Mount Hope, the head quarters of Philip, were the first who felt the effects of this war. Philip, encouraged by the numbers who were daily enlisting under his banners, and despairing of discovering cause that could justify him in the commencement of hostilities against his "friends and brothers," as he had termed them, resolved to provoke them to war by killing their cattle, firing their barns, &c. This plan had its desired effect, as the inhabitants, determined to save their property or perish in the attempt, fired upon the Indians, which was deemed cause sufficient by the latter to commence their bloody work. The war whoop was immediately thereupon sounded, when the Indians commenced an indiscriminate murder of the defenceless inhabitants of Swanzey, sparing not the tender infant at the breast; but three of seventy-eight persons which the town contained made their escape. Messengers were despatched with the melancholy tidings of this bloody affair to the governor, who, by and with the advice and consent of the council, despatched a company of militia with all possible speed to the relief of the distressed inhabitants residing near the head quarters of Philip. As soon as they could be raised, three companies more were despatched, under the command of Captains Henchman, Prentice, and Church, who arrived in the neighborhood of Swanzey on the 28th of June, where they were joined by four more companies from Plymouth colony. It was found that the Indians had pillaged and set fire to the village, and with their booty had retired to Mount Hope. A company of cavalry were sent, under the command of Captain Prentice, to reconnoitre them; but before they arrived at a convenient place for this purpose they were ambushed and fired upon by the enemy, who killed six of their number and wounded ten. The report of their guns alarming the remaining companies of the English, they hastened to the relief of the cavalry, who at this moment were completely surrounded by about six hundred Indians, between whom and the English a warm contest now ensued. The savages fought desperately, and more than once nearly succeeded in overpowering the English; but, very fortunately for the latter, when nearly despairing of victory, a fresh company of militia from Boston arrived, which, flanking the enemy on the right and left and exposing them to two fires, soon overpowered them and caused them to seek shelter in an adjoining wood inaccessible to the English. The English had in this severe engagement forty-two killed, and seventy-three wounded, many of them mortally. The enemy's loss was supposed to be much greater.

On the 30th Major Savage, who by his excellency the governor had been appointed commander-in-chief of the combined English forces, arrived with an additional company of cavalry, who with the remaining companies the following day commenced their march for Mount Hope, the head quarters of Philip. On their way the English were affected with a scene truly distressing. The savages, not content with bathing their tomahawks in the blood of the defenceless inhabitants of Swanzey, had, it was discovered, in many instances detached their limbs from their mangled bodies and affixed them to poles which were extended in the air — among which were discovered the heads of several infant children; the whole of which, by order of Major Savage, were collected and buried.

The English arrived at Mount Hope about sunset; but the enemy, having received information of their approach, had deserted their wigwams and retired into a neighboring wood. Major Savage, to pursue the enemy with success, now divided his men into separate companies, which he ordered to march in different directions, stationing forty at Mount Hope. On the 4th of July the men under the command of Captains

Church and Henchmen fell in with a body of the enemy to the number of two hundred, whom they attacked. The English being but thirty-two in number, including officers, victory for a considerable length of time appeared much in favor of the savages; but very fortunately for the former, being commanded by bold and resolute officers, they defended themselves in the most heroic manner until relieved by a company of cavalry under the command of Captain Prentice. The Indians, now in turn finding the fire of the English too warm for them, fled in every direction, leaving thirty of their number dead and about sixty severely wounded on the field of action. The English in this engagement had seven killed and twenty-two wounded, five of whom survived the action but a few hours.

This action, so far from daunting the bold and resolute Captain Church, seemed to inspire him with additional bravery. Unwilling that any of the enemy should escape, he boldly led his men into an almost impenetrable forest, into which those who survived the action had fled. The Indians, perceiving the English approaching, concealed themselves from their view by lying flat on their bellies, in which situation they remained concealed until the English had advanced within a few rods of them, when each, unperceived, fixing upon his man, discharged a shower of arrows among them. This unexpected check threw the English into confusion, which the Indians perceiving, rushed furiously upon them with their knives and tomahawks, shouting horribly. The English, their cavalry being unable to afford them assistance, were now in a very disagreeable situation; the trees being so very large as to render it difficult to use their firearms with any effect, and they were very soon so encompassed by the savages as to render almost every effort to defend themselves useless. Of sixty-four who entered the swamp but twenty-seven escaped, among whom very fortunately was their valuable leader, Captain Church.

The English, finding that they could neither bring their enemies to action in open field nor engage them with any success in the forest in which they were lodged, returned home, with the exception of three companies who were stationed by Major Savage near the borders of a swamp, into which it was strongly suspected that Philip, with a number of his tribe, had fled. This swamp was two miles in length, and to the English inaccessible. Philip, who had been watching the motion of his enemies, perceiving the greater part of them marching off, conjectured that their object was to obtain a reenforcement: impressed with this belief, he resolved to improve the first opportunity to escape, with a few chosen men, by water, which he with little difficulty effected the succeeding night, taking the advantage of a low tide. The enemy were soon after their escape discovered and pursued by the inhabitants of Rehoboth, accompanied by a party of the Mohegans, who had volunteered their services against Philip.

The Rehoboth militia came up with the rear of the enemy about sunset, and killed twelve of them, without sustaining any loss on their part: night prevented their engaging the whole force of Philip; but early the succeeding morning they continued the pursuit. The Indians had, however, fled with such precipitancy that it was found impossible to overtake them. They bent their course to the westward, exhorting the different tribes through which they passed to take up arms against the English.

The United Colonies became now greatly alarmed at the hostile views and rapid strides of Philip. The general court was constantly in sitting, and endeavoring to plan means to cut him off before he should have an opportunity to corrupt the minds of too many of his countrymen.

While the court was thus employed, information was received that Philip had arrived in the neighborhood of Brookfield, situated about sixty-five miles from Boston, and that a number of its inhabitants had been inhumanly butchered by his adherents.  Orders were immediately thereupon issued for the raising ten companies of foot and horse, to be despatched to the relief of the unfortunate inhabitants of Brookfield; but before they could reach that place Philip and his party had entered the town and indiscriminately put to death almost every inhabitant which it contained; the few that escaped having taken the precaution, previous to the attack, to assemble together in one house, which they strongly fortified.  This house was furiously attacked by the savages, and several times set on fire; and the besieged were on the point of surrendering when Major Willard happily arrived to their relief.  Between the English and the Indians a desperate engagement now ensued: the former, by the express command of their officers, gave no quarter, but in a very heroic manner rushed upon the savages with clubbed muskets.  The action continued until near sunset, when the few Indians that remained alive sought shelter in the neighboring woods.  In this engagement the English had twenty-two killed and seventy-five wounded.  The enemy's loss was two hundred and seventeen killed, and between two and three hundred wounded, who, by way of retaliation for their barbarity exercised towards the defenceless inhabitants of Brookfield, were immediately put to death.

The governor and council, on learning the fate of the unfortunate inhabitants of Brookfield, despatched a reënforcement of three companies of cavalry to Major Willard, and ordered the like number to be sent him from Hartford, in Connecticut colony, with which he was directed to pursue Philip with fire and sword to whatever part of the country he should resort.

It being discovered that a part of Philip's forces had fled to Hatfield, two companies of English, under command of Captain Lathrop and Captain Beers, were sent in pursuit of them, who, within about three miles of Hatfield, overtook and attacked them; but the force of the English being greatly

inferior to that of the enemy, the former were defeated and
driven back to the main body, which enabled the enemy,
who had in the late engagement been detached from their
main body, to join Philip. On the 18th of September information was received by Major Willard that the enemy
had successfully attacked and defeated the troops under the
command of Captain Lathrop; that they were ambushed and
unexpectedly surrounded by one thousand of the enemy, to
whom they all, except three who escaped, fell a sacrifice.
The defeat of Captain Lathrop took place in the neighborhood of Deerfield, for the defence of which there was an
English garrison, which the Indians were about to attack
when Major Willard happily arrived, on the approach of
whom the Indians fled.

On the 10th of October following a party of Philip's Indians successfully assaulted the town of Springfield, which
they pillaged and set fire to, killing about forty of the inhabitants. On the 14th they assaulted the town of Hatfield, in
which two companies, under the command of Captain Mosely
and Captain Appleton, were stationed. The enemy continued
the attack about two hours, when, finding the fire of the English too warm for them, they fled, leaving a number of their
party behind them dead.

Philip, now finding himself closely pursued by a large and
formidable body of the English, deemed it prudent to bend
his course towards his old place of residence, there to remain
until the ensuing spring.

But the commissioners of the United Colonies, duly reflecting on the deplorable situation of their defenceless brethren
throughout the country, aware that there were then a much
greater number of their savage enemies imbodied than at
any former period, who, if suffered peaceably to retire into
winter quarters, might prove too powerful for them the spring
ensuing, resolved to attack the whole force under Philip in
their winter encampment; for the purpose of which every

Englishman capable of bearing arms was commanded, by proclamation of the governor, to hold himself in readiness to march at the shortest notice. The 10th of December was the day appointed by the commissioners on which the decisive blow was to be given. Six companies were immediately raised in Massachusetts, consisting in the whole of five hundred and twenty-seven men, to the command of which were appointed Captains Mosely, Gardener, Davenport, Oliver, and Johnson. Five companies were raised in Connecticut, consisting of four hundred and fifty men, to the command of which were appointed Captains Siely, Mason, Gallop, Watts, and Marshall. Two companies were likewise raised in Plymouth, consisting of one hundred and fifty men, who were commanded by Captains Rice and Goram. Three majors of the three respective divisions were also appointed; to wit, Major Appleton, of Massachusetts; Major Treat, of Connecticut; and Major Bradford, of Plymouth. The whole force, consisting of eleven hundred and twenty-seven men, were commanded by Major General Winslow, late governor of the colonies. On the 7th of December the combined forces commenced their march for the head quarters of the enemy. At this inclement season it was with the utmost difficulty that the troops were enabled to penetrate through a wild and pathless wood. On the morning of the 9th, having travelled all the preceding night, they arrived at the border of an extensive swamp, in which, they were informed by their guides, the enemy were encamped to the number of four thousand. The English, after partaking of a little refreshment, formed for battle. Captain Mosely and Captain Davenport led the van, and Major Appleton and Captain Oliver brought up the rear of the Massachusetts forces. General Winslow, with the Plymouth troops, formed the centre. The Connecticut troops, under the command of their respective captains, together with about three hundred of the Mohegans, commanded by Oneco, the son of Uncus, brought up the rear.

It was discovered by an Indian, sent for that purpose, that
in the centre of the swamp the enemy had built a very strong
fort, of so wise construction that it was with difficulty that
more than one person could enter at one time.  About 10
o'clock, A. M., the English, with the sound of the trumpet,
entered the swamp, and, when within about fifty rods of their
fort, were met and attacked by the enemy.  The Indians, in
their usual manner, shouting and howling like beasts of prey,
commenced the attack with savage fury : but with a hideous
noise the English were not to be intimidated.  Charging them
with unequalled bravery, the enemy were soon glad to seek
shelter within the walls of their fort.  The English, having
closely pressed upon the enemy as they retreated, now in turn
found themselves in a very disagreeable situation, exposed to
the fire of the Indians, who were covered by a high breastwork : they were not even enabled to act on the defensive.
At this critical juncture the lion-hearted Oneco, with the assent of General Winslow, offered with the men under his
command to scale the walls of the fort; which being approved
of by the English commanders, Oneco, with about sixty picked
men, in an instant ascended to the top of the fort, where, having a fair chance at the enemy, they hurled their tomahawks
and discharged their arrows with such success among them
as in a very short time to throw them into the utmost confusion : those who attempted to escape from the fort were instantly cut in pieces by the troops without.  The enemy, finding themselves thus hemmed in and attacked on all sides, in
the most abject terms begged for quarter, which was denied
them by the English.  A great proportion of the troops being
now mounted on the walls of the fort, they had nothing to do
but load and fire; the enemy being penned up and huddled
together in such a manner that there was scarcely a shot lost.
This bloody contest was of near six hours' continuance, when
the English, perceiving the fort filled with nought but dead or
such as were mortally wounded of the enemy, closed the
bloody conflict.

The scene of action, at this instant, was indeed such as could not fail to shock the stoutest hearted. The huge logs of which the fort was constructed were completely crimsoned with the blood of the enemy, while the surrounding woods resounded with the dying groans of the wounded. The number of slain of the enemy in this severe engagement could not be ascertained; it was, however, immense. Of four thousand, which the fort was supposed to contain at the commencement of the action, not two hundred escaped; among whom, unfortunately, was the treacherous Philip.

After the close of this desperate action, the troops, having destroyed all in their power, left the enemy's ground, and, carrying about three hundred wounded men, marched back to the distance of sixteen miles to head quarters. The night proved cold and stormy; the snow fell deep; and it was not until midnight or after that the troops were enabled to reach their place of destination: many of the wounded, who probably otherwise might have recovered, perished with the cold and inconvenience of a march so fatiguing.

Although the destruction of so great a number of the enemy was considered of the greatest importance to the English, yet it proved a conquest dearly bought. It was obtained at the expense of the lives of not only a great number of privates, but a great proportion of their most valuable officers; among whom were Captains Davenport, Gardner, Johnson, Siely, and Marshall. On enumerating their number of slain and wounded, it was found as follows: —

Of the companies commanded by
Captains Mosely, . . 10 killed, 40 wounded.
" Oliver, . . . 20 " 48 "
" Gardner, . . 11 " 82 "
" Johnson, . . . 18 " 88 "
" Davenport, . . 15 " 19 "
" Gallop, . . . 28 " 48 "

| Captains Siely, | . | . | . | 82 killed, | 50 wounded. |
|---|---|---|---|---|---|
| "      Watts, | . | . | . | 19 " | 83 " |
| "      Mason, | . | . | . | 40 " | 50 " |
| "      Marshall, | . | . | . | 25 " | 87 " |
| "      Goram, | . | . | . | 80 " | 41 " |
| Sachem Oneco, | . | . | . | 51 " | 82 " |
| Total, | . |  |  | 299 " | 513 " |

The courage displayed during the action by every part of the army, the invincible heroism of the officers, the firmness and resolution of the soldiers when they saw their captains falling before them, and the hardships endured before and after the engagement, are hardly credible, and rarely find a parallel in ancient or modern ages.   The cold the day preceding the action was extreme, and in the night of which the snow fell so deep as to render it extremely difficult for the army to move the day succeeding : four hundred of the soldiers were so completely frozen as to be unfit for duty. The Connecticut troops were the most disabled, having endured a tedious march, without halting, from Stonington to the place of public rendezvous ; they sustained, too, a much greater loss in the action, in proportion to their numbers, than the troops of the other colonies.   The bold and intrepid Captain Mason, who received a fatal wound in the action, of which he died in about three months after, was the first after the Mohegans to mount the walls of the fort ; nor did the troops under his command fail to follow the noble example.

The loss of the troops from Connecticut was so great that Major Treat conceived it absolutely necessary to return immediately home.   Such of the wounded as were not able to travel were put on board a vessel and conveyed to Stonington. The troops, on their return, killed and captured about thirty of the enemy.

The Massachusetts and Plymouth forces kept the field the greater part of the winter.   They ranged the country, took a number of prisoners, destroyed about three hundred wigwams, but achieved nothing brilliant or decisive.

The Nipnet and Narraganset tribes being by the late action nearly exterminated, the few that survived, by the direction of Philip, fled in small parties to different parts of the country, improving every opportunity that presented to revenge the untimely fate of their brethren. On the 10th of February, 1678, about one hundred of them surprised the inhabitants of Lancaster, Massachusetts, a part of whom, as a place of greater safety, had the day previous resorted to the dwelling of the Rev. Mr. Rowland : this, however, being constructed of dry logs, was set fire to by the Indians, which the unfortunate English within being unable to extinguish, they fell victims to the devouring flames. On the 21st the enemy attacked the inhabitants of Medfield, thirty-two of whom they killed, and of the remainder made captives.

On the 3d of March, the Indians still continuing their depredations, two companies of cavalry, under the command of Captain Pierce and Captain Watkins, were ordered out for the purpose of affording protection to the defenceless inhabitants of towns most exposed to their incursions. On the 5th they marched to Pautuxet, near where there was a considerable body of Indians encamped, whom, on the morning of the 5th, they fell in with and attacked. The enemy at first appeared but few in number ; but these were only employed to decoy the English, who, on a sudden, found themselves surrounded by near three hundred Indians, who, with their tomahawks and scalping knives, rushing furiously upon them, threatened them with instant destruction. The English, now acting upon the defensive, although surrounded by five times their number, fought with their usual spirit, and were resolved to sell their lives at as dear rate as possible : they were very soon, however, compelled to yield to the superior force of their savage enemies : but five escaped. This victory, though of considerable importance to the savages, cost them a number

5 *

of their bravest warriors, ninety-three of whom were the succeeding day found dead upon the field of action: there were in this engagement about twenty friendly Indians with the English, who fought like desperadoes: one of them, observing Captain Pierce unable to stand, in consequence of the many wounds he had received, for nearly two hours bravely defended him; when, perceiving his own imminent danger, and that he could afford the captain no further assistance, by blacking his face as the enemy had done, he escaped unnoticed.

On the 25th of March a party of Indians attacked and burned the towns of Weymouth and Warwick, killing a great number of the inhabitants. On the 10th of April following they pillaged and burned Rehoboth and Providence.

On the 1st of May a company of English and one hundred and fifty Mohegans, under command of Captain George Dennison, were sent in pursuit of a body of the enemy commanded by the son of Miantinomi. On the 8th they met with and attacked them near Groton. The Indians, apparently determined on victory or death, displayed an unusual degree of courage; but the English and Mohegans proved too strong for them, who, after destroying the greater part with their muskets and tomahawks, drove the remainder into a neighboring river, where they soon perished.

On the 23d Cononchet, sachem of the few scattered remains of the Narragansets, proposed to his council that the lands bordering on Connecticut River not inhabited by the English should be by them planted with corn for their future subsistence; which being approved of by the latter, two hundred of the Narragansets were despatched for this purpose: the governor, being apprised of their intentions, despatched three companies of cavalry to intercept them. About one hundred of the Mohegans, under the command of Oneco, accompanied the English. The enemy were commanded by Cononchet in person, who first proceeded to Seconk to procure seed corn: it was in the neighborhood of this place that they were first met with and engaged by the English and Mohegans. The enemy, with becoming bravery, for a long time withstood the attack; but, being but poorly provided with weapons, they were at length overpowered and compelled to yield to the superior power of their enemies. In the midst of the action Cononchet, fearful of the issue, deserted his men and attempted to seek shelter in a neighboring wood; but, being recognized by the Mohegans, they pursued him. Cononchet, perceiving himself nearly overtaken by his pursuers, to facilitate his flight first threw away his blanket, and then his silver-laced coat, with which he had been presented by the English a few weeks previous; but, finding that he could not escape from his pursuers by flight, he plunged into a river, where he was even followed by half a dozen resolute Mohegans, who, laying hold of him, forced him under water and there held him until he was drowned. The loss of the English and Mohegans in this engagement was twelve killed and twenty-one wounded; that of the enemy was forty-three killed and about eighty wounded.

The inhabitants of New London, Norwich, and Stonington, having frequently discovered a number of the enemy lurking about in small bodies in the adjacent woods, by joint agreement voluntarily enlisted themselves, to the number of three hundred, under the command of Major Palmer and Captains Dennison and Avery, who, with the assistance of the Mohegans and a few friendly Narragansets, in three expeditions destroyed near one thousand of the enemy.

On the 8th of June the Indians assaulted and burned Bridgewater, a small settlement in the colony of Massachusetts: forty of its inhabitants fell victims to savage barbarity.

The governor and council of Massachusetts colony, aware of the danger to which many of the inland settlements were exposed by frequent incursions of the enemy, and finding it extremely difficult to raise a sufficient force to oppose them in the many parts to which the fragments of the broken tribes had resorted, adopted the policy of sending among them, as spies, such Indians as were friendly and could be depended on; which plan had its desired effect. These Indians, representing the force of the English much greater than it really was, and warning the enemy of danger which did not at that time exist, deterred them from acting in many instances on the offensive. One of the friendly Indians, returning to Boston on the 10th of July, reported as follows: " That a large number of Indians were imbodied in a wood near Lancaster, which village they intended to attack and burn in a few days; that they had been encouraged to continue the war with the English by Frenchmen from the great lake, who had supplied them with firearms and ammunition."

On the receipt of this important information the governor despatched three companies of cavalry, under the command of Major Savage, for the defence of Lancaster, who unfortunately, by mistaking the road, fell into an ambush of about three hundred and fifty Indians, by whom they were instantly surrounded. The English exhibited great presence of mind, and repelled the attack of the enemy in a very heroic manner. The savages being, however, well provided with firearms, soon gained a complete victory over the English, whose loss in this unfortunate engagement was fifty-four. The number of killed and wounded of the enemy could not be ascertained, as they remained masters of the field of action.

On the 15th a severe engagement took place between a company of English cavalry and about three hundred of the enemy near Groton. The latter were not perceived by the former until they were within a few paces of them, the Indians having concealed themselves in the bushes; when, suddenly issuing forth with a hideous yell, the cavalry were thrown into confusion; but instantly forming and charging the enemy with great spirit, they fled in every direction. The cavalry, in attempting to pursue them, were once more ambushed. The contest now became close and severe: the Indians, having succeeded in decoying the English into a thick wood, attacked them with great fury and success. The commander of the English being killed, every man sought his own safety. Of forty-five of which the company was composed, but twelve escaped. The loss of the enemy was, however, supposed to be much greater.

On the 12th of August a party of Indians entered the town of Westfield, killed and took several of the inhabitants prisoners, and burned several houses. Three of them soon after made their appearance at a house near said town and fired at a man at his door, who fell. They ran towards him, and one of them stooping to scalp him, he was saluted by the man's wife with a stroke from a large hatchet, which went so completely into his body that at three different efforts she could not disengage it; and the Indian made off with it sticking in him. A second Indian also made an attempt; when she, by a well-directed stroke with a stick she had got, laid him on the ground. The third then run; and the other, as soon as he had recovered his feet, followed the example; on which the woman took her husband in her arms and carried him into the house, where he soon after recovered.

On the 17th a party of Indians commenced an attack on Northampton; but there being a number of English soldiers therein stationed, the enemy were repulsed.

On the 20th a number of the inhabitants of Springfield were attacked by a party of Indians as they were returning from divine service; and although the former were provided with firearms, the enemy succeeded in making prisoners of two women and several children, whom they soon after inhumanly tomahawked and scalped; in which situation they were the succeeding day found by a party of English sent out in pursuit of the enemy. One of the unfortunate women, although shockingly mangled, was found still alive, and, when so far recovered as to be enabled to speak, gave the following account of the fate of her unfortunate companions, to wit:

"That they were first conveyed by the savages to a thick wood, where they were severally bound with cords; that the Indians soon after built a fire and regaled themselves with what they had previously stolen from the English; that soon after a warm dispute arose between them relative to the prisoners, each claiming the women for their squaws, (or wives;) that they at length proceeded to blows; and, after beating each other for some time with clubs, it was agreed by both parties, to prevent further altercation, that the women should be put to death; which they, as they supposed, carried immediately into execution. The unfortunate narrator received a severe blow on the head, which brought her senseless to the ground, and, while in this situation, was scalped and left for dead by her savage enemies."

The inhabitants of Sudbury, with a company of soldiers under the command of Lieutenant Jacobs, of Marlborough, alarmed at the near approach of the enemy, who to the number of about two hundred were encamped near that place, resolved to attack them at night. Accordingly, on the 6th of September they marched within view of them, and at night, as they lay extended around a large fire, approached them, unperceived, within gunshot, when they gave them the contents of their muskets. Many of those that remained unhurt, being suddenly aroused from their slumber by the yells of their wounded brethren, and imagining that they were completely surrounded by the English, whom the darkness of the night prevented their seeing, threw themselves into the fire which they had enkindled, and there perished. But few if any escaped. In this attack the English sustained no loss.

On the 25th a considerable body of the enemy attacked the inhabitants of Marlborough, many of whom they killed, and set fire to their houses. A company of English, who had been ordered from Concord for the defence of this place, were cut off by the savages and totally destroyed. Two other companies, despatched from Boston for the like purpose, met with the same fate.   It appeared that the governor, on learning the situation of the unfortunate inhabitants of Marlborough, despatched to their relief two companies, under the command of Captains Wadsworth and Smith, who, before they arrived at their place of destination, were informed that the savages had quitted Marlborough and proceeded for Sudbury, twelve miles distant; which induced the English to alter their course and proceed immediately for the latter place.   Of this it appeared that the enemy had been apprised by their runners, and had lain a plan to cut them off ere they should reach Sudbury; which they in the following manner completely effected.   Learning the course which the English would take, they within a few rods thereof stationed fifty or sixty of their number in an open field, who were ordered to retreat into a neighboring thicket as soon as discovered and pursued by the English.   In this thicket the remainder of the Indians, to the number of about three hundred, concealed themselves by lying prostrate on their bellies.   The English, on their arrival, espying the Indians in the field, and presuming them to be but few in number, pursued and attacked them, who very soon retreated to the fatal spot where their treacherous brethren lay concealed, and prepared to give their pursuers a warm if not a fatal reception: here they were closely pursued by the English, who too late discovered the fatal snare which had been laid for them.   In an instant they were completely surrounded and attacked on all sides by the savages.   The English for several hours bravely defended themselves, but at length were borne down by numbers far superior to their own.   Thus fell the brave Captain Wadsworth and Captain Smith, as well as most of the troops under their command.

The Indians bordering on the River Merrimack, feeling themselves injured by the encroachments of the English, once more reassumed the bloody tomahawk, which had been buried for a number of years.   On the 1st of November they in a considerable body entered the villages of Chelmsford and

Woburn, and indiscriminately put to death every inhabitant they contained, not sparing the infant at the breast. On the 9th they burned the house of a Mr. Eames, near Concord, killed his wife and threw her body into the flames, and made captives of his children. On the 15th they took prisoner a young woman, sixteen years of age, who, by the family with whom she resided, had been placed on a hill in the neighborhood of their dwelling to watch the motions of the enemy. The account which the young woman gave of her capture and escape was as follows: "That on the morning of her capture, the family having been informed that a party of Indians had the day previous been discovered in a neighboring wood, she, by their request, ascended a hill near the house to watch their motions, and alarm the family if seen approaching the house; that about noon she discovered a number of them ascending the hill in great haste; that she immediately thereupon attempted to evade them by retiring into a thicket; but that the Indians, who it appeared had before observed her, found her after a few moments' search, and compelled her to accompany them to their settlement, about forty miles distant. It was here they gave her to understand she must remain and become their squaw, and dress and cook their victuals; that she remained with them about three weeks, during which time they made several expeditions against the English, and returned with a great number of human scalps; that on the night of the 6th of December they returned with six horses which they had stolen from the English, which having turned into a small enclosure, they set out on a new expedition; that she viewed this as a favorable opportunity to escape, to effect which she caught and mounted one of the horses, and, making use of a strip of bark as a bridle, penetrated a wild and pathless wood, and arrived at Concord at seven o'clock the morning succeeding, having travelled all the preceding night to evade the pursuit of the enemy." In like manner did one of the children of Mr. Eames, of whose capture mention is made in the preceding page, escape from the Indians.   Although but ten years of age, he travelled sixty miles through an uninhabited wood, subsisting on acorns.

On the 12th of December a party of Indians attacked and killed several of the inhabitants of Bradford.   The governor of Massachusetts colony, for the protection of the defenceless inhabitants of the Merrimack, ordered the raising and equipping of four companies of cavalry; to the command of which were appointed Captains Sill, Holyoke, Cutler, and Prentice.

On the 23d the above troops proceeded for the borders of the Merrimack, and on the 26th fell in with a considerable body of the enemy, whom they engaged and completely defeated.   On the 4th of January, 1679, Captain Prentice, detached from the main body, fell in with and engaged about one hundred of the enemy in the neighborhood of Amherst, whom he likewise defeated, but with considerable loss on his part.

On the 6th a son of the brave Captain Holyoke, of Springfield, receiving information that a number of the enemy in small bodies were skulking about in the woods bordering on that town, with twenty resolute young men marched out to attack them.   Falling in with a considerable body of them, an engagement ensued, which, though severe, terminated at length in favor of the English.   The Indians, being furnished with muskets, were unwilling to give ground, and would probably have remained masters of the field had not the English received a reënforcement which put them to flight. The loss of the English in the engagement was five killed and nine wounded, and that of the enemy twenty-three killed, and between thirty and forty wounded.

The savages were no longer confined to any particular tribe or place, but, in parties from fifty to three hundred, were scattered all over the thinly-inhabited parts of New England: a considerable body of them were yet in the neighborhood of Hadley, Deerfield, and Northampton, where they were con-

tinually committing their wanton acts of barbarity. Several
of the inhabitants of the towns above mentioned, duly reflecting on the danger to which they and their families were daily
exposed, formed themselves into several companies, and made
choice of their commanders. On the 4th of February, receiving information that there were near two hundred Indians
imbodied in a swamp in the neighborhood of Deerfield, the
above-mentioned force marched to attack them. Arriving
within view of them about daybreak, they discovered them
in a profound sleep, stretched out upon the ground around
their fire. The cavalry immediately thereupon alighted, and,
after forming themselves, approached them within pistol shot
before they were discovered by the enemy, who, being suddenly aroused from their slumber, and astonished at the unexpected appearance of so many of their enemies, fell an
easy prey to the English, who, without the loss of a man,
killed one hundred and twenty of them; the remainder, as
the only means of escape, having plunged into a river, where
probably many of them perished.

Although the English achieved this action without any loss
on their part, they were on their return unhappily ambushed
by about four hundred of the enemy. The English, having
expended all their ammunition in the late engagement, and
being much fatigued, were now in turn likely to fall an easy
prey to their enemies, who with their bloody knives and tomahawks, for the space of an hour, attacked them with the
greatest success. Not one of the English, it is probable, would
have survived this bloody and unexpected attack, had it not
been for the presence of mind of their brave commander,
Captain Holyoke, who, by a stratagem, succeeded in saving a
part of them. Captain Holyoke had his horse killed under
him, and at one time was attacked by five of the enemy, whom
he beat off with his cutlass. The loss of the English in this
unfortunate action was fifty-one killed and eighty-four wounded; many of the latter survived the action but a few days.

The defeat and destruction of the English in this engagement were much to be lamented, as among the slain were the heads of several families who had volunteered their services in defence of their infant settlements.

On the 10th several hundreds of the enemy, encouraged by their late success, appeared before Hatfield and fired several dwelling houses without the fortification of the town. The inhabitants of Hadley being seasonably apprised of the situation of their brethren at Hatfield, a number of them volunteered their services and marched to their relief. The Indians, as they were accustomed to do on the approach of the English, lay flat on their bellies until the latter had advanced within bowshot, when, partly rising, they discharged a shower of arrows among them, which wounded several of the English; but they, having wisely reserved their fire, now in turn levelled their pieces with the best effect before the savages had time to recover their legs, about thirty of whom were instantly despatched, and the remainder dispersed.

On the 15th of February the governor of Massachusetts colony, receiving information that the Indians were collecting in great numbers, under the immediate guidance of Philip, near Brookfield, despatched Captain Henchman, with fifty men, to dislodge them, who, proceeding first to Hadley, was joined by a company of cavalry from Hartford. On the 20th they discovered and attacked a party of Indians near Lancaster: they killed fifty of them, and took between fifty and sixty of their squaws and children prisoners. Captain Henchman, on his way to Brookfield, discovered the dead bodies of several of his countrymen half consumed by fire, who, it appeared, had a few days previous fallen victims to the wanton barbarity of the savages.

The scattered remains of the enemy being now so completely harassed and driven from place to place by the English, a number of them resorted to the western country, then inhabited by the Mohawks; but the latter, being on friendly terms with the English and Dutch, who were settling among them, were unwilling to harbor their enemies, and consequently attacked a considerable body of them on the 5th of March. The engagement was a severe one. The fugitive Indians, being furnished with firearms, repelled the attack of the Mohawks with a becoming spirit, but were at length overpowered and completely defeated: the loss on both sides was very great.

On the 20th the Indians took a Mr. Willet prisoner near Swanzey, and, after cutting off his nose and ears, set him at liberty. On the 23d they made prisoners of the family of a Mr. Barney, of Rehoboth, consisting of himself, wife, and six children: two of the youngest of the latter they killed and scalped, and threw their mangled bodies to their dogs to devour.

On the 28th a negro man, who had been for several months a prisoner among the savages, escaped from them and returned to the English, to whom he gave the following information; to wit, that the enemy were concerting a plan to attack Taunton and the villages adjacent; that for this purpose there were then imbodied near Worcester one thousand of them, at the head of whom was Philip, and that near one hundred of them were furnished with firearms; that, a few days previous to his escape, a scouting party arrived and brought in with them two prisoners and three human scalps. To frustrate the intentions of the enemy, the governor of Massachusetts colony despatched three companies of cavalry for the defence of Taunton.

The English of Connecticut colony, although but little troubled with the enemy since the destruction of the Pequots, were not unwilling to afford their brethren all the assistance possible in a protracted and bloody war with the common enemy. They accordingly furnished three companies of cavalry, who, under command of the experienced Major Talcott, on the 5th of April, proceeded to the westward in search of the enemy.   On the 11th they fell in with, attacked, and defeated a considerable body of them.   Apparently, by the special direction of divine Providence, Major Talcott arrived in the neighborhood of Hadley in time to preserve the town and save its inhabitants from total destruction.   The savages, to the number of five hundred, were on the eve of commencing an attack when they were met by the major with the troops under his command.   This unexpected relief animating the few inhabitants which the town contained, they hastened to the assistance of the cavalry, who, at this moment, were seriously engaged with the whole body of the enemy.   The savages having gained some signal advantages, victory for a considerable length of time appeared likely to decide in their favor.   Fortunately, the inhabitants of Hadley having for their defence, a few weeks previous, procured from Boston an eight pounder, it was at this critical period loaded by the women, and, being mounted, was by them conveyed to the English, which, being charged with small shot, nails, &c., was by the latter discharged with the best effect upon the enemy, who immediately thereupon fled in every direction. Thus it was that the English in a great measure owed the preservation of their lives to the unexampled heroism of a few women.

The governor and council of the United Colonies, taking under serious consideration the miraculous escape of the inhabitants of Hadley from total destruction and the recent success of the arms of the English in various parts of the country, appointed the 27th day of August, 1679, to be observed throughout the colonies as a day of public thanksgiving and praise to Almighty God.   This, it may be well to observe, was the commencement of an annual custom of our forefathers, which to the present day is so religiously observed by their descendants throughout the New England States.

On the 3d of September the Connecticut troops, under command of Major Talcott and Captains Dennison and New-

bury, proceeded to Narraganset in quest of the enemy, who,
to the number of about three hundred, had been discovered in
a piece of woods. The English were accompanied by their
faithful friend Oneco, with one hundred Mohegans·under his
command. In the evening of the 5th they discovered the
enemy encamped at the foot of a steep hill; on which Major
Talcott made arrangements for an attack. The Mohegans
were ordered by a circuitous route to gain the summit of the
hill, to prevent the flight of the enemy: two companies of
cavalry were ordered to flank them on the right and left;
while Major Talcott, with a company of foot, stationed himself in their rear. Having thus disposed of his forces, a signal was given by the major for the Mohegans to commence
the attack, which they did, and with such spirit, accompanied
by their savage yells, that, had the enemy been renowned for
their valor, they must have been to the highest degree appalled at so unexpected an onset. After contending a few
moments with the Mohegans, the enemy were attacked on the
right and left by the cavalry, who, with their cutlasses, made
great havoc among them: they were, however, unwilling to
give ground until they had lost nearly one half their number,
when they attempted a flight to a swamp in their rear; but
here they were met by Major Talcott, with the company of
foot, who gave them so warm a reception that they once more
fell back upon the Mohegans, by whom they were very soon
overpowered, and would have been totally destroyed had not
Major Talcott humanely interfered in their behalf and made
prisoners of the few that remained alive: among the latter
was their leader, a squaw, commonly termed the Queen of
Narraganset; and among them an active young fellow, who
begged to be delivered into the hands of the Mohegans, that
they might put him to death in their own way, and sacrifice
him to their cruel genius of revenge, in which they so much
delighted. The English, although naturally averse to acts
of savage barbarity, were not, in this instance, unwilling to

comply with the voluntary, although unnatural, request of the prisoner; as it appeared that he had, in presence of the Mohegans, exultingly boasted of having killed nineteen of the English with his gun since the commencement of the war, and after loading it for the twentieth, there being no more of the latter within reach, he levelled at a Mohegan, whom he killed; which completing his number, he was willing to die by their hands. The Mohegans accordingly began to prepare for the tragical event. Forming themselves into a circle, admitting as many of the English as were disposed to witness their savage proceedings, the prisoner was placed in the centre; when one of the Mohegans, who, in the late engagement, had lost a son, with his knife cut off the prisoner's ears, then his nose, and then the fingers of each hand; and after the lapse of a few moments dug out his eyes, and filled their sockets with hot embers. Although the few English present were overcome with a view of a scene so shocking to humanity, yet the prisoner, so far from bewailing his fate, seemed to surpass his tormentors in expressions of joy. When nearly exhausted with the loss of blood, and unable longer to stand, his executioner closed the tragic scene by beating out his brains with a tomahawk.

The few Indians that now remained in the neighborhood of Plymouth colony, being in a state of starvation, surrendered themselves prisoners to the English; one of whom, being recognized as the person who had a few days previous inhumanly murdered the daughter of a Mr. Clarke, was, by order of the governor, publicly executed: the remainder were retained and treated as prisoners of war. By the assistance of one of the prisoners, who served as guide, twenty more of the enemy were, on the following day, surprised and taken prisoners by the English.

The troops, under the command of Major Bradford and Captains Mosely and Brattle, on the 15th of September surprised and took one hundred and fifty of the enemy prisoners

near Pautuxet, among whom was the squaw of the celebrated
Philip; and on the day following, learning that the enemy
in considerable bodies were roving about in the woods near
Dedham, Major Bradford despatched Captain Brattle with
fifty men to attack them, who, the day following, fell in with
and engaged about one hundred of them.  As hatchets were
the only weapons with which they were provided, they made
but a feeble defence, and were soon overpowered by the English, who took seventy-four of them prisoners, the remainder
having fallen in the action.  The loss of the English was
two killed and five wounded.  The above party was commanded by a bloodthirsty sachem called Pomham, renowned
for his bodily strength, which exceeded that of any of his
countrymen ever met with.  He bravely defended himself to
the last: being wounded in the breast and unable to stand,
he seized one of the soldiers while in the act of despatching
him with the but of his gun, and by whom he would have
been strangled had he not been fortunately rescued by one
of his comrades.

A general famine now prevailing among the enemy, in consequence of being deprived of an opportunity to plant their
lands, numbers were daily compelled by hunger to surrender
themselves prisoners to the English, among whom was a Nipnet sachem, accompanied by one hundred and eighty of his
tribe.

On the 12th of October Captain Church, with fifty soldiers
and a few friendly Indians under his command, attacked and
defeated a party of the enemy near Providence; and on the
day following, conducted by Indian guides, discovered a considerable body of the enemy encamped in a swamp near Pom-
fret: a friendly Indian first espying them, commanded them
to surrender; but the enemy did not appear disposed to obey.
Being sheltered by large trees, they first discharged their
arrows among the English, and then, with a terrible yell, attacked them with their long knives and tomahawks.  The

English, meeting with a much warmer reception than what
they expected, gave ground; but being rallied by their old and
experienced commander, Captain Church, they rushed upon
them with such impetuosity that the enemy were thrown into
confusion and dislodged from their coverts.   The action continued about an hour and a quarter.   The English had seven
men killed and fourteen wounded; among the latter their
brave commander, who received an arrow through his left
arm.   The loss of the enemy was thirty-two killed and between sixty and seventy wounded.

On the 20th information was forwarded the governor and
council that the famous Philip, who had been for a long time
skulking about in the woods near Mount Hope, much disheartened by the ill success of his countrymen, was, the morning
preceding, discovered in a swamp near that place, attended by
about ninety Seaconet Indians; on which the brave Captain
Church, with his little band of invincibles, was immediately
despatched in pursuit of him.   Captain Church was accompanied, as usual, by a number of the Mohegans and a few
friendly Seaconet Indians.   On the 27th they arrived in the
neighborhood of the swamp, near the border of which he
stationed several of the Mohegans to intercept Philip in case
he should attempt an escape therefrom.   Captain Church, at
the head of his little band, now with unconquerable resolution plunged into the swamp, and, wading nearly to his waist
in water, discovered and attacked the enemy.   The Indians
were nearly one hundred strong; but being unexpectedly attacked they made no resistance, but fled in every direction;
the inaccessible state of the swamp, however, prevented the
English from pursuing them with success.   Their dependence
was now upon their friends stationed without; nor did it
appear that those faithful fellows suffered so good an opportunity to pass unimproved.   The report of their muskets
convinced Captain Church that they were doing their duty;
in confirmation of which, he was very soon after presented
with the head of King Philip.

Philip, it appeared, in attempting to fly from his pursuers, was recognized by one of the English who had been stationed with the Mohegans to intercept him, and at whom he levelled his piece; but the priming being unfortunately wet and preventing the discharge thereof, the cunning sachem would yet have escaped had not one of the brave sons of Uncus at this instant given him the contents of his musket. The ball went directly through his heart; and thus fell, by the hands of a faithful Mohegan, the famous Philip, who was the projector and instigator of a war which not only proved the cause of his own destruction, but that of nearly all his tribe, once the most numerous of any inhabiting New England.

It was at this important instant that the English were made witnesses of a remarkable instance of savage custom. Oneco, on learning that Philip had fallen by the hand of one of his tribe, urged that, agreeable to their custom, he had an undoubted right to the body, and a right to feast himself with a piece thereof; which the English not objecting to, he deliberately drew his long knife from his girdle, and with it detached a piece of flesh from the bleeding body of Philip of about one pound weight, which he broiled and ate, in the mean time declaring that "he had not for many moons eaten any thing with so good an appetite!" The head of Philip was detached from his body and sent by Captain Church to Boston, to be presented to the governor and council as a valuable trophy.

The few hostile Indians that now remained within the United Colonies, conscious that, if so fortunate as to evade the vigilance of the English, they must soon fall victims to the prevailing famine, fled with their families far to the westward. The English were disposed rather to facilitate than prevent their flight. Having been for a number of years engaged in a destructive and bloody war with them, they were willing that the few that remained alive should escape to a country so far distant that there was no probability of their returning to

resume the bloody tomahawk.    Impressed with this idea, and
that the enemy were completely exterminated, they were
about to bury the hatchet and turn their attention to agricul-
tural pursuits, when, by an express, they were informed that
the natives in the eastern part of the country, Province of
Maine, had unprovokedly attacked and killed a considerable
number of the English in that quarter.

To quench the flame which appeared to be enkindling in
the east, the governor despatched four companies of cavalry
to the relief of the unfortunate inhabitants.    The enemy, who
were of the Kennebeck and Amoscoggin tribes, first attacked
with unprecedented fury the defenceless inhabitants settled
on Kennebeck River, the most of whom were destroyed or
dispersed by them.

On the 2d of November about seven hundred of the enemy attacked with their accustomed fury, accompanied by
their savage yells, the inhabitants of Newchewannick, an
English settlement, situated a few miles from the mouth of
the River Kennebeck.    Before they had fully accomplished
their hellish purpose they were surprised by the troops sent
from Boston, between whom a most bloody engagement now
ensued.    The Indians, encouraged by their numbers, repelled
the attack of the English in so heroic a manner that the latter were very soon thrown into disorder and driven out of
town, where they again formed, faced about, and in turn
charged the enemy with unconquerable resolution.    The contest now became close and severe : the savages, with their
terrific yells, dexterously hurled their tomahawks among the
English ; while the latter, with as much dexterity, attacked and
mowed them down with their cutlasses.    Each were apparently determined on victory or death.    The English at one
moment, unable to withstand the impetuosity of the savages,
would give ground ; at the next, the latter, hard pushed by
the cavalry, would fall back.    Thus for the space of two hours
did victory appear balancing between the two contending

parties. The field of action was covered with the slain, while the adjacent woods resounded with the shrieks and groans of the wounded. At this critical juncture the English, when on the very point of surrendering, were providentially preserved by a stratagem. In the heat of the action Major Bradford despatched a company of cavalry by a circuitous route to attack the enemy in the rear, which had the most happy effect. The enemy, suspecting this company a reënforcement of the English, fled in every direction, leaving the English masters of the field. Thus, after two hours' hard fighting, did the English obtain a victory at the expense of the lives of more than half their number. Their killed and wounded amounted to ninety-nine. The loss of the enemy was not ascertained; it was, however, probably three times greater than that of the English.

The day succeeding this bloody engagement a lieutenant with twelve men was sent by the commander to the place of action to bury their dead; when they were a few rods therefrom unexpectedly attacked by about one hundred of the enemy who had lain in ambush. The lieutenant ordered his men to reserve their fire until they could discharge with the best effect upon the enemy, by whom they were soon surrounded and furiously attacked on all sides. The savages, yelling horribly, brandished their long knives in the air, yet crimsoned with the blood of their countrymen. The brave little band, however, remained firm and undaunted; and as the savages approached them, each taking proper aim, discharged with so good effect upon them that the Indians, amazed at the instantaneous destruction of so many of their comrades, fled in every direction. The English sustained no loss.

On the 5th the enemy successfully attacked the inhabitants of the village of Casco, thirty of whom they killed, and made prisoners of the family of a Mr. Bracket, who on the 7th, in the following manner, made their escape. The Indians, on their return to their wigwams, learning that a detached party of their brethren had attacked with success and plundered the village of Arowsick, to enjoy a share of the spoil hastened to join them, leaving the prisoners in the care of two old men and three squaws. Mr. Bracket, whose family consisted of himself, wife, three small children, and a negro lad, viewed this as a favorable opportunity to escape; to effect which, he requested the lad to attempt an escape by flight, which, being uncommonly active, he easily effected. The plan of Mr. Bracket had now its desired effect; as the old men, pursuing the negro, left him and his family guarded only by the three squaws, whom, being intoxicated, he soon despatched, and returned the day succeeding with his family to Casco, where the negro lad had arrived some hours before.

On the 15th the Indians attacked the dwelling house of a Captain Bonithon and Major Philips, situated on the east side of Casco River. They having seasonable notice of the hostile views of the enemy, the family of the former, as a place of greater safety, had resorted to the house of the latter a few moments previous to the attack. The savages first, communicating fire to the house of Captain Bonithon, next proceeded furiously to attack the dwelling of Major Philips, in which there were about twenty persons, by whom it was most gallantly defended. The enemy had their leader and a number of their party killed by the fire of the English. Despairing of taking the house by assault, they adopted a new plan to communicate fire thereto. They procured a carriage, on which they erected a stage, in front of which was a barricade rendered bullet proof, and to which long poles were attached nearly twenty feet in length, to the ends of which were affixed every kind of combustible, such as birch rinds, straw, pitch, pine, &c. The Indians were sheltered by the barricade from the fire of the English while they approached the walls of the house with their carriage. The English were now on the eve of despairing, when fortunately one of the wheels of the carriage, being brought in contact with a rock, was turned completely round, which exposed the whole body of Indians to their fire. This unexpected opportunity was improved with the greatest advantage by the English, who with a few rounds soon dispersed the enemy with no inconsiderable loss.

The day following the Indians attacked and set fire to the house of a Mr. Wakely, whom with his whole family they murdered. A company of English, apprised of their dangerous situation, marched to their relief, but arrived too late to afford them assistance. They found the house reduced to ashes, among which they discovered the mangled bodies of the unfortunate family half consumed by fire.

The savages, emboldened by their late success, on the 20th attacked a small English settlement on Piscataqua River, and succeeded in murdering a part and carrying away the remainder of the inhabitants into captivity. As an instance of their wanton barbarity, it should be here mentioned, that, after tomahawking and scalping one of the unfortunate women of the above place, they bound to the dead body her little infant, in which situation it was the succeeding day discovered by the English, attempting to draw nourishment from its mother's breast.

The governor and council of the United Colonies, conceiving it their duty, if possible, to put a final stop to the ravages of the enemy in the east, and to prevent the further effusion of innocent blood, despatched Major Wallis and Major Bradford, with six companies under their command, to destroy, "root and branch," the common enemy. On the 1st of December they arrived in the neighborhood of Kennebeck, near where they were informed the main body of the enemy were encamped. On the morning of the 3d they fell in with and attacked them. The enemy, who were about eight hundred strong, appeared disposed to maintain their ground. They fought with all the fury of savages, and even assailed the

MURDER OF MR. WAHELY'S FAMILY.   Page 74.

English from the tops of lofty trees which they ascended for the purpose. They were possessed of but few firearms, but hurled their tomahawks with inconceivable exactness, and checked the progress of the cavalry with long spears. Victory for a long time remained doubtful. The ground, being covered with snow, greatly retarded the progress of the troops, who probably would have met with a defeat had not a fresh company of infantry arrived in time to change the fortune of the day. These having remained inactive as a body of reserve, the commander found himself under the necessity of calling for their aid. The enemy, disheartened at the unexpected arrival of an additional number of the English, fled with precipitancy to the woods; but very few of them, however, escaped: more than two hundred of them remained dead upon the field of action, and double that number mortally wounded. The loss of the English was twenty-five killed and forty-four wounded. This engagement, which proved a decisive one, was of the greatest importance to the English. The great and arduous work was now completed. The few remaining Indians that inhabited the eastern country now expressed a desire to bury the bloody hatchet and to make peace with the English. Their request was cheerfully complied with, and they continued ever after the faithful friends of the English.

From this important period — which, being the 5th day of December, 1679 — ought the peace and prosperity of the now flourishing states of New England to receive their date. It was at this period that her hardy sons quitted the sanguine field and exchanged their implements of death for such as were better calculated for the cultivation and tillage of their farms. The forests with which they were encompassed no longer abounded with fierce and untutored savages. The Indian death song and war whoop was no longer heard. The greater part of the Indians that survived the many bloody engagements had sought peace and retirement far westward. The prisoners which the English had captured were liberated upon condition of resorting to and remaining with them. They proved faithful to their promise; they took possession of the country bounding on the great lakes, and in possession of which their descendants remain to the present day — a description of whose manners and customs will be found in the succeeding chapter.

We shall close this with a few remarks relative to the state, customs, and ludicrous opinions of the Indians in New England when first visited by our forefathers, and of their rapid depopulation since that period.

We cannot even hazard a conjecture respecting the Indian population of New England at the time of its first settlement by the English. Captain Smith, in a voyage to this coast in 1614, supposed that on Massachusetts Island there were about three thousand Indians. All accounts agree that the sea coast and neighboring islands were thickly inhabited.

Three years before the arrival of the Plymouth colony a very mortal sickness, supposed to have been the plague, or perhaps the yellow fever, raged with great violence among the Indians in the eastern parts of New England. Whole towns were depopulated. The living were not able to bury the dead; and their bones were found lying above ground many years after. The Massachusetts Indians are said to have been reduced from thirty thousand to three hundred fighting men. In 1633, the small pox swept off great numbers of the Indians in Massachusetts.

In 1763, on the Island of Nantucket, in the space of four months the Indians were reduced by a mortal sickness from three hundred and twenty to eighty-five souls. The hand of Providence is notable in these surprising instances of mortality among the Indians to make room for the whites. Comparatively few have perished by wars; and the descendants of the few that were not driven to the westward by the English waste and moulder away and in a manner unaccountable disappear.

The number of Indians in the State of Connecticut, in 1774, was one thousand three hundred and sixty-three; but their number is now doubtless much lessened. The principal part of their population in this state is at Mohegan, in the county of New London. These are the descendants of the Mohegans, of whom frequent mention is made in the foregoing pages as being very serviceable, under the command of Uncus, to the English, in their many engagements with the natives. The Mohegans have ever exhibited great reverence for the descendants of their royal sachem. After the death of Uncus, his body was conveyed, by his request, to Norwich, and there interred in the neighborhood of one of his forts. This spot was selected by him previous to his death; and it was his dying request that the whole family of Uncus should be there buried — a request which has been strictly complied with by the Mohegans, who, although the distance is seven miles from their own burying ground, have deposited, and continue to deposit there, the descendants of their revered sachem.

The number of Indians in Rhode Island, in 1783, was only five hundred and twenty-five. More than half of these live in Charleston, in the county of Washington. In 1774 the number of Indians in Rhode Island was one thousand four hundred and eighty-two; so that, in nine years, the decrease was nine hundred and fifty-seven. We have not been able to ascertain the exact state of the Indian population in Massachusetts and New Hampshire. In 1784 there was a tribe of about forty Indians at Norridgewalk, in the Province of Maine, with some few other scattering remains of tribes in other parts, and a number of towns thinly inhabited round Cape Cod.

When the English first arrived in America, the Indians had no time or places set apart for religious worship. The first settlers in New England were at great pains to introduce among them the habits of civilized life and to instruct them in the Christian religion. A few years' intercourse with the

7 *

Indians induced them to establish several good and natural regulations.

The Rev. Mr. Elliot, of Roxbury, near Boston, who has been styled the great "Indian apostle," with much labor learned the Natic dialect of the Indian languages. He published an Indian grammar, and preached in Indian to several tribes, and, in 1664, translated the Bible and several religious books into the Indian language. He relates several pertinent queries of the Indians respecting the Christian religion; among others, whether Jesus Christ, the Mediator, or Interpreter, could understand prayer in the Indian language. If the father be bad and the child good, why should God, in the second commandment, be offended with the child? How the Indians came to differ so much from the English in the knowledge of God and Jesus Christ, since they all sprang from one father. Mr. Elliot was indefatigable in his labors, and travelled through all parts of Massachusetts and Plymouth colonies as far as Cape Cod. The colony had such a veneration for him, that, in an act of the General Assembly relating to Indians, they express themselves thus: " By the advice of the said magistrates and of Mr. Elliot."

Concerning the religion of the untaught natives of New England, who once held a plurality of deities, after the arrival of the English they supposed there were only three, because they saw people of three kinds of complexions; viz., English, negroes, and themselves.

It was a notion pretty generally prevailing among them that it was not the same God made them who made us, but that they were created after the white people; and it is probable they supposed their God gained some special skill by seeing the white people made, and so made them better. For it is certain they looked upon themselves and their methods of living, which they say their God expressly prescribed for them, as vastly preferable to the white people and their methods.

With regard to a future state of existence, many of them
imagined that the *chichung*, that is, the shadow, or what survived the body, would at death go southward, and in an unknown but curious place; would enjoy some kind of happiness, such as hunting, feasting, dancing, and the like. And
what they supposed would contribute much to their happiness
was, that they should there never be weary of those enter-
tainments.

The natives of New England believed not only a plurality
of gods, who made and governed the several nations of the
world, but they made deities of every thing they imagined to
be great, powerful, beneficial, and hurtful to mankind : yet
they conceived an almighty Being, whom they called Kichtau, who at first, according to their tradition, made a man
and woman out of stone; but upon some dislike destroyed
them again, and then made another couple out of a tree, from
whom descended all the nations of the earth; but how they
came to be scattered and dispersed into countries so remote
from one another, they could not tell. They believed their
supreme God to be a good Being, and paid a sort of acknowl-
edgment to him for plenty, victory, and other benefits.

The immortality of the soul was universally believed among
them. When good men died they said their souls went to
Kichtau, where they met with their friends and enjoyed all
manner of pleasures. When the wicked died they went to
Kichtau also, but were commanded to walk away, and so
wander about in restless discontent and darkness forever.

The natives of New England, in general, were quick of
apprehension, and ingenious ; and, when pleased, nothing could
exceed their courtesy and friendship. Gravity and eloquence
distinguished them in council, address and bravery in war.
They were not more easily provoked than the English; but
when once they had received an injury it was never forgotten.
In anger they were not like the English, talkative and boisterous, but sullen and revengeful. The men declined all

labor, and spent their time in hunting, fishing, shooting, and warlike exercises. They imposed all the drudgery upon their women, who gathered and brought home their wood, planted, dressed, and gathered their corn. When they travelled the women carried their children, packs, and provisions. The women submitted patiently to such treatment : this ungenerous usage of their husbands they repaid with smiles and good humor.

The clothing of the natives was the skins of wild beasts. The men threw a mantle of skins over them, and wore a small flap, which were termed Indian breeches. The women were much more modest : they wore a coat of skins, girt about their loins, which reached down to their hams, which they never put off in company. If the husband chose to dispose of his wife's beaver petticoat, she could not be persuaded to part with it until he had provided another of some sort. In the winter their blanket of skins, which hung loose in summer, was tied or wrapped more closely about them. The old men in the severe seasons also wore a sort of trousers, made of skins and fastened to their girdles ; and on their feet they wore moccasons made of moose leather ; and their chiefs, or sachems, wore on their heads a cap decorated with feathers.

Their houses, or wigwams, were at best but miserable cells. They were constructed generally like arbors, or small young trees bent and twisted together, and so curiously covered with mats or bark that they were tolerably dry and warm. The natives made their fires in the centre of the house ; and there was an opening at the top, which emitted the smoke. For the convenience of wood and water these huts were commonly erected in groves, near some river, brook, or living spring ; when either failed, the family removed to another place.

They lived in a poor, low manner ; their food was coarse and simple, without any kind of seasoning ; they had neither spice, salt, or bread. Their food was principally the entrails of moose, deer, bears, and all kinds of wild beasts and fowls : of fish and snakes they were extremely fond. They had strong stomachs, and nothing came amiss. They had no set meals, but, like other wild creatures, ate when they were hungry and could find any thing to satisfy the cravings of nature. They had but little food from the earth except what it spontaneously produced. Indian corn, beans, and squashes were the only eatables for which the natives of New England labored.

Their household furniture was of but small value. Their beds were composed of mats or skins. They had neither chairs nor stools; but commonly sat upon the ground, with their elbows upon their knees. A few wooden and stone vessels and instruments served all the purposes of domestic life. Their knife was a sharp stone, shell, or kind of reed, which they sharpened in such a manner as to cut their hair, make their bows and arrows, &c. They made their axes of stone, which they shaped somewhat similar to our axes, but with the difference of theirs being made with a neck instead of an eye, and fastened with a with like a blacksmith's chisel.

The manner of the courtship and marriage of the natives manifested the impurity of their morals. When a young Indian wished for marriage, he presented the girl with whom he was enamoured with bracelets, belts, and chains of wampum. If she received his presents they cohabited together for a time upon trial; if they pleased each other they were joined in marriage; but if, after a few weeks, they were not suited, the man, leaving his presents, quitted the girl and sought another mistress, and she another lover. In this manner they courted until two met who were agreeable to each other.

The natives of New England, although they consisted of a great number of different nations and clans, appear to have spoken radically the same language : from Piscataqua to Connecticut it was so nearly the same that the different tribes could converse tolerably together. The Mohegan, or Pequot, language was essentially that of all the Indians in New England. The word *Mohegan* is a corruption of *Muhhekaneew* in the singular, or of *Muhhekaneek* in the plural number. The Penobscots bordering on Nova Scotia, the Indians of St. Francis in Canada, the Delawares in Pennsylvania, the Shawanese on the Ohio, and the Chippewaus at the westward of Lake Huron, all now speak the same radical language.

# WASHINGTON'S EXPEDITION IN 1753;

## AND

# DEFEAT OF GENERAL BRADDOCK, BY THE INDIANS, IN 1755.

In 1753 the French and Indians began to make inroads on our western frontiers along the Ohio. Governor Dinwiddie, of Virginia, was very desirous to get a letter of remonstrance to their commander-in-chief. He had applied to several young gentlemen of his acquaintance; but they were all so deficient in courage that they could not be prevailed on for love or money to venture out among the savages. Our beloved Washington, happening to hear of it, instantly waited on his excellency and offered his services, but not without being terribly afraid lest his want of a beard should go against him. However, the governor was so charmed with his modesty and manly air that he never asked him a syllable about his age; but, after thanking him for "a noble youth," and insisting on his taking a glass of wine with him, slipped a commission into his hand. The next day, accompanied by an interpreter and a couple of servants, he set out on his expedition, which was, from start to pole, as disagreeable and dangerous as any thing Hercules himself could have wished. Soaking rains, chilling blasts, roaring floods, pathless woods, and mountains clad in snows opposed his course, but opposed in vain. The glorious ambition to serve his country imparted an animation to his nerves which rendered him superior to all difficulties,

Returning homewards he was waylaid and shot at by a French Indian; and though the copper-colored ruffian was not fifteen steps distant when he fired at him, yet not even so much as the smell of lead passed on the clothes of our young hero. On his return to Virginia it was found that he had executed his negotiations, both with the French and Indians, with such fidelity and judgment that he received the heartiest thanks of the governor and council for the very important services he had done his country.

He was now, in the twentieth year of his age, appointed major and adjutant general of the Virginia forces. Soon after this, the Indians continuing their encroachments, orders were given by the English government for the colonies to arm and unite in one confederacy. Virginia took the lead, and raised a regiment of four hundred men, at the head of which she placed her darling Washington.

With this handful of brave fellows Colonel Washington, not yet twenty-three years of age, boldly pushed out into the Indian country, and there, for a considerable time, Hannibal-like, maintained the war against three times the number of French and Indians. At the Red Stones he came up with a strong party of the enemy, whom he engaged and effectually defeated, after having killed and taken thirty-one men. From his prisoners he obtained undoubted intelligence that the French forces on the Ohio consisted of upwards of a thousand regulars and many hundreds of Indians. But, notwithstanding this disheartening advice, he still pressed on undauntedly against the enemy, and at a place called the Little Meadows built a fort, which he called Fort Necessity. Here he waited, hourly and anxiously looking for succors from New York and Pennsylvania; but he looked in vain. Nobody came to his assistance. Not long after this, his small force, now reduced to three hundred men, were attacked by an army of eleven hundred French and Indians. Never did the true Virginian valor shine more gloriously than on this trying occasion.

To see three hundred young fellows, commanded by a smoothfaced boy, all unaccustomed to the terrors of war; far from home and from all hopes of help; shut up in a dreary wilderness, and surrounded by four times their number of savage foes; and yet, without sign of fear, without thought of surrender, preparing for mortal combat, — O, it was a noble sight! Scarcely since the days of Leonidas and his three hundred deathless Spartans had the sun beheld its equal. With hideous whoops and yells the enemy came on like a host of tigers. The woods, and rocks, and tall tree tops, as the Indians, climbing to the tops of the trees, poured down their bullets into the fort, were in one continued blaze and crash of firearms. Nor were our young warriors idle, but, animated by their gallant chief, plied their rifles with such spirit that their little fort represented a volcano in full blast, roaring and discharging thick sheets of liquid fire and of leaden deaths among their foes. For three glorious hours, salamander-like, enveloped in smoke and flame, they sustained the attack of the enemy's whole force, and laid two hundred of them dead on the spot. Discouraged by such desperate resistance, the French general, the Count de Villiers, sent in a flag to Washington, extolling his gallantry to the skies, and offering him the most honorable terms. It was stipulated that Colonel Washington and his little band of heroes should march away with all the honors of war, and carry with them their military stores and baggage.

In the spring of 1755 Washington, while busied in the highest military operations, was summoned to attend General Braddock, who, in the month of February, arrived at Alexandria with two thousand British troops. The Assembly of Virginia appointed eight hundred provincials to join him. The object of this army was to march through the country, by the way of Will's Creek, to Fort Du Quesne, now Pittsburg, or Fort Pitt. As no person was so well acquainted with the frontier country as Washington, and none stood so

high in military fame, it was thought he would be infinitely
serviceable to General Braddock.   At the request of the
governor and council he cheerfully quitted his own command
to act as volunteer aid-de-camp to that very imprudent and
unfortunate general.   The army, near three thousand strong,
marched from Alexandria, and proceeded unmolested within
a few miles of Fort Pitt.   On the morning of the day in
which they expected to arrive the provincial scouts discovered a large party of French and Indians lying in ambush.
Washington, with his usual modesty, observed to General
Braddock what sort of enemy he had now to deal with — an
enemy who would not, like the Europeans, come forward to a
fair contest in the field, but, concealed behind rocks and trees,
carry on a deadly warfare with their rifles.   He concluded
with begging that General Braddock would grant him the
honor to let him place himself at the head of the Virginia
riflemen and fight them in their own way.   And it was generally thought that our young hero and his eight hundred
hearts of hickory would very easily have beaten them too ;
for they were not superior to the force which, with only three
hundred, he had handled so roughly a twelvemonth before.
But General Braddock, who had all along treated the American officers and soldiers with infinite contempt, instead of following this truly salutary advice, swelled and reddened with
most unmanly rage.   " High times, by G—d ! " he exclaimed,
strutting to and fro, with arms akimbo.   " High times, when
a young buckskin can teach a British general how to fight ! "
Washington withdrew, biting his lips with grief and indignation to think what numbers of brave fellows would draw short
breath that day through the pride and obstinacy of one epau-
letted fool.   The troops were ordered to form and advance
in columns through the woods.   In a little time the ruin
which Washington had predicted ensued.   This poor, devoted
army, pushed on by their madcap general, fell into the fatal
snare which was laid for them.   All at once a thousand rifles

INDIANS AND FRENCH ATTACKING BRADDOCK'S ARMY.   Page 87.

began the work of death. The ground was instantly covered with the dying and the dead. The British troops, thus slaughtered by hundreds, and by an enemy whom they could not see, were thrown irrecoverably into panic and confusion; and in a few minutes their haughty general, with twelve hundred of his brave but unfortunate countrymen, bit the ground. Poor Braddock closed the tragedy with great decency. He was mortally wounded in the beginning of the action, and Washington had him placed in a cart ready for retreat. Close on the left, where the weight of the French and Indian fire principally fell, Washington and his Virginia riflemen, dressed in blue, sustained the shock. At every discharge of their rifles the wounded general cried out, "O my brave Virginia blues, would to God I could live to reward you for such gallantry!" But he died. Washington buried him in the road, and, to save him from discovery and the scalping knife, ordered the wagons on their retreat to drive over his grave. O God, what is man? Even a thing of nought.

Amidst all this fearful consternation and carnage, amidst all the uproar and horrors of a rout, rendered still more dreadful by the groans of the dying, the screams of the wounded, the piercing shrieks of the women, and the yells of the furious assaulting savages, Washington, calm and self-collected, rallied his faithful riflemen, led them on to the charge, killed numbers of the enemy who were rushing on with tomahawks, checked their pursuit, and brought off the shattered remains of the British army.

With respect to our beloved Washington we cannot but mention here two very extraordinary speeches that were uttered about him at this time, and which, as things have turned out, look a good deal like prophecies. A famous Indian warrior, who assisted in the defeat of Braddock, was often heard to swear that Washington was not born to be killed by a bullet; "for," continued he, "I had seventeen fair fires at him with my rifle; and, after all, I could not bring him to the ground." And indeed, whoever considers that a good rifle, levelled by a proper marksman, hardly ever misses its aim, will readily enough conclude, with this unlettered savage, that some invisible hand must have turned aside his bullets.

The Rev. Mr. Davies, in a sermon occasioned by General Braddock's defeat, has these remarkable words: "I beg leave to point the attention of the public to that heroic youth, Colonel George Washington, whom I cannot but hope Providence has preserved for some great service to this country."

# EXPEDITION AND DEFEAT OF GENERAL HARMER BY THE INDIANS, 1790.

ALTHOUGH a peace was happily effected between the two contending parties, Great Britain and America, in 1783, yet the savages, who had been persuaded to take a part with the former, were unwilling to bury the bloody hatchet. They had not sufficiently bathed that destructive weapon in the blood of the Americans. Without any pretext whatever, they continued to exercise towards them the most wanton acts of barbarity. It appeared from respectable evidence that from the year 1783 until the month of October, 1790, the time the United States commenced offensive operations against the said Indians, that on the Ohio and the frontiers on the south side thereof, they killed, wounded, and took prisoners about one thousand five hundred men, women, and children, besides carrying off upwards of two thousand horses and other property to the amount of fifty thousand dollars.

The particulars of many of the instances of barbarity exercised upon the prisoners of different ages and sexes, although supported by indisputable evidence, are of too shocking a nature to be presented to the public. It is sufficient here to observe that the scalping knife and tomahawk were the mildest instruments of death; that in some cases torture by fire and other execrable means were used.

But the outrages which were committed upon the frontier inhabitants were not the only injuries that were sustained. Repeated attacks upon detachments of the troops of the United States were at different times made. The following, from

8 *                                        (89)

its peculiar enormity, deserves recital: In April, 1790, Major Doughty, in service of the United States, was ordered to the friendly Chicasaws on public business. He performed this duty in a boat, having with him a party of fifteen men. While ascending the Tennessee River he was met by a party of forty Indians in four canoes, consisting principally of Shawanese and outcast Cherokees. They approached under a white flag, the well-known emblem of peace. They came on board the major's boat, received his presents, continued with him nearly an hour, and then departed in the most friendly manner. But they had scarcely cleared his oars before they poured in a fire upon his crew, which was returned as soon as circumstances would permit, and a most unequal combat was sustained for several hours, when they abandoned their design, but not until they had killed and wounded eleven out of fifteen of the boat's crew.

All overtures of peace failing, and the depredations still continuing, an attempt at coercion became indispensable. Accordingly, on the 30th of September, 1790, the president, by and with the consent and advice of the Congress of the United States, despatched General Harmer, with three hundred and twenty federal troops and eleven hundred and thirty-three militia under his command, to attack and destroy their principal villages.

The troops, after seventeen days' march from Miami, reached the great Miami village without any other molestation than that of having a number of their packhorses stolen. On their arrival they found the village deserted, and all the valuable buildings in flames, set on fire by the Indians. After a short tarry they proceeded to the neighboring villages without molestation and destroyed five of them and a large quantity of corn, computed at fifteen thousand bushels, which they found buried in different places, and very large quantities of vegetables of every kind.

The first opposition that was met with, a party of about one hundred and fifty Kentucky militia and thirty regular troops, all under the command of Colonel Harding, of Kentucky, were detached from the main body lying in the great Miami village, to pursue the trail of a party of Indians which had the day before been discovered.   After a pursuit of about six miles they came up with and were attacked on surprise by a body of Indians who were concealed in the thickets on every side of a large plain; and on the first onset the militia, without exchanging a single shot, made a most precipitate retreat, and left the regular troops to stand the whole charge of the Indians.   The conflict was short and bloody; the troops were soon overpowered by numbers; and all fell, except two officers and two or three privates, after defending themselves at their bayonet points with the greatest possible obstinacy. Ensign Hartshorn was one of the officers who providentially escaped; and his escape appeared to depend more on a lucky circumstance of faltering over a log in his retreat, and by that means screening himself from the eye of his pursuers, than from any other circumstance.   Captain Armstrong, who commanded the party, likewise made his escape by plunging himself into a pond, or swamp, up to his neck, within two hundred yards of the field of action, where he remained the whole night a spectator to the horrid scene of the war dance performed over the dead and wounded bodies of the poor soldiers that had fallen the preceding day; where their shrieks, mixed with the horrid yells of the savages, rendered his situation shocking.

After this some few skirmishes succeeded, but nothing material until the second capital action, which happened two days after the army left the Miami village.   At ten miles' distance from the town the general ordered a halt, and detached from four to five hundred militia and about sixty regular soldiers, under the command of Major Wyllys and Colonel Harding, who were ordered to march back to the town. On their first entrance there appeared a small body of Indians, who immediately fled at the first onset, and by that means decoyed the whole body of the militia, by making their flight in different directions and encouraging the militia to pursue. By this stratagem the few regular troops were left alone, and the Indians had effected their design; for, the moment they found the small handful of regular troops detached from the main body of the militia, they commenced the attack with their whole force, excepting the flying parties that had divided the militia; and although they soon found some part of the militia returning on their backs, pursued their object of routing and destroying the troops as the only sure plan of success, which, after a most bloody conflict on each side, they effected.

Nothing could exceed the intrepidity of the savages on this occasion. The militia they appeared to despise, and, with all the undauntedness conceivable, threw down their guns and rushed upon the bayonets of the regular soldiers. A number of them fell, but being so far superior in numbers the regulars were soon overpowered; for, while the poor soldier had his bayonet in one Indian, two more would sink their tomahawks in his head. The defeat of the troops was complete; the dead and wounded were left on the field of action in possession of the savages.

The following is a copy of the official return of the killed and wounded in the expedition:—

### Killed of the Federal Troops.

1 major, 1 lieutenant, 73 rank and file; total, 75. Wounded, 3 rank and file.

### Killed of the Militia.

1 major, 3 captains, 2 lieutenants, 4 ensigns, 98 rank and file; total, 180. Wounded, 2 lieutenants, 1 ensign, 25 rank and file; total, 28.

The regular troops, all but nine, including two commissioned officers, were killed.   Among the slain was Major Wyllys and a number of brave and valuable soldiers.   The Indians, it appeared from some cause, did not think it prudent to pursue their successes from the field of action; as most of the troops that were not killed or badly wounded made their escape, which they could not have effected had the enemy pursued with their usual fury.

# EXPEDITIONS OF GENERALS SCOTT AND WILKINSON, IN MAY AND AUGUST, 1791.

## GENERAL SCOTT TO THE SECRETARY OF WAR.

SIR,—In prosecution of the enterprise, I marched with eight hundred and fifty troops under my command, four miles from the banks of the Ohio, on the 23d of May; and on the 24th I resumed my march and pushed forward with the utmost industry, directing my route to Ouiattannan in the best manner my guides and information enabled me, though I found myself greatly deficient in both.

By the 31st I had marched one hundred and thirty-five miles over a country cut by four large branches of White River, and many smaller streams with steep, muddy banks. During this march I traversed a country alternately interspersed with the most luxurious soil and deep clayey bogs, from one to five miles wide, rendered almost impervious by brush and briers. Rain fell in torrents every day, with frequent blasts of wind and thunder storms. These obstacles impeded my progress, wore down my horses, and destroyed my provisions.

On the morning of the 1st instant, as the army entered an extensive prairie, I perceived an Indian on horseback a few miles to the right. I immediately made a detachment to intercept him; but he escaped. Finding myself discovered, I determined to advance with all the rapidity my circumstances would permit, rather with the hope than the expectation of reaching the object sought that day; for my guides were strangers to the country which I occupied.  At one o'clock, having marched by computation one hundred and fifty-five miles from the Ohio, as I penetrated a grove which bordered on an extensive prairie, I discovered two small villages to my left, at two and four miles' distance.

My guides now recognized the ground, and informed me that the main town was four or five miles in front, behind a point of wood which jutted into the prairie.  I immediately detached Colonel John Hardin with sixty mounted infantry, and a troop of light horse under Captain M'Coy, to attack the villages to the left, and moved on briskly with my main body in order of battle towards the town, the smoke of which was discernible.  My guides were deceived with respect to the situation of the town; for, instead of standing at the edge of the plain through which I marched, I found in the low ground bordering on the Wabash, on turning the point of woods, one house presented in my front.  Captain Price was ordered to assault that with forty men.  He executed the command with great gallantry, and killed two warriors.

When I gained the summit of the eminence which overlooks the villages on the banks of the Wabash, I discovered the enemy in great confusion, endeavoring to make their escape over the river in canoes.  I instantly ordered Lieutenant Colonel Commandant Wilkinson to rush forward with the first battalion.  The order was executed with promptitude, and this detachment gained the bank of the river just as the rear of the enemy had embarked; and, regardless of a brisk fire kept up from a Kickapoo town on the opposite bank, they in a few minutes, by a well-directed fire from their rifles, destroyed all the savages with which five canoes were crowded.

The enemy still kept possession of the Kickapoo town. I determined to dislodge them, and for the purpose ordered Captains King's and Logsdon's companies to march down the river below the town and cross, under the conduct of

Major Barbee. Several of the men swam the river, and others passed in a small canoe. This movement was unobserved, and my men had taken post on the bank before they were discovered by the enemy, who immediately abandoned the village. About this time word was brought me that Colonel Hardin was encumbered with prisoners, and had discovered a stronger village, farther to my left, than those I had observed, which he was proceeding to attack. I immediately detached Captain Brown, with his company, to support the colonel; but the distance being six miles, before the captain arrived the business was done, and Colonel Hardin joined me little before sunset, having killed six warriors and taken fifty-two prisoners. Captain Bull, the warrior who discovered me in the morning, had gained the main town and given the alarm a short time before me; but the villages to the left were uninformed of my approach, and had no retreat. The next morning I determined to detach my lieutenant colonel commandant with five hundred men to destroy the important town of Kethlipecanunk, at the mouth of the Eel River, eighteen miles from my camp, and on the west side of Wabash. But on examination I discovered my men and horses to be crippled and worn down by a long, laborious march, and the active exertions of the preceding day; that three hundred and sixty men only could be found in capacity to undertake the enterprise, and they prepared to march on foot.

Colonel Wilkinson marched with this detachment at half past five in the evening, and returned to my camp the next day at one o'clock, having marched thirty-six miles in twelve hours, and destroyed the most important settlement of the enemy in that quarter of the federal territory.

The following is Colonel Wilkinson's report respecting the enterprise : —

SIR, — The detachment under my command, destined to attack the village Kethlipecanunk, was put in motion at half past five o'clock last evening. Knowing that an enemy, whose chief dependence is in his dexterity as a marksman, and alertness in covering himself behind trees, stumps, and other impediments to fair sight, would not hazard an action in the night, I determined to push my march until I approached the vicinity of the villages where I knew the country to be champaign. I gained my point without a halt twenty minutes before eleven o'clock, lay upon my arms until four o'clock, and half an hour after assaulted the town at all quarters. The enemy was vigilant, gave way on my approach, and in canoes crossed Eel Creek, which washed the north-east part of the town; that creek was not fordable. My corps dashed forward with the impetuosity becoming volunteers, and were saluted by the enemy with a brisk fire from the opposite side of the creek. Dauntless they rushed on to the water's edge, and, finding the river impassable, returned a volley which so galled and disconcerted their antagonists that they threw away their fire without effect. In five minutes the Indians were driven from their covering and fled with precipitation. I have three men slightly wounded. At half past five the town was in flames, and at six o'clock I commenced my retreat.

I am, sir, yours, &c.,

JAMES WILKINSON.

Brigadier General Scott.

Many of the inhabitants of Kethlipecanunk were French, and lived in a state of civilization. Misunderstanding the object of a white flag, which appeared on an eminence opposite to me in the afternoon of the first, I liberated an aged squaw, and sent with her a message to the savages, that, if they would come in and surrender, their towns should be spared and they should receive good treatment. It was afterwards found that this white flag was not intended as a signal of parley, but was placed there to mark the spot where a person of distinction among the Indians, who had died some time before,

9

was interred. On the 4th I determined to discharge sixteen of the weakest and most infirm of my prisoners with a talk to the Wabash tribes, a copy of which follows. My motives to this measure were, to rid the army of a heavy encumbrance, to gratify the impulses of humanity, to increase the panic my operations had produced, and, by distracting the council of the enemy, to favor the views of government.

On the same day, after having burned the towns and adjacent villages and destroyed the growing corn and pulse, I began my march for the rapids of Ohio, where I arrived the 14th, without the loss of a single man by the enemy, and five only wounded, having killed thirty-two, chiefly warriors of size and figure, and taken fifty-eight prisoners.

---

*To the various Tribes of the Peankashaws and all the Nations of Red People living on the Waters of the Wabash River.*

The sovereign council of the thirteen United States, having long patiently borne your depredations against their settlements on this side of the great mountains, in hopes that you would see your error and correct it, by entering into bonds of amity and lasting peace, moved by compassion, and pitying your misguided councils, have not unfrequently addressed you on this subject, but without effect. At length their patience is exhausted, and they have stretched forth the arm of power against you. Their mighty sons and chief warriors have at length taken up the hatchet; they have penetrated far into your country, to meet your warriors and punish them for their transgressions. But you fled before them and decline the battle, leaving your wives and children to their mercy. They have destroyed your old town, Ouiattanau, and the neighboring villages, and have taken many prisoners. Resting here two days, to give you time to collect your strength, they have proceeded to your town of Kethli-pecanunk; but you again fled before them; and that great town has been destroyed. After giving you this evidence of their power they have stopped their hands, because they are as merciful as strong; and they again indulge the hope that you will come to a sense of your true interest, and determine to make a lasting peace with them and all their children for-ever. The United States have no desire to destroy the red people, although they have the power to do it; but should you decline this invitation and pursue your unprovoked hos-tilities, their strength will again be exerted against you, your warriors will be slaughtered, your wives and children carried into captivity; and you may be assured that those who escape the fury of our mighty chiefs shall find no resting-place on this side the great lakes. The warriors of the United States wish not to distress or destroy women and children or old men; and although policy obliges them to retain some in cap-tivity, yet compassion and humanity have induced them to set others at liberty, who will deliver you this talk. Those who are carried off will be left in the care of our great chief and warrior General St. Clair, near the mouth of the Miami and opposite to the Licking River, where they will be treated with humanity and tenderness. If you wish to recover them, repair to that place by the first day of July next. Determine with true hearts to bury the hatchet and smoke the pipe of peace: they will then be restored to you, and you may again set down in security at your old towns, and live in peace and happiness, unmolested by the people of the United States, who will become your friends and protectors, and will be ready to furnish you with all the necessaries you may require. But should you foolishly persist in your warfare, the sons of war will be let loose against you, and the hatchet will never be buried until your country is desolated and your people humbled to the dust.

(Signed)    CHARLES SCOTT, *Brig. Gen.*

# GENERAL WILKINSON'S EXPEDITION.

## GENERAL WILKINSON TO GOVERNOR ST. CLAIR.

"SIR, — Having carried into complete effect the enterprise which you were pleased to direct against L'Anguille, and having done the savages every other damage on the Wabash to which I conceived my force adequate, I embrace the first moment's recess from active duty to detail to your excellency the operations of the expedition intrusted to my command.

I left the neighborhood of Fort Washington on the 1st instant at one o'clock, and, agreeably to my original plan, feinted boldly at the Miami villages by the most direct course the nature of the ground over which I had to march would permit. I persevered in this plan until the morning of the 4th instant, and thereby avoided the hunting ground of the enemy and the paths which led direct from White River to the Wabash, leaving the head waters of the first to my left. I then, being about seventy miles advanced of Fort Washington, turned north-west. I made no discovery until the 5th, about nine o'clock, A. M., when I crossed three much frequented paths within two miles of each other, and all bearing east of north. My guides were urgent for me to follow these paths, which betrayed their ignorance of the country, and convinced me I had to depend on my own judgment only. In the afternoon of that day I was obliged to cross a deep bog, which injured several of my horses exceedingly, and a few miles beyond I struck a path, bearing north by west, marked by the recent footsteps of five or six savages. My guides renewed their application to me to follow this path; but I pursued my own course. I had not got clear of my encampment next morning before my advance reported an impassable bog in my front, extending several miles on either hand; and the guides asserted that the whole country to the Wabash was cut by such bogs, and that it would be impossible for me to proceed unless I followed the Indian paths, which avoided these bogs, or led through them at places where they were least difficult. Although I had little regard to this information, as delay was dangerous, and every thing depended on the preservation of my horses, I determined to return to the right and fall into the path I had passed the evening before, which varied in its course from north by west to northeast. The country had now become pondy in every direction. I therefore resolved to pursue this path until noon, in the hope that it would conduct me to better ground, or to some devious trace, which might lead to the object sought.

At seven o'clock I crossed an east branch of the Calumet River about forty yards wide, and about noon my advance guard fired on a small party of warriors and took a prisoner; the rest ran off to the eastward. I halted about a mile beyond the spot where this affair happened, and, on examining the prisoner, found him to be a Delaware, living near the site of the late Miami village, which, he informed, was about thirty miles distant. I immediately retrograded four miles, and filed off by the right over some rising ground, which I had observed between the east branch of the Calumet River and a creek four or five miles in advance of it, taking my course north, sixty degrees west. This measure fortunately extricated me from the bogs and ponds, and soon placed me on firm ground. Late in the afternoon I crossed one path running from north to south, and shortly after fell in with another varying from north-west to north. I pursued this about two miles, when I encamped; but, finding it still inclining northward, I determined to abandon it in the morning. I

9 *

resumed my march on the 6th at four o'clock.  The Calumet being to the westward of me, I was fearful I should strike the Wabash too high up, and, perhaps, fall in with the small town, which you mentioned to me, at the mouth of the former river.   I therefore steered a due west course, and at six o'clock A. M. crossed a road much used both by horse and foot, bearing due north.  I now knew that I was near a Shawanese village, generally supposed to be on the waters of White River, but actually on the waters of the Calumet, and was sensible that every thing depended on the celerity and silence of my movements, as my real object had become manifest.  I therefore pushed my march vigorously, leaving an officer and twenty men in ambush to watch the road, in order to intercept or beat off any party of the enemy which might casually be passing that way, and thereby prevent, as long as possible, the discovery of my real intentions.

At eight o'clock I crossed Calumet River, now eighty yards wide, and running down north north-west.  I was now sensible from my reckoning, compared with my own observations during the late expedition under General Scott and the information received from your excellency and others, that I could not be very far from L'Anguille.   The party left at the road soon fell in with four warriors encamped half a mile from the right of my line of march, killed one, and drove off the others to the northward.  My situation had now become extremely critical; the whole country to the north being in alarm, which made me greatly anxious to continue my march during the night: but I had no path to direct me, and it was impossible for me to keep my course, or for horsemen to march through a thick, swampy country in utter darkness.  I quitted my camp on the 7th as soon as I could see my way ; crossed one path at three miles' distance, bearing north-east ; and at seven miles fell into another very much used, bearing north-west by north, which I at once adopted as the direct route to my object, and pushed forward with the utmost despatch.  I

halted at twelve o'clock to refresh the horses and examine
the men's arms and ammunition, marched again at half past
one, and at fifteen minutes before five struck the Wabash
at one and a half leagues above the mouth of Eel River,
being the very spot for which I had aimed from the commencement of my march. I crossed the river, and, following
the path a north by east course, at the distance of two and a
half miles my reconnoitring party announced Eel River in
front and the town on the opposite bank. I dismounted, ran
forward, and examined the situation of the town as far as
was practicable without exposing myself; but the whole face
of the country, from the Wabash to the margin of Eel River,
being a continued thicket of brambles, blackjacks, weeds, and
shrubs of various kinds, it was impossible for me to get a
satisfactory view without endangering a discovery. I immediately determined to post two companies near the bank of
the river opposite to the town and above the ground I then
occupied, to make a detour with Major Caldwell and the
second battalion until I fell into the Miami trace, and by that
route to cross the river above and gain the rear of the town,
and to leave directions with Major M'Dowell, who commanded
the first battalion, to lie perdu until I commenced the attack;
then to dash through the river with his corps and the advanced guard and assault the house in front and upon the left.

In the moment I was about to put this arrangement into
execution, word was brought me that the enemy had taken
the alarm and were flying, I instantly ordered a general
charge, which was obeyed with alacrity: the men, forcing their
way over every obstacle, plunged through the river with vast
intrepidity. The enemy was unable to make the smallest resistance. Six warriors, and, in the hurry and confusion of
the charge, two squaws and a child, were killed; thirty-four
prisoners were taken, and an unfortunate captive released;
with the loss of two men killed and one wounded. I found
this town scattered along Eel River for full three miles, on

an uneven, shrubby, oak barren, intersected alternately by bogs almost impassable and impervious thickets of plum and hazel. Notwithstanding these difficulties, if I may credit the report of the prisoners, very few who were in town escaped: expecting a second expedition, their goods were generally packed up or buried. Sixty warriors had crossed the Wabash to watch the paths leading from the Ohio. The head chief, with all the prisoners and a number of families, was out digging a root, which they substitute in the place of the potato; and about one hour before my arrival, all the warriors except eight had mounted their horses and rode up the river to a French store to purchase ammunition. This ammunition had arrived from the Miami village that very day, and the squaws informed me was stored about two miles from town. I detached Major Caldwell in quest of it; but he failed to make any discovery, although he scoured the country for seven or eight miles up the river. I encamped in the town that night, and the next morning I cut up the corn scarcely in the milk, burned the cabins, mounted my young warriors, squaws, and children in the best manner in my power, and, leaving two infirm squaws and a child with a short talk, (which will be found annexed,) I commenced my march for the Kickapoo town in the prairie. I felt my prisoners a vast encumbrance; but I was not in force to justify a detachment, having barely five hundred and twenty-three rank and file, and being then in the bosom of the Ouiattanau country, one hundred and eighty miles removed from succor, and not more than one and a half days' forced march from the Pattawamees, Shawanese, and Delawares.

Not being able to discover any path in the direct course to the Kickapoo town, I marched by the road leading to Tippecanoe, in the hope of finding some diverting trace which might favor my design. I encamped that evening about six miles from Kenapacomaque, the Indian name for the town I had destroyed, and marched the next morning at four o'clock.

My course continued west till about nine o'clock, when I turned to the north-west on a small hunting path, and at a short distance launched into the boundless prairies of the west, with the intention to pursue that course until I should strike a road which leads from the Pattawamees of Lake Michigan immediately to the town I sought. With this view I pushed forward through bog after bog, to the saddle skirts, in mud, and water, and after persevering for eight hours I found myself environed on all sides with morasses which forbade my advancing, and at the same time rendered it difficult for me to extricate my little army. The way by which we had entered was so much beat and softened by the horses that it was almost impossible to return by that route, and my guides pronounced the morass in front impassable. A chain of thin groves extending in the direction to the Wabash at this time presented to my left; it was necessary I should gain these groves, and for this purpose I dismounted, went forward, and, leading my horse through a bog to the armpits in mud and water, with difficulty and fatigue I accomplished my object, and, changing my course to south by west, regained the Tippecanoe road at five o'clock, and encamped on it at seven o'clock, after a march of thirty miles, which broke down several of my horses.

I am the more minute in detailing the occurrences of this day, because they produced the most unfavorable effect. I was in motion at four next morning; and at eight o'clock my advanced guard made some discoveries, which induced me to believe we were near an Indian village. I immediately pushed that body forward in a trot, and followed with Major Caldwell and the second battalion, leaving Major M'Dowell to take charge of the prisoners. I reached Tippecanoe at twelve o'clock, which had been occupied by the enemy, who watched my motions and abandoned the place that morning. After the destruction of this town in June last, the enemy had returned and cultivated their corn and pulse, which I found in high perfection and in much greater quantity than at L'Anguille. To refresh my horses and give time to cut down the corn, I determined to halt until the next morning, and then resume my march to the Kickapoo town in the prairie by the road which leads from Ouiattanau to that place. In the course of the day I had discovered some murmurings and discontent among the men, which I found, on inquiry, to proceed from their reluctance to advance into the enemy's country. This induced me to call for a state of the horses and provisions, when to my great mortification two hundred and seventy horses were returned lame and tired, with barely five days' provision for the men.

Under these circumstances I was compelled to abandon my designs upon the Kickapoos of the prairie; and, with a degree of anguish not to be comprehended but by those who have experienced similar disappointments, I marched forward to a town of the same nation, situate about three leagues west of Ouiattanau. As I advanced to the town the enemy made some show of fighting me, but vanished at my approach. I destroyed this town, consisting of thirty houses, with a considerable quantity of corn in the milk; and the same day I moved on to Ouiattanau, where I forded the Wabash, and proceeded to the site of the villages on the margin of the prairie, where I encamped at seven o'clock. At this town and the villages destroyed by General Scott in June we found the corn had been replanted and was now in high cultivation; several fields being well ploughed, all which we destroyed. On the 12th I resumed my march, and, falling into General Scott's return trace, I arrived without material accident at the rapids of the Ohio on the 21st instant, after a march, by accurate computation, of four hundred and fifty-one miles from Fort Washington.

The services which I have been able to render fall short of my wishes, my intention, and expectation. But, sir, when you reflect on the causes which checked my career, and blasted my designs, I flatter myself you will believe every thing has been done which could be done in my circumstances. I have destroyed the chief town of the Ouiattanau nation, and made prisoners the sons and sisters of the king. I have burned a respectable Kickapoo village, and cut down at least four hundred and thirty acres of corn chiefly in the milk. The Ouiattanaus left without horses, home, or provision, must cease to war, and will find active employ to subsist their squaws and children during the impending winter.

Should these services secure to the country which I immediately represented, and the corps which I had the honor to command, the favorable consideration of government, I shall infer the approbation of my own conduct, which, added to a consciousness of having done my duty, will constitute the richest reward I can enjoy.

With the most perfect respect, I have the honor to be your excellency's obedient and most humble servant,

JAMES WILKINSON.

Governor St. Clair.

---

### A Talk from Colonel Wilkinson to the Indian Nations living on the River Wabash.

The arms of the United States are again exerted against you, and again your towns are in flames, and your wives and children made captives. Again you are cautioned to listen to the voice of reason, to sue for peace, and submit to the protection of the United States, who are willing to become your friends and fathers; but, at the same time, are determined to punish you for every injury you may offer to their children. Regard not those evil counsellors who, to secure to themselves the benefits of your trade, advise you to measures which involve you, your women, and children in trouble and distress. The United States wish to give you peace, because it is good in the eyes of the Great Spirit that all his children should unite and live like brothers; but if you foolishly prefer war, their warriors are ready to meet you in battle, and will not be the first to lay down the hatchet. You may find your squaws and your children under the protection of our great chief and warrior General St. Clair, at Fort Washington; to him you will make all applications for an exchange of prisoners or for peace.

JAMES WILKINSON.

# DEFEAT OF GENERAL ST. CLAIR BY THE INDIANS, 1791.

GENERAL ST. CLAIR TO THE SECRETARY OF WAR.

FORT WASHINGTON, November 9, 1791.

SIR,— Yesterday afternoon the remains of the army under my command got back to this place; and I have now the painful task to give an account of as warm and as unfortunate an action as almost any that has been fought, in which every corps was engaged and worsted except the first regiment, that had been detached upon a service I had the honor to inform you of in my last despatch, and had not joined me.

On the 3d instant the army had reached a creek about twelve yards wide, running to the southward of west, which I believe to have been the River St. Mary, that empties into the Miami of the lake, arrived at the village about four o'clock in the afternoon, having marched near nine miles, and were immediately encamped upon a very commanding piece of ground in two lines, having the above-mentioned creek in front. The right wing, composed of Butler's, Clarke's, and Patterson's battalions, commanded by Major General Butler, formed the first line; and the left wing, consisting of Bedinger's and Gaither's battalions and the second regiment, commanded by Colonel Drake, formed the second line, with an interval between them of about seventy yards, which was all the ground would allow.

The right flank was pretty well secured by the creek, a

10

steep bank, and Faulkener's corps : some of the cavalry and their pickets covered the left flank.   The militia were thrown over the creek, and advanced about one quarter of a mile, and encamped in the same order.   There were a few Indians who appeared on the opposite side of the creek, but fled with the utmost precipitation on the advance of the militia.   At this place, which I judged to be about fifteen miles from the Miami village, I had determined to throw up a slight work, the plan of which was concerted that evening with Major Ferguson, wherein to have deposited the men's knapsacks and every thing else that was not of absolute necessity, and to have moved on to attack the enemy as soon as the first regiment was come up.   But they did not permit me to execute either; for on the 4th, about half an hour before sunrise, and when the men had been just dismissed from the parade, — for it was a constant practice to have them all under arms a considerable time before light, — an attack was made upon the militia. Those gave way in a very little time, and rushed into camp through Major Butler's battalion, which, together with part of Clarke's, they threw into considerable disorder, and which, notwithstanding the exertions of both these officers, was never altogether remedied : the Indians followed close at their heels. The fire, however, of the front line checked them ; but almost instantaneously a very heavy attack began upon that line, and in a few minutes it was extended to the second likewise. The great weight of it was directed against the centre of each, where the artillery was placed, and from which the men were repeatedly driven with great slaughter.   Finding no great effect from the fire, and confusion beginning to spread from the great number of men who were fallen in all quarters, it became necessary to try what could be done by the bayonet.

Lieutenant Colonel Drake was accordingly ordered to make a charge with a part of the second line and to turn the left flank of the enemy. This was executed with great spirit. The Indians instantly gave way, and were driven back three or four hundred yards; but, for want of a sufficient number of riflemen to pursue this advantage, they soon returned, and the troops were obliged to give back in their turn. At this moment they had entered our camp by the left flank, having pursued back the troops that were posted there.

Another charge was made here by the second regiment, Butler's and Clarke's battalions, with equal effect; and it was repeated several times, and always with success. But in all of them many men were lost, and particularly the officers, which, with some raw troops, was a loss altogether irremediable. In that I just spoke of, made by the second regiment and Butler's battalion, Major Butler was dangerously wounded, and every officer of the second regiment fell except three, one of which, Captain Greaton, was shot through the body.

Our artillery being now silenced, and all the officers killed except Captain Ford, who was badly wounded,—more than half of the army fallen, being cut off from the road,—it became necessary to attempt the regaining it, and to make a retreat, if possible. To this purpose the remains of the army were formed, as well as circumstances would admit, towards the right of the encampment; from which, by the way of the second line, another charge was made upon the enemy, as if with the design to turn their right flank, but, in fact, to gain the road. This was effected; and as soon as it was open the militia took along it, followed by the troops, Major Clarke with his battalion covering the rear.

The retreat in those circumstances was, you may be sure, a precipitate one; it was, in fact, a flight. The camp and the artillery were abandoned; but that was unavoidable, for not a horse was left alive to have drawn it off had it otherwise been practicable. But the most disgraceful part of the business is, that the greatest part of the men threw away their arms and accoutrements, even after the pursuit, which continued about four miles, had ceased.

I found the road strewed with them for many miles, but was not able to remedy it; for, having had all my horses killed, and being mounted upon one that could not be pricked out of a walk, I could not get forward myself; and the orders I sent forward, either to halt the front or prevent the men from parting with their arms, were unattended to.

The route continued quite to Fort Jefferson, twenty-nine miles, which was reached a little after sunsetting. The action began about half an hour before sunrise, and the retreat was attempted at half an hour after nine o'clock.

I have not yet been able to get returns of the killed and wounded. But Major General Butler, Lieutenant Colonel Oldham, of the militia, Major Ferguson, Major Hart, and Major Clarke are among the former.

I have now, sir, finished my melancholy tale — a tale that will be felt, sensibly felt, by every one that has sympathy for private distress or for public misfortune. I have nothing, sir, to say to the charge of the troops but their want of discipline, which, from the short time they had been in service, it was impossible they should have acquired, and which rendered it very difficult, when they were thrown into confusion, to reduce them again to order; and is one reason why the loss has fallen so heavy upon the officers, who did every thing in their power to effect it. Neither were my own exertions wanting; but worn down with illness, and suffering under a painful disease, unable either to mount or dismount a horse without assistance, they were not so great as they otherwise would, or perhaps ought to have been.

We were overpowered by numbers. But it is no more than justice to observe, that, though composed of so many different species of troops, the utmost harmony prevailed through the whole army during the campaign.

At Fort Jefferson I found the first regiment, which had returned from the service they had been sent upon without either overtaking the deserters or meeting the convoy of provisions. I am not certain, sir, whether I ought to consider the absence of this regiment from the field of action as fortunate or otherwise. I incline to think it was fortunate; for I very much doubt whether, had it been in the action, the fortune of the day had been turned; and if it had not, the triumph of the enemy would have been more complete, and the country would have been destitute of every means of defence.

Taking a view of the situation of our broken troops at Fort Jefferson, and that there were no provisions in the fort, I called on the field officers for their advice what would be proper further to be done; and it was their unanimous opinion that the addition of the first regiment, unbroken as it was, did not put the army on so respectable a footing as it was in the morning, because a great part of it was now unarmed; that it had been found unequal to the enemy, and should they come on, which was probable, would be found so again; that the troops could not be thrown into the fort, both because it was too small and that there was no provision in it; that provisions were known to be upon the road at the distance of one, or at most two, marches; that therefore it would be proper to move without loss of time to meet the provisions, when the men might have the sooner an opportunity of some refreshment; and that a proper detachment might be sent back with it, to have it safely deposited in the fort.

This advice was accepted, and the army was put in motion again at ten o'clock, and marched all night, and the succeeding day met with a quantity of flour. Part of it was distributed immediately, part taken back to supply the army on the march to Fort Hamilton, and the remainder, about fifty horseloads, sent forward to Fort Jefferson.

I have said, sir, in the former part of my communication,

10 *

that we were overpowered by numbers; of that, however, I have no other evidence but the weight of the fire, which was always a most deadly one, and generally delivered from the ground; few of the enemy showing themselves on foot, except when they were charged, and that in a few minutes our whole camp, which extended above three hundred and fifty yards in length, was entirely surrounded and attacked on all quarters.

The loss, sir, the public has sustained by the fall of so many officers, particularly General Butler and Major Ferguson, cannot be too much regretted; but it is a circumstance that will alleviate the misfortune, in some measure, that all of them fell most gallantly doing their duty.

I have the honor to be, sir, your most obedient servant,

ARTHUR ST. CLAIR.

Honorable secretary of war.

--------

The defeat of General St. Clair took place within six miles of the Miami village. The loss on this occasion was about six hundred killed and wounded, (said to be nearly equal to Braddock's defeat,) with seven pieces of artillery and all the stores. General St. Clair had about twelve hundred men; had reason to expect an attack; and kept his men under arms all night, drawn up in a square. The attack commenced about dawn of day on all the lines, but principally on the rear lines, which were composed of the militia. The Indians gave one fire and rushed on, tomahawk in hand. The militia gave way to the centre; and before the artillery could be brought into action the matrosses were all killed, and it fell into the hands of the enemy. It was retaken; but was useless, for want of men to manage the pieces.

The action was continued obstinately until nine o'clock, when the troops gave way. St. Clair rallied his men, and brought them off in tolerable order, with most of the wounded,

to Fort Jefferson, thirty miles in the rear of the action.    The
enemy pursued five miles.

The following is a copy of a return of the officers killed
and wounded in the engagement : —

*Killed.* — 1 major general, 1 lieutenant colonel, 4 majors,
11 captains, 10 lieutenants, 9 ensigns, 1 surgeon; total, 37.

*Wounded.* — 2 lieutenant colonels, 1 major, 11 captains,
6 lieutenants, 6 ensigns, 1 surgeon; total, 27.

Beside the above there were about five hundred and fifty
privates killed, and many more wounded.    Few officers of
distinction escaped except General St. Clair, who had many
narrow escapes; eight balls passed through his clothes.    The
attack was conducted with astonishing intrepidity on the part
of the Indians.    In a few moments the general's tent was
surrounded : however, he was rescued by a party of regular
soldiers, who repelled the enemy with fixed bayonets.    There
was a party of the Chickasaw nation on their way to join
General St. Clair, but did not arrive in season.    There was
but one fellow only of that nation in the action, who killed
and scalped eleven of the enemy with his own hands, and
engaging with the twelfth he fell, greatly lamented by the
Americans.

Major General Butler was wounded and carried to a convenient place to have his wounds dressed; but an Indian, having discovered the place to which he was conveyed, broke
through the troops who attended him, and tomahawked and
scalped the former before he was killed by the troops.

Agreeably to the statement of the Indians, they killed six
hundred and fifty of the American troops, and took seven
pieces of cannon, two hundred oxen, and a great number of
horses, but no prisoners; and that their loss was only fifty-
six warriors killed.    They stated that they were four thousand
strong, and were commanded by one of the Missasago In-

dians, who had been in the British service in the late war; that he plánned and conducted the attack, which was even contrary to the opinion of a majority of the chiefs; and that, after the Americans began their retreat, he told the Indians they had killed enough, and that it was proper to give over the pursuit, and return and enjoy the booty they had taken. He was six feet in height, about forty-five years of age, of a very sour and morose countenance, and apparently very crafty and subtle. His dress was Indian hose and moccasons, a blue petticoat that came half way down his thighs, a European waistcoat and surtout: his head was bound with an Indian cap, that hung half way down his back, and was almost entirely filled with plated silver broaches to the number of more than two hundred. He had two earrings to each ear; the upper part of each was formed of three silver medals about the size of a dollar; the lower part was formed of quarter dollars, and fell more than twelve inches from his ear; one from each ear over his breast, the other over his back. He had three very large nose jewels of silver that were curiously painted.

The party of friendly Chickasaws, who were on their way to join the American troops, arrived at Fort Jefferson two days after the bloody action. They were commanded by Piomingo, or the Mountain Leader. On their way they discovered that the troops had been defeated, but saw but one of the enemy, who, mistaking Piomingo's party for some of his own comrades, made up to them. He perceived his mistake, but too late to retreat. He was accosted by Piomingo with " Ráscal, you have been killing white men." He endeavored to exculpate himself; but Piomingo ordered two of his warriors to expand his arms, and a third, an old man, ("for," says Piomingo, "none of my young men shall disgrace themselves so much as to kill a wretch like thee,") to shoot him through the heart, which was accordingly executed: they afterwards took off his scalp.

During St. Clair's bloody engagement Adjutant Burgess received two wounds, the second of which proved mortal. After the receipt of the first he continued to fight with distinguished gallantry; the second unfortunately stopped his progress. Faint with the loss of blood, he fell: a woman, who attended him and was particularly attached to him, raised him up, and, while supporting him in her arms, received a ball in her breast, which put an immediate end to her existence.

# DEPREDATIONS OF THE INDIANS ON THE FRONTIERS IN 1791, 1792, AND 1793.

On the 10th of December, 1791, as two men and three boys were fishing on Floyd's fork of Salt River, they were suddenly attacked by a party of Indians, who killed the two men and made prisoners of the boys. Soon after they liberated one of the lads, first presenting him with a tomahawk, which they desired him to carry to his friends and inform them what had become of his companions.

About the 20th a party of Indians attacked the house of a Mr. Chenoweth, situated near the mouth of the Wabash: they killed and scalped two of his children, and tomahawked and scalped his wife, whom they left for dead. Mr. C., who had his arm broken by the fire of the savages, with the remainder of the family made his escape. A sick daughter, who was confined to her chamber, and who, during the bloody affray, had been forgotten by her father, remained ignorant of the horrid massacre until the succeeding day; when, no one of the family coming to her assistance, she succeeded in crawling down stairs, where she was inexpressibly shocked at the sight of a beloved parent stretched upon the floor, almost lifeless, and beside of whom lay the mangled bodies of her dear brothers. Fortunately her unhappy father returned the succeeding day to the house, and conveyed the two surviving members of his family to the house of a friend, where they finally recovered.

On the 24th a party of Indians attacked the dwelling house of a Mr. John Merril, in Nelson county, Kentucky. Mr.

Merril, who was first alarmed by the barking of his dog, hastened to the door to discover the cause, on opening of which he received the fire of the Indians, which broke his right leg and arm. The Indians now attempted to enter the house, but were prevented by the doors being immediately closed and secured by Mrs. Merril and her daughter. The Indians succeeded in hewing away a part of the door, through which passage one of them attempted to enter; but the heroic mother, in the midst of her screaming children and groaning husband, seized an axe and gave the ruffian a fatal blow; after which she hauled him through the passage into the house. The others, unconscious of the fate of their companion, supposing that they had now nearly succeeded in their object, rushed forward, four of whom Mrs. Merril in like manner despatched before the others discovered their mistake. The remaining Indians, after retiring for a few moments, returned and renewed their efforts to enter the house. Despairing of succeeding at the door, they got on the top of the house and attempted to descend the chimney; to prevent which Mr. Merril directed his little son to empty upon the fire the contents of a feather bed, which had the desired effect, as the smoke and heat caused thereby soon brought down rather unexpectedly two of the enemy. Mr. Merril, exerting every faculty at this critical moment, seized a billet of wood, with which he soon despatched the two half-smothered Indians; while in the mean time his heroic wife was busily engaged in defending the door against the efforts of the only remaining one, whom she so severely wounded with an axe that he was soon glad to retire.

A prisoner, who escaped from the enemy soon after the transaction, informed that the wounded savage above mentioned was the only one that escaped of the party, which consisted of eight; that on his return, being asked by the prisoner, " What news ? " he answered, " Bad news for poor Indian; me lose a son, me lose a brother: the squaws have taken the breach clout, and fight worse than the Long Knives."

*Copy of a Letter from a Gentleman in Marietta to his Friend
in Washington.*

MARIETTA, March 4, 1793.

About eight weeks since two brothers, by the name of
Johnson, one twelve the other nine years old, were playing
on the western bank of Short Creek, about twelve miles from
Wheeling, skipping stones in the water.    At a distance they
discovered two men, who appeared to be settlers, being dressed
with coats and hats.    These men, to amuse and deceive the
children, as they even showed, engaged in the same sport,
advancing towards the boys, till by degrees they got so near
that the children discovered them to be Indians; but it was
then too late to make their escape.  The Indians seized and
carried them six miles into the woods, where they made a fire
and took up their lodgings for the night: their rifles and tomahawks they rested against a tree, and then laid down, each
Indian with a boy on his arm.    The children, as may be supposed, kept awake.    The oldest began to move, and, finding
his Indian sound asleep, by degrees disengaged himself and
went to the fire, which had then got low, and stirred it up.
The Indian not waking, he whispered to his brother, who
likewise crept away, and both of them went to the fire.    The
oldest boy then observed to his brother, "I think we can kill
these Indians and get away from them." The youngest agreed
in the proposal of attempting it.    The oldest then took one
of the rifles, and placed the muzzle, which he rested on a
small stick that he found for the purpose, close to the head
of one of the Indians, and, committing the execution of this
part of the business to his brother, ordered him to pull the
trigger at the moment he saw him strike the other Indian
with one of the tomahawks.    The oldest gave the signal ; the
youngest pulled trigger.    The rifle shot away the lower part
of the Indian's face and left him senseless.    He then told his

GOING TO DIVINE SERVICE IN THE TIMES OF THE EARLY INDIAN WARS

brother to lay on, for he had done for his; after which he snatched up the gun and ran. The boy with the tomahawk gave the stroke with the wrong end: the Indian started on his seat: the boy found the mistake, and, turning the tomahawk in his hand, gave him another blow, which brought him to the ground: he repeated his strokes until he had despatched him, and then made the best of his way after his brother. When the boys had found the path which they recollected to have travelled before, the oldest fixed his hat on a bush, as a directory to find the scene of action the next day. The tomahawked Indian was found near the place where the boys had left him. The other was not there, but was tracked by his blood, and although so weakened by his wounds that he could not raise his rifle to fire at his pursuers, the whites, they suffered him to escape: but it is supposed he must have died of his wounds. These two Indians were sent out to reconnoitre the best place for an attack, which was to have been made by a body of warriors waiting in the neighborhood.

11

# DEFEAT OF THE INDIANS BY GENERAL WAYNE, AUGUST 20, 1794.

## GENERAL WAYNE TO THE SECRETARY OF WAR.

SIR,—It is with infinite pleasure that I announce to you the brilliant success of the federal army under my command, in a general action with the combined force of the hostile Indians, and a considerable number of the volunteers and militia of Detroit, on the 20th of August, on the banks of the Miamis, in the vicinity of the British post and garrison at the foot of the Rapids.

The army advanced from Fort Washington on the 15th, and arrived at Roach de Bout on the 18th; and the 19th we were employed in making a temporary post for the reception of our stores and baggage, and in reconnoitring the position of the enemy, who were encamped behind a thick bushy wood and the British fort.

At eight o'clock on the morning of the 20th the army again advanced in columns agreeably to the standing order of the march, the legion on the right, its right flank covered by the Miamis; one brigade of mounted volunteers on the left, under Brigadier General Todd, and the other in the rear, under Brigadier General Barbee. A select battalion of mounted volunteers moved in front of the legation, commanded by Major Price, who was directed to keep sufficiently advanced, and to give timely notice for the troops to form in case of action, it being yet undetermined whether the Indians would decide for peace or war.

After advancing about five miles, Major Price's corps received so severe a fire from the enemy, who were secreted in the woods and high grass, as to compel them to retreat.

The legion was immediately formed in two lines, principally in a close, thick wood, which extended for miles on our left and for a very considerable distance in front, the ground being covered with old fallen timber, probably occasioned by a tornado, which rendered it impracticable for the cavalry to act with effect, and afforded the enemy the most favorable covert for their mode of warfare.   The savages were formed in three lines, within supporting distance of each other, and extending for near two miles at right angles with the river. I soon discovered, from the weight of the fire and extent of their lines, that the enemy were in full force in front, in possession of their favorite ground, and endeavoring to turn our left flank.   I therefore gave orders for the second line to advance to support the first, and directed Major General Scott to gain and turn the right flank of the savages, with the whole of the mounted volunteers, by a circuitous route.   At the same time I ordered the front line to advance and charge with trailed arms, and rouse the Indians from their coverts at the point of the bayonet, and, when up, to deliver a close and well-directed fire on their backs, followed by a brisk charge, so as not to give them time to load again or to form their lines.

I also ordered Captain M. Campbell, who commanded the legionary cavalry, to turn the left flank of the enemy next the river, and which afforded a favorable field for that corps to act in.   All those orders were obeyed with spirit and promptitude; but such was the impetuosity of the charge by the first line of infantry that the Indians and Canadian militia and volunteers were driven from all their coverts, in so short a time, that, although every possible exertion was used by the officers of the second line of the legion, and by Generals Scott, Wood, and Barbee, of the mounted volunteers, to gain their proper positions, but part of each could get up in season to participate in the action; the enemy being driven in the course of one hour more than two miles through the thick woods already mentioned by less than one half their number.

From every account the enemy amounted to two thousand combatants; the troops actually engaged against them were short of nine hundred. This horde of savages, with their allies, abandoned themselves to flight and dispersed with terror and dismay, leaving our victorious army in full and quiet possession of the field of battle, which terminated under the influence of the guns of the British garrison.

The bravery and conduct of every officer belonging to the army, from the generals down to the ensigns, merit my approbation.

Lieutenant Covington, upon whom the command of the cavalry devolved, Captain Campbell being killed, cut down two savages with his own hand, and Lieutenant Webb one, in turning the enemy's left flank. .

The wounds received by Captains Slough, Prior, Van Ranselaer, and Rawlins, and Lieutenants M'Kenny and Smith, bear honorable testimony of their bravery and conduct. In fact, every officer and soldier who had an opportunity to come into action displayed that true bravery which will always insure success. And here permit me to declare that I have never discovered more true spirit and anxiety for action than appeared to pervade the whole of the mounted volunteers; and I am well persuaded, that, had the enemy maintained their favorite ground for one half hour longer, they would have most severely felt the prowess of that corps.

But whilst I pay this just tribute to the living, I must not neglect the gallant dead, among whom we have to lament the early death of those worthy and brave officers, Captain Campbell and Lieutenant Towles, who fell in the first charge.

The loss of the enemy was more than double to that of the federal army. The woods were strewed for a considerable distance with dead bodies of Indians and their white auxiliaries, the latter armed with British muskets and bayonets. We remained three days and nights on the banks of the Miamis, in front of the field of battle, during which time all the houses and cornfields were consumed and destroyed for a considerable distance above and below the garrison, among which were the houses, stores, and property of Colonel M'Kee, the British Indian agent and principal stimulator of the war now existing between the United States and the savages.

The army returned to head quarters on the 27th by easy marches, laying waste the villages and cornfields for about fifty miles on each side of the Miamis. It is not improbable but that the enemy may make one desperate effort against the army, as it is said a reënforcement was hourly expected at Fort Miamis from Niagara, as well as numerous tribes of Indians living on the margins and islands of the lakes. This is an event rather to be wished for than dreaded whilst the army remains in force ; their numbers will only tend to confuse the savages, and the victory will be the more complete and decisive, and may eventually insure a permanent and happy peace.

The following is a return of the killed and wounded and missing of the federal army in the late action, to wit: —

*Killed.* — 1 captain, 1 lieutenant, 3 sergeants, 28 privates; total, 33.

*Wounded.* — 4 captains, 2 lieutenants, 1 ensign, 4 sergeants, 3 corporals, 2 musicians, 84 privates ; total, 100.

I have the honor to be your most obedient and very humble servant,

ANTHONY WAYNE.

To the secretary of war.

The following circumstances, which took place previous to and during General Wayne's engagement, are worthy of record.

At the instant Captain Campbell was attempting to turn the left flank of the enemy, three of them plunged into the river. Two friendly negroes, being on the opposite side and observing the Indians making for the shore, placed themselves on the bank behind a log, and, as soon as the Indians approached within shot, one of the negroes fired and killed one of the Indians. The other two got hold of him to drag him out, when the other negro fired and killed another. The remaining Indian got hold of both those dead to pull them ashore; when the negro who killed the first, having again reloaded, fired and killed the third, and they all floated down the river.

Another circumstance is also related; viz., a soldier, soon after the conclusion of the action, proceeding some distance from the camp, met an Indian. They attacked each other, the soldier with his bayonet and the Indian with his tomahawk. Some of the soldiers passing by that way two days after found them both dead — the soldier with his bayonet in the body of the Indian, and the Indian with his tomahawk in the soldier's head.

The following circumstance took place previous to the action: A Mr. Wells, who, when very young, was taken prisoner by the Indians, and had resided several years among them, had made his escape, and was employed by General Wayne as a spy. The day before the action he was taken by the Indians, who determined to put him to death. Finding it impossible to escape, he informed them that General Wayne had not five hundred men under his command, and did not expect an attack. On hearing this, the Indians attacked General Wayne with a confidence inspired by their supposed superiority of numbers, and were repulsed as before mentioned. After the action, Major Campbell, in whose custody the Indians had left Wells, inquired his motives for deceiving them. He answered, " For the good of my country." For this heroic action he was unfeelingly delivered to the

Indians, in whose hands it is supposed he experienced every torture that savage ·barbarity could invent or inflict. The circumstances respecting Mr. Wells were related by a British drummer who deserted from the fort to General Wayne.

A council of Indians was held a few days after their defeat by General Wayne, in which British agents endeavored to persuade them to risk another action; but this they refused to do, expressing a willingness to bury the bloody hatchet and return to their homes. Their loss they declared to be two hundred, and that their whole force at the commencement of the action amounted to fifteen thousand Indians and eighty Canadians. The body of the collector of Niagara was found among the slain.

# A NARRATIVE OF THE CAPTIVITY OF MRS. JOHNSON.

### *Notices of the Willard Family.*

To trace the progress of families from their origin to the present day, when, perhaps, they are spread over the four quarters of the globe, and no memorandums are found except in the uncertain pages of memory, is a task which can be but feebly performed. In noticing the name of Willard, which was my family name, I cannot pretend to accuracy; but the information which I have collected will, perhaps, be of some service to others who possess a greater stock; and if the various branches of families would contribute their mites, it would be an easy way of remedying the deficiency which at present exists in American genealogy.

The first person by the name of Willard who settled in this country was Major Willard, whose name is recorded in the history of New England wars. In the year 1675, in the time of "Philip's war," (a notorious Indian, who lived within the present limits of the State of Rhode Island,) Major Willard, who then lived in the town of Lancaster, in Massachusetts, commanded a troop of horse; and among his vigorous services he relieved the town of Brookfield from the Nipnet Indians, who had burned every house but one, and had almost reduced that to capitulation. When Lancaster was destroyed by the Indians Major Willard removed to Salem, where he spent the rest of his days. He had two sons; one of whom was a settled minister in the town of Groton, from which place he was driven by the Indians, and was afterwards installed in Boston. His other son, Simon, established' himself on Still River, since taken from Lancaster and incorporated into the town of Harvard. He had nine sons; Simon, Henry, Hezekiah, John, Joseph, Josiah, Samuel, Jonathan, and James. Josiah removed to Winchester, in New Hampshire, and afterwards commanded Fort Dummer; the rest inherited the substance of their father, and lived to very advanced ages in the vicinity of their birth. They all left numerous families, who spread over the United States. His eldest son, Simon, was my grandfather. He had two sons, Aaron and Moses: Aaron lived in Lancaster, and Moses, my father, removed to Lunenburg. I ought to remark, that my grandmother Willard, after the death of her husband, married a person by the name of Farnsworth, by whom she had three sons, who were the first settlers of Charlestown, No. 4. One of them was killed by the Indians.

My father had twelve children. He removed to Charlestown, No. 4, in 1742, and soon had the pleasure to find his children settled around him. He was killed by the Indians in 1756. My mother died in March, 1797,* and had lived to see twelve children, ninety-two grandchildren, one hundred and twenty-three great-grandchildren, and four great-great-grandchildren. The whole that survive are now settled on Connecticut River.

### Notices of Mr. James Johnson.

In the year 1730 my great-uncle, Colonel Josiah Willard, while at Boston, was invited to take a walk on the Long Wharf to view some transports who had just landed from Ireland. A number of gentlemen present were viewing the

---

* At the age of eighty-four she busied herself in making a coverlid, which contains something of the remarkable; she did not quite complete it. It now contains upwards of five thousand pieces.

exercise of some lads, who were placed on shore to exhibit their activity to those who wished to purchase. My uncle spied a boy of some vivacity, of about ten years of age, and who was the only one in the crew who spoke English. He bargained for him. I have never been able to learn the price; but as he was afterwards my husband, I am willing to suppose it a considerable sum. He questioned the boy respecting his parentage and descent. All the information he could get was, that young James, a considerable time previous, went to sea with his uncle, who commanded a ship and had the appearance of a man of property; that this uncle was taken sick at sea and died: immediately after his death they came in sight of this ship of Irish transports, and he was put on board. His being the only one of the crew who spoke English and other circumstances have led his friends to conclude that this removal on board the Irish ship was done to facilitate the sequestration of his uncle's property. He lived with Colonel Willard until he was twenty years old, and then bought the other year of his time. In 1748 Governor Shirley gave him a lieutenant's commission under Edward Hartwell, Esq.

### Situation of the Country in 1744.

It is an old maxim, that, after a man is in possession of a small, independent property, it is easy for him to acquire a great fortune. Just so with countries: possess them of a few inhabitants, and let those be unmolested by Indians and enemies, the land will soon swarm with inhabitants. But when a feeble band only are gathered together and obliged to contend with pestilence, famine, and the sword, their melancholy numbers will decrease and waste away. The situation of our ancestors has often been described in language that did honor to the hearts that conceived it. The boisterous ocean, with unknown shores, hemmed them in on one side; and a forest, swarming with savages yelling for their blood, threat-

ened on the other.   But the same undaunted spirit which has
defended them in so many perils buoyed them above despair
in their early struggles for safety and liberty.   I shall be
pardoned for the digression when I observe that I have in all
my travels felt a degree of pride in recollecting that I belonged to a country whose valor was distinguished and whose
spirit had never been debased by servile submission.

At the age of fourteen, in 1744, I made a visit from Leominster to Charlestown to visit my parents.   Through a long
wilderness from Lunenburg to Lower Ashuelot, now Swanzey, we travelled two days: a solitary house was all the
mark of cultivation that occurred on the journey.   Guided
by marked trees, we travelled cautiously through the gloomy
forest where now the well-tilled farms occupy each rod of
ground.   From Ashuelot to Charlestown the passage was
opposed, now by the Hill of Difficulty, and now by the
Slough Despond.   A few solitary inhabitants, who appeared
the representatives of wretchedness, were scattered on the way.

When I approached the town of Charlestown, the first object that met my eyes was a party of Indians holding a war
dance: a cask of rum, which the inhabitants had suffered
them to partake of, had raised their spirits to all the horrid
yells and feats of distortion which characterize the nation.
I was chilled at the sight, and passed tremblingly by.   At this
time Charlestown contained nine or ten families, who lived
in huts not far distant from each other.   The Indians were
numerous, and associated in a friendly manner with the whites.
It was the most northerly settlement on Connecticut River,
and the adjacent country was terribly wild.   A saw mill was
erected, and the first boards were sawed while I was there.
The inhabitants commemorated the event with a dance, which
took place on the new boards.   In those days there was such
a mixture on the frontiers of savages and settlers, without
established laws to govern them, that the state of society cannot be easily described; and the impending dangers of war,

where it was known that the savages would join the enemies of our country, retarded the progress of refinement and cultivation. The inhabitants of Charlestown began to erect a fort, and took some steps towards clearing their farms; but war soon checked their industry.

## Charlestown.

In the year 1740 the first settlement was made in the town of Charlestown, then known by the name of No. 4, by three families, who emigrated from Lunenburg, by the name of Farnsworth: that part of New Hampshire west of Merrimack River was then a trackless wilderness. Within a few years past instances have been known of new townships, totally uninhabited, becoming flourishing and thick-settled villages in the course of six or seven years. But in those days, when government was weak, when savages were on our borders and Frenchmen in Canada, population extended with timorous and tardy paces: in the course of twelve years the families increased only to twenty-two or three. The human race will not flourish unless fostered by the warm sunshine of peace.

During the first twenty years of its existence as a settled place, until the peace between Great Britain and France, it suffered all the consternation and ravages of war; not that warfare which civilized nations wage with each other, but the cruel carnage of savages and Frenchmen. Sometimes engaged in the duties of the camp, at others sequestering themselves from surrounding enemies, they became familiar with danger, but not with industrious husbandry.

In the year 1744 the inhabitants began to erect a fort for their safety. When the Cape Breton war commenced the Indians assumed the hatchet and began their depredations on Charlestown on the 19th of April, 1746, by burning the mills and taking Captain John Spafford, Isaac Parker, and Stephen Farnsworth prisoners. On the 2d of May following Seth Putnam was killed. Two days after Captain Payne arrived with a troop of horse, from Massachusetts, to defend the place. About twenty of his men had the curiosity to view the place where Putnam was killed, and were ambushed by the Indians. Captain Stevens, who commanded a few men, rushed out of the fort to their relief: a sharp combat ensued, in which the Indians were routed. They left some guns and blankets on the field of action; but they carried their dead off with them, which is a policy they never omit. Ensign Obadiah Sartwell was captured; and Samuel Farnsworth, Elijah Allen, Peter Perin, Aaron Lyon, and Joseph Massey fell victims to Indian vengeance.

On the 19th of June a severe engagement took place. Captain Brown, from Stow, in Massachusetts, had previously arrived with some troops: a party of his joined a number of Captain Stevens's soldiers to go into the meadow after their horses. The dogs discovered an ambush, which put them into a posture for action and gave them the advantage of the first fire. This disconcerted the savages, who, being on higher ground, overshot and did but little damage to the English. The enemy were routed, and even seen to drag several dead bodies after them. They left behind them guns, spears, and blankets, which sold for forty pounds, old tenor. During the time Captain Josiah Brown assisted in defending the fort Jedediah Winchel was killed; Samuel Stanhope, Cornet Baker and David Parker were wounded. During this summer the fort was entirely blockaded, and all were obliged to take refuge within the pickets. On the 3d of August one Philips was killed within a few feet of the fort as he accidentally stepped out: at night a soldier crept to him with a rope, and he was drawn into the fort and interred. In the summer of the year 1746 Captain Ephraim Brown, from Sudbury, arrived with a troop of horse to relieve Captain Josiah Brown. The Sudbury troop tarried about a month, and were relieved by a company commanded by Captain Winchester, who defended the place till autumn, when the inhabitants, fatigued

12

with watching and weary of the dangers of the forest, deserted the place entirely for about six months. In the month of August, previous to the evacuation, the Indians, assisted by their brethren the French, were very troublesome and mischievous: they destroyed all the horses, hogs, and cattle. An attack was made on the fort which lasted two days. My father at this time lost ten cattle; but the people were secured behind their wooden walls, and received but little damage.

In this recess of the settlement of No. 4 the Indians and French were icelocked in Canada, and the frontiers suffered only in apprehension. In March, 1747, Captain Phinehas Stevens, who commanded a ranging party of about thirty men, marched to No. 4 and took possession of the fort. He found it uninjured by the enemy; and an old spaniel and a cat, who had been domesticated before the evacuation, had guarded it safely through the winter, and gave the troops a hearty welcome to their tenement.

Captain Stevens was of eminent service to the infant settlement. In 1748 he moved his family to the place, and encouraged the settlers by his fortitude and industry. In the early part of his life, when Rutland suffered by savage vengeance, when the Rev. Mr. Willard was murdered, he was taken prisoner and carried to St. Francis. This informed him of the Indian customs and familiarized him with their mode of warfare. He was an active, penetrating soldier, and a respectable, worthy citizen.

In a few days after the fort was taken possession of by Captain Stevens's troops a party of five hundred French and Indians, commanded by Monsieur Debelcie, sallied from their den in Canada and made a furious attack on the fort. The battle lasted five days, and every stratagem which French policy or Indian malice could invent was practised to reduce the garrison. Sometimes they made an onset by a discharge of musketry; at others they discharged fire arrows, which communicated fire to several parts of the fort. But these were insufficient to daunt the courage of the little band that were assailed. Their next step was to fill a cart with combustibles, and roll it against the walls, to communicate fire; but the English kept up such a brisk, incessant fire that they were defeated in the project. At length the monsieurs, tired with fighting, beat a parley. Two Indians, formerly acquainted with Captain Stevens, came as negotiators, and wished to exchange some furs for corn: this Captain Stevens refused, but offered a bushel of corn for each hostage they would leave to be exchanged at some future day. These terms were not complied with; and on the fifth day the enemy retreated, at which time the soldiers in the garrison honored them with as brisk a discharge as they could afford, to let them know that they were neither disheartened nor exhausted in ammunition. The garrison had none killed; and only one, by the name of Brown, was wounded.

Perhaps no place was ever defended with greater bravery than this fort during this action. Thirty or forty men, when attacked by five hundred, must have an uncommon degree of fortitude and vigilance to defend themselves during a siege of five days. But Captain Stevens was equal to the task, and will be applauded by posterity. After the battle he sent an express to Boston with the tidings. Governor Charles Knowles happened then to be at Boston, and rewarded Captain Stevens with a handsome sword; in gratitude for which the place was afterwards called Charlestown.

In November, 1747, a body of the troops set out from the fort to return to Massachusetts. They had not proceeded far before the Indians fired on them. Isaac Goodale and Nathaniel Gould were killed, and one Anderson taken prisoner. From this period until the end of the Cape Breton war the fort was defended by Captain Stevens. Soldiers passed and repassed to Canada; but the inhabitants took sanctuary in the fort, and made but little progress in cultivation. During the Indian wars, which lasted till the year 1760, Charlestown was noted more for its feats of war than a place of rapid improvement. Settlers thought it more prudent to remain with their friends in safety than risk their scalps with savage power. Since that period it has become a flourishing village, and contains all that a rural situation affords of the useful and the pleasant. Numerous farms and stately buildings now flourish where the savage roamed the forest. The prosperity of the town was greatly promoted by the Rev. Bulkely Olcott, who was a settled minister there about thirty-two years. In the character of this good man were combined the agreeable companion, the industrious citizen, and the unaffected Christian. During the whole of his ministry his solicitude for the happiness of his parishioners was as conspicuous in the benefits they received from his assistance as in their sincere attachment to his person. As a divine he was pathetic, devout, and instructive, and may with propriety be said to have

Shown the path to heaven, and led the way.

He was highly respected through life. In June, 1793, he died, much lamented.

### Removal to Charlestown, &c.

In May, 1749, we received information of the cessation of arms between Great Britain and France. I had then been married about two years, and Mr. Johnson's enterprising spirit was zealous to remove to Charlestown. In June we undertook the hazardous and fatiguing journey. We arrived safe at the fort, and found five families, who had ventured so far into the woods during hostilities. But the gloomy forest and the warlike appearance of the place soon made me homesick. Two or three days after my arrival orders came from Massachusetts to withdraw the troops. Government placed confidence in the proffered peace of Frenchmen, and withdrew even the appearance of hostility. But French treachery and savage malice will ever keep pace with each other. Without even the suspicion of danger, the inhabitants went about their business of husbandry. The day the soldiers left the fort Ensign Obadiah Sartwell went to harrow some corn, and took Enos Stevens, the fourth son of Phinehas Stevens, Esq., to ride horse : my father and two brothers were at work in the meadow. Early in the afternoon the Indians appeared and shot Ensign Sartwell and the horse, and took young Stevens a prisoner. In addition to this my father and brothers were in the meadow, and we supposed they must be destroyed. My husband was gone to Northfield. In the fort were seven women and four men : the anxiety and grief we experienced were the highest imaginable. The next night we despatched a post to Boston to carry the news of our disaster; but my father and brothers did not return. The next day but one my husband and five or six others arrived from Northfield. We kept close in the garrison, suffering every apprehension for ten or twelve days, when the sentry from the box cried out that troops were coming : joyful at the relief, we all mounted on the top of the fort, and among the rest discovered my father. He, on hearing the guns, supposed the fort was destroyed, left his team in the meadow, and made the best of his way to Northfield with my two brothers. The soldiers were about thirty in number, and headed by Major Josiah Willard, of Fort Dummer. Enos Stevens was carried to Montreal; but the French commander sent him back directly by the way of Albany. This was the last damage done the frontiers during the Cape Breton war.

## Cursory Notices.

A detail of the miseries of a " frontier man " must excite the pity of every child of humanity. The gloominess of the rude forest, the distance from friends and competent defence, and the daily inroads and nocturnal yells of hostile Indians, awaken those keen apprehensions and anxieties which conception only can picture. If the peaceful employment of hus-

12 *

bandry is pursued, the loaded musket must stand by his side; if he visits a neighbor, or resorts on Sundays to the sacred house of prayer, the weapons of war must bear him company; at home the distresses of a wife and the tears of lisping children often unman the soul that real danger assailed in vain. Those who can recollect the war that existed between France and England fifty years ago may figure to themselves the unhappy situation of the inhabitants on the frontiers of New Hampshire : the malice of the French in Canada, and the exasperated savages that dwelt in their vicinity, rendered the tedious days and frightful nights a season of unequalled calamities. The daily reports of captured families and slaughtered friends mingled grief with fear. Had there been an organized government to stretch forth its protecting arm in any case of danger, the misery might have been in a degree alleviated. But the infancy of our country did not admit of this blessing. While Governor Shirley, of Massachusetts, was petitioning to England for a fleet and an army, Benning Wentworth, the supine governor of New Hampshire, obeyed implicitly the advice of his friend Shirley, and remained inactively secure at his seat at Portsmouth. At the commencement of the year 1745 the Quixotic expedition to Louisburg was projected, the success of which originated from the merest accident rather than from military valor or generalship : this drained the thinly inhabited State of New Hampshire of most of its effective men. From that period till the peace, which took place in the year 1749, the visionary schemes of Shirley kept the best soldiers imbodied in some remote place, as a force to execute some impolitic project. The conquest of Canada and the attack upon Crown Point are recorded as specimens of the wild projects which were to employ the infant forces of New England. During this time the frontiers sustained additional miseries by having the small forces of the state deducted for purposes which could be of no immediate service to them. The savages committed frequent depredations on the defenceless inhabitants; and the ease with which they gained their prey encouraged their boldness, and by scattering in small parties they were able to infest the whole frontier of New Hampshire, from Fort Dummer, on Connecticut River, to the lowest settlement on the Merrimack. During this war, which is known by the name of the Cape Breton war, the town of No. 4 could hardly be said to be inhabited: some adventurers had made a beginning, but few were considered as belonging to the town. Captain Stevens, whose valor is recorded as an instance of consummate generalship, part of the time kept the fort, which afforded a shelter to the enterprising settlers in times of imminent danger. But even his vigilance did not save the town from numerous scenes of carnage. At the commencement of the peace, in 1749, the enterprising spirit of New England rose superior to the dangers of the forest, and they began to venture innovation. The Indians, still thirsty for plunder and rapine, and regardless of the peace which their masters the French had concluded, kept up a flying warfare, and committed several outrages upon lives and property. This kept the increasing inhabitants in a state of alarm for three or four years: most of the time they performed their daily work without molestation, but retreated to the fort at each returning night.

Our country has so long been exposed to Indian wars that recitals of exploits and sufferings, of escapes and deliverances, have become both numerous and trite. The air of novelty will not be attempted in the following pages: simple facts, unadorned, are what the reader must expect: pity for my sufferings and admiration at my safe return is all that my history can excite. The aged man, while perusing, will probably turn his attention to the period when the facts took place; his memory will be refreshed with the sad tidings of his country's sufferings, which gave a daily wound to his feelings, between the years 1740 and 1760. By contrasting those days with the present he may rejoice that he witnesses those times which many have "waited for, but died without the sight." Those "in early life," while they commiserate the sufferings which their parents and ancestors endured, may felicitate themselves that their lines fell in a land of peace, where neither savages nor neighboring wars molest their happiness

---

### Situation until August 31, 1754.

Some of the soldiers who arrived with Major Willard, with the inhabitants who bore arms, were commanded by Captain Stevens the rest of the year 1749 and part of the following spring; after which the inhabitants resided pretty much in the fort until the spring or fall of the year 1752. They cultivated their lands in some degree, but they put but little confidence in the savages.

The continuation of peace began by degrees to appease the resentment of the Indians, and they appeared to discover a wish for friendly intercourse. The inhabitants in No. 4 and its vicinity relaxed their watchfulness and ventured more boldly into their fields. Every appearance of hostility at length vanished. The Indians expressed a wish to traffic; the inhabitants laid by their fears, and thought no more of tomahawks or scalping knives. Mr. Johnson now thought himself justified in removing to his farm, a hundred rods distant from the fort, which was then the uppermost settlement on Connecticut River. He pursued his occupation of trade, and the Indians made frequent visits to traffic their furs for his merchandise. He frequently credited them for blankets and other necessaries, and in most instances they were punctual in payment. During the year 1753 all was harmony and safety; settlements increased with tolerable rapidity; and the new country began to assume the appearance of cultivation.

The commencement of the year 1754 began to threaten another rupture between the French and English; and as the dividing line between Canada and the English colonies was the object of contention, it was readily seen that the frontier towns would be in imminent danger. But as immediate war was not expected, Mr. Johnson thought that he might risk the safety of his family while he made a tour to Connecticut for trade. He set out the last of May; and his absence of three months was a tedious and a bitter season to me. Soon after his departure every body was "tremblingly alive" with fear. The Indians were reported to be on their march for our destruction; and our distance from sources of information gave full latitude for exaggeration of news before it reached our ears. The fears of the night were horrible beyond description; and even the light of day was far from dispelling painful anxiety. While looking from the windows of my log house and seeing my neighbors tread cautiously by each hedge and hillock lest some secreted savage might start forth to take their scalp, my fears would baffle description. Alarms grew louder and louder, till our apprehensions were too strongly confirmed by the news of the capture of Mr. Malloon's family on Merrimack River. This reached us about the 20th of August. Imagination now saw and heard a thousand Indians; and I never went round my own house without first looking with trembling caution by each corner to see if a tomahawk was not raised for my destruction.

On the 24th of August I was relieved from all my fears by the arrival of my husband. He brought intelligence from Connecticut that a war was expected the next spring, but that no immediate danger was contemplated. He had made preparations to remove to Northfield as soon as our stock of hay was consumed and our dozen of swine had demolished our ample stores of grain, which would secure his family and property from the miseries and ravages of war. Our eldest son, Sylvanus, who was six years old, was in the mean time

to be put to school at Springfield. Mr. Johnson brought home
a large addition to his stores, and the neighbors made frequent
parties at our house to express their joy for his return; and
time passed merrily off by the aid of spirit and a ripe yard
of melons. As I was in the last days of pregnancy, I could
not join so heartily in their good cheer as I otherwise might.
Yet in a new country pleasure is often derived from sources
unknown to those less accustomed to the woods. The return
of my husband, the relief from danger, and the crowds of
happy friends combined to render my situation peculiarly
agreeable. I now boasted with exultation that I should, with
husband, friends, and luxuries, live happy in spite of the fear
of savages.

On the evening of the 29th of August our house was visited by a party of neighbors, who spent the time very cheerfully with watermelons and flip till midnight. They all then
retired in high spirits except a spruce young spark, who
tarried to keep company with my sister. We then went to
bed with feelings well tuned for sleep, and rested with fine
composure till midway between daybreak and sunrise, when
we were roused by neighbor Labarree's knocking at the door,
who had shouldered his axe to do a day's work for my husband. Mr. Johnson slipped on his jacket and trousers and
stepped to the door to let him in. But by opening the door
he opened a scene terrible to describe. "Indians! Indians!"
were the first words I heard. He sprang to his guns; but
Labarree, heedless of danger, instead of closing the door to
keep them out, began to rally our hired men up stairs for
not rising earlier. But in an instant a crowd of savages,
fixed horribly for war, rushed furiously in. I screamed and
begged my friends to ask for quarter. By this time they
were all over the house — some up stairs, some hauling my
sister out of bed; another had hold of me; and one was approaching Mr. Johnson, who stood in the middle of the floor
to deliver himself up. But the Indian, supposing that he

would make resistance and be more than his match, went to
the door and brought three of his comrades, and the four
bound him. I was led to the door, fainting and trembling.
There stood my friend Labarree bound. Ebenezer Farnsworth, whom they found up chamber, they were putting in
the same situation; and, to complete the shocking scene, my
three little children were driven naked to the place where I
stood. On viewing myself I found that I, too, was naked.
An Indian had plundered three gowns, who, on seeing my
situation, gave me the whole. I asked another for a petticoat; but he refused it. After what little plunder their hurry
would allow them to get was confusedly bundled up, we were
ordered to march. After going about twenty rods we fell
behind a rising ground, where we halted to pack the things
in a better manner: while there a savage went back, as we
supposed, to fire the buildings. Farnsworth proposed to my
husband to go back with him, to get a quantity of pork from
the cellar to help us on our journey; but Mr. Johnson prudently replied, that, by that means, the Indians might find the
rum, and in a fit of intoxication kill us all. The Indian presently returned with marks of fear in his countenance,* and
we were hurried on with all violence. Two savages laid hold
of each of my arms, and hurried me through thorny thickets
in a most unmerciful manner. I lost a shoe and suffered
exceedingly. We heard the alarm guns from the fort. This
added new speed to the flight of the savages. They were
apprehensive that soldiers might be sent for our relief. When

---

* This, as we afterwards found, was occasioned by his meeting Mr.
Osmer at the door of the house, who lodged in the chamber and had
secreted himself behind a box, and was then making his escape. He
ran directly to the fort, and the alarm guns were fired. My father,
Mr. Moses Willard, was then second in command. Captain Stevens
was for sallying out with a party for our relief; but my father begged
him to desist, as the Indians made it an invariable practice to kill
their prisoners when attacked.

we had got a mile and a half my faintness obliged me to sit. This being observed by an Indian, he drew his knife, as I supposed, to put an end to my existence. But he only cut some band with which my gown was tied, and then pushed me on. My little children were crying, my husband and the other two men were bound, and my sister and myself were obliged to make the best of our way with all our might. The loss of my shoe rendered travelling extremely painful. At the distance of three miles there was a general halt. The savages, supposing that we as well as themselves might have an appetite for breakfast, gave us a loaf of bread, some raisins, and apples which they had taken from the house. While we were forcing down our scanty breakfast a horse came in sight, known to us all by the name of Scoggin, belonging to Phinehas Stevens, Esq. One of the Indians attempted to shoot him, but was prevented by Mr. Johnson. They then expressed a wish to catch him, saying, by pointing to me, for squaw to ride. My husband had previously been unbound to assist the children; he, with two Indians, caught the horse on the banks of the river. By this time my legs and feet were covered with blood, which being noticed by Mr. Labarree, he, with that humanity which never forsook him, took his own stockings and presented them to me, and the Indians gave me a pair of moccasons. Bags and blankets were thrown over Scoggin, and I mounted on the top of them, and on we jogged about seven miles to the upper end of Wilcott's Island. We there halted and prepared to cross the river. Rafts were made of dry timber. Two Indians and Farnsworth crossed first; Labarree, by signs, got permission to swim the horse; and Mr. Johnson was allowed to swim by the raft that I was on, to push it along. We all arrived safe on the other side of the river about four o'clock in the afternoon. A fire was kindled, and some of their stolen kettles were hung over it and filled with porridge. The savages took delight in viewing their spoil, which amounted to forty or fifty pounds in value. They then with a true savage yell gave the war whoop and bade defiance to danger. As our tarry in this place lasted an hour, I had time to reflect on our miserable situation. Captives, in the power of unmerciful savages, without provision and almost without clothes, in a wilderness where we must sojourn as long as the children of Israel did for aught we knew; and, what added to our distress, not one of our savage masters could understand a word of English. Here, after being hurried from home with such rapidity, I have leisure to inform the reader respecting our Indian masters. They were eleven * in number, men of middle age except one, a youth of sixteen, who in our journey discovered a very mischievous and troublesome disposition. According to their national practice, he who first laid hands on a prisoner considered him as his property. My master, who was the one that took my hand when I sat on the bed, was as clever an Indian as ever I saw. He even evinced, at numerous times, a disposition that showed he was by no means void of compassion. The four who took my husband claimed him as their property; and my sister, three children, Labarree, and Farnsworth had each a master. When the time came for us to prepare to march I almost expired at the thought of leaving my aged parents, brothers, sisters, and friends, and travel with savages through a dismal forest to unknown regions, in the alarming situation I then was in, with three small children. The eldest, Sylvanus, was but six years old; my eldest daughter, Susanna, was four; and Polly, the other, two. My sister Miriam was fourteen. My husband was barefoot, and otherwise thinly clothed. His master had taken his jacket, and nothing but his shirt and trousers remained. My two daugh-

---

* Mr. Labarree is very positive, and I think Mr. Johnson was of the same opinion, that seventeen Indians attacked the house. The other six might have been a scouting party, that watched till we were out of danger, and then took another route.

ters had nothing but their shifts, and I only the gown that was handed me by the savages. In addition to the sufferings which arose from my own deplorable condition, I could not but feel for my friend Labarree. He had left a wife and four small children behind to lament his loss and to render his situation extremely unhappy. With all these misfortunes lying heavily upon me, the reader can imagine my situation. The Indians pronounced the dreadful word " munch," march ; and on we must go. I was put on the horse; Mr. Johnson took one daughter; and Mr. Labarree, being unbound, took the other. We went six or eight miles and stopped for the night. The men were made secure by having their legs put in split sticks, somewhat like stocks, and tied with cords, which were tied to the limbs of trees too high to be reached. My sister, much to her mortification, must lie between two Indians, with a cord thrown over her and passing under each of them. The little children had blankets ; and I was allowed one for my use. Thus we took lodging for the night, with the sky for a covering and the ground for a pillow. The fatigues of the preceding day obliged me to sleep several hours, in spite of the horrors which surrounded me. The Indians observed great silence, and never spoke but when really necessary ; and all the prisoners were disposed to say but little. My children were much more peaceable than could be imagined ; gloomy fear imposed a deadly silence.

*History of our Journey through the Wilderness till we came to the Waters that enter Lake Champlain.*

In the morning we were roused before sunrise : the Indians struck up a fire, hung on their stolen kettles, and made us some water gruel for breakfast. After a few sips of this meagre fare I was again put on the horse, with my husband by my side to hold me on. My two fellow-prisoners took the little girls, and we marched sorrowfully on for an hour or two, when a keener distress was added to my multiplied afflictions. I was taken with the pangs of childbirth. The Indians signified to us that we must go on to a brook. When we got there they showed some humanity by making a booth for me. Here the compassionate reader will drop a fresh tear for my inexpressible distress; fifteen or twenty miles from the abode of any civilized being, in the open wilderness, rendered cold by a rainy day, in one of the most perilous hours, and unsupplied with the least necessary that could yield convenience in the hazardous moment. My children were crying at a distance, where they were held by their masters, and only my husband and sister to attend me. None but mothers can figure to themselves my unhappy fortune. The Indians kept aloof the whole time. About ten o'clock a daughter was born. They then brought me some articles of clothing for the child which they had taken from the house. My master looked into the booth and clapped his hands with joy, crying, "Two moneys for me! two moneys for me!" I was permitted to rest the remainder of the day. The Indians were employed in making a bier for the prisoners to carry me on, and another booth for my lodging during night. They brought a needle, and two pins, and some bark to tie the child's clothes, which they gave my sister, and a large wooden spoon to feed it with. At dusk they made some porridge, and brought a cup to steep some roots in, which Mr. Labarree had provided. In the evening I was removed to the new booth. For supper they made more porridge and some johnny cakes. My portion was brought me in a little bark. I slept that night far beyond expectation.

In the morning we were summoned for the journey, after the usual breakfast of meal and water. I, with my infant in my arms, was laid on the litter, which was supported alternately by Mr. Johnson, Labarree, and Farnsworth. My sister and son were put upon Scoggin, and the two little girls rode on their masters' backs. Thus we proceeded two miles, when my carriers grew too faint to proceed any farther. This being observed by our sable masters, a general halt was called, and they imbodied themselves for council. My master soon made signs to Mr. Johnson that if I could ride on the horse I might proceed, otherwise I must be left behind. Here I observed marks of pity in his countenance; but this might arise from the fear of losing his two moneys. I preferred an attempt to ride on the horse rather than to perish miserably alone. Mr. Labarree took the infant, and every step of the horse almost deprived me of life. My weak and helpless condition rendered me, in a degree, insensible to every thing. My poor child could have no sustenance from my breast, and was supported entirely by water gruel. My other little children, rendered peevish by an uneasy mode of riding, often burst into cries; but a surly check from their masters soon silenced them. We proceeded on with a slow, mournful pace. My weakness was too severe to allow me to sit on the horse long at a time. Every hour I was taken off and laid on the ground to rest. This preserved my life during the third day. At night we found ourselves at the head of Black River Pond. Here we prepared to spend the night. Our supper consisted of gruel and the broth of a hawk they had killed the preceding day. The prisoners were secured as usual, a booth was made for me, and all went to rest. After encampment we entered into a short conversation. My sister observed, that, if I could have been left behind, our trouble would have been seemingly nothing. My husband hoped, by the assistance of Providence, we should all be preserved. Mr. Labarree pitied his poor family; and 'Farnsworth summed the whole of his wishes by saying, that, if he could have got a layer of pork from the cellar, we should not be in fear of starvation. The night was uncommonly dark, and passed tediously off.

In the morning, half chilled with a cold fog, we were ordered from our places of rest, were offered the lean fare of meal and water, and then prepared for the journey. Every thing resembled a funeral procession. The savages preserved their gloomy sadness. The prisoners, bowed down with grief and fatigue, felt little disposition to talk; and the unevenness of the country, sometimes lying in miry plains, at others rising into steep and broken hills, rendered our passage hazardous and painful. Mr. Labarree kept the infant in his arms and preserved its life. The fifth day's journey was an unvaried scene of fatigue. The Indians sent out two or three hunting parties, who returned without game. As we had in the morning consumed the last morsel of our meal, every one now began to be seriously alarmed; and hunger, with all its horrors, looked us earnestly in the face. At night we found the waters that run into Lake Champlain, which was over the height of land. Before dark we halted; and the Indians, by the help of their punk, which they carried in horns, made a fire. They soon adopted a plan to relieve their hunger. The horse was shot, and his flesh was in a few moments broiling on embers; and they, with native gluttony, satiated their craving appetites. To use the term politeness, in the management of this repast, may be thought a burlesque; yet their offering the prisoners the best parts of the horse certainly bordered on civility. An epicure could not have catered nicer slices, nor in that situation served them up with more neatness. Appetite is said to be the best sauce; yet our abundance of it did not render savory this novel steak. My children, however, ate too much, which made them very unwell for a number of days. Broth was made for me and my child, which was rendered almost a luxury by the seasoning of roots. After supper countenances began to brighten. Those who had relished the meal exhibited new strength, and those who had only snuffed its effluvia confessed themselves regaled. The evening was employed in drying and smoking what remained for future use. The night was a scene of distressing fears to me; and my extreme weakness had affected my mind to such a degree that every difficulty appeared doubly terrible. By the assistance of Scoggin I

13 *

had been brought so far; yet so great was my debility that every hour I was taken off and laid on the ground, to keep me from expiring. But now, alas! this conveyance was no more. To walk was impossible. Inevitable death, in the midst of woods one hundred miles wide, appeared my only portion.

### Our Arrival at East Bay, in Lake Champlain.

In the morning of the sixth day the Indians exerted themselves to prepare one of their greatest dainties. The marrow bones of old Scoggin were pounded for a soup; and every root, both sweet and bitter, that the woods afforded, was thrown in to give it a flavor. Each one partook of as much as his feelings would allow. The war whoop then resounded, with an infernal yell, and we began to fix for a march. My fate was unknown, till my master brought some bark and tied my petticoats as high as he supposed would be convenient for walking, and ordered me to " munch." With scarce strength to stand alone, I went on half a mile with my little son and three Indians. The rest were advanced. My power to move then failed; the world grew dark, and I dropped down. I had sight enough to see an Indian lift his hatchet over my head; while my little son screamed, " Ma'am, do go; for they will kill you." As I fainted, my last thought was, that I should presently be in the world of spirits. When I awoke my master was talking angrily with the savage who had threatened my life. By his gestures I could learn that he charged him with not acting the honorable part of a warrior, by an attempt to destroy the prize of a brother. A whoop was given for a halt. My master helped me to the rest of the company, where a council was held, the result of which was, that my husband should walk by my side and help me along. This he did for some hours; but faintness then overpowered me, and Mr. Johnson's tenderness and solicitude were unequal to the task of aiding me farther. Another council was held:

while in debate, as I lay on the ground gasping for breath, my master sprang towards me with his hatchet. My husband and fellow-prisoners grew pale at the sight, suspecting that he by a single blow would rid themselves of so great a burden as myself. But he had yet too much esteem for his "two moneys." His object was to get bark from a tree, to make a pack saddle for my conveyance on the back of my husband. He took me up, and we marched in that form the rest of the day. Mr. Labarree still kept my infant. Farnsworth carried one of the little girls, and the other rode with her master. They were extremely sick and weak, owing to the large portion of the horse which they ate; but if they uttered a murmuring word, a menacing frown from the savages soon imposed silence. None of the Indians were disposed to show insults of any nature except the youngest, which I have before mentioned. He often delighted himself by tormenting my sister, by pulling her hair, treading on her gown,. and numerous other boyish pranks, which were provoking and troublesome. We moved on, faint and wearily, till night. The Indians then yelled their war whoop, built a fire, and hung over their horse broth. After supper my booth was built as usual, and I reposed much better than I had the preceding nights.

In the morning I found myself greatly restored. Without the aid of physicians, or physic, Nature had begun the cure of that weakness to which she had reduced me but a few days before. The reader will be tired of the repetition of the same materials for our meals; but if my feelings can be realized, no one will turn with disgust from a breakfast of steaks which were cut from the thigh of a horse. After which Mr. Johnson was ordered to take the infant and go forward with part of the company. I "munched" in the rear till we came to a beaver pond, which was formed in a branch of Otter Creek. Here I was obliged to wade. When half way over, up to the middle in cold water, my little strength failed, and my

power to speak or see left me.  While motionless and stiff-
ened, in the middle of the pond, I was perceived from the
other side by Mr. Johnson, who laid down the infant and
came to my assistance.  He took me in his arms; and when
the opposite side was gained, life itself had apparently for-
saken me.  The whole company stopped; and the Indians,
with more humanity than I supposed them possessed of,
busied themselves in making a fire to warm me into life.  The
warm influence of the fire restored my exhausted strength by
degrees; and in two hours I was told to munch.  The rest
of the day I was carried by my husband.  In the middle of
the afternoon we arrived on the banks of one of the great
branches of Otter Creek.  Here we halted; and two savages,
who had been on a hunting scout, returned with a duck.  A
fire was made, which was thrice grateful to my cold, shiver-
ing limbs.  Six days had now almost elapsed since the fatal
morn in which we were taken; and by the blessing of that
Providence whose smiles give life to creation we were still
in existence.  My wearied husband, naked children, and helpless infant formed a scene that conveyed severer pangs to my
heart than all the sufferings I endured myself.  The Indians
were sullen and silent; the prisoners were swollen with gloomy
grief; and I was half the time expiring.  After my feelings
were a little quickened by warmth, my sad portion was brought
in a bark, consisting of the duck's head and a gill of broth.
As I lifted the unsavory morsel with a trembling hand to my
mouth, I cast my thoughts back a few days to a time when,
from a board plentifully spread in my own house, I ate my
food with a merry heart.  The wooden spoon dropped from
my feeble hand.  The contrast was too affecting.  Seated on
a ragged rock, beneath a hemlock, as I then was, emaciated
by sickness, and surrounded by my weeping and distressed
family, who were helpless prisoners, despair would have
robbed me of life, had I not put my whole confidence in that
Being who has power to save.  Our masters began to prepare

to ford the stream.  I swallowed most of my broth, and was taken up by my husband.  The river was very rapid and passing dangerous.  Mr. Labarree, when half over with my child, was tripped up by its rapidity, and lost the babe in the water : little did I expect to see the poor thing again ; but he fortunately reached a corner of its blanket and saved its life. The rest got safe to the other shore ; another fire was built, and my sister dried the infant and its clothes.

\*        \*        \*        \*        \*

Here the savages for the first time gave loud tokens of joy, by hallooing and yelling in a tremendous manner.  The prisoners were now introduced to a new school.  Little did we expect that the accomplishment of dancing would ever be taught us by the savages.  But the war dance must now be held, and every prisoner that could move must take its awkward steps.  The figure consisted of circular motion round the fire ; each sang his own music, and the best dancer was the one most violent in motion.  The prisoners were taught each a song ; mine was, *Danna witchee natchepung ;* my son's was, *Narwiscumpton.*  The rest I cannot recollect. Whether this task was imposed on us for their diversion, or a religious ceremonial, I cannot say ; but it was very painful and offensive.  In the forenoon seven Indians came to us, who were received with great joy by our masters, who took great pleasure in introducing their prisoners.  The war dance was again held ; we were obliged to join and sing our songs, while the Indians rent the air with infernal yelling.  We then embarked, and arrived at Crown Point about noon.  Each prisoner was then led by his master to the residence of the French commander.  The Indians kept up their infernal yelling the whole time.  We were ordered to his apartment, and used with that hospitality which characterizes the best part of the nation.  We had brandy in profusion, a good dinner, and a change of linen.  This was luxury indeed, after what we had suffered for the want of these things.  None but ourselves could prize their value. We, after dinner, were paraded before Mr. Commander and underwent examination; after which we were shown a convenient apartment, where we resided four days, not subject to the jurisdiction of our savage masters. Here we received great civilities and many presents. I had a nurse, who in a great measure restored my exhausted strength. My children were all decently clothed, and my infant in particular. The first day, while I was taking a nap, they dressed it so fantastically, *à la France*, that I refused to own it when brought to my bedside, not guessing that I was the mother of such a strange thing.

On the fourth day, to our great grief and mortification, we were again delivered to the Indians, who led us to the water side, where we all embarked in one vessel for St. John's. The wind shifted after a short sail, and we dropped anchor. In a little time a canoe came alongside of us, in which was a white woman, who was bound for Albany. Mr. Johnson begged her to stop a few minutes while he wrote to Colonel Lydius, of Albany, to inform him of our situation, and to request him to put the same in the Boston newspapers, that our friends might learn that we were alive. The woman delivered the letter, and the contents were published, which conveyed the agreeable tidings to our friends, that, although prisoners, we were then alive.

The following letter, in return for the one we sent to Colonel Lydius, was the first we received from New England : —

ALBANY, November 5, 1754.

SIR, — I received yours of the 5th of October, with a letter or two for New England, which I have forwarded immediately, and have wrote to Boston, in which I urged the government to endeavor your and family's redemption as soon as conveniency would admit.

I am quite sorry for your doleful misfortune, and hope the just God will endue you with patience to undergo your troubles, and justly use his rewards on the evil doers and authors of your misfortune. Present my service to all the prisoners with you, from him who subscribes himself to be

Your very humble servant,

JOHN W. LYDIUS.

Lieutenant James Johnson, Montreal.

After a disagreeable voyage of three days, we made St. John's the 16th of September, where we again experienced the politeness of a French commander. I, with my child, was kindly lodged in the same room with himself and lady. In the morning we still found misfortune treading close at our heels: we must again be delivered to our savage masters, and take another passage in the boats for Chamblee; when within three miles of which, Labarree, myself and child, with our two masters, were put on shore. We were ignorant of our destiny; and parting from my husband and friends was a severe trial, without knowing whether we were ever to meet them again. We walked on to Chamblee; here our fears were dissipated by meeting our friends. In the garrison of this place we found all the hospitality our necessities required. Here for the first, after my captivity, I lodged on a bed. Brandy was handed about in large bowls, and we lived in high style. The next morning we were put in the custody of our old masters, who took us to the canoes, in which we had a painful voyage that day and the following night to Sorell, where we arrived on the 19th. A hospitable friar came to the shore to see us, and invited us to his house. He gave us a good breakfast, and drank our better healths in a tumbler of brandy. He took compassionate notice of my child, and ordered it some suitable food. But the Indians hurried us off before it could eat. He then went with us to the shore, and ordered his servant to carry the food, prepared for the child, to the canoe, where he waited till I fed it. The friar was a very genteel man, and gave us his benedic-

tion at parting in feeling language. We then rowed on till
the middle of the afternoon, when we landed on a barren
heath, and by the help of a fire cooked an Indian dinner;
after which the war dance was held and another infernal
yelling. The prisoners were obliged to sing till they were
hoarse, and dance round the fire.

We had now arrived within a few miles of the village of
St. Francis, to which place our masters belonged. Whenever
the warriors return from an excursion against an enemy,
their return to the tribe or village must be designated by warlike ceremonial; the captives or spoil, which may happen to
crown their valor, must be conducted in a triumphant form,
and decorated to every possible advantage. For this end we
must now submit to painting: their vermilion, with which
they were ever supplied, was mixed with bear's grease, and
every cheek, chin, and forehead must have a dash. We then
rowed on within a mile of the town, where we stopped at a
French house to dine: the prisoners were served with soup
meagre and bread. After dinner two savages proceeded to
the village to carry the glad tidings of our arrival. The
whole atmosphere soon resounded from every quarter with
whoops, yells, shrieks, and screams. St. Francis, from the
noise that came from it, might be supposed the centre of
pandemonium. Our masters were not backward; they made
every response they possibly could. The whole time we were
sailing from the French house the noise was direful to be
heard. Two hours before sunset we came to the landing at
the village. No sooner had we landed than the yelling in the
town was redoubled; a cloud of savages, of all sizes and
sexes, soon appeared running towards us. When they reached
the boats they formed themselves into a long parade, leaving
a small space through which we must pass. Each Indian
then took his prisoner by his hand, and, after ordering him to
sing the war song, began to march through the gantlet. We
expected a severe beating before we got through; but were

agreeably disappointed when we found that each Indian only gave us a tap on the shoulder. We were led directly to the housés, each taking his prisoner to his own wigwam. When I entered my master's door his brother saluted me with a large belt of wampum, and my master presented me with another. Both were put over my shoulders, and crossed behind and before. My new home was not the most agreeable: a large wigwam, without a floor, with a fire in the centre, and only a few water vessels and dishes to eat from, made of birch bark, and tools for cookery, made clumsily of wood, for furniture, will not be thought a pleasing residence to one accustomed to civilized life.

### Residence at St. Francis. — Sale of most of the Prisoners to the French, and Removal to Montreal.

Night presently came after our arrival at St. Francis. Those who have felt the gloomy, homesick feelings which sadden those hours which a youth passes when first from a father's house, may judge of part of my sufferings; but when the rest of my circumstances are added, their conception must fall infinitely short. I now found myself, with my infant, in a large wigwam, accompanied with two or three warriors and as many squaws, where I must spend the night, and perhaps a year. My fellow-prisoners were dispersed over the town, each one, probably, feeling the same gloominess with myself. Hasty pudding presently was brought forward for supper. A spacious bowl of wood, well filled, was placed in a central spot, and each one drew near with a wooden spoon. As the Indians never use seats, nor have any in their wigwams, my awkwardness in taking my position was a matter of no small amusement to my new companions. The squaws first fall upon their knees, and then sit back upon their heels. This was a posture that I could not imitate. To sit in any other was thought by them indelicate and unpolite. But I advanced to my pudding with the best grace I could; not,

however, escaping some of their funny remarks.  When the
hour for sleep came on, for it would be improper to call it
bedtime where beds were not, I was pointed to a platform,
raised half a yard, where upon a board covered with a blanket
I was to pass the night.  The Indians threw themselves down
in various parts of the building in a manner that more resembled cows in a shed than human beings in a house.  In
the morning our breakfast consisted of the relics of the last
night.  My sister came to see me in the forenoon; and we
spent some hours in observations upon our situation while
washing some apparel at a little brook.  In the afternoon I,
with my infant, was taken to the grand parade, where we
found a large collection of the village inhabitants.  An aged
chief stepped forward into an area, and after every noise was
silenced and every one fixed in profound attention he began
to harangue : his manner was solemn; his motions and expression gave me a perfect idea of an orator.  Not a breath was
heard, and every spectator seemed to reverence what he said.
After the speech my little son was brought to the opposite
side of the parade, and a number of blankets laid by his side.
It now appeared that his master and mine intended an exchange of prisoners.  My master, being a hunter, wished for
my son to attend him on his excursions.  Each delivered his
property with great formality; my son and blankets being an
equivalent for myself, child, and wampum.  I was taken to
the house of my new master, and found myself allied to the
first family.  My master, whose name was Gill, was son-in-
law to the grand sachem, was accounted rich, had a store of
goods, and lived in a style far above the majority of his tribe.
He often told me that he had an English heart, but his wife
was true Indian blood.  Soon after my arrival at his house
the interpreter came to inform me that I was adopted into his
family.  I was then introduced into the family, and was told
to call them brothers and sisters.  I made a short reply, ex-
pressive of gratitude for being introduced to a house of high

rank, and requested their patience while I should learn the customs of the nation. This was scarce over when the attention of the village was called to the grand parade, to attend a rejoicing occasioned by the arrival of some warriors who had brought some scalps. They were carried in triumph on a pole. Savage butchery upon murdered countrymen! The sight was horrid. As I retired to my new residence I could hear the savage yells that accompanied the war dance. I spent the night in sad reflection.

My time now was solitary beyond description. My new sisters and brothers treated me with the same attention that they did their natural kindred; but it was an unnatural situation to me. I was a novice at making canoes, bunks, and tumplines, which was the only occupation of the squaws; of course, idleness was among my calamities. My fellow-prisoners were as gloomy as myself; ignorant whether they were to spend their days in this inactive village, to be carried into a war campaign, to slaughter their countrymen, or to be dragged to the cold lakes of the north in a hunting voyage. We visited each other daily, and spent our time in conjecturing our future destiny.

The space of forty-two years having elapsed since my residence in St. Francis, it is impossible to give the reader a minute detail of events that occurred while there: many of them are still forcibly impressed upon my memory; but dates and particulars are now inaccurately treasured up by faint recollection. Mr. Johnson tarried but a few days with me before he was carried to Montreal to be sold. My two daughters, sister, and Labarree were soon after carried to the same place at different times. Farnsworth was carried by his master on a hunting scout; but not proving so active in the chase and ambush as they wished, he was returned and sent to Montreal. I now found an increase to my trouble: with only my son and infant in this strange land, without a prospect of relief, and with all my former trouble lying heavy upon me, disappointment and despair came well nigh being my executioners. In this dilemma, who can imagine my distress when my little son came running to me one morning, swóllen with tears, exclaiming that the Indians were going to carry him into the woods to hunt? He had scarcely told the piteous story before his master came to pull him away. He threw his little arms around me, begging, in the agony of grief, that I would keep him. The inexorable savage unclinched his hands and forced him away: the last words I heard, intermingled with his cries, were, "Ma'am, I shall never see you again." The keenness of my pangs almost obliged me to wish that I had never been a mother. "Farewell, Sylvanus," said I; "God will preserve you."

\*　　\*　　\*　　\*　　\*

Mr. Johnson and my daughter were taken with the small pox; and I obtained permission to go to the hospital and see them, after which I never returned to the Indians. It is a singular instance of divine interposition that we all recovered from this malignant disease. We were remanded to prison, but were not compelled to our former rigid confinement. Mr. Johnson was allowed, at certain times, to go about the city in quest of provision. But, on the 20th of October, St. Luc Lucorne arrived from Montreal with the news of Dieskau's defeat: he had, ever since my husband's misfortune about his parole, been his persecuting enemy. By his instigation we were all put directly to close prison.

The ravages of the small pox reduced us to the last extremity; and the fetid prison, without fire or food, added bitterness to our distress. Mr. Johnson preferred a petition to the lord intendant, stating our melancholy situation. I had the liberty of presenting it myself; and by the assistance of Mr. Perthieur, the interpreter, in whom we ever found a compassionate friend, we got some small relief. About the 1st of November I was taken violently ill of a fever, and was carried to the hospital with my daughter Captive. After a month's residence there, with tolerably good attendance, I recovered from my illness and went back to my husband.  While at the hospital I found an opportunity to convey the unwelcome tidings of our deplorable situation to my sister at Montreal, charging her to give my best love to my daughter Susanna, and to inform our fellow-prisoners, Labarree and Farnsworth, that our good wishes awaited them.  Not a word had we yet heard from poor Sylvanus.

Winter now began to approach, and the severe frosts of Canada operated keenly upon our feelings.  Our prison was a horrid defence from the blasts of December: with two chairs, and a heap of straw, and two lousy blankets, we may well be supposed to live uncomfortably: but in addition to this, we had but one poor fire a day, and the iron grates gave free access to the chills of the inclement sky.  A quart basin was the only thing allowed us to cook our small piece of meat and dirty crusts in; and it must serve at the same time for table furniture.  In this sad plight, — a prisoner, in jail, winter approaching, — conceive, reader, for I cannot speak, our distress.

Our former benevolent friends, Captains Stowbrow and Vambram, had the peculiar misfortune to be cast into a prison opposite to us.  Suspicion of having corresponded with their countrymen was the crime with which they were charged.  Their misfortune did not preclude the exertion of generosity: they frequently sent us, by the waiting maid, bottles of wine and articles of provision.  But the malice of Frenchmen had now arrived to such a pitch against all our country that we must be deprived of these comforts.  These good men were forbidden their offices of kindness, and our intercourse was entirely prohibited.  We, however, found means by a stratagem to effect in some measure what could not be done by open dealing.  When the servants were carrying in our daily supplies, we slipped into the entry and deposited our letters in an ash box, which were taken by our friends, they leaving

14*

one at the same time for us: this served in some measure to amuse a dull hour.  Sometimes we diverted ourselves by the use of Spanish cards: as Mr. Johnson was ignorant of the game, I derived no inconsiderable pleasure from instructing him.  But the vigilance of our keepers increased, and our paper and ink were withheld.  We had now been prisoners seventeen months, and our prospects were changing from bad to worse.  Five months had elapsed since our confinement in this horrid receptacle, except the time we lingered in the hospital.  Our jailer was a true descendant from Pharaoh; but, urged by impatience and despair, I softened him so much as to get him to ask Mr. Perthieur to call on us.  When the good man came we described our situation in all the moving terms which our feelings inspired, which, in addition to what he saw, convinced him of the reality of our distress.  He proposed asking an influential friend of his to call on us, who, perhaps, would devise some mode for our relief.  The next day the gentleman came to see us: he was one of those good souls who ever feel for others' woes.  He was highly affronted with his countrymen for reducing us to such distress, and declared that the lord intendant himself should call on us and see the extremities to which he had reduced us.  He sent from his own house that night a kettle, some candles, and each of us a change of linen.

The next day, January 8, 1756, Mr. Intendant came to see us.  He exculpated himself by saying that we were put there by the special order of Monsieur Vaudrieul, the governor-in-chief, and that he had no authority to release us.  But he would convey a letter from Mr. Johnson to monsieur, which might have the desired effect.  The letter was accordingly written, stating our troubles and beseeching relief; likewise praying that our son might be got from the Indians and sent to us, with our daughter and sister from Montreal.  The governor returned the following obliging letter : —

TRANSLATION.

I have received, sir, your letter, and am much concerned for the situation you are in. I write to Mr. Longieul to put you and your wife in the civil jail. Mr. L. Intendant will be so good as to take some notice of the things you stand in need of, and to help you. As to your boy, who is in the hands of the Indians, I will do all that is in my power to get him; but I do not hope to have a good success in it. Your child in town and your sister-in-law are well. If it is some opportunity of doing you some pleasure I will make use of it, unless some reason might happen that hinder and stop the effects of my good will. If you had not before given some cause of being suspected, you should be at liberty.

I am, sir, your most humble servant,

VAUDRIEUL.

From the receipt of this letter we dated our escape from direful bondage. Mr. Intendant ordered us directly to the new jail, called the civil prison, where our accommodations were infinitely better. We had a decent bed, candles, fuel, and all the conveniences belonging to prisoners of war. Mr. Johnson was allowed fifteen pence per day, on account of a lieutenant's commission which he held under George II.; and I was permitted to go once a week into the city to purchase necessaries, and a washerwoman was provided for my use. We were not confined to the narrow limits of a single room, but were restrained only by the bounds of the jail yard. Our situation formed such a contrast with what we endured in the gloomy criminal jail that we imagined ourselves the favorites of fortune and in high life.

*Residence in the Civil Jail, and Occurrences till the 20th of July,* 1757.

To be indolent from necessity has ever been deemed a formidable evil. No better witnesses than ourselves can testify to the truth of the remark, although our lodgings were now such as we envied a month before; yet to be compelled to continual idleness was grievous to be borne. We derived some amusement from the cultivation of a small garden within the jail yard; but a continued sameness of friends and action rendered our time extremely wearisome.

About a month after our arrival at this new abode, one Captain Milton, with his crew, who with their vessel were taken at sea, were brought prisoners of war to the same place. Milton was lodged in our apartment. He had all the rude, boisterous airs of a seaman, without the least trait of a gentleman, which rendered him a very troublesome companion. His impudence was consummate; but that was not the greatest evil: while some new recruits were parading before the prison one day, Milton addressed them in very improper language from our window, which was noticed directly by city authority, who, supposing it to be Mr. Johnson, ordered him into the dungeon. Deeply affected by this new trouble, I again called on my friend Mr. Perthieur, who, after having ascertained the facts, got him released. Mr. Milton was then put into other quarters.

A new jailer, who had an agreeable lady for his wife, now made our situation still more happy. My little daughters played with hers and learned the French language. But my children were some trouble; the eldest, Polly, could slip out into the street under the gate, and often came nigh being lost. I applied to the sentinel, and he kept her within proper bounds.

Captain M'Neil and his brother, from Boston, were brought to us as prisoners. They informed us of the state of politics in our own country, and told us some interesting news about some of our friends at home.

In the morning of the 13th of August, our jailer, with moon eyes, came to congratulate us on the taking of Oswego by the French. We entered little into his spirit of joy, preferring much to hear good news from the other side. We were soon visited by some of the prisoners who had surrendered. Colonel Schuyler was in the number, who, with the gentlemen in his suit, made us a generous present.

The remainder of the summer and fall of 1756 passed off without any sensible variation. We frequently heard from Montreal. My sister was very well situated in the family of the lieutenant governor, and my eldest daughter was caressed by her three mothers. Could I have heard from my son, half my trouble would have ended.

In December I was delivered of a son, who lived but a few hours, and was buried under the Cathedral Church.

In the winter I received a letter from my sister, containing the sad tidings of my father's death, who was killed by Indians on his own farm the preceding June, at the age of fifty-three. Savage vengeance fell heavily upon our family. I had a brother wounded at the same time, who ran to the fort with the spear sticking in his thigh. Too much grief reduced me to a weak condition. I was taken sick and carried to the hospital, where, after a month's lingering illness, I found myself able to return.

The commencement of the year 1757 passed off without a prospect of liberty. Part of our fellow-prisoners were sent to France, but we made no voyage out of the jail yard. About the 1st of May we petitioned Mons. Vaudrieul to permit our sister to come to us. Our prayer was granted; and in May we had the pleasure of seeing her, after an absence of two years. She had supported herself by her needle in the family of the lieutenant governor, where she was treated extremely well, and received a present of four crowns at parting.

Impatient of confinement, we now made another attempt to gain our liberty. Mr. Perthieur conducted us to the house of the lord intendant, to whom we petitioned in pressing terms, stating that we had now been prisoners almost three

years, and had suffered every thing but death; and that would
be our speedy portion, unless we had relief. His lordship
listened with seeming pity, and promised to lay our case before the head man at Montreal and give us an answer in
seven days; at the expiration of which time we had a permit to leave the prison. It is not easy to describe the effect
of such news; those only who have felt the horrors of confinement can figure to themselves the happiness we enjoyed
when breathing once more the air of liberty. We took lodgings in town, where we tarried till the 1st of June, when a
cartel ship arrived to carry prisoners to England for an exchange. Mr. Johnson wrote an urgent letter to Mons. Vaudrieul, praying that his family might be included with those
who were to take passage. Monsieur wrote a very encouraging letter back, promising that he and his family should
sail, and that his daughter, Susanna, should be sent to him.
He concluded by congratulating him on his good prospects,
and ordering the governor of Quebec to afford us his assistance. This letter was dated June the 27th.

This tide of good fortune almost wiped away the remembrance of three years' adversity. We began our preparations for embarkation with alacrity. Mr. Johnson wrote St.
Luc Lucorne for the seven hundred livres due on Mr. Cuy-
ler's order; but his request was, and still is, unsatisfied. This
was a period big with every thing propitious and happy.
The idea of leaving a country where I had suffered the keen-
est distress during two months and a half with the savages,
been bowed down by every mortification and insult which
could arise from the misfortunes of my husband in New England, and where I had spent two years in sickness and despair in a prison too shocking to mention, contributed to fill
the moment with all the happiness which the benevolent
reader will conceive my due after sufferings so intense. To
consummate the whole, my daughter was to be returned to
my arms who had been absent more than two years. There

was a good prospect of our son's being released from the Indians. The whole formed such a lucky combination of fortunate events that the danger of twice crossing the ocean to gain our native shore vanished in a moment. My family were all in the same joyful mood, and hailed the happy day when we should sail for England.

But little did we think that this sunshine of prosperity was so soon to be darkened by the heaviest clouds of misfortune. Three days before the appointed hour for sailing, the ship came down from Montreal without my daughter. In a few moments I met Mr. Perthieur, who told me that counter orders had come, and Mr. Johnson must be retained a prisoner; only my two little daughters, sister, and myself could go. This was calamity indeed. To attempt such a long, wearisome voyage, without money and without acquaintance, and to leave a husband and two children in the hands of enemies, was too abhorrent for reflection. But it was an affair of importance, and required weighty consideration. Accordingly, the next day a solemn council of all the prisoners in the city was held at the coffee house. Colonel Schuyler was president; and after numerous arguments for and against were heard, it was voted, by a large majority, that I should go. I, with hesitation, gave my consent. Some, perhaps, will censure the measure as rash, and others may applaud my courage; but I had so long been accustomed to danger and distress, in the most menacing forms they could assume, that I was now almost insensible to their threats; and this act was not a little biased by desperation. Life could no longer retain its value if lingered out in the inimical regions of Canada. In Europe I should, at least, find friends, if not acquaintance; and among the numerous vessels bound to America I might chance to get a passage. But then, to leave a tender husband, who had so long, at the hazard of his life, preserved my own, — to part, perhaps forever, from two children, — put all my resolution to the test and shook my boasted firmness.

Colonel Schuyler, whom we ever found our benevolent friend, promised to use his influence for Mr. Johnson's release and for the redemption of our children.

On the 20th of July we went on board the vessel, accompanied by Mr. Johnson, who went with us to take leave. We were introduced to the captain, who was a gentleman and a person of great civility. He showed us the best cabin, which was to be the place of our residence; and after promising my husband that the voyage should be made as agreeable to me as possible, he gave orders for weighing anchor. The time was now come that we must part. Mr. Johnson took me by the hand; our tears imposed silence. I saw him step into the barge; but my two little children, sister, and myself were bound for Europe.

We fell down the River St. Lawrence but a small distance that night. The next morning the captain, with a cheerful countenance, came to our cabin and invited us to rise and take our leave of Quebec. None but myself complied; and I gazed, as long as sight would permit, at the place where I had left my dearest friend.

While in the custody of the Canadians, a number of circumstances occurred with which my memory is not strongly impressed; but a dream which I had while in the civil jail will never be forgotten. Methought that I had two rings on one finger; the one a plain, and the other a diamond mourning ring. The plain ring broke and fell from my finger, while the other remained. My family was now broke, and I left to mourn.

*Voyage to Plymouth. — Occurrences. — Sailing from Plymouth to Portsmouth; from thence, by the Way of Cork, to New York.*

All my fears and affliction did not prevent my feeling some little joy at being released from the jurisdiction of Frenchmen. I could pardon the Indians for their vindictive spirit, because they had no claim to the benefits of civilization. But the French, who give lessons of. politeness to the rest of the world, can derive no advantage from the plea of ignorance. The blind superstition which is inculcated by their monks and friars doubtless stifles, in some measure, the exertion of pity towards their enemies; and the common herd, which includes almost seven eighths of their number, have no advantages from education. To these sources I attribute most of my sufferings. But I found some benevolent friends, whose generosity I shall ever recollect with the warmest gratitude.

The commencement of the voyage had every favorable presage; the weather was fine, the sailors cheerful, and the ship in good trim. My accommodations in the captain's family were very commodious. A boy was allowed me for my particular use. We sailed with excellent fortune till the 19th of August, when we hove in sight of old Plymouth, and at four o'clock in the afternoon dropped anchor.

The next day all but myself and family were taken from the vessel. We felt great anxiety at being left, and began to fear that fortune was not willing to smile on us even on these shores. We waited in despair thirty or forty hours and found no relief. The captain, observing our despondency, began his airs of gayety to cheer us. He assured us that we should not suffer; that, if the English would not receive us, he would take us to France and make us happy. But at last an officer came on board to see if the vessel was prepared for the reception of French prisoners. We related to him our situation. He conducted us on shore and applied to the admiral for directions, who ordered us lodgings and the king's allowance of two shillings sterling per day for our support. Fortunately we were lodged in a house where resided Captain John Tufton Mason, whose name will be familiar to the inhabitants of New Hampshire on account of his patent. He very kindly interested himself in our favor, and wrote to Messrs. Thomlinson and Apthorp, agents at London for the

Province of New Hampshire, soliciting their assistance in my behalf. We tarried at Plymouth but a fortnight, during which time I received much attention, and had to gratify many inquisitive friends with the history of my sufferings.

Captain Mason procured me a passage to Portsmouth in the Rainbow man-of-war, from whence I was to take passage in a packet for America. Just as I stepped on board the Rainbow, a good lady, with her son, came to make me a visit. Her curiosity to see a person of my description was not abated by my being on my passage. She said she could not sleep till she had seen the person who had suffered such hard fortune. After she had asked all the questions that time would allow of she gave me a guinea, and a half guinea to my sister, and a muslin handkerchief to each of our little girls. On our arrival at Portsmouth the packet had sailed. The captain of the Rainbow, not finding it convenient to keep us with him, introduced us on board the Royal Ann.

Wherever we lived we found the best friends and the politest treatment. It will be thought singular that a defenceless woman should suffer so many changes without meeting with some insults and many incivilities. But during my long residence on board the various vessels I received the most delicate attention from my companions. The officers were assiduous in making my situation agreeable, and readily proffered their services.

While on board the Royal Ann I received the following letters. The reader will excuse the recitation. It would be ingratitude not to record such conspicuous acts of benevolence.

PLYMOUTH, September 13, 1757.

MADAM,—Late last postnight I received an answer from Mr. Apthorp, who is partner with Mr. Thomlinson, the agent for New Hampshire, with a letter enclosed to you, which gave you liberty to draw on him for fifteen guineas. As Madam Hornech was just closing her letter to you, I gave it her to enclose for you. I now write again to London on your behalf. You must immediately write Mr. Apthorp what you intend to do, and what further you would have him and our friends at London do for you.

I hope you have received the benefaction of the charitable ladies in this town. All friends here commiserate your misfortunes and wish you well, together with your sister and children.

Your friend and countryman to serve,<br>
JOHN T. MASON.

Mrs. Johnson.

LONDON, September 7, 1757.

MADAM, — I received a letter from Captain Mason, dated the 80th of last month, giving an account of your unfortunate situation; and yesterday Mr. Thomlinson, who is ill in the country, sent me your letter, together with Captain Mason's, to him, with the papers relative to you. In consequence of which I this day applied to a number of gentlemen in your behalf, who very readily gave their assistance; but as I am a stranger to the steps you intend to pursue, I can only give you liberty at present to draw on me for ten or fifteen guineas, for which sum your bill shall be paid; and when you furnish me with information I shall very cheerfully give any furtherance in my power to your relief, when I shall also send you a list of your benefactors.

I am, madam,<br>
Your most humble servant,<br>
JOHN APTHORP.

Mrs. Susanna Johnson.

### LETTER FROM H. GROVE.

I have now the pleasure to let dear Mrs. Johnson know the goodness of Mrs. Hornech. She has collected seven pounds for you, and sent it to Mrs. Brett, who lives in the yard at

Portsmouth, to beg her favors to you in any thing she can do to help or assist you. She is a good lady: do go to her and let her know your distress. Captain Mason has got a letter this post, but he is not at home; cannot tell you further. You will excuse this scrawl, likewise my not enlarging, as Mr. Hornech waits to send it away. Only believe me, madam, you have my earnest prayers to God to help and assist you. My mamma's compliments with mine, and begs to wait on you; and believe me, dear Mrs. Johnson, yours in all events to serve you,

HANNAH GROVE.

Sunday eve, 10 o'clock.

I received the donation, and Mr. Apthorp sent me the fifteen guineas. I sincerely lament that he omitted sending me the names of my benefactors.

The captain of the Royal Ann, supposing my situation with him might not be so convenient, applied to the mayor for a permit for me to take lodgings in the city; which was granted. I took new lodgings, where I tarried three or four days, when orders came for me to be on board the Orange man-of-war in three hours, which was to sail for America. We made all possible despatch; but when we got to the shore we were astonished to find the ship too far under way to be overtaken. No time was to be lost. I applied to a waterman to carry us to a merchantman, which was weighing anchor at a distance to go in the same fleet. He hesitated long enough to pronounce a chapter of oaths, and rowed us off. When we came to the vessel I petitioned the captain to take us on board till he overtook the Orange. He directly flew into a violent passion, and offered greater insults than I had ever received during my whole voyage. He swore we were women of bad fame, who wished to follow the army, and that he would have nothing to do with us. I begged him to calm his rage, and we would convince him of his error. But fortunately the victualler of the fleet happened to be in the ship, who at this moment stepped forward with his roll of names and told the outrageous captain that he would soon convince him whether we deserved notice by searching his list. He soon found our names, and the captain began to beg pardon. He took us on board and apologized for his rudeness.

When within half a dozen miles of Springfield, Mr. Ely, a benevolent friend of Mr. Johnson's, sent his two sons with a sleigh to convey me to his house, where I proposed staying till some of my friends could hear of my arrival. Fortunately Mr. Johnson about the same time arrived at Boston; but misfortune had not yet filled the measure of his calamity. He had no sooner landed than he was put under guard, on suspicion of not performing his duty in the redemption of the Canada prisoners, which suspicion was occasioned by his remissness in producing his vouchers. But the following certificate procured his liberty : —

This is to certify whom it may concern, that the bearer, Lieutenant James Johnson, inhabitant in the town of Charlestown, in the Province of New Hampshire, in New England, who, together with his family, were taken by the Indians on the 30th of August, 1754, has ever since continued a steady and faithful subject to his majesty King George, and has used his utmost endeavors to redeem his own family, and all others belonging to the province aforesaid, that were in the hands of the French and Indians, which he cannot yet accomplish; and that both himself and family have undergone innumerable hardships and afflictions since they have been prisoners in Canada.

In testimony of which, we, the subscribers, officers in his Britannic majesty's service, and now prisoners of war at Quebec, have thought it necessary to grant him this certificate, and do recommend him as an object worthy the aid and compassion of every honest Englishman.

(Signed,)           PETER SCHUYLER,
                            ANDREW WATKINS,
                            WILLIAM MARTIN,
                            WILLIAM PADGETT.

QUEBEC, September 16, 1757.

To compensate him for this misfortune, Governor Pownall recommended a grant, which the general court complied with, and gave him one hundred dollars from the treasury; and he was recorded a faithful subject of King George.

After his dismission from the guards in Boston he proceeded directly for Charlestown. When within fifteen miles of Springfield he was met by a gentleman who had just before seen me, who gave him the best news he could have heard: although it was then late at night, he lost not a moment. At two o clock in the morning of the 1st of January, 1758, I again embraced my dearest friend. Happy New Year! With pleasure would I describe my emotions of joy, could language paint them sufficiently forcible; but the feeble pen shrinks from the task.

Charlestown was still a frontier town, and suffered from savage depredations, which rendered it an improper residence for me; consequently I went to Lancaster. Mr. Johnson in a few days set out for New York to adjust his Canada accounts. But on his journey he was persuaded by Governor Pownall to take a captain's commission and join the forces bound for Ticonderoga, where he was killed on the 8th of July following, in the battle that proved fatal to Lord How, while fighting for his country. Humanity will weep with me. The cup of sorrow was now replete with bitter drops. All my former miseries were lost in the affliction of a widow.

In October, 1758, I was informed that my son Sylvanus was at Northampton sick of a scald. I hastened to the place and found him in a deplorable situation. He was brought there by Major Putnam, (afterwards General Putnam,) with Mrs. How and her family, who had returned from captivity. The town of Northampton had taken the charge of him. His situation was miserable : when I found him he had no recollection of me ; but after some conversation he had some confused ideas of me, but no remembrance of his father. It was four years since I had seen him ; he was then eleven years old. During his absence he had entirely forgotten the English language, spoke a little broken French, but was perfect in Indian. He had been with the savages three years, and one year with the French ; but his habits were somewhat Indian. He had been with them in their hunting excursions and suffered numerous hardships ; he could brandish a tomahawk or bend the bow ; but these habits wore off by degrees. I carried him from that place to Lancaster, where he lived a few years with Colonel Aaron Willard.

I lived in Lancaster till October, 1759, when I returned to old Charlestown. The sight of my former residence afforded a strange mixture of joy and grief ; while the desolations of war, and the loss of a number of dear and valuable friends, combined to give the place an air of melancholy. Soon after my arrival Major Rogers returned from an expedition against the village of St. Francis, which he had destroyed, and killed most of the inhabitants. He brought with him a young Indian prisoner, who stopped at my house : the moment he saw me he cried, " My God ! my God ! here is my sister ! " It was my little brother Sabatis, who formerly used to bring the cows for me when I lived at my Indian masters. He was transported to see me, and declared that he was still my brother, and I must be his sister. Poor fellow ! The fortune of war had left him without a single relation ; but with his country's enemies he could find one who too sensibly felt his miseries. I felt the purest pleasure in administering to his comfort.

I was extremely fortunate in receiving, by one of Major Rogers's men, a bundle of Mr. Johnson's papers, which he found in pillaging St. Francis. The Indians took them when we were captivated, and they had lain at St. Francis five years.

Sabatis went from Charlestown to Crown Point with Major Rogers. When he got to Otter Creek he met my son Sylvanus, who was in the army with Colonel Willard. He recognized him, and, clasping him in his arms, "My God!" says he, "the fortune of war!" I shall ever remember this young Indian with affection: he had a high sense of honor and good behavior: he was affable, good natured, and polite.

My daughter Susanna was still in Canada; but as I had the fullest assurances that every attention was paid to her education and welfare by her three mothers, I felt less anxiety than I otherwise might have done.

Every one will imagine that I have paid Affliction her utmost demand: the pains of imprisonment, the separation from my children, the keen sorrow occasioned by the death of a butchered father, and the severe grief arising from my husband's death, will amount to a sum perhaps unequalled. But still my family must be doomed to further and severe persecutions from the savages. In the commencement of the summer of 1766, my brother-in-law, Mr. Joseph Willard, son of the Rev. Mr. Willard, of Rutland, who was killed by the Indians in Lovell's war, with his wife and five children, who lived but two miles distant from me, were taken by a party of Indians. They were carried much the same route that I was to Montreal. Their journey of fourteen days through the wilderness was a series of miseries unknown to any but those who have suffered Indian captivity: they lost two children, whose deaths were owing to savage barbarity. The history of their captivity would almost equal my own; but the reader's commiseration and pity must now be exhausted. No more of anguish; no more of sufferings.

They arrived at Montreal a few days before the French surrendered it to the English, and after four months' absence returned home, and brought my daughter Susanna to my arms. While I rejoiced at again meeting my child, whom I had not seen for above five years, I felt extremely grateful to the Mrs. Jaissons for the affectionate attention they had bestowed on her. As they had received her as their child, they had made their affluent fortune subservient to her best interest. To give her the accomplishments of a polite education had been their principal care: she had contracted an ardent love for them, which never will be obliterated. Their parting was an affecting scene of tears. They never forgot her during their lives: she has eight letters from them, which are proofs of the warmest friendship. My daughter did not know me at her return, and spoke nothing but French: my son spoke Indian; so that my family was a mixture of nations.

Mr. Farnsworth, my only fellow-prisoner whose return I have not mentioned, came home a little before.

Thus, by the goodness of Providence, we all returned in the course of six painful years to the place from whence we were taken. The long period of our captivity and the severity of our sufferings will be called uncommon and unprecedented. But we even found some friends to pity among our most persecuting enemies; and from the various shapes in which mankind appeared, we learned many valuable lessons. Whether in the wilds of Canada, the horrid jails of Quebec, or in our voyage to Europe, daily occurrences happened to convince us that the passions of men are as various as their complexions. And although my sufferings were often increased by the selfishness of this world's spirit, yet the numerous testimonies of generosity I received bid me suppress the charge of neglect or want of benevolence. That I have been an unfortunate woman, all will grant; yet my misfortunes, while they enriched my experience and taught me the value of patience, have increased my gratitude to the Author of all blessings, whose goodness and mercy have preserved my life to the present time.

During the time of my widowhood, misfortune and disappointment were my intimate companions. When New England was ruled by a few men who were the creatures of a king, the pleasures of dissipation were preferred to the more severe attention to business; and the small voice of a woman was seldom heard. Hence, in the settlement of my husband's estate, the delay and perplexity were distressing. I made three journeys to Portsmouth, fourteen to Boston, and three to Springfield, to effect the settlement. Whether my captivity had taught me to be ungrateful, or whether imagination formed a catalogue of evils, I will not pretend to say; but from the year 1754 to the present day, greater misfortunes have apparently fallen to my share than to mankind in general, and the meteor happiness has eluded my grasp. The life of a widow is peculiarly afflictive; but my numerous and long journeys over roads imminently bad, and incidents that seemed to baffle all my plans and foresight, render mine more unfortunate than common.

But I found many attentive friends, whose assistance and kindness will always claim my gratitude. Colonel White, of Leominster, with whom I had lived from the time I was eight years old until I married, was extremely affectionate and kind: in his house I found a welcome home. Mr. Samuel Ely, of Springfield, who was the friend of my husband, rendered me numerous kindnesses. Colonel Murray, of Rutland, and Colonel Chandler, of Worcester, were very friendly and kind. Mr. Clarke, deputy secretary, Governor Pownall, and Governor Wentworth, exerted their influence for me in attempting to procure a grant from the general assembly.

In one of my journeys to Portsmouth I conversed with Captain Adams, who was in Europe at the time I was. He informed me that while there Mr. Apthorp gave him fourteen pounds sterling, for the purpose of conveying me and my family to America. My sailing with the convoy prevented my receiving this kindness.

During the four years of my widowhood I was in quite an unsettled situation; sometimes receiving my children who were returning from captivity, and at others settling the estate of my deceased husband. In October, 1759, I moved to Charlestown and took possession of my patrimony, consisting of a house which Colonel Whiting had generously assisted my mother in building. In copartnership with my brother, Moses Willard, I kept a small store, which was of service in supporting my family and settling my husband's estate. I have received, by petitioning, from the general assembly of New Hampshire forty-two pounds, to indemnify myself and family for losses sustained by our country's enemies. This was of eminent service to me. Mr. Johnson left with Mr. Charles Apthorp, of Boston, the sum which my son's redemption cost, for Colonel Schuyler, who had paid the same. But the general assembly of Massachusetts afterwards paid Colonel Schuyler his demand for redeeming my son.

By Mr. Johnson I had seven children: two sons and a daughter died in infancy. Sylvanus, with whom the reader is acquainted, now lives in Charlestown. Susanna married Captain Samuel Wetherbee, and has been the mother of fifteen children, among whom were five at two births. Polly married Colonel Timothy Bedel, of Haverhill: she died in August, 1789. Captive married Colonel George Kimball. In the year 1762 I married Mr. John Hastings, my present husband. He was one of the first settlers in Charlestown. I recollect to have seen him when I visited the place in the year 1744. He suffered much by the Indians, and assisted in defending the town during the wars. By him I have had seven children: one daughter and four sons died in their infancy. Theodosia is married to Mr. Stephen Hasham. Randilla died at the age of twenty-two. She lived from her infancy with Mr. Samuel Taylor, of Rockingham, by whom she was treated with great affection.    I have had thirty-nine grandchildren and four great-grandchildren.

I am now in the winter of life, and feel sensibly the effects of old age.   I live on the same spot where the Indians took us from in 1754; but the face of Nature has so changed that old savage fears are all banished.   My vacant hours I often employ in reflecting on the various scenes that have marked the different stages of my life.   When viewing the present rising generation, in the bloom of health and enjoying those gay pleasures which shed their exhilarating influence so plentifully in the morn of life, I look back to my early days, when I, too, was happy and basked in the sunshine of good fortune. Little do they think that the meridian of their lives can possibly be rendered miserable by captivity or a prison: as little, too, did I think that my gilded prospects could be obscured: but it was the happy delusion of youth; and I fervently wish there was no deception.   But that Being who "sits upon the circle of the earth and views the inhabitants as grasshoppers" allots all our fortunes.

Although I have drunk so largely from the cup of sorrow, yet my present happiness is a small compensation.   Twice has my country been ravaged by war since my remembrance. I have detailed the share I bore in the first: in the last, although the place in which I live was not a field of bloody battle, yet its vicinity to Ticonderoga and the savages that ravaged the Coos country rendered it perilous and distressing.   But now no one can set a higher value on the smiles of peace than myself.  The savages are driven beyond the lakes, and our country has no enemies.  The gloomy wilderness, that forty years ago secreted the Indian and the beast of prey, has vanished away, and the thrifty farm smiles in its stead; the Sundays, that were then employed in guarding a fort, are now quietly devoted to worship; the tomahawk and scalping knife have given place to the sickle and ploughshare; and prosperous husbandry now thrives where the terrors of death once chilled us with fear.

My numerous progeny often gather around me to hear the sufferings once felt by their aunt or grandmother, and wonder at their magnitude. My daughter Captive still keeps the dress she appeared in when brought to my bedside by the French nurse at the Ticonderoga hospital, and often refreshes my memory with past scenes when showing it to her children. These things yield a kind of melancholy pleasure.

Instances of longevity are remarkable in my family. My aged mother, before her death, could say to me, " Arise, daughter, and go to thy daughter ; for thy daughter's daughter has got a daughter ; " a command which few mothers can make and be obeyed.

And now, reader, after sincerely wishing that your days may be as happy as mine have been unfortunate, I bid you adieu.

CHARLESTOWN, June 20, 1798.

---

*Names of Persons killed by the Indians in Charlestown, No. 4.*

Seth Putnam, May 2, 1748.

Samuel Farnsworth,
Joseph Allen,
Peter Perin,
Aaron Lyon,
Joseph Massey, } May 24, 1746.

Jedediah Winchel, June or July, 1746.

———— Philips, August 3, 1746.

Isaac Goodale,
Nathaniel Gould, } October, 1747.

Obadiah Sartwell, June, 1749.

Lieutenant Moses Willard, June 18, 1756.

Asahel Stebbins, August, 1758.

Josiah Kellogg, 1759.

16

*Number taken Prisoners by the Indians from Charlestown,*
*No. 4.*

Captain John Spafford, ⎫
Isaac Parker,          ⎬ April 19, 1746.
Stephen Farnsworth,   ⎭
———— Anderson, October, 1747.
Enos Stevens, June 17, 1749.

James Johnson,        ⎫
Susanna Johnson,      ⎪
Sylvanus Johnson,     ⎪
Susan Johnson,        ⎬ August 29, 1754.
Polly Johnson,        ⎪
Miriam Willard,       ⎪
Peter Labarree,       ⎪
Ebenezer Farnsworth,  ⎭

Sampson Colefax,      ⎫
David Farnsworth,     ⎪
Thomas Robins,        ⎬ May, 1756.
Thomas Robins,        ⎪
Asa Spafford,         ⎭

Mrs. Robins,          ⎫
Isaac Parker,         ⎬ August, 1758.
David Hill,           ⎭

Joseph Willard,       ⎫ June 7, 1760.
Wife, and five children, ⎭

# BURNING OF ROYALTON.

As a union of interest always strengthens the bonds of affection, so a participation in extreme sufferings will never fail to produce a mutual sensibility. Prompted by a generous glow of filial love and affection, we generally take delight in surveying whatever gave our forefathers joy, and are ready to drop a sympathetic tear when we review the sufferings which they have undergone. But, contrary to the laws of sympathy and justice, the attention of the public is often engrossed with accounts of the more dreadful conflagrations of populous cities in foreign countries or the defeat of armies in the field of carnage; while the destruction of small frontier settlements by the Indian tribes in our own country is at the same time little known, if not entirely forgotten. Thus the miseries of our neighbors and friends around us, whose bitter cries have been heard in our streets, are too often suffered to pass unnoticed down the current of time into the tomb of oblivion.

The burning of Royalton was an event most inauspicious and distressing to the first settlers of that town. Nor is it a little strange that, among the numerous authors who have recorded the events of the American revolution, some of them have not given place in their works to a more full detail of that afflictive scene.

Laboring under all the difficulties and hardships to which our infant settlements were subject, and striving by persevering industry to soar above every obstacle which might present itself to obstruct their progress, they had filled their barns with the fruits of the land, their storehouses were crowded with the comforts of life, and all nature seemed to wear a propitious smile. All around them promised prosperity. They were far removed from the noise of war; and, though conscious of their danger, fondly hoped they should escape the ravages of a savage foe.

Royalton was chartered in the year 1779. A considerable settlement, however, had taken place previous to that time, and the town was in a thriving condition. Large stocks of cattle, which would confer honor upon the enterprise of farmers in old countries, were here seen grazing in their fields.

United by common interest, living on terms of friendship, and manifesting that each one in a good degree "loved his neighbor as himself," harmony prevailed in their borders, social happiness was spread around their firesides, and plenty crowned their labors. But, alas! the dreadful reverse remains to be told. While joys possessed were turned to sorrows, their hopes for joys to come were blasted. And as the former strongly marked the grievous contrast between a state of prosperity and affliction, the latter only showed the fallacy of promising ourselves the future.

On the morning of the 16th of October, 1780, before the dawn of day, the inhabitants of this town were surprised by the approach of about three hundred Indians of various tribes. They were led by the Caghnewaga tribe, and had left Canada intending to destroy Newbury, a town in the eastern part of Vermont, on Connecticut River. A British lieutenant, by the name of Horton, was their chief commander; and one Le Mott, a Frenchman, was his second. Their pilot, or leader, was a despicable villain, by the name of Hamilton, who had been made prisoner by the Americans at the taking of Burgoyne in 1777. He had been at Newbury and Royalton the preceding summer on parole of honor, left the latter place with several others under pretence of going to survey lands in the northern part of this state, and went directly to the enemy. He was doubtless the first instigator of those awful depredations which were the bitter fruits of this expedition, and which ought to stamp his name with infamy and disgrace.

On their way thither, it is said, they came across several men from Newbury, who were engaged in hunting near the place where Montpelier village now stands, and made them prisoners. They made known their object to these hunters, and inquired of them whether an armed force was stationed at Newbury. Knowing the defenceless state of that town, and hoping they should be able to induce the Indians to relinquish their object and return to Canada, they told them that such an armed garrison was kept at Newbury as would render it extremely dangerous for them to approach — thus artfully dissembling by ambiguity of expression the true condition of their fellow-townsmen, and, like Rahab the harlot, saved their father's house from destruction.

Unwilling, however, that their expedition should prove wholly fruitless, they turned their course to Royalton. No arguments which the prisoners could adduce were sufficient to persuade them from that determination.

Following up Onion River as far as the mouth of Stevens's branch, which empties into the river at Montpelier, they steered their course through Barre, at that time called Wildersburg; proceeded up Gaol branch, which forms a part of Stevens's branch, and travelled over the mountains through Orange and Washington; thence down the first branch of White River, through Chelsea and Tunbridge, to Royalton. They laid in their encampment at Tunbridge, not far distant from Royalton, during the Sabbath, the day preceding their attack upon the latter place, for the purpose of concerting measures to carry into effect their atrocious and malignant designs. Here were matured those diabolical seeds of depredation and cruelty from which sprung bitterness, sorrow, and death.

16*

As they entered the town before daylight appeared darkness covered their approach, and they were not discovered till Monday morning at dawn of day, when they entered the house of Mr. John Hutchinson, who resided not far from the line separating Royalton from Tunbridge. He was totally ignorant of their approach and wholly unsuspicious of danger till they burst the door upon him.

Here they took Mr. John Hutchinson, and Abijah Hutchinson, his brother, prisoners, and plundered the house; crossed the first branch and went to the house of Mr. Robert Havens, who lived at a small distance from Mr. Hutchinson's. Mr. Havens had gone out into his pasture in pursuit of his sheep, and having ascended a hill about forty rods from his house, hearing his neighbor Hutchinson's dog bark, halted, and stood in pensive silence. Here he listened with deep anxiety to know the extent of the evil he feared. But, alas! he little expected to find a herd of savage men. It was his only fear that some voracious animal was among his sheep, which so disturbed the watchful dog. While he listened in silence, with his thoughts suspended, he heard a noise as of sheep or cattle running with full speed through the water. Casting his eye to the west, towards his own dwelling, he beheld a company of Indians just entering the door. Seeing his own danger, he immediately laid down under a log and hid himself from their sight. But he could not hide sorrow from his mind. Here he wept. Tears trickling down his withered cheeks bespoke the anguish of his soul while he thought upon the distress of his family. With groanings unutterable he lay a while, heard the piercing shrieks of his beloved wife, and saw his sons escaping for their lives.

Laden with the weight of years, decrepit and infirm, he was sensible if he appeared in sight it would prove his death. He therefore resolved not to move until a favorable opportunity presented. His son, Daniel Havens, and Thomas Pember, were in the house, and made their appearance at the door a little before the Indians came up. Beholding the foe but few rods distant, they ran for their lives. Daniel Havens made his escape by throwing himself over a hedge fence down the bank of the branch and crawling under a log, although a large number of the Indians passed directly over it in pursuit of him. Who can tell the fears that agitated his bosom while these savage pursuers stepped upon the log under which he lay? and who can tell the joys he felt when he saw them pass off, leaving him in safety? — a quick transition from painful fear and imminent danger to joyful peace and calm retirement. They pursued Thomas Pember till they came so near as to throw a spear at him, which pierced his body and put an end to his existence. He ran some time, however, after he was wounded, till by loss of blood he fainted, fell, and was unable to proceed farther. The savage monsters came up, several times thrust a spear through his body, took off his scalp, and left him food for worms. While they were tearing his scalp from his head, how did his dying groans pierce the skies and call on Him who holds the scales of justice to mark their cruelty and avenge his blood!

He had spent the night previous at the house of Mr. Havens, engaged in amorous conversation with a daughter of Mr. Havens, who was his choice companion, the intended partner of his life. .

By imagination we view the fair survivor surrounded by the savage tribe, whose frightful aspect threatened ruin; her soul overwhelmed with fear, and stung with grief, bereft of her dearest friend.

They made the house of Mr. Havens their rallying point, or post of observation, and stationed a part of their company there to guard their baggage and make preparations for retreat when they had completed their work of destruction. Like the messenger of death, silent and merciless, they were scarcely seen till felt; or, if seen, filled the mind with terror, nor often afforded opportunity for escape. Moving with violent steps, they proceeded down the first branch to its mouth ; while a number, armed with spears, led the van, and were followed by others, armed with muskets and scalping knives. The former they called *runners*, who were directed to kill all those who should be overtaken in an attempt to escape ; while the latter were denominated *gunners*, took charge of the prisoners, and scalped those who were killed.

They had not proceeded far before a young man, by the name of Elias Button, being ignorant of their approach, made his appearance in the road but a few rods from them. Espying his danger, he turned and ran with the greatest possible speed in his power to escape their cruel hands. The savage tribe pursued him with their usual agility, soon overtook the trembling youth, pierced his body with their spears, took off his scalp, and left him weltering in his gore. Young, vigorous, and healthy, and blessed with the brightest hopes of long life and good days, he was overtaken by the merciless stroke of death without having a minute's warning. Innocence and bravery were no shield, nor did activity secure him a safe retreat.

That they might be enabled to fall upon the inhabitants unawares, and thereby secure a greater number of prisoners as well as procure a greater quantity of plunder, they kept profound silence till they had arrived at the mouth of the branch.

After killing Pember and Button and taking such plunder as most pleased their fancy, they proceeded to the house of Joseph Kneeland, who resided about half a mile distant from the house of Mr. Havens. Here they found Messrs. Simeon Belknap, Giles Gibbs, and Jonathan Brown, together with Joseph Kneeland and his aged father, all of whom they made prisoners. They then went to the house of Mr. Elias Curtis, where they took Mr. Curtis, John Kent, and Peter Mason. Mrs. Curtis had just waked from the slumbers of the night, and was about dressing herself as she sat upon her bed, when the savage monsters entered the door; and one of them instantly flew at her, with a large knife in his hand, and seized her by the neck, apparently intending to cut her throat. While in the very attitude of inflicting the fatal wound the murderous wretch discovered a string of gold beads around her neck, which attracted his attention and prevented the dreadful stroke of death. Thus his avidity for gold allayed his thirst for human blood. His raging passions were suddenly cooled; curiosity restrained his vengeance and spared the life of the frightened object of his cruelty. He had put the knife to her throat, and eternity seemed open to her view; but instead of taking her life he only took her beads, and left her rejoicing at her deliverance. The barbarous looks of the wicked crew bespoke their malignant designs, and caused horror and dismay to fill the minds of all who beheld them. But, alas! who can tell what horror thrilled the bosom of this trembling woman? What fearful pangs were made to pierce her soul! Behold the tawny wretch, with countenance wild and awful grimaces, standing by her bedside, holding her by the throat with one hand, and the weapon of death in the other! See standing around her a crowd of brutal savages, the sons of violence, foul tormentors! In vain do I attempt to paint the scene. Nor will I pretend to describe the feelings of a kind and tender mother, who, reposing in the arms of sleep, with her infant at her bosom, is roused from her slumbers by the approach of a tribe of savage Indians at her bedside.

To prevent an alarm from being sounded abroad, they commanded the prisoners to keep silence on pain of death. While the afflicted inhabitants beheld their property wasted and their lives exposed to the arrows of death, it caused their hearts to swell with grief. But they were debarred the privilege of making known their sufferings to their nearest friends, or even to pour out their cries of distress, while surrounded by the savage band, whose malevolent appearance could not fail to spread fear and distress in every bosom. They plundered every house they found till they arrived at the mouth of the branch. Here the commander, a British officer, took his stand with a small party of Indians, while some went up and others down on each side of the river to complete the work of destruction. They had already taken several horses, which some of them rode, to facilitate their march and enable them to overtake those who attempted to make their escape. Frightened at the horrible appearance of their riders, who were in no way qualified to manage them, the horses served rather to impede than hasten their progress.

Instigated by "the powers of darkness," fired with rage, eager to obtain that booty which they acquired by the pillage of houses, and fearful, at the same time, that they should themselves fall a prey to the American forces, they pursued their ravages with infuriated zeal, and violence and horror attended their movement.

General Elias Stevens, who resided in the first house on the river above the mouth of the branch, had gone down the river about two miles, and was engaged at work with his oxen and cart. While busily employed loading his cart, casting his eye up the river he beheld a man approaching, bareheaded, with his horse upon the run, who, seeing General Stevens, cried out, "For God's sake, turn out your oxen, for the Indian's are at the mill!" * General Stevens hastened to unyoke his oxen, turned them out, and immediately mounted his horse and started to return to his family, filled with fearful apprehensions for the fate of his beloved wife and tender offspring. He had left them in apparent safety, reposing in the arms of sleep. Having proceeded on his return about half way home he met Captain Joseph Parkhurst, who informed him that the Indians were but a few rods distant, in

* The mills to which he referred, owned by a Mr. Morgan, were situated on the first branch, near its mouth.

swift pursuit down the river, and that, unless he returned immediately, he would inevitably fall into their hands.

Apprised of his danger, he turned and accompanied the captain down the river. Conjugal and parental affection alone can suggest to the imagination of the reader what were the feelings of General Stevens when compelled for his own safety to leave the wife of his bosom and their little ones to the mercy of a savage foe. What pains did he feel when he found himself deprived of all possible means to afford them relief! Nor could he expect a more favorable event than to find them all sacrificed at the shrine of savage barbarity. Who, not totally devoid of sympathy, can refrain to drop a tear as he reflects upon those painful emotions which agitated the general's breast when he was forced to turn his back upon his beloved family while thus exposed to danger? Indeed, it was his only source of consolation that he might be able to afford assistance to his defenceless neighbors; and as they soon came to the house of Deacon Daniel Rix, he there found opportunity to lend the hand of pity. General Stevens took Mrs. Rix and two or three children with him upon his horse; Captain Parkhurst took Mrs. Benton and several children upon his horse with him; and they all rode off as fast as possible, accompanied by Deacon Rix and several others on foot, till they arrived at the place where the general first received the alarm. Filled with anxiety for his family, and not having seen any Indians, General Stevens here concluded again to return, hoping he should be able to reach home in time to secure his household from danger before the Indians arrived. Leaving Mrs. Rix and children in the care of a Mr. Burroughs, he started for home, and had proceeded about half a mile when he discovered the Indians in the road ahead of him, but a few rods distant. He quickly turned about, hastened his retreat, soon overtook the company he had left, and entreated them immediately to leave the road and take to the woods, to prevent being taken. Those who were on foot

jumped over the fence, hastened to the woods out of sight of
the Indians, where they remained in safety, undiscovered by
the savage foe, who kept the road in pursuit of General Stevens. He passed down the road about half a mile, and came
to the house of Mr. Tilly Parkhurst, his father-in-law. Seeing his sister engaged in milking by the barn, he "told her to
leave her cow immediately, or the Indians would have her,"
and left her to secure her own retreat. They were now in
plain sight, not more than eighty or a hundred rods off. The
road was full of them, running like bloodhounds. The general rode to the house, told them to run for their lives, and
proceeded to warn others who lived contiguous. By this
time the way was filled with men, women, and children, and
a large body of Indians in open view but just behind them.
The savage tribe now began to make the surrounding wilderness reëcho with their frightful yells. Frightened and alarmed
for their safety, children clung to their parents; and half-dis-
tracted mothers, filled with fearful apprehensions of approaching destruction, were heard to make the air resound with their
cries of distress. General Stevens endeavored to get them
into the woods, out of sight of the Indians. Fear had usurped
the power of reason, and Wisdom's voice was drowned in the
torrent of distraction. There was no time for argument: all
was at stake: the enemy hard by, and fast approaching:
defenceless mothers, with helpless infants in their arms, fleeing for their lives. Despair was spread before them, while
the roaring flood of destruction seemed rolling behind them.
Few could be persuaded to go into the woods; and most of
them kept the road till they arrived at the house of Captain
E. Parkhurst, in Sharon. Here they halted a moment to
take breath, hoping they should not be pursued any farther. The Indians, being taken up in plundering the houses,
had now fallen considerably in the rear. But the unhappy
victims of distress had not long been here when the cruel
pursuers again appeared in sight.

GENERAL STEVENS SAVING MRS. RIX.　Page 191.

Screaming and crying now witnessed the horrors of that
dreadful scene. Groans and tears bespoke the feelings of a
heart agitated with fear and swollen with grief. There was
no time to be lost. While they waited they waited for destruction. Children hanging to their mothers' clothes; mothers inquiring what they should do, and calling for assistance;
floods of tears and piercing shrieks, — all presented to view
a most painful scene. Seeing the Indians approaching with
hideous yells that thrilled the heart of every one, General
Stevens put his mother and his sister upon his own horse.
Captain Joseph Parkhurst put Mrs. Rix and three of her
children upon another horse, without a bridle, and ordered
them to hasten their flight. There yet remained the wife
of Captain E. Parkhurst, who stood in the most critical situation in which a woman can be placed, begging and crying
for help, surrounded by six small children clinging to her
clothes and pleading with her for protection. Alas! how
awful was the spectacle, how affecting the scene, to see a
woman in this deplorable condition pleading for succor when
none could help, when safety and support had fled and dangers were rushing upon her! A heart not devoid of sympathy could not fail to weep. Conscious of her wretched situation, feeling for her dear children, being told there was no
probability for her escape, gathering her little ones around
her she wept in bitterness of soul; tears of pity ran down
her cheeks while she waited the approach of the savage
tribe to inflict upon her whatever malice could invent or
inhumanity devise. .

Her husband, to whom she fain would have looked for protection, was gone from home when all her woes fell upon her.
Well might she say, " Therefore are my loins filled with pain;
pangs have taken hold upon me as the pangs of a woman
that travaileth; my heart panted; fearfulness affrighted me;
the night of my pleasure hath he turned into fear unto me."
While Mrs. Parkhurst saw her friends and neighbors fleeing

17

from her, and beheld the Indians approaching with impetuous
step, her bosom throbbed with anguish; horror seized her
soul; and death, immediate death, both to her and her children,
" stood thick around her," threatening to thrust his dagger
into her aching heart.   There was no time to decide on the
priority of claims to pity or the demands of justice.   Those
who were nearest at hand first received assistance; not, however, without regard to that affection which arises from con-
sanguinity or matrimonial connection; and these relations not
only unite the hearts but connect the hands in scenes of distress.

At the time General Stevens put his mother and his sister
upon his horse the Indians were not eight rods from him:
they, in company with Mrs. Rix and her children, rode off
as fast as possible: the general followed with several others
on foot.   Part of the Indians pursued them, while others entered the house and plundered it of its furniture.   They took
her eldest son from her; then ordered her, with the rest of her
children, to leave the house.   She accordingly repaired into
the fields back of the house with five of her children, and
remained in safety till they had left the place.   Soon after
General Stevens started his dog came in his way and caused
him to stumble and fall, which so retarded his progress that
he was obliged to flee to the woods for safety, leaving the
women and children to make the best of their retreat.   The
Indians pursued down the road after them with frightful yells,
and soon overtook those who were on foot.   They took Gardner Rix, son of Deacon Rix,* a boy about fourteen years old,
just at the heels of his mother's horse, while she was compelled to witness the painful sight.   Alas! what distress and
horror filled her bosom, when she, with three of her children
no less dear than herself, fleeing from the savage foe, mounted upon a horse snorting with fear, having nothing but a

* Captain Rix then lived where Mr. Phelps now lives, 1853.

pocket handkerchief in his mouth for a bridle, saw her wearied son, faint for want of breath, fall a captive to this barbarous crew ! Cruel fate ! The trembling youth, overwhelmed with fear and bathed in tears, was now torn from his tender parents and compelled to roam the wilderness to unknown regions. Nor was the disconsolate mother, with her other little ones, left in a much more safe condition. Exposed and expecting every step to fall to the ground, which, if it proved not their death, would leave them a prey to the savage monsters, no tongue can tell the pains she felt, nor pen describe the horrors of her soul. To behold her little son, while fleeing for his life, fall into the hands of these sons of cruelty, what kind and tender mother would not feel her heart to bleed ? May we not listen to the voice of Imagination, and hear her say, —

> " O infinite distress ! such raging grief
> Should command pity, and despair relief;
> Passion, methinks, should rise from all my groans,
> Give sense to rocks and sympathy to stones " ?

The Indians pursued the women and children as far as the house of Mr. Benedict, the distance of about a mile. They effected their escape, though surrounded with dangers and pursued with impetuous and clamorous steps. Here they discovered Mr. Benedict on the opposite side of a stream, called Broad Brook, which ran near the house. They beckoned to have him come over to them : choosing, however, not to hazard the consequences of yielding obedience to their request, he turned and ran a short distance and hid himself under a log. He had not long been in this situation when these bloodthirsty wretches came and stood upon the same log, and were heard by him to exclaim, in angry tone, " If we could find him he should feel the tomahawk."

After standing upon the log some time and endeavoring to espy the concealed, trembling object of their pursuit, they left

him and returned to the house. Ah, what joy filled his
bosom when he saw these messengers of death pass away,
leaving him in safety! How must his heart have glowed
with gratitude towards the " great Preserver of men " at this
unexpected deliverance from the most imminent danger!

His joys, however, were not unmingled with sorrow, as the
fell destroyers were still at his house committing ravages and
wasting his property. But no man can be supposed to put
his property in competition with his life.

The Indians pursued down the river about forty rods farther, where they made a young man, by the name of Avery,
prisoner, and then concluded to return.

While they were at the house of Tilly Parkhurst, afore-
mentioned, (which was about six miles from the place they
entered Royalton,) his son, Phineas Parkhurst, who had been
to alarm the people on the east side of the river, just as he
entered the stream on his return discovered the Indians at
his father's door. Finding himself in danger he immediately
turned to go back; and the Indians just at this time happened
to see him, and fired upon him. This was the first gun they
fired after they entered the town. The ball entered his back,
went through his body, came out under his ribs, and lodged in
the skin: notwithstanding the wound, he was, however, able
to ride, and continued his retreat to Lebanon, in the State of
New Hampshire, the distance of about sixteen miles, with
very little stop, supporting the ball between his fingers. He
now resides in that town, and sustains the character of a useful physician, and an industrious, independent farmer.

That party of Indians which went down on the east side of
the river extended their ravages as far as the house of Captain Gilbert, in Sharon, where a public house is now kept by
Captain Dana. Here they took a nephew of Captain Gilbert, by the name of Nathaniel Gilbert, a boy about fifteen
years of age. They now resolved to return, and commenced
that waste of property which tracked their progress. As

INDIANS CARRYING OFF PRISONERS.   Page 197.

they retraced their steps, they set fire to all the buildings they found of every description. They spread desolation and distress wherever they went. Houses filled with furniture and family supplies for the winter, barns stored with the fruits of industry, and fields stocked with herds of cattle were all laid waste.

They shot and killed fourteen fat oxen in one yard, which, in consequence of the inhabitants being dispersed, were wholly lost. Cows, sheep, and hogs, and, indeed, every creature designed by the God of nature to supply the wants of man, which came within their sight, fell a prey to these dreadful spoilers. Parents torn from their children, husbands separated from their wives, and children snatched from their parents presented to view an indescribable scene of wretchedness and distress. Some were driven from their once peaceful habitations into the adjacent wilderness for safety, there to wait the destruction of their property; stung with the painful reflection that their friends, perhaps a kind father and affectionate brother, were made captives, and compelled to travel with a tawny herd of savage men into the wild regions of the north, to be delivered into the hands of enemies and undergo the fatigues and dangers of a wretched captivity; or, what was scarcely more to be deplored, learn with pain that they had fallen the unhappy victims to the relentless fury of the savage tribe, and were weltering in their gore where there was no eye to pity or friendly hand to administer relief.

The third party of Indians who went up the river first came to the house of General Stevens. Daniel Havens, whose escape I have mentioned, went directly there and warned the family of their danger. Trembling with fear, he only stepped into the house, told them that "the Indians were as thick as the d—l at their house," and turned and went directly out, leaving the family to secure their own retreat.

Mrs. Stevens and the family were in bed excepting her husband, who, as before stated, had gone down the river, about two miles from home. She immediately arose from her bed, flung some loose clothes over her, took up her child, and had scarcely got to the fire when a large body of Indians rushed in at the door. They immediately ransacked the house in search of men, and then took the beds and bedding, carried them out of doors, cut open the bed ticks, and threw the feathers into the air. This made them sport enough. Nor did they fail to manifest their infernal gratification by their tartarean shouts and disingenuous conduct.

Mrs. Stevens entreated them to let her have some clothes for herself and child; but her entreaties were in vain. They were deaf to the calls of the needy and disregarded the demands of justice. Her cries reached their ears; but nothing could excite one single glow of sympathy. Her destitute and suffering condition was plain before their eyes; but they were blind to objects of compassion. Alas! what bitterness of soul, what anguish, what heartrending pangs of fear distressed her tender bosom! Surrounded by these pitiless, terrific monsters in human shape, with her little offspring in her arms, whose piercing shrieks and tender age called for compassion; exposed to the raging fire of savage jealousy, unquenchable by a mother's tears; anxious for the safety and mourning the absence of her bosom friend, the husband of her youth,— it is beyond the powers of imagination to conceive or language to express the sorrows of her heart.

At one moment securely reposing in the arms of sleep, with her darling infant at her breast; the next amid a savage crew, whose wicked hands were employed in spreading desolation and mischief, whose mortal rage exposed her to the arrows of death. After plundering the house they told Mrs. Stevens to "begone, or they would burn." She had been afraid to make any attempt to escape, but now gladly embraced the opportunity. She hastened into the adjacent wilderness, carrying her child, where she tarried till the Indians had left the town.

A boy by the name of Daniel Waller, about fourteen years old, who lived with General Stevens, hearing the alarm given by Mr. Havens, set out immediately to go to the general and give him the information. He had proceeded about half a mile when he met the Indians, was taken prisoner, and carried to Canada.

They left the house and barn of General Stevens in flames and proceeded up the river as far as Mr. Durkee's, where they took two of his boys prisoners, Adan and Andrew, and carried the former to Canada, who died there in prison.

Seeing a smoke arise above the trees in the woods adjacent, the hostile invaders directed their course to the spot, where they found a young man, by the name of Prince Haskell, busily engaged in chopping, for the commencement of a settlement. Haskell heard a rustling among the leaves behind him, and, turning round, beheld two Indians but a few feet from him. One stood with his gun pointed directly at him, and the other in the attitude of throwing a tomahawk. Finding he had no chance to escape, he delivered himself up as a prisoner, and was also carried to Canada. He returned in about one year, after enduring the most extreme sufferings in his wanderings through the wilderness on his way home.

A Mr. Chafee,* who lived at the house of Mr. Hendee started early in the morning to go to the house of Mr. Elias Curtis to get his horse shod. On his way he saw Mr. John Kent ahead of him, who was upon the same business. Wishing to put in his claim before Mr. Chafee, he rode very fast, and arrived at the house first. He had scarcely dismounted from his horse when the Indians came out of the house, took him by the hair of his head, and pulled him over backwards. Seeing this, Mr. Chafee immediately dismounted, jumped behind the shop, hastened away, keeping such a direction as would cause the shop to hide his retreat. Thus he kept out

---

* Mr. Chafee lived near where Mr. Dewey now lives, 1851.

of sight of the Indians, effected his escape, and returned to
the house of Mr. Hendee.* On receiving the alarm given
by Mr. Chafee, Mr. Hendee directed his wife to take her little
boy, about seven years old, and her little daughter, who was
still younger, and hasten to one of their neighbors for safety,
while he should go to Bethel, the town west of Royalton, and
give the alarm at the fort.

Mrs. Hendee had not proceeded far when she was met by
several Indians upon the run, who took her little boy from
her. Feeling anxious for the fate of her child, she inquired
what they were going to do with him. They replied that they
should make a soldier of him; and then hastened away, pulling him along by the hand, leaving the weeping mother with
her little daughter to witness the scene and hear the piercing
shrieks of her darling son.

This leads me to notice one instance of female heroism,
blended with benevolence, displayed by Mrs. Hendee, whose
name deserves ever to be held in remembrance by every
friend of humanity.

She was now separated from her husband, and placed in
the midst of a savage crew, who were committing the most
horrid depredations and destroying every kind of property
that fell within their grasp. Defenceless, and exposed to the
shafts of envy or the rage of a company of despicable tories
and brutal savages, the afflicted mother, robbed of her only
son, proceeded down the river with her tender little daughter
hanging to her clothes, screaming with fear, pleading with her
mother to keep away the Indians.

In this condition, possessing uncommon resolution and great
presence of mind, she determined again to get possession of
her son. As she passed down the river she met several tories
who were with the Indians, of whom she continued to inquire
what they intended to do with the children they had taken,

* Mr. Hendee lived near where Milo Dewey now lives, 1853.

and received an answer that they should kill them. Still determined not to part with her son, she passed on and soon discovered a large body of Indians stationed on the opposite side of the river. Wishing to find the commanding officer, and supposing him to be there, she set out to cross the river, and just as she arrived at the bank an old Indian stepped ashore. He could not talk English, but requested by signs to know where she was going. She signified that she was going to cross; when he, supposing she intended to deliver herself up to them as a prisoner, kindly offered to carry her and her child across on his back. But she refused to be carried. He then insisted upon carrying her child; to which she consented. The little girl cried, and said "she didn't want to ride the old Indian." She was, however, persuaded to ride him; and they all set out to ford the river.

Having proceeded about half way across they came to deeper and swifter water; and the old Indian, patting the mother upon the shoulder, gave her to understand that if she would tarry upon a rock near them, which was not covered with water, till he had carried her child over, he would return and carry her also. She therefore stopped and sat upon the rock till he had carried her daughter and set it upon the opposite shore, when he returned and took her upon his back, lugged her over, and safely landed her with her child.

Supported by a consciousness of the justice of her cause, braving every danger, and hazarding the most dreadful consequences, not excepting her own life and that of her children, she now sat out to accomplish her object.

She hastened to the commanding officer and boldly inquired of him what he intended to do with her child. He told her that it was contrary to orders to injure women or children. "Such boys as should be taken," he said, "would be trained for soldiers, and would not be hurt."

"You know," said she, in reply, "that these little ones cannot endure the fatigues of a march through the vast extent of wilderness which you are calculating to pass. And when their trembling limbs shall fail to support their feeble bodies, and they can no longer go, the tomahawk and the scalping knife will be the only relief you will afford them. Instead of falling into a mother's arms and receiving a mother's tender care, you will yield them into the arms of death, and earth must be their pillow where the howling wilderness shall be their only shelter. Truly a shelter from a mother's tears, but not from the jaws of wild beasts or a parent's grief. And give me leave to tell you," added she, "were you possessed of a parent's love, could you feel the anguish of a mother's heart at the loss of her first born, her darling son, torn from her bosom by the wicked hands of savage men, no entreaties would be required to obtain the release of my dear child."

Horton replied, "that the Indians were an ungovernable race, and would not be persuaded to give up any thing they should see fit to take."

"You are their commander," continued she, "and they must and will obey you. The curse will fall upon you for whatever crime they may commit; and all the innocent blood they shall here shed will be found in your skirts ‘ when the secrets of men's hearts shall be made known;’ and it will then cry for vengeance on your head!"

Melted into tears at this generous display of maternal affection, the infamous destroyer felt a relenting in his bosom, bowed his head under the weight of this powerful eloquence and simple boldness of the brave heroine, and assured her that he would deliver her child up when the Indians arrived with him. The party who took him had not yet returned. When he arrived, Horton, with much difficulty, prevailed on the Indians to deliver him up. After she had gained possession of him she set out, leading him and her little girl by the hand, and hastened away with speed, while the mingled sensations of fear, joy, and gratitude filled her bosom. She had not gone more than ten rods when Horton followed and told her to go back and stay till the scouting parties had returned, lest they should again take her boy from her. She accordingly returned and tarried with the Indians till they all arrived and started for Canada. While she was there, several of her neighbors' children, about the same age of her own, were brought there as captives. Possessing benevolence equal to her courage, she now made suit for them; and, by her warm and affectionate entreaties, succeeded in procuring their release. While she waited for their departure, sitting upon a pile of boards, with the little objects of charity around her holding fast to her clothes, with their cheeks wet with tears, an old Indian came and took her son by the hand and endeavored to get him away. She refused to let him go, and held him fast by the other hand till the savage monster violently waved his cutlass over her head, and the piercing shrieks of her beloved child filled the air. This excited the rage of the barbarous crew so much as to endanger her own and the lives of the children around her, and compelled her to yield him into his hands. She again made known her grievances to Horton, when, after considerable altercation with the Indians, he obtained her son and delivered him to her a second time, though he might be said to "fear not God nor regard man." Thus, like the importunate widow who "troubled the unjust judge," this young woman * obtained the release of nine small boys from a wretched captivity which doubtless would have proved their death. She led eight of them away, together with her daughter, all hanging to her own clothes and to each other, mutually rejoicing at their deliverance. The other, whose name was Andrew Durkee, whom the Indians had carried to the house of Mr. Havens, was there released according to the agreement of Horton with Mrs. Hendee, and sent back on account of his lameness.

Being told that the great bone in his leg had been taken

---

* Mrs. Hendee was at this time aged twenty-seven years.

out in consequence of a fever sore, an old Indian examined it and cried out, "No boon! no go!" and, giving him a blanket and a hatchet, sent him back.

Mrs. Hendee carried two of the children across the river on her back, one at a time, and the others waded through the water with their arms around each other's neck. After crossing the river she travelled about three miles with them and encamped for the night, "gathering them around her as a hen gathereth her chickens under her wings." The names of the children who were indebted to her for their release from the savage tribe were Michael Hendee, Roswell Parkhurst, son of Captain Ebenezer Parkhurst, Andrew and Sheldon Durkee, Joseph Rix, Rufus and ———— Fish, Nathaniel Evans, and Daniel Downer. The latter received such an affright from the horrid crew that he was ever afterwards unable to take care of himself, wholly unfit for business, and lived for many years wandering from place to place, a solemn though silent witness of the distress and horror of that dreadful scene.

Mrs. Hendee now (1818) lives in Sharon, where the author visited her and received the foregoing statement of this noble exploit from her own mouth. It is also corroborated by several gentlemen, now living, who were eye witnesses.

She has buried her first and second husbands, and now lives a widow, by the name of Moshier. Her days are almost gone. May her declining years be crowned with the reward due to her youthful deeds of benevolence. She has faced the most awful dangers for the good of mankind, and rescued many from the jaws of death.

In view of the exceeding riches of that mercy which has protected her through such scenes of danger, may she devote her life to the service of the mighty God, and, at last, find a happy seat at the right hand of Him "who gave himself a ransom for all." And thus let the children, who are indebted to her bravery and benevolence for their lives, "rise up and call her blessed." Gratitude forbids their silence; for to maternal affection and female heroism alone, under God, they owe their deliverance from savage cruelty. The boldest hero of the other sex could never have effected what she accomplished. His approach to the savage tribe to intercede in behalf of those defenceless children most surely would have brought upon himself a long and wretched captivity, and perhaps even death itself.

The Indians, having accomplished their nefarious designs, returned to the house of Mr. Havens with their prisoners and the plunder of houses which they had devoted to destruction. Here was the place where they had commenced their ravages. The old man, as before observed, having concealed himself under a log, at the time he espied the Indians in the morning while hunting for his sheep, still remained in sorrowful silence undiscovered. He had considered it unsafe to move, as a party of the crew had continued there during the day, and had twice come and stood upon the log under which he lay without finding him.

After collecting their plunder together and distributing it among them they burned the house and barn of Mr. Havens and started for Canada. It was now about two o'clock in the afternoon. They carried off twenty-six prisoners from Royalton, who were all delivered up to the British as prisoners of war.

They all obtained their release and returned in about one year excepting Adan Durkee, who died in camp at Montreal.

Twenty-one dwelling houses, and sixteen good new barns, well filled with hay and grain, the hard earnings of industrious young farmers, were here laid in ashes by the impious crew. They killed about one hundred and fifty head of neat cattle and all the sheep and swine they found. Hogs in their pens and cattle tied in their stalls were burned alive. They destroyed all the household furniture except what they carried with them. They burned the house of Mr. John

18

Hutchinson; and giving his wife a hatchet and a flint, together with a quarter of mutton, told her to "go and cook for her men." This they said to aggravate her feelings and remind her of her forlorn condition.

Women and children were left entirely destitute of food and every kind of article necessary for the comforts of life, almost naked, and without a shelter. Wandering from place to place, they beheld their cattle rolling in their blood, groaning in the agonies of death, and saw their houses laid in ruins. Disconsolate mothers and weeping orphans were left to wander through the dreadful waste and lament the loss of their nearest friends, comfortless and forlorn.

The Indians took away about thirty horses, which were however of little use to them, but rather served to hinder their progress. Their baggage was composed of almost every article commonly found among farmers; such as axes and hoes, pots, kettles, shovels and tongs, sickles, scythes and chains, old side saddles, and bed ticks emptied of their feathers, warming pans, plates, and looking glasses, and indeed nearly all kinds of articles necessary for the various avocations of life.

On their return they crossed the hills in Tunbridge, lying west of first branch, and proceeded to Randolph, where they encamped for the first night, near the second branch, a distance of about ten miles. They had, however, previously despatched old Mr. Kneeland, a prisoner whom they considered would be of the least service to them, with letters to the militia, stating that, " if they were not followed, the prisoners should be used well; but should they be pursued, every one of them would be put to death."

The alarm had by this time spread through the adjacent towns; and the scattering, undisciplined militia shouldered their muskets and hastened to pursue them. They collected at the house of Mr. Evans, in Randolph, about two miles south of the encampment of the Indians. Here they formed a company, consisting of about three hundred in number, and made choice of Colonel John House, of Hanover, New Hampshire, for their commander. They supposed the Indians had gone to Brookfield, about ten miles from that place, up the second branch. With this expectation they took up their march about twelve o'clock at night, hoping they should be able to reach Brookfield before light and make them prisoners. They had scarcely started when the American front guard, to their utter surprise, were fired upon by the rearguard of the enemy. Several fires were exchanged and one of the Americans wounded; when Colonel House, through cowardice or want of skill, commanded them to halt and cease firing. He then ordered them to make a stand, and kept them in suspense till the Indians had made their escape. To hasten their flight, the savage tribe were compelled to leave at their encampment a considerable quantity of their plunder, nearly all the horses, and made good their retreat.

Here they killed two of the prisoners, by the names of Joseph Kneeland and Giles Gibbs. The former was found dead, with his scalp taken off, and the latter with a tomahawk in his head.

At daylight Colonel House courageously entered the deserted camp and took possession of the spoil; but, alas! the enemy were gone he knew not where. Urged by his brave soldiers, who were disgusted at his conduct, he proceeded up the second branch, as far as Brookfield, in pursuit of the enemy, and, not finding them, disbanded his men and returned.

Had Colonel H. possessed courage and skill adequate to the duties of his station he might have defeated the enemy, it is thought, without the least difficulty, and made them all prisoners. His number was equal to that of the enemy, well armed with muskets and furnished with ammunition. The enemy, though furnished with muskets, had little ammunition, and were cumbered with the weight of much guilt and a load of plunder. They had encamped upon a spot of ground which gave the Americans all the advantage, and their only safety rested in their flight. The American force consisted of undisciplined militia, who promiscuously assembled from different quarters, but were full of courage, animated by the principles of justice and determined to obtain redress for the injuries they had received from the barbarous crew.

Many of them likewise had friends and connections then in possession of the Indians, to obtain whose freedom they were stimulated to action. But, alas! their determination failed, their hopes were blasted. They were forced to relinquish the object, and suffer their friends to pass on and endure a wretched captivity. They, however, forced the Indians to leave the stream and take their course over the hills, between the second and third branch, which brought them directly and unexpectedly to the house of Zadock Steele, whom they made prisoner and took to Canada.

To his "captivity and sufferings," as related by himself in the following pages, the reader is referred for a further account of the expedition of the Indians and its dreadful consequences.

# CAPTIVITY OF ZADOCK STEELE.

BEFORE the mind of the indulgent reader is engaged in a perusal of the sufferings of my maturer years, it may not be improper to direct the attention to scenes of nativity and youth.

The day of my birth, and the events which transpired to bring upon me the miseries I have undergone, will not be uninteresting, I think, to those who may feel disposed to read the following pages.

As, in the evening of a tempestuous day, with solemn yet pleasing emotions we look back on the dangers through which we have been preserved, so, when man has passed through scenes of fatigue, endured the hardships of a savage captivity, as well as the pains of a prison, and again obtained his freedom, it is a source of pleasure to cause those scenes to pass in review before his imagination, and cannot fail to excite his gratitude to the Power that afforded him relief.

I was born at Tolland, Connecticut, on the 17th of December, 1758. In 1776 my father, James Steele, Esq., moved from Tolland to Ellington, a town adjoining, where he kept a house of entertainment several years. During the years of my childhood the American colonies were put in commotion by what is generally termed the French war.

The colonies had hardly recovered from the convulsions of that war when the American revolution commenced. My father had been actively engaged in the former war, and now received a lieutenant's commission in the revolutionary army. The importance of the contest in which the colonies were engaged called upon every friend to the rights of man to be actively employed. Being in my eighteenth year in May, 1776, I enlisted into the army for one year as waiter to my father. Soon after I enlisted he was visited with a severe fit of sickness, which prevented him from entering the army, and compelled me to go into the ranks, leaving him behind. My two older brothers, Aaron and James, also enlisted the same year. Aaron died in March following at Chatham, New Jersey, in the twenty-third year of his age. Bereft of a brother whom I held dear, after serving the term of my enlistment I returned to Ellington.

The next year I served one campaign in the militia, and the year following as a teamster, which closed my services in the army. I was now about nineteen years of age. I had been favored with very little opportunity, as yet, to acquire an education; as the infantile state of the colonies and the agitation of public affairs at that time afforded little encouragement to schools, and caused a universal depression of literature in general.

I, however, acquired an education sufficient to enable me to transact the business of a farmer and regulate my own concerns in my intercourse with mankind. But long have I deeply regretted the want of that knowledge of letters requisite to prepare for the press a narrative of my own sufferings and those of my fellow-captives which should be read with interest and receive the approbation of an indulgent public.

No hope of pecuniary gain or wish to bring myself into public notice has induced me to publish a narrative of my sufferings. A desire that others as well as myself might learn wisdom from the things I have suffered is the principal cause of its publication. The repeated instances of my deliverance from threatened death, in which the finger of God was visible, call for the deepest gratitude, and have made an impression upon my mind which I trust will remain as long as the powers of my recollection shall endure. I was sensible it might also furnish a lesson of instruction to my fellow-men and to future generations duly to prize the privileges and blessings they may enjoy, by observing the dreadful contrast which is brought to view in this narrative.

Desirable, however, as it might be, I had long since relinquished all idea of ever seeing an account of my sufferings in print. But by the earnest solicitations and friendly though feeble assistance of others, I have thought fit at this late period of my life, yet with humble deference to the good sense of an enlightened public, to give a short narrative of what I have endured in common with many of my fellow-men who were my fellow-prisoners.

Among the evils resulting from the destruction of Royalton, my own captivity was far from being the least. That event was the precursor of all my sorrows — the fountain from which sprung streams of wretchedness and want. Nor will the channel be forgotten, though the raging flood cease to roll. As small streams are swallowed up by larger ones, so many serious and sore trials are doubtless lost in that dreadful current of distress through which I was called to pass.

The attention of the reader is, however, requested to a simple statement of facts, as they occur to my mind, while I relate the circumstances of my captivity by the Indians, the treatment I received from them, my privations while a prisoner to the British, my wonderful escape from their hands, and extreme sufferings in the wilderness on my way home. Truth will not easily permit, nor have I any desire, to enlarge or exaggerate upon the things I suffered. Guided by the principles of justice, and wishing no ill to any man or set of men, I hope I shall not be found disposed to calumniate or reproach.

It is not my intention to speak of any individual or nation with less respect than is due to their true character and conduct.

I shall, however, be under the necessity of noticing many

cruelties that were inflicted upon the prisoners, by men who enjoyed the advantages of civilization, which were sufficient to put the rudest savage to the blush.

But the long lapse of time and the effects of old age have, no doubt, blotted from my memory incidents which would have been no less, and perhaps more, interesting and instructive than many circumstances which I shall be able to recollect. This, together with the inexperience of the writer, must be the only apology for the imperfections of the following pages.

In April, 1780, being in my twenty-second year, I started from my father's house in Ellington, leaving all my friends and relatives, and came to Randolph, in the State of Vermont, a town south of Brookfield, a distance of nearly two hundred miles. I there purchased a right of land, lying in the north part of the town, on which was a log house and a little improvement. Suffering the privations and hardships common to those who dwell in new countries, I spent the summer in diligent labor, subsisting upon rather coarse fare, and supported by the fond hopes of soon experiencing better days.

The young man who drove my team from Connecticut, with provisions, farming utensils, &c., labored with me through the summer and fall seasons till October, when he returned to Ellington just in time to escape the danger of being taken by the Indians.

A small settlement had commenced in the south-westerly part of Randolph, on the third branch of White River, about six miles from my own. A little settlement had also commenced on the second branch of the same river in Brookfield, in the easterly part of the town, and at about an equal distance from my abode. As there were in Randolph a number of families situated in different parts of the town, and our country being engaged in a war, which rendered our frontier settlements exposed to the ravages of an exasperated foe, we had taken the necessary precaution to establish alarm posts, by which we might announce to each other the approach of an enemy.

But our Brookfield brethren, though in a town adjoining, were beyond the hearing of the report of our alarm guns.

On the 16th of October we were apprised of the arrival of the Indians at Royalton, a town about ten miles south of Randolph. They entered that town on the morning of the 16th, and were committing ravages, taking and killing the inhabitants, sparing the lives of none whom they could overtake in an attempt to escape, destroying property, burning all the buildings that they discovered, killing the cattle, pillaging the houses, and taking captives.

It was expected they would follow up either the second or third branch on their return to Canada, as these two branches run to the south and nearly parallel to each other; the former of which empties itself into the river at Royalton, and the latter a few miles west.

I was employed during the sixteenth day till nearly night in assisting the settlers on the third branch in Randolph to move their families and effects into the woods such a distance as was thought would render them safe, should the Indians pursue that stream up on their return.

I then requested that some one of them should accompany me to go and notify the Brookfield settlers of their danger. Being unable to persuade any to go with me, I started alone. I had only time to arrive at my own dwelling, which was on my direct course, before I was overtaken by the approach of night. As there was no road and nothing but marked trees to guide my way, I tarried all night. Having prepared some food for breakfast I lay down to sleep, little knowing what awaited my waking hours. At the dawn of day on the morning of the 17th I set out to prosecute the object for which I started, though in a violent tempest, attended with snow. I had not proceeded far before the storm greatly increased, which I found would not only much endanger my life, but so retard my progress that I could not

arrive in time seasonably to warn my friends of their danger
or escape myself from the hands of the enemy should they
follow the second branch instead of the third.  I therefore
returned to my house.  Soon after I arrived within doors,
filled with anxiety for the unsuspecting inhabitants of Brookfield, I heard a shocking cry in the surrounding woods; and,
trembling for my own safety, I ran to the door, when, to my
utter astonishment, and the reader may judge my feelings, I
beheld a company of Indians, consisting of not less than three
hundred in number, not ten rods distant, approaching with
hideous cries and frightful yells!

"O how unlike the chorus of the skies!"

There was no way of escape.  I had only to stand still,
wait their approach, and receive my miserable destiny.  Indeed, I could now say with David, "The sorrows of death
compassed me, and the floods of ungodly men made me
afraid."  I had nowhere to flee but to the "great Preserver
of men, who was my only hiding-place," "my goodness and
my fortress, my high tower and my deliverer, my shield,
and he in whom I trust."

"They came upon me as a wide breaking of waters; in
the desolation they rolled themselves upon me."

Their leader came up and told me I must go with them.
They asked me if any other persons were to be found near
that place.  I told them it was probable there were none to
be found.  They then inquired if any cattle were near; to
which I answered in the negative.  But they seemed to choose
rather to take the trouble to search than to confide in what I
told them.

After taking every thing they found worthy to carry with
them, and destroying all that was not likely to suffer injury
by fire, they set the house on fire and marched on.  One of
them took a bag of grass seed upon his back, and, cutting a
hole in the bag, scattered the seed as he marched, which took

root, stocked the ground, and was for many years a sad memento of my long captivity.

The chief who came up to me could talk English very well, which was a circumstance much in my favor, as he became my master, under which name I shall have frequent occasion to speak of him in the course of this narrative.

They took all my clothes, not excepting the best I had on, and distributed them amongst themselves. They, however, furnished me with blankets sufficient to defend me against the cold, but deprived me of my own property; the bitter consequences of which I felt in my subsequent confinement with the British, and on my return to resume my settlement at Randolph.

The Indians had encamped the night preceding on the second branch in Randolph, on which the Brookfield settlers lived, and not more than ten miles below them, but during the night had been put to rout by a party of Americans, consisting of about two hundred and fifty in number, who were commanded by Colonel John House, of Hanover, New Hampshire. To make their escape, they left the stream and took a course which brought them directly to my dwelling.

Had they not been molested, but permitted to pursue their intended course up the stream, the defenceless inhabitants of Brookfield would doubtless have shared the miserable fate of the inhabitants of Royalton, themselves taken prisoners, and doomed to suffer a long and wretched captivity, and their property destroyed by the devouring element. This prevention, which, however, was the cause of my captivity, the subject of the following narrative, was probably the only good that Colonel H. effected; and this he did unwittingly, for which he can claim no thanks.

Soon after we started from my house my master, who was the principal conductor and chief of the whole tribe, discovered that I had a pair of silver buckles in my shoes, and attempted to take them from me; but, by promising to let him have them when we arrived at our journey's end, I persuaded him to let me keep them. But we had not travelled far before another Indian espied them, and crying out, "*Wah stondorum!*" (Ah, there's silver!) took them from me, and furnished me with strings for my shoes as substitutes.

We travelled the first day to Berlin and encamped on Dog River, not many miles from the place where Montpelier village now stands. They built a fire of some rods in length, to which opportunity was afforded for all to approach. They then placed sentinels around, which rendered it impossible for any one to move unnoticed. But this precaution was not sufficient to satisfy their minds to prevent the escape of their captive prisoners. Therefore, to render our escape less easy to be effected, as we lay down upon the ground they tied a rope around our bodies, and, extending it each way, the Indians laid upon it on our right and on our left, not suffering any two prisoners to lie next each other. I could, however, crawl so far out of the rope as to be able to sit upright, but always found some of the Indians sitting up, either to prepare their clothing for the following day's march, or intentionally to set as additional guards; and I never found the favored moment when all were at rest.

As they had told me before we encamped that if they were overtaken by the Americans they should kill every prisoner, I felt the more anxious to make my escape; and they seemed, in view of their danger, more desirous to keep us within reach of the tomahawk, and secure us against a flight in case the Americans should approach. I watched with trembling fear and anxious expectation during the night we lay at Berlin, seeking an opportunity to escape, which I found utterly impossible, and looking every moment for the arrival of a company of Americans, whose approach I was assured would be attended with death to every prisoner.

They compelled many of the prisoners to carry their packs, enormous in size and extremely heavy, as they were filled with the plunder of pillaged houses and every thing which attracted their curiosity or desire to possess. Looking glasses, which by the intention or carelessness of the prisoners became broken in a short time, pots, spiders, frying pans, and old side saddles, which were sold on their arrival at St. John's for one dollar, composed a part of their invaluable baggage.

On the morning of the 18th they first ordered me to eat my breakfast, urging me to eat as much as I wanted; while, on account of the loss of their provisions at Randolph, they had scarce half an allowance for themselves. I knew not whether to attribute this conduct to their feelings of charity and generosity, a desire to secure my friendship, or a wish to preserve my life under a prospect of procuring gain, or to . some other cause.

Indeed, they seemed at all times to be willing to "feed the hungry," not even seeing one of the prisoners leisurely pick a berry by the way, as they passed along, without offering them food, considering this as a token of our hunger.

Their food, however, was very unsavory, insomuch that nothing but extreme hunger would have induced me to eat of it, though I always had a share of their best.

Habituated to a partial covering themselves and excited by curiosity, they took from me all my best clothes, and gave me blankets in exchange. They often travelled with the utmost celerity in their power to try my activity, viewing me with looks of complacency to find me able to keep pace with them.

We this day passed down Dog River till we came to Onion River, into which the former empties itself, and then kept the course of the latter during the day, steering nearly a north-west direction. At night we came to a very steep mountain, which was extremely difficult of access, not far from the place now called Bolton, in the county of Chittenden. Upon the top of this mountain the Indians, on their way to Royalton, had secreted a number of bags of fine flour which they brought with them from Canada, and now regained. This greatly re-

19

plenished their stores, and afforded a full supply of wholesome
bread. The manner of making their bread is curious, and
exhibits useful instruction to those who may be called to make
their bread in the wilderness without enjoying the privilege
of household furniture.

They took their dough, wound it around a stick in the form
of a screw, stuck it into the ground by the fire, and thus
baked their bread, without receiving injury by the smoke or
rendering it more filthy than it came from their hands.

Their fear that they should be overtaken by the Americans had by this time greatly abated, and this was considered
by the prisoners grounds for less apprehension of the danger
of being put to death by the Indians. Till now, however, it
is beyond the power of language to express, nor can imagination paint, the feelings of my heart, when, torn from my
friends and all I held dear on earth, compelled to roam the
wilderness to unknown parts, obliged to ford rivers, and then
lie down at night upon the cold ground with scarcely a dry
thread in my clothes, having a rope fastened around my
body, surrounded by a tribe of savage Indians, from whose
very friendship I could expect nothing but wretchedness and
misery, and whose brutal rage would be sure to prove my
death.

Nor was this rage only liable to be excited by a sense of
real danger, but, from conscious guilt, equally liable to be put
in force by the most slight, false, and trifling alarm.

> " 'Tis a prime part of happiness to know
> How much unhappiness must prove our lot —
> A part which few possess."

On the fourth day we arrived at Lake Champlain. We
here found some bateaux, in which the Indians had conveyed
themselves thither on their way to Royalton. On their arrival at the lake, and regaining their bateaux, they gave a
shout of exultation and laughter, manifesting their joy and
triumph.

My master, who was about to take a different route from the rest of the tribe, took me aside, and, in a dissembling tone, told me with great professions of friendship, with little credit, however, that I had better take off my coat and let him have it, for which he would give me a blanket in exchange, assuring me that the Indians would take it from me if I did not do it. Dreading the consequences of a refusal more than the loss of the coat, I let him have it, and received a blanket in return. We crossed over and encamped on Grand Isle that night. The next morning we reëmbarked in our bateaux, and safely landed at the Isle Aux Noix before night. Here the Indians found a supply of rum, which gave them an opportunity to make market for a part of their plunder and satiate their thirst. Nor, indeed, was the opportunity unimproved. Irritated by the force of intoxication, they were all in confusion: savage yells and shrill outcries filled the surrounding atmosphere, and death seemed to stare every captive full in the face.

> " So sung Philander, as a friend went round
> In the rich ichor, in the generous blood
> Of Bacchus, purple god of joyous wit."

At length, however, their senses became drowned in the torrent of inebriety; they sank into a helpless state, and reposed in the arms of insensibility. As we had now arrived within the dominions of the British, and were not only guarded by a number of the Indians who were not under the power of intoxication, but watched by the enemy's subjects resident at that place, we could find no opportunity to make our escape.

The next morning, which was the sixth day of our march, we started for St. John's, and arrived there that day. At this place, likewise, the Indians found a plenty of ardent spirits, by a too free use of which they became more enraged, if possible, than before.

They now began to threaten the lives of all the captives

whose faces were not painted, as the face being painted was a distinguishing mark put upon those whom they designed not to kill.

As I was not painted, one of the Indians, under the influence of intoxication and brutal rage, like many white people, more sagacious than humane, came up to me, and, pointing a gun directly at my head, cocked it, and was about to fire, when an old Indian, who was my new master, knocked it aside, pushed him backwards upon the ground, and took a bottle of rum, and, putting it to his mouth, turned down his throat a considerable quantity, left him, and went on.

The punishment seemed in no way to displease the criminal: he wished he would continue to punish him through the day in the same manner; regarding the momentary gratification of appetite more than all other blessings of life, or even life itself.

They now procured some paint and painted my face, which greatly appeased the rage of those who, before, had been apparently determined to take my life. I now received their marks of friendship, nor felt myself in danger of becoming the subject of their fatal enmity. Clothed with an Indian blanket, with my hands and my face painted, and possessing activity equal to any of them, they appeared to be willing I should live with them and be accounted as one of their number.

We arrived at Caghnewaga on the seventh day of our march. Thus I found myself, within the space of seven days, removed from my home and from all my relatives the distance of about three hundred miles, almost destitute of clothing, entirely without money, with no other associates than a race of savage Indians, whose language I could not understand, whose diet was unsavory and unwholesome, whose "tender mercies are cruel," barbarism their civility, no pardon to an enemy their established creed, and presented with no other prospect for the future than a captivity for life, a final separation from all earthly friends, and situated in an enemy's country.

In short, stripped of every comfort that sweetens life except the "one thing needful, which the world can neither give nor take away," my temporal prospects were banished and lost forever. No earthly friends to administer consolation or with whom to sympathize, nor hope of escape to feed upon, truly, humble submission to the will of Heaven, and an entire "trust in the Lord," was the only balm afforded me.

> " A soul prepared for such a state as this
> Is heir expectant to immortal bliss."

Some days after we arrived at Caghnewaga, an old man by the name of Philips, whose silver locks bespoke the experience of many winters; whose visage indicated the trials, sorrows, and afflictions of a long and wretched captivity; whose wrinkled face and withered hands witnessed the sufferings of many hardships, and presented to me a solemn and awful token of what I myself might expect to suffer,—came and told me that I was about to be adopted into one of the Indian families, to fill the place of one whom they had lost on their expedition to Royalton.

Mr. Philips was taken prisoner in the western part of the State of New York, by the Indians, in his youthful days, and, having been adopted into one of their families, had always lived with them. He had retained his knowledge of the English language, and served as an interpreter for the tribe.

The ceremony of my own adoption, as well as that of many other of the prisoners, afforded no small degree of diversion. The scene presented to view a spectacle of an assemblage of barbarism assuming the appearance of civilization.

All the Indians, both male and female, together with the prisoners, assembled and formed a circle, within which one of their chiefs, standing upon a stage erected for the purpose, harangued the audience in the Indian tongue. Although I could not understand his language, yet I could plainly discover a great share of native eloquence. His speech was of

considerable length, and its effect obviously manifested weight
of argument, solemnity of thought, and at least human sensibility.   I was placed near by his side, and had a fair view of
the whole circle.   After he had ended his speech an old
squaw came and took me by the hand and led me to her wigwam, where she dressed me in a red coat, with a ruffle in my
bosom, and ordered me to call her mother.   She could speak
English tolerably well; but was very poor, and therefore unable to furnish me with very sumptuous fare.   My food was
rather beneath a savage mediocrity; though no doubt my new
mother endeavored as far as lay in her power to endear the
affections of her newly-adopted yet ill-natured son.

I found the appellation of *mother* highly pleased the tawny
jade, which proportionably increased my disgust, already in-
tolerable; and, instead of producing contentment of mind,
added disquietude to affliction and sorrow.

As I was blessed with an excellent voice for singing, I was
the more beloved by, and, on that account, received much
better treatment from, my new mother, as well as from other
Indians.

'I was allowed the privilege of visiting any part of the village in the daytime, and was received with marks of fraternal
affection and treated with all the civility an Indian is capable
to bestow.

A prisoner, by the name of Belknap, was set about hewing
some poles for a stable floor while his Indian master held
them for him. As he hewed, the Indian, sitting upon the pole,
suffered it gradually to turn over, though unperceived by him;
which occasioned the workman, who saw its operation, laugh-
ing in his sleeves, to hew quite round the stick, in hewing
from end to end.   Thinking that Belknap knew no better, the
Indian endeavored to instruct him.   After trying several poles
with the same success, the Indian, filled with impatience for
this untractable pupil, with his eyes on fire, left him and called
his interpreter to make his wishes more distinctly known; to

whom Belknap declared, that he did well understand the wishes of the Indian, and was determined to avoid doing his will.

After remaining in this condition a few weeks, finding the prisoners very incorrigible, and wishing for the reward they might obtain for them, information was given the prisoners that they might be delivered over to the British at Montreal as prisoners of war, or continue with the Indians, as they should choose.

We sought the advice of an English gentleman, by the name of Stacy, resident in the village of Caghnewaga, who had married a squaw for his wife, and was extensively acquainted, not only with the affairs of the Indians, but with the citizens of Montreal. He appeared to be a man of integrity and veracity, was employed in merchandise, and also served as one of their interpreters.

I was advised by Mr. Stacy to be delivered into the hands of the British. He said I might doubtless obtain leave to dwell in some family of a private gentleman until I should be exchanged.

Encouraged by the prospect of enjoying the company of civilized people, and flattered with the idea of being soon exchanged, and thereby enabled to return once more to see my friends in Connecticut, I made choice to be given up to the British. All the captives did likewise.

We were all conducted to Montreal, by the Indians, in the latter part of November, 1780, and there "sold for a half joe" each. Most of the captives were young, and remarkably robust, healthy, and vigorous. I was now almost twenty-two years of age. To be compelled to spend the vigor of my days in useless confinement was a source of grief and pain to my mind; but I could see no way of escape. The wisdom of God I found to be unsearchable indeed. I felt, however, a good degree of submission to the providence of the Most High, and a willingness to " accept of the punishment of mine iniquities."

We found at the city of Montreal about one hundred and seventy prisoners, some of whom were made captives by the Indians in different parts of America, and others had been taken prisoners of war in forts by capitulation and by conquest. Here we could see women and children, who had fallen the victims of savage captivity, weeping and mourning their fate, whose tears, trickling down their cheeks, bespoke the language of their hearts. It was enough to melt the heart of stone with grief to behold the bosoms of the "poor widows" heaving with sighs and to hear their groans; while the companions of their youth, their bosom friends and partners in life, were no more, having spilled their blood and laid down their lives in defence of their country, their families, and their firesides.

Here I beheld the orphan, fatherless and motherless, whose tender age called for compassion and required the kind protection of an affectionate mother, whose infantile mind rendered it incapable of telling its name, the place of its birth, or giving any information respecting itself or its parents.

This led me to consider my own sufferings comparatively small; and a sense of my own wretched condition became lost in the feelings of compassion for these unhappy widows and orphans.

We were put into a large building, called the Old Regal Church, with the other prisoners, in which we were kept several days, when we were removed into a large stone building, fitted up for the purpose, in the suburbs of the city, upon the shore of the River St. Lawrence.

I often made application for liberty to take quarters in the family of some private gentleman, where I might enjoy the advantages of a common slave until I should be able to procure a ransom or be exchanged, urging the manner of my being taken and my destitute situation as arguments in my favor, having been stripped of all my property by the Indians and deprived of all my change of clothes. But all my efforts proved only a witness to myself and my fellow-sufferers of that deafness to the calls of humanity which is always the characteristic of tyranny and despotism.

Many of the prisoners as well as myself had only one shirt, and were obliged to go without any while we washed that. Indolence and disregard for cleanliness prevented many from doing this, which may be reckoned among the many causes that brought our subsequent evils upon us. We were allowed, or rather said to be allowed, one pound of bread and one pound of fresh beef per day. But, through the injustice and dishonesty of the person who dealt out our allowance, we were robbed even of a part of this humble pittance. Had we been able to obtain our full allowance in provisions of good quality, we should have been able to have furnished ourselves with other necessary articles; but now we were deprived of the privilege by the curtailment of our rations. We were obliged by the calls of hunger to pound up the beef bones, which composed no small share of our rations of meat, and boil them for broth. We had no butter, cheese, flour, nor any kind of sauce during the winter. We were kept almost totally without firewood, having scarcely enough to enable us to cook our meat. Our beds consisted principally of blankets, which they brought from the hospital in all their filth. This was an apparent manifestation of their disregard at least for the prisoners, if not a malevolent design to introduce that contagion which should spread disease, desolation, and death throughout our camp.

Pinched with hunger, half naked, and chilled with the cold, we were forced to have recourse to our beds, and occupy them a great part of the time, though they were the habitations of filthy vermin, tainted with the infections of mortal distempers, and scented with the nauseous smell of the dying and the dead.

The complicated collection of people of different habits, comprising almost every kind of foul and vicious character, and the combination of so many events, either of which should seem alone sufficient to create disease, caused a general and universal prevalence of the itch.

Our close confinement was, to some of the prisoners, a source of grief; to others a cloak of indulgence in laziness; while to all it was the mother of disease, the harbinger of pain.

We suffered so much with hunger that we should have thankfully "fed upon the crums that fell from the rich man's table;" and so great were our afflictions that we should have gladly caressed the "dog that had come and licked our sores."

While I was a captive with the Indians I was in sorrow, and "desired a better country." And I had not experienced the "trial of cruel mockings and scourgings, of bonds and imprisonment," sufficiently to enable me to say with Paul, "I have learned in whatsoever state I am therewith to be content." When we were put into the hands of the British "we looked for peace, but no good came; and for a time of health, and beheld trouble." Indeed, it may justly be said of them, "They turned the needy out of the way; they caused the naked to lodge without clothing, that they have no covering in the cold; they pluck the fatherless from the breast, and take a pledge of the poor; they cause him to go naked without clothing, and they take away the sheaf from the hungry." (Job xxiv. 4–7, 10.) I pleaded that they would "make me as one of their hired servants;" but they would not.

In the spring, after being "brought low, through oppression, affliction, and sorrow," we were supplied with salt pork, bread, oatmeal, and peas in abundance. As we had long been almost starved, our avidity for the food which was now before us may more easily be imagined than described. Let it suffice us to say, that none ate sparingly, but all greedily. Indeed, some seemed not only anxious to satisfy hunger, but determined to revenge for their past sufferings. This sudden repletion of our wants produced the scurvy among the prisoners, which threatened death to every one.    Reiterated sighs and dying groans now filled our camp.

To such an alarming degree did this dreadful disease prevail that many were obliged to be removed to the hospital for relief; distress and anguish pervaded the whole body of the prisoners ; and the citizens of Montreal, alarmed, perhaps, for their own safety, seemed to feel anxious for our relief. But justice requires I should state that we received at this time all that kind attention which was due to our wretched condition and every favor in the power of our keepers to bestow ; while the inhabitants manifested a humane disposition, and displayed the generous/feelings of pity and tender compassion.    In short, conscious that they, in truth, had all partially contributed to increase our miseries, they seemed to feel a relenting for their past misconduct, which excited them to use their utmost exertion to exonerate themselves from guilt by their subsequent good offices for our relief.

They furnished us with green herbs and every thing which was adapted to our disorders or calculated for our comfort and recovery.    By these means our health was fully restored, gratitude and joy sat smiling on every countenance, and songs of deliverance dwelt on every tongue.    Pain now gave place to pleasure, sorrow fled as happiness approached, murmurs and complaints which had long been the universal cry now were heard no more, and quietude was felt in every breast.

After our recovery we were allowed the privilege of a yard, of some rods square in extent, by which we were enabled to exercise for the preservation of our health.    But at length some of the prisoners made their escape, which occasioned all the rest to be put into close confinement and kept under lock and key.    We were supplied, however, with all the comforts of life, so far as our close confinement would permit.

In October, 1781, all the prisoners were removed to an island in the River St. Lawrence, called Prison Island, about forty-five miles above the city of Montreal, and opposite to a place called Cateau du Lac. Here we were furnished with a full supply of wholesome food during our confinement on the island.

This island is situated a little below the Lake St. Francis, which is formed by a large swell in the River St. Lawrence, and was considered a very eligible place for the confinement of the prisoners. Indeed, it was thought impossible that any person destitute of boats should be able to escape without being drowned, as the water ran with the utmost velocity on each side of the island. We were, therefore, allowed the liberty of traversing the whole island, which contained about twenty acres.

Guarded by a company of refugees and tories possessing as little humanity as patriotism, and having long been the miserable sufferers of a wretched captivity and painful imprisonment, many of the prisoners attempted to make their escape by swimming down the current the distance of three miles. But few succeeded, while some were drowned in the hazardous attempt. The captain of the guard, whose name was M'Daniel, was a tory, and as totally devoid of humanity and generosity as the Arab who traverses the deserts of Africa. His conduct towards the prisoners was such as ought to stamp his character with infamy and disgrace. Cruelty to the prisoners seemed to be his greatest delight. I once saw one of the prisoners plunge into the river in the daytime and swim down the current the distance of three miles, but was discovered by M'Daniel soon after he started, who ordered him to be shot before he should ever reach shore; but a British soldier, possessing more humanity than his commander, waded into the river and took hold of the trembling prisoner, almost exhausted, declaring, "if the prisoner was shot, he would be likewise."

The malignant disposition of M'Daniel and the invidious character of the guard induced the prisoners to seek opportunity and confront almost every danger to effect their escape.

But time soon rolled away, till winter approached, without bringing to our view that propitious moment which could afford the slightest hope of success in the attempt. On the one hand, the eye of an implacable foe was upon us, with rancor, malice, and revenge in his bosom, and the implements of destruction in his hand; and on the other, the rapid current of the stream threatened us with death if we approached; while the foaming billows, roaring in a voice like thunder, bade us beware.

Desperate, indeed, must be the attempt for any one knowingly to plunge himself into the jaws of death to escape from trouble.

At the approach of winter, the ice below the island rendered it visibly and utterly impossible to escape alive. We were, therefore, now forced into submission, and had only to consult together upon those measures which should be most likely to promote our own happiness while we waited the return of spring.

In January we were ordered by M'Daniel to shovel the snow for a path, in which the guard were to travel while on their duty.

Regarding the proverb of Solomon as worthy of our notice, that "it is an honor for a man to cease from strife," we complied with the demand, thus sacrificing our rights on the altar of peace. But now, finding by ocular demonstration the verity of a like proverb of the same wise man, that "every fool will be meddling," we unanimously agreed to disobey all similar orders and every command which should be afterwards given contrary to right. We were not insensible that the prisoner, though unable to defend, was possessed of certain inalienable rights, which we resolved to assert, and refuse obedience to the tyrant who should attempt to encroach upon them. The time soon arrived when duty called us boldly to assert our rights, and manly firmness forbade submission.

We were again commanded by M'Daniel to shovel the

snow, to make a path for the guard to travel in; while they themselves had nothing to do but to wait our toil. Disdaining to become slaves, we had universally determined to reject their unauthorized servitude. I therefore informed the infamous M'Daniel what was our unanimous resolution, and told him I feared less what he should dare to do than I did the consequences of yielding to the lawless requisitions of a petty tyrant. Enraged at the opposition of the prisoners to his arbitrary commands, and more highly exasperated against me as the organ, he directed me to be put in irons and carried to the guard house. After uttering the most dreadful threats and horrid imprecations, and finding I was not easily terrified nor readily forced to abandon my rights, he carried his order into execution, took me to the guard house, put me in irons, and kept me there during the whole day till night, when he came and repeated his threats of torture and death in case I continued to refuse compliance. But still finding me unmoved in my determination, and that "hatred stirreth up strifes," he ordered me to be kept in irons till nine o'clock at night without food and then sent back to my barrack.

This was accordingly done, though some Dutchmen, terrified at my fate, consented to his requirements and performed the service while I was confined in the guard house. In consequence of our refusal to comply with his unjust and illegal demands, the most severe punishments and barbarous cruelties were inflicted upon the prisoners.

"To revenge upon," he said, "no prisoner should be allowed to have a fire another night while they remained on the island."

Accordingly the guard came into our barracks every night with large quantities of snow and put out all the fires, using as much caution not to leave a spark unquenched as though the lives of thousands and the wealth of a metropolis were at stake.

"Though seen, we labor to believe it true."

What malice is manifest in the breasts of those who labor with diligence and toil with pain to increase the misery of those who are already wretched and groaning in sorrow!

Here we beheld the depravity of man. Here we could see the fulfilment of that passage of holy writ which declares that, "because sentence against an evil work is not executed speedily, therefore the heart of the sons of men is fully set in them to do evil."

Here we could behold a full display of the seven abominations in the sight of God: "A proud look, a lying tongue, and hands that shed innocent blood, a heart that deviseth wicked imaginations, feet that be swift in running to mischief, a false witness that speaketh lies, and him that soweth discord among brethren." (Prov. vi. 16, &c.)

Here we could see monsters in human shape feeding upon revenge; for the labor which they unjustly required of us was not a tenth part of what they performed every night by putting out our fires to punish us for non-compliance with their tyrannical demands. But, possessing the spirit of freemen, we "chose rather to suffer affliction" than to become the slaves of a set of despicable refugees and tories, feeling assured that our affliction would afford us more consolation in the hour of reflection than could be found in a servitude imposed upon us by an infamous renegado.

As our barracks were very cold and open, and being scantily clothed, we suffered greatly for want of fire, to support which we were willing to get wood ourselves. But our keepers chose rather to suffer pain themselves than to permit us to enjoy comfort.

M'Daniel, however, was called away, and succeeded by one M'Kelpin in command. He was also a refugee, the son of a tory, and had the appearance of a raw boy not more than eighteen or nineteen years old, whose very visage portended evil and bade the prisoners prepare for trouble.

His father, he said, had received very ill treatment from

the American army, and he had also shared with his father in the abuse for not engaging in the rebellion against the British government.   As "the rod is for the back of him that is void of understanding," we doubted not the truth of his statement, nor felt disposed to question but that he received very severe treatment, and more especially when the station in which he was found was taken into consideration; for this, together with the littleness of his mind and the malignity of his temper, will forever prove his want of patriotism and stamp his indignant character with infamy and disgrace as long as evil shall be had in remembrance.

His immature age can be no palliation of his crimes, nor admit of much hope of his reformation by repentance ; for, like all other fools, "he hated knowledge, and was wise in his own conceit."   Inheriting from his father all the qualities of a knave, and the cowardice of a western savage, who looks for security from danger in his own flight only or in the strength of his allies, he perverted the power put into his hands to do good ; used it as a weapon of revenge and an instrument of cruelty.   His paternal education was, at the best, toryism, perfectly congenial to his natural disposition.   In short, " he was wise to do evil; but to do good he had no knowledge." His first steps towards tyranny and oppression met no opposition ; as we wished to enjoy peace, and were willing to yield a portion of our rights to the enjoyment of so invaluable a blessing.   But our indulgence served only to stimulate him in the course of revengeful tyranny; and he seemed the more angry, as if " coals of fire were heaped upon his head."

Manifesting a desire to meet with opposition, by using every exertion to provoke to rage, he ordered the prisoners to shovel the snow from the door of his own house.   As the prisoners discovered in him a settled determination to pursue compliance with greater and more grievous burdens until he could meet a refusal to comply, we resolved to reject all further encroachments upon our rights.   We therefore refused to obey

his arbitrary commands any longer.    As there was a fort directly opposite the island where a company of soldiers were
stationed, we feared the consequences of a revolt, and could
only refuse our obedience without making any actual resistance.    The prisoner to whom he addressed himself possessed
courage equal to the most trying scene, and, choosing rather
to suffer an honorable death in defence of his rights than to
endure an ignominious life of captive slavery, he met the infamous M'Kelpin with firmness and intrepidity, although he
had no prospects of any thing but to endure extreme torture,
if not death itself.    And this he was the more inclined to do,
since it was the avowed object of the infamous villain "to
wreak his vengeance upon the unhappy prisoners for injuries,"
which he said he had received from men who were entire
strangers to us, and in which abuse he well knew we took no
agency or even had any knowledge.

When the prisoner refused compliance, M'Kelpin came up
with a bayonet pointing directly at him, and thrust it within
a few inches of his breast, threatening to run him through
the heart if he did not immediately comply.    But the prisoner, continuing firm in his obstinacy, replied with dauntless
courage and deliberate coolness, "Run me through if you
dare; I fear you not."    Enraged at this reply, M'Kelpin repeated his threats with redoubled vehemence and infuriated
madness, and again rushed at the prisoner with the greatest
violence, thus endeavoring to terrify him into submission to
his will.    But the prisoner, with all the appearance of a full
sense of death and supported by the rectitude of his motives,
met M'Kelpin with manly firmness and true heroism, putting
his hand upon his breast, and telling the impertinent fugitive
that "he had resolved to die before he should yield obedience to the arbitrary commands of one whose name was sy-
nonymous with disgrace, and whose very visage bespoke the
corruptions of a heart loaded with every thing that is requisite to fit a soul to become an inhabitant of the regions of

20 *

blackness and darkness forever." After repeating his threats and menaces several times, and each time receiving the most unqualified denials from the prisoner, he proceeded to punish all such as refused compliance with his request. He associated with threats the most daring oaths and awful imprecations, as if he would endeavor to establish his own authority by manifesting to the world his want of the fear of God and a disregard of every thing that is good.

Like many of the present day, he appeared to imagine that he should be thought to possess uncommon courage and power unlimited if he dared, openly and without fear, to blaspheme the name of Him who is the Ruler of all people, of every language, tongue, and nation. Finding all his threatenings in vain, and discovering that no one would yield obedience to his requirements, forgetting or disregarding the injustice of his claim, and lost in the torrent of anger and revenge, he came, with a guard of soldiers possessing feelings in perfect coincidence with his own, and took the defenceless yet dauntless prisoner whom he had threatened to run through with his bayonet, conveyed him to the barrack, which was used for an ash house, put him in irons, and left him to suffer in the cold the malicious gratification of his malignant and revengeful disposition; telling the innocent and unfortunate victim of his relentless fury that "he was glad he refused to comply with his demands, because he had long wanted and had anxiously sought opportunity to wreak his vengeance on him, and gave the order to shovel the snow from his own door for no other purpose but to excite the opposition of the prisoners, and thus find occasion to punish them, and at the same time take revenge on them for the abuse he had received from the Americans." He then proceeded to order others to shovel the snow; and, being still refused compliance, he threatened and confined in the same manner as he did the first, until he had collected together and confined in that cold barrack the number of twenty-one, who were all handcuffed and chained to the posts of the barrack. This was in January, 1782, when the cold was exceeding severe, and hardly permitted a comfortable seat by the fireside, or admitted of a lodging free from suffering in our closed barracks with a large quantity of blankets.

Here they were ordered to be kept in this barrack, with the windows and doors open to the wind and snow, all that day and the next night. But most of them made their escape to their own barracks before the next morning, some with frozen hands and feet, others with their ears and faces frozen; and, indeed, all having some part of their bodies frozen, and bearing the miserable tokens of their wretched sufferings.

But their escape, notwithstanding the visible and abiding marks of their pain and distress, only exasperated the mind of the unfeeling M'Kelpin, and so enraged the desperate villain that he the next day morning selected the same prisoners, and, with a heart harder than adamant and hands more cruel than the grave, again confined them all in irons and ordered them to be put into the chamber of one of the barracks, there to be kept during that day, the next night, and the following day, without provision, any food, or even a quid of tobacco.

Destitute of any clothing except their wearing apparel, which was poor; confined in irons, in a small, cold room; having no food of any kind; deprived of a luxury which habit had rendered necessary to preserve health; and groaning under the severe pains of their frozen bodies, — their sufferings cannot easily be imagined, far less described.

It was my happy lot, however, not to fall into this number of miserable sufferers of human depravity who were put into the ash house and in the chamber. But the sufferings which I have mentioned were only a prelude to more painful torments and greater barbarities. They were taken from the barrack chamber one by one, carried to the guard house, and tor· red in the most cruel manner. Some were surrounded with soldiers, armed with guns and bayonets pointing directly at them, and so near as to render the prisoners unable to move without being pierced with the bayonets; while the infamous M'Kelpin whipped the prisoners and caned them till he had glutted his vengeance. Who can describe the inhuman scene? To see a prisoner, the victim of cruelty and wretchedness, guiltless and defenceless, confined in irons with his hands behind him, ready to faint for want of food, groaning under the excruciating pains of his frozen limbs, bathed in blood which gushed from his mangled body, tears flowing from his eyes in streams, which bespoke in language more forcible than a voice like thunder, as they trickled down his frozen cheeks, the sorrows of a heart swollen with grief and racked with pain. I could say with Job, "Mine eye is also dim by reason of sorrow, and all my members are as a shadow."

Others of this unhappy number were hung up by the neck till nearly dead, while their hands were confined in irons and their faces black with death, when they were taken down, and the irons which had bound their hands jammed into their mouths till they were filled with blood. Who could behold this and not weep and mourn for the depravity of man left to himself? Who can witness a scene like this without acknowledging with self-application the truth of those words which fell from our Savior's lips to the unbelieving Jews, "Ye are of your father the devil, and the lusts of your father ye will do"? After enduring these horrid barbarities and inhuman tortures, inflicted by men professing the principles of humanity, the unhappy sufferers were sent back to their barracks, there to weep and bewail their miserable fate. Often have my cheeks been wet with tears of commiseration, while my heart ached within me, for these unfortunate sufferers of the unrestrained vengeance of a depraved villain. Nor was I left to be reminded of their torture and distress only by a recollection of the past; but my eyes could witness the scars of wounds and behold the palefaced visage of death abiding on the countenance of many, which were received by the cruelties of this horrid scene. And, alas! I needed only to look at myself and all around me to remind me of the woful case of those whose lot it is to fall into the hands and become the victims of a revengeful tyrant, and suffer the wrath of a man totally devoid of mercy, unrestrained either by the authority of a superior, the laws of his country, or the fear of God. Doubtless many will wear the marks, and thus bear witness of his cruelty, to their graves.

Emaciated countenances, scars, and impediment of speech were the visible marks of the savage and inhuman treatment which they received from the hand of M'Kelpin. Let detestation be written upon his character as legibly as the marks of depravity are to be seen in his visage, and it shall be a lesson to his posterity to flee from iniquity and follow the path of virtue. He excelled in nothing but cruelty and inhumanity, and was superior to none except in the most nefarious acts of iniquity, tyranny, and oppression. His highest ambition appeared to be to " heap up wrath against the day of wrath," and prepare himself to receive " vengeance due to them that know not God, and obey not the gospel of our Lord Jesus Christ, who shall be punished with everlasting destruction." He appeared, involuntarily, to verify the truth of the proverb, " He that is soon angry dealeth foolishly; and a man of wicked devices is hated." Out of the abundance of the heart he publicly declared "that he had taken more comfort in afflicting the prisoners four days than he had four years' time previous." This declaration requires no additional proof to convince every mind susceptible of the least sympathetic affection that he was possessed of no better disposition than the infernal spirits, and must be sufficient to stamp his name with infamy; and, at the same time, excite commiseration in the heart of every person who realizes it is by grace, and not by works, that he is saved from falling into the like wickedness. Nor let any man boast of his good works, knowing it is the gift of God to possess charity.

When we review this awful though faint description of the conduct of M'Kelpin, who enjoyed the advantages of civilization and was favored with the joyful tidings of "peace on earth and good will towards men," filled with anger and revenge, nature cries within us, "Curse the wretch!" But when the meekness and pity of the Savior in his dying agonies upon the shameful and accursed tree are suffered to find a place in our bosoms, we are led to cry, with him, "Father, forgive!" And though the conflict between revenge and forgiving mercy be strong, yet the latter will surely prevail whenever she is properly commanded and led by the Spirit of truth.

I would not intimate that I have the power of necromancy, or pretend to possess a spirit of divination; but, from the authority of holy writ, "this is the portion of a wicked man with God, and the heritage of oppressors, which they shall receive of the Almighty. If his children be multiplied, it is for the sword; and his offspring shall not be satisfied with bread. Those that remain of him shall be buried in death, and his widows shall not weep. Though he heap up silver as the dust, and prepare raiment as the clay, he may prepare it, but the just shall put it on, and the innocent shall divide the silver." I shall therefore leave this great disturber of peace and oppressor of the afflicted to receive from the hand of "Him, who doeth all things well," the punishment due to his wickedness, or share in the mercy offered to the truly penitent, hoping that he may have already, by deep repentance, found forgiveness, or will, before his death, if he is yet living, taste the sweetness of redeeming grace.

He tarried not long on the island, though much longer than he was desired, when another took his office whose name I do not recollect, who manifested a disposition for peace, established good order, appeared to have a regard to the laws of justice, humanity, and benevolence, restored tranquillity among the prisoners, and reconciliation between them and the guard.

Could I recollect the name of this person, I would present him to the public as a character worthy of imitation; and as "peacemakers shall be called the children of God," I think I am authorized by the Holy Scriptures to call him by that dignified and honorable title.

In the spring, complaint was made to the British provincial government against the base M'Kelpin, which resulted only in his exclusion from the service of the army with disgrace. The long and successful rebellion of the colonies had greatly exasperated the British; and M'Kelpin, being a strong adherent to their government, loyal to his majesty, and having been harshly treated for his toryism, doubtless the court by which he was tried was strongly though unjustly biased in his favor, which greatly ameliorated his punishment.

In seedtime we were allowed the privilege to sow garden seeds and plant corn. This gave us a prospect of being furnished with not only a more full supply but a greater variety of food, if it should prove our unhappy lot to be kept in confinement another winter. It also gave the prisoners an opportunity to use proper exercise to preserve health and prevent disease — a consideration of no small importance. But, disaffected by our former treatment, and fearing that the afflictions we had once received would again be laid upon us, many chose to hazard their lives by an attempt to swim down the rapids. Some thus succeeded in making their escape, while others only plunged themselves into the jaws of death.

This caused the confinement of all who were left behind. The British now set about encompassing our barracks with pickets or barricades, by setting posts in the ground adjoining each other and fastening them together.

Discovering what they were about to do, several of the prisoners, among whom I was myself one, resolved to make our endeavors to effect our escape before they had completed the barricade and encircled our camp, which would deprive us of the liberty of the island. We accordingly collected some logs together on the lower part of the island for a raft, carried some provisions for our sustenance on the way home, secreted it near the logs, and, at an hour when we supposed all were at rest, we started, but had not gone far when we espied one of the soldiers upon the bank of the river employed in dressing some fish. We then returned to our barracks. Our attempt to escape now became known to some of our fellow-prisoners by discovering our absence, who betrayed our object to our keepers, thus courting favor by the deeds of treachery. Having these suspicions, we improved an opportunity to bring back our provisions; and the next day gave proof that our suspicions were well founded, as they then went and rolled all the logs off that part of the island.

We still were determined to use every exertion and watch for an opportunity to effect our escape from confinement while we saw their labors to prevent us. We sought, but sought in vain. Time rolled away, till we found ourselves enclosed with pickets, which rendered it almost impossible to make our escape, as we were not allowed to go without this enclosure unattended by the guard, and that, too, in the daytime only.

We were allowed to go in the daytime, attended by one or two of the guard, and hoe our corn and garden roots. But this afforded us no opportunity for escape, as it was impossible to swim the current on either side of the island undiscovered by the guard or the soldiers stationed in the fort opposite the island. The prisoners, as may well be supposed, had long been very uneasy and discontented; but, as is usually the case, a sense of being confined caused still more disquietude in their minds, and excited an eager desire to be freed from bondage.

The yard which was surrounded by the pickets was about ten or fifteen rods wide and nearly forty rods long, extending lengthwise of the stream. They completed the yard some time in the month of July, 1782. Having encouragement of receiving our discharge, by exchange, often held out to us, and seeing little prospect of succeeding in the hazardous attempt to escape from our confinement, we long waited with great impatience for the approach of that desirable event, and wholly neglected to use any exertion to gain our liberty by flight. But we at length perceived that their object in giving us repeated encouragement of being exchanged was only to dally us with the fond hopes of soon seeing better days, and thus amuse our minds with fancied prospects, while they should be enabled to rivet our chains or privately assassinate some undistinguished number of us. Of this design we had abundant proof, or at least of a disposition to abuse their power by rendering it subservient to the most despicable actions and wicked purposes; for, finding one of the prisoners alone in the evening, a gang of them took him, put a rope round his neck, threatening to stab him to the heart if he made any noise, and were about to hang him, when one of the company, staring him in the face, with a tone of disappointment cried out, "O, this is not the one!" They then took the rope off his neck and let him go.

This manifested to the prisoners either a determination among the guard to waylay some of us, or a wish to trifle with their authority by creating fear in our minds and thus torment the afflicted.

As we were sensible that the guard, if disposed, which we little doubted, might assassinate one or more of the prisoners, and, consigning the body to the waters of the river, keep the transaction hid from the knowledge of any person who should not be engaged in the horrid deed, we were led ever afterwards to take the precaution never to be found alone in the dark unarmed with a large scalping knife, which we kept in our camp, and which served as a dagger and weapon of defence against a violent attack of nocturnal enemies. Having long been flattered with the prospect of soon being set at liberty, and discovering an intention among the guard privately to assassinate some unknown number of us, we resolved to make another attempt to effect our escape, and thus free ourselves from their brutal tyranny and unhallowed pretences.

We had once paid several dollars to one of the guard to suffer us to pass through the gate, should he find an opportunity; but never had the good fortune even to see him again.

The plan we adopted was in itself extremely precarious as to its success, and afforded so little encouragement, even to those who seemed to be most anxious to obtain their freedom, that few would engage in the enterprise, believing it would be a fruitless attempt to obtain our object, which would only cost us pain and bring upon us more sore trials and far greater afflictions.

Had we been confined upon the main land, where liberty from the prison would have afforded us a chance to retreat from danger, though we should be obliged even to pass the gates of a city surrounded with enemies, having our hands bound in irons and our feet fettered with chains, yet our prospects of success in our attempt to escape had still been brighter than now presented to our view; for then our deliverance from prison might have given us a passport to the wilderness free from danger; but now our freedom from those walls of wretchedness incurred the penalty of death, which was annexed to our escape if overtaken, and brought us to "troubled waters," which seemed to promise death inevitable to all who should attempt to pass the current even with well-fitted boats; while we had nothing in our power but logs, fastened together with ropes.

Our plan was, to dig a passage under ground that should extend beyond the pickets, which stood about twenty feet from the barracks. It had been our practice during the summer to hang up blankets around the bunks in which we slept, to prevent the flies from troubling us while we reposed upon our couch in the daytime.

We now again hung up the blankets around one of our bunks in a corner of the room, though not to prevent being disturbed by flies, but to hide ourselves from the face of "serpents that will bite without enchantment; and a babbler, which is no better."

Fearing the consequence of making our object known to the prisoners generally, we determined to keep it a profound secret to all except the number who belonged to our room, consisting of twelve. Accordingly, we took up the floor, both of the bunk and barrack, and commenced digging. If any of our fellow-prisoners or the guard happened to come in while one was at work, others would drown the noise of his digging by making some noise with a stick or with their feet, which was easily done without being suspected of the design.

We dug in a perpendicular direction deep enough to have a horizontal course leave the earth between the barracks and the pickets, of sufficient depth to render it safe for the guard to travel over the hole without breaking through. As they had dug a ditch along the back side of the barracks between them and the pickets in order to bank up the walls of the barracks, it became necessary for us to dig a perpendicular course of considerable depth before we could dig horizontally, to prevent any person who might chance to travel in the ditch from breaking in and discovering our plan.

We had no other tool to dig with except a large jackknife; nor, indeed, could we use any other instrument with any advantage when we came to dig in a horizontal line. And, like the animal that makes his abode in the bosom of the earth by digging a subterraneous passage to his gloomy cell, after we had dug a quantity of earth loose, so that we had no room to dig more, we returned backwards, drawing or scraping the dirt we had dug with our hands and arms, which we put under the floor of the barracks.

Our progress, as must readily be perceived, was very slow; though some one of us kept constantly digging except in the hours of sleep and time of taking refreshment, alternately following each other in our turns;.having a dress prepared for the purpose which each one wore while at work in this dreary cavern, where we were groping in darkness at noonday. Here we had an opportunity to reflect upon our wretched condition, while our labor itself witnessed our sufferings and discontentment. Here we could perceive the comparative state of him who spiritually "walketh in darkness and hath no light." Here it might, indeed, with propriety be said that silence wept. We succeeded, however, in the prosecution of our design extremely well, finding no obstacle in our way till we had dug under the ditch before mentioned, when a heavy rain fell and filled the ditch full of water, which soaked through the ground into our subterraneous way and filled the hole we had dug completely full. This was truly a great misfortune, which dampened the feelings of every one who had been engaged in the arduous undertaking.

As we had dug considerable distance and advanced nearly to the pickets, had toiled with diligence and expended much labor, we were unwilling to relinquish the task and submit to the idea of continuing in bondage another winter. And we were the more anxious to pursue the undertaking and effect our escape, because the infamous M'Daniel, of whom I have spoken, had now returned and resumed his command over us, which gave us greater reason to fear that we should again be compelled to undergo those tortures which he had once inflicted.

But it now became impossible any longer to keep the matter secret as we had done. We therefore made known our object to all the prisoners who were stationed in our line of barracks; and, receiving their universal and respective promises not to divulge the secret to any of the prisoners who were stationed in the other line of barracks, — although few would assist us, considering it labor in vain, — we resolved to persevere in the plan, and, if possible, effect our escape.

We now commenced dipping out the water into a barrel, which we emptied into a ditch that was made to convey our wash water from the barracks into the river. We dipped six barrels' full and emptied it into the ditch, besides a considerable quantity which we put into a clay pit under the barracks where they dug clay for their chimneys; and still there was much left in our way.

The guard, no doubt, supposed we were washing, or they would have suspected us. Nor yet can I account for their stupidity while they saw we were in possession of such a quantity of water, which we brought out of, without carrying into, our barracks.

We were now obliged to lie half buried in mud and water while digging, which chilled our bodies, benumbed our senses, and depressed our spirits.

To prevent being discovered, when we returned from our toil we were under the necessity of washing ourselves in a large tub of water, which we had also placed behind our blankets that were hung up around our bunk; as we now were forced, on account of the mud, to enter upon our subterraneous labor entirely naked. Vain would be the attempt to give a description of my feelings while at work in this dreary cavern, twenty feet under ground, wholly without clothing, half buried in mud, and struggling for liberty.

I was removed from all my friends and relatives the distance of more than three hundred miles, and placed upon an island in the river, on both sides of which the water moved over the ragged rocks with such velocity as to appear white to the eye like a foaming billow, not less than three miles in length. Here I was confined within the power, and exposed to the envy, malice, and resentment, of an implacable enemy. Shrouded in darkness, in the heart of the earth where light was unapproachable, my body lay in the mire, and my mind

21 *

was overwhelmed with sorrow. If we refrained from digging, we seemed to be threatened with death on every side; and if we continued to dig, our prospect appeared as melancholy as the grave. Fear and trouble were before us; while our absence from the barracks exposed us to the danger of having our plan discovered, which would be sure to bring upon us the most awful tortures, and perhaps even death itself. We chose, however, rather to hazard our lives in an attempt to escape, though doubtful of success, than to risk the consequences of remaining in confinement.

When we arrived to the picket we found it was placed upon a large stone. We then dug to the right, where we found another, which formed an angle with the first. Then, turning to the left, we also found a third. All which seemed to discourage my fellow-laborers, and led them entirely to give up the object. But, being in perfect health and in good spirits myself, I went in with a determination to remove one of these obstacles, if possible, before I returned. We had, by this time, made quite a large cavern near the pickets, which gave me considerable chance to work. After laboring in this cold, dismal place during the space of two hours, I succeeded in removing one of the stones out of the way, and, to my great joy, found that the picket was hollow up a few inches above the ground, which emitted light into this before gloomy but now delightful place. I could verily say with Solomon, "Truly the light is sweet; and a pleasant thing it is to behold the sun."

I then returned and informed my fellow-prisoners of my success, which occasioned transports of joy, raised the desponding, encouraged the faithless, confirmed the doubting, and put new vigor in every breast.

The work was now prosecuted in earnest and soon completed. Animated at the prospect of gaining our liberty, the one who dug last undesignedly broke through the ground and rendered the hole visible to any person who should happen to

pass on the outside of the pickets. It now became necessary
to devise a plan to secrete the hole from the observation of
the guard. To effect this, Mr. Belknap, one of our fellow-
prisoners, went to the guard, and, in a dissembling tone, represented to M'Daniel the little prospect we had of being
exchanged; that we had long been flattered, and as long
waited with anxious expectation, for the approach of such
a happy event, but, finding ourselves disappointed, were
forced to abandon all hopes of deliverance by exchange that
fall; that, under these considerations, the prisoners were resolved to be contented during their confinement on the island
till they should find themselves actually set at liberty, when
all their hopes would be swallowed up in the full fruition of
the object we had so long sought. Consequently we desired
the indulgence of an opportunity to secure all our garden
seeds, some of which, such as lettuce and mustard, were then
ripe and fit to harvest, that we might be enabled to supply
ourselves with the like articles the ensuing year, should it be
our unhappy case to remain on the island another season.

Pleased with the idea that the prisoners were resolved to
be submissive to his requirements, he readily ordered one of
the guard to go and attend us while we gathered our lettuce
and mustard, whose duty it was to see that no one absconded.
Having cut and tied up in small bundles these vegetables, we
proceeded to hang them up so as to fill the space between the
pickets, and also place them over the hole we had dug, to
hide our escape from the sight of the sentinel, who walked
over the hole between the pickets and the barracks in which
we were stationed. This we accomplished while our unsuspecting attendant was lounging about at a distance from us.

Here we beheld an example of selfishness, discontentment,
fear, and deception, actually assuming the appearance of hon-
esty, contentment, and submission.

Knowing that we must separate ourselves into small companies and take different rafts, in order to render our passage

down the rapids more safe, we now made choice of our associates to pass the dangerous scene before us. I associated myself with William Clark, of Virginia, John Sprague, of Ballston, New York, and Simeon Belknap, of Randolph, Vermont. We had prepared some food for our sustenance on the way by taking a quantity of flour and mixing it with melted butter, which we put into a small bag made for the purpose. We also had a little salt pork and bread, together with some parched corn and black pepper.

Those of us who had been engaged in digging had previously furnished ourselves with ropes, by cutting our blankets into strings and twisting them together; while those who had believed our attempt to be vain and foolish had neither provided themselves with provisions, ropes, or materials for a raft, and were, therefore, unable to improve the opportunity which now presented to effect their escape.

But they could not forbear collecting in small companies and whispering together to devise plans for escape, which raised suspicions in the minds of the guard that the prisoners were entering into some plot either to make their escape or to raise a mutiny in the camp. Under these apprehensions, which took rise from no other source but from the conduct of those who had been made privy to our undertaking, and would neither assist us in the work nor prepare themselves to make their escape, M'Daniel ordered that, "if any prisoner should be found attempting to make his escape or be guilty of any misconduct that night, he should not be spared alive."

We commenced digging on the 24th of August, 1782; and having dug a passage under ground the distance of twenty-two feet and a half with no other tool but a jackknife, on the night of the 10th of September following, after waiting till nine o'clock, when the roll was called and all was still, we tied our ropes to our packs and crawled out, drawing our packs after us. I was preceded by six of my fellow-prisoners, who, after crawling through the hole, which was nearly half filled with mud, made a path in the grass, as they crawled down the banks of the river, which resembled that of a log having been drawn through the mud.

The moon shone bright. The sentinel was walking directly across the hole just as I was about to crawl out, when he cried out, "All's well!" Thought I, "Be it so; continue the cry, if you please." My head at this time was not more than a yard from his feet. I crawled on, and was followed by about twenty more, who were our fellow-laborers.

As we had been allowed to go out of our enclosure in the daytime to hoe our corn and garden roots and get our wood, attended by one of the guard, we had improved the opportunity, and selected some logs for a raft to which we could go without difficulty. Clark, Belknap, Sprague, and myself now separated ourselves from the rest of the prisoners and remained together, sharing equally in all the sufferings through which we were called to pass.

We took a large scalping knife with us and a pocket compass, together with a tinder box and fireworks. We rolled a large log into the river on the upper part of the north side of the island, on each side of which we placed another; then, putting sticks across both ends of them, underneath and on the upper side, opposite each other, we tied all of them together with our blanket ropes, and fastening our packs thereon, which contained our provision, &c., we then sat one on each corner and set sail down the rapids.

Death in its most frightful form now seemed to threaten us, and the foaming billows pointed us to a watery grave. Guided only by the current, sometimes floating over rocks, sometimes buried in the water, with little hope of again being carried out alive, we passed down the raging stream with the greatest rapidity imaginable, clinging to our logs respectively, sensible that, under the guidance of divine Providence, our only ground of hope rested in our adhesion to the raft.

We passed down the river about nine miles, when we were

enabled to reach shore. We landed on the north side of the river about two hours before day, with not a dry thread in our clothes, chilled with the cold and trembling with fear. Our bread had all washed to a jelly and been rendered wholly unfit to eat. None of our provision remained fit to carry with us except a little parched corn, which was in a small, wooden bottle, some salt pork, and our buttered flour, which we found to be waterproof. Our compass was also rendered useless; which was indeed a great misfortune to us, as the want of it protracted our journey through the woods many days. We marched up the river till daybreak, when we discovered that we were near the fort opposite the island. We then turned north into the woods, which led us into a swamp, where we encamped under some old tree tops that had fallen together, about one mile from the fort, which formed no shelter from rain, but merely hid us from our expected pursuers. We plainly heard the report of the alarm guns on the morning of the 11th of September, which announced to us the discovery of what had cost us great pains, and evinced, to all who should behold the place, our love of liberty and resolution to obtain it.

We remained under these tree tops three days and two nights without going ten rods from the place, having nothing to eat but salt pork, parched corn, and our buttered flour, together with a few kernels of black pepper; for the want of which last I think we must have perished, as it rained with a mixture of snow every day and night sufficiently to keep us completely wet all the time.

Having been so harshly treated by the British, and knowing that "confidence in an unfaithful man in time of trouble is like a broken tooth and a foot out of joint," we resolved to make ourselves known to no one; and like the Ishmaelites of old, while we had reason to suppose that every man's hand was against us, we were determined to put our own hands against every man who should come in our way.

Destitute of food sufficient to supply us through the long woods we were to pass to reach our homes, we were determined to replenish our stores before we crossed the River St. Lawrence, as there were but few settlements on the south side of the river in that part of the country. We were, therefore, under the necessity of staying about there till they had done searching for us.

On the night of the third day after our escape we ventured to take up our march, and travelled till we came to a stream which we supposed emptied into the River St. Lawrence at the fort; but we afterwards found it to be only a branch of that stream. I waded into it, and found it was so deep that we could not ford it. I therefore returned, and we encamped for the night. Our sufferings this night were almost insupportable; as it was a cold, frosty night, and we were wholly exposed, having nothing about us except what was completely wet, without a shelter, and destitute of fire.

On the morning of the 14th, benumbed and chilled with the cold, we found a place where we forded the stream, and travelled till we came to another; and by mistaking the former, we supposed this to empty itself into the river above the fort. We followed the current of this stream till about dark, when we came in sight of a settlement. After waiting till about nine o'clock at night we ventured to approach a little nearer, when to our utter astonishment we heard the drum beat, which gave us assurance that we were near the fort. Finding ourselves so near, we concluded to cross the stream at the nearest fording-place. In passing off we went through the commanding officer's garden; and I pulled up a hill of his potatoes and carried them along with me.

We then went into the road and followed up the River St. Lawrence about four miles. We had not proceeded far, however, before we came to a boat lying at anchor in the river, near the shore. I waded in towards it till I heard men in it snoring in their sleep, when I quickly made my retreat. We then went on till we came to the house of a Frenchman, as we supposed by his speech, who, just as we came up, opened the door and hailed us. Turning into his lot, we went to his barn and endeavored to find some creature to kill. We found one cow. As we were approaching towards her, two large dogs came at us with great rage, and, barking most furiously, appeared to be determined to bite us. The old Frenchman again came to the door and hailed us. Fearing that soldiers might be quartered there, we retreated as fast as we could, keeping an eye upon the dogs, and swinging our staves at them to keep them from biting us, while the old Frenchman was trying to set them on. The ground was descending as we retreated; and while we were all moving together very fast, having our eyes partially turned upon the dogs, we ran against a fence, slightly laid up, and threw down many lengths, which made such a rattling that it terrified the dogs and immediately put them upon their retreat, as much affrighted as they had been outrageous.

Trembling for our safety, we kept in the fields back of the street; while the dogs continued their barking as if determined to arouse our enemies from their slumbers and cause us to be taken. They succeeded, at least, in exciting all the dogs in the neighborhood to engage in the general alarm, and seemed anxious to maintain a constant echo in the surrounding atmosphere. They were busily employed at every house, and sometimes in great earnest, as we passed along the distance of several miles.

At length we came to a number of cattle in a field not far from the road, among which we found a two-year-old heifer, very tame and in good flesh.

We had long been lurking about, waiting for the agitation of the public mind to abate, that we might have opportunity to obtain some provision before we entered into the wide wilderness through which we were expecting to pass; and as the favored moment had now arrived, we agreed that Belknap

should go in search of a boat to convey us over the Lake St.
Francis, near which we found the cattle; that Sprague should
stand with our scalping knife to defend against every foe;
while Clark and myself should kill the heifer and procure a
quantity of meat.  By the help of a little salt I soon succeeded in catching the heifer; and, taking her by the horns
and nose, I instantly flung her down, when Clark cut her
throat with a large jackknife; and, not waiting for her to die
or even spending time to skin her, we took off a gammon and
left her bleeding.  Belknap had now returned and informed
us that he had found a boat, to which we immediately resorted,
carrying with us our unskinned beef, the booty we had desired for many days, leaving the owner of the heifer to seek
his recompense where he could find it; willing, however, he
should share with us in his beef by taking what we left.

We were not insensible that, if he were a British subject, we
had abundantly compensated his loss to his government by
our own starvation; or, if he were a friend to the unfortunate,
he could not lament his loss, since he had thus far contributed
to feed the hungry without even knowing what his right hand
did.  Nor, indeed, did we trouble ourselves, while we rumi-
nated upon the affair, concerning what might be the cogitations
of the owner; since we had obtained the meat, and thus answered our own purpose.

Having entered the boat with all our baggage, the moon
shining bright, we set out upon the lake, steering for the south
shore.  We had advanced but little distance when a breeze
arose from the north-west and drifted us ahead with great
violence, every wave dashing the water into our boat.

It now became necessary that two of us should dip the
water from our boat with our hats as fast as possible, while
the other two rowed for the shore with the greatest exertion.
The wind increased.  The boat was fast filling in spite of all
we could do.  Every wave, to human view, brought us by
rapid strides to the arms of death and presented to us a

watery grave. But, through the wonderful goodness of the great Preserver of men, we succeeded in landing just as our boat had filled with water. Having fastened it to the shore we went into the woods, struck up a fire, skinned our beef and cut it into thin slices, which we partially roasted on sticks by the fire, and then lay down to sleep. This was the first time we had been to any fire since we left Prison Island. We had lain secreted in bushes and old tree tops; wandered in the darkness of the night, exposed to the inclemency of the weather; forded streams of water up to our necks, constantly and completely wet; hungry, and chilled with cold; filled with fear and anxiety for our safety during the space of four days and five nights, including the night in which we made our escape.

Destruction and misery often appeared in our way. Death frequently stared us in the face, threatening to make us his prey, but seemed to be held from falling upon us by the finger of God.

On the morning of the 15th of September, (the fifth day after we escaped,) supposing we had landed upon an island, we began to seek how we should get off without being discovered by the inhabitants on the northern shores of the lake or by those who might happen to be upon the waters. Happily. we found, by travelling into the woods, that we were upon a peninsula, joined to the main land by an isthmus not more than eight or ten feet wide. This was a circumstance greatly in our favor, as we should otherwise have been under the necessity of exposing ourselves to the view of our enemies, or waiting for the night to cover our escape.

We now set out, directing our course nearly south-east, for the American fort at Pittsford, a town situated on Otter Creek, in the western part of the State of Vermont.

Our companion, Mr. Clark, had been much accustomed to travelling in the woods, having been engaged in the business of surveying in the western part of the United States at the time he was taken by the Indians. We therefore cnose him to be our leader through the wilderness and our pilot to a more favored country.

We travelled all the first day over low, marshy land, timbered with cedar, but were unable to find any water to drink either in running brooks or by digging; for the want of which we suffered much, being thirsty as well as hungry, and greatly fatigued. Wishing to escape the vigilance of our expected pursuers, we travelled with great speed, which, together with our living on flesh alone, doubtless occasioned a far greater degree of thirst than we should have felt had we been supplied with bread. The next day we found water in great plenty. We crossed many streams of considerable size; some by fording, although of such depth as to reach to our shoulders: others we crossed by making a small raft sufficient to bear one of us with our baggage; while the other three stripped, and, hanging by one hand to the raft, swam by her side.

After wandering in the wilderness during the space of ten days, — sometimes progressing on our journey, sometimes lounging in suspense, doubting which course to take, and waiting for the clouds to be dispelled, that the sun might appear to enlighten our path and guide our way, — we arrived at Lake Champlain with our clothes nearly torn from our bodies, emaciated with hunger and fatigued with the daily toil and long deprivation of the comforts of civilized life. During these ten days we saw no other human being, nor heard his voice, beheld his footsteps, or the works of his hand. We lived almost wholly on flesh, like the carnivorous race, and, like them, reposed upon the ground, equally fearing the face of man, suspicious of his design, and dreading his approach as we did the instrument of death.

While we one day lay encamped by the fire, waiting for the appearance of the sun, we were aroused from our sleep by the supposed report of a musket. Ignorant of the source whence it came, and fearing to make immediate flight lest we should flee into the hands of our enemies, we prepared ourselves to march, and were endeavoring to espy the foe, when a similar noise, proceeding from the bursting of a stone heated by the fire, relieved our minds from fear, and filled our bosoms with joy at the happy disappointment of expected danger.

Soon after we arrived at Lake Champlain we found a part of an old flat-bottomed boat, which we fitted up, for the purpose of conveying us across the lake, by lashing a log on each side with bark and withs.

At about sunset we went aboard and set sail to cross the lake. We had proceeded nearly half way across, when the wind arose against us and baffled all our exertions to proceed farther. After laboring till about midnight without success, and fearing we should be taken by the British if we remained on the water till light, we concluded to row back to the shore we left and relinquish the idea of crossing the lake that night. We had continued upon the water till a tempest arose, and the wind blew from various directions, shifting its course every few minutes; and our strength had become almost exhausted, being faint for want of food, insomuch that we could hardly move. We labored with diligence and with all our might till daybreak, having nothing to use for oars except such sticks as we found in the woods and prepared for the purpose with a jackknife. We were now enabled to reach the same shore from which we started, though several miles farther north. Our clothes were completely wet, and our strength so far gone that neither of us could scarcely go.

In this wretched state, stupefied and chilled with the cold, so faint and tired that we could hardly move, we crept a few rods into the woods, built a fire, and laid down upon the ground.

I never suffered so much fatigue, in the same space of time in my life, as I did this night; nor would I have believed I could endure as much, with so little strength, without perishing. Language is too feeble to express, nor can imagination conceive, the sufferings we underwent.

We had but little provision left, and were compelled to curtail our former allowance, so that we should be enabled to subsist and continue our journey till we could reach the desired country.

Having rested from the wearisome and fruitless labors of the night till nearly sunset the next day, we resolved to travel on the west side of the lake till we should come to a narrow place where we could well hope for success in an attempt to cross. We resumed our march and travelled a few miles that night, then camped down and waited for the morning.

The next day we came to the River Saranac, which empties into Lake Champlain at a place now called Plattsburg, in the State of New York. We heard the noise of the British engaged in chopping a few rods up the river, while we crossed it between them and the lake, not far from its mouth.

After we crossed the river we travelled a small distance and encamped for the night in a valley which was in the form of a basin. We followed up the lake upon the western shore; crossed Duck Creek, River-au-Sable, Salmon River, and Gilliland's Creek; when we came to a place called Split Rock, where the lake is narrow, which afforded us a prospect of succeeding if we attempted to cross. We then went to work to build a raft, and while engaged, a little before sunset, espied a British armed vessel making towards us from the south. We went into the bushes and lay secreted from their view, though they were so visible to us that we could see their red coats, and even count the buttons upon them, while they sailed around at a small distance from us, apparently for amusement, and then returned again to the south, out of our sight, without discovering us.

We then went to work, completed our raft at dark, set sail across the lake, and safely landed in a few hours at a place now called Charlotte, in the State of Vermont. We were, however, ignorant at that time both of the name of the place

22 *

and of its local situation. Being yet in a strange wilderness, we knew not which way to direct our course to reach inhabitants. Indeed, all that prompted us to go forward was the information we had received that there were settlements near some part of this lake. But we were wholly ignorant what way to take that should enable us to find them. Supposing ourselves to be between the mouth of Onion River and Otter Creek, we concluded to steer in a south-east direction, which we supposed would bring us to Pittsford Fort. We travelled into the woods a few rods and lay down for the night. In the morning we resumed our march, and had not gone far before we came to an old log house, which had long been abandoned, and, by the long continuance of the war, had become greatly decayed.

We however found a few beans, which had probably been there a number of years, and were covered with mould. As our provision was mostly gone and we were extremely hungry, we took and parched them, as we would corn, by the fire, which gave some relish to the twigs, roots, and berries that had already, for some days, composed our principal food.

Our clothes were almost torn from our mangled bodies by the bushes, logs, and trees; and the blood that gushed from our naked and wornout feet witnessed, in every track we made, the pains we suffered.

Parts of our stockings still remained about our feet; and, having a needle (but no thread) with us, we ravelled off the tops of them and sewed our tattered rags together as much as possible, to defend our bodies from the inclemency of the weather.

Our daily allowance of the food we brought with us from Prison Island was now reduced to about an inch square of salt pork and as much of our buttered flour as we could twice put upon the point of a large jackknife. We had eaten all our beef and parched corn.

We dug roots of various kinds and ate them, together with

birch and other twigs.  Spikenard roots, which we roasted by
the fire, comprised the greatest part of our subsistence.  We
found several small frogs, which we killed and ate with great
delight.  But we could find only a few of them, though we
searched diligently.  Their meat tasted exceedingly sweet and
delicious.  We also found means to catch several small fish
from a little rivulet which we crossed; but could not obtain
more than two or three, although we spent much time and
used every exertion in our power.

Some time after we had dressed our fish and had advanced
considerable distance, we espied a bear upon a tree a few rods
ahead of us.  We hastened to the foot of the tree, in view of
killing her, as she descended, by stabbing her with our large
scalping knife.  But, on examination, we found the knife was
left at the place of dressing the fish, which frustrated our plan
and blighted our hopes of obtaining any meat.

Disappointment was now added to hunger and distress, and
our faint and wearied bodies were hardly able to support the
dreadful weight of sorrow which hung over our minds.

We however continued to keep a south-east course till we
reached the top of the mountains lying between Onion River
and Otter Creek, when, looking back, we could see the lake
in fair view.  Being so faint for want of food that we could
hardly step, and seeing no prospect of obtaining any, it
seemed as if death must be our inevitable fate.  We had
travelled seven or eight days, and had subsisted the whole
time mostly upon the spontaneous productions of the country.
The season for berries was nearly gone, though we were able
to find some.

Our natures seemed to waste away and leave nothing but
death to stare us in the face.  Winter was fast approaching,
while we were almost naked, destitute, and forlorn.  O the
wretched condition of those whose lot it is to be cast into the
wilderness and left to wander upon the dark mountains of
despair!  I could feelingly adopt the language of Job, and

say, "Terrors are turned upon me: they pursue my soul as
the wind; and my welfare passeth away as a cloud. When
I looked for good, then evil came unto me; and when I
waited for light, there came darkness. I am a brother to
dragons and a companion to owls; for I have eaten ashes
like bread and mingled my drink with weeping."

Had we seen any prospect of soon finding the house of a
friend, or of obtaining provision in any other way before we
should arrive among inhabitants, we could not have denied
ourselves at once to eat the little provision we had in our
packs while we suffered so much by hunger on our way.

The barren mountains and rocky cliffs of Bristol, Ripton,
and Hancock, the dismal plain of Chataugua, and the waters
of Champlain witnessed the cries of our sufferings; while our
steps traced in blood the distress we endured.

We wandered from mountain to mountain and from valley
to valley, keeping at a distance from the lake, lest we should
fall into the hands of the British, who had command of the
lake at that time. Sorrow, hunger, and bitterness of soul
were our constant attendants through the day; and the approach of the night only increased our miseries and multiplied our sighs and groanings.

Though we slept, it was for trouble; and if we continued to
roam the wilderness we found no comfort, and our strength
failed. If we slumbered, it was upon the brink of the grave,
and it would not feed us. While our hunger increased, our
hopes of relief grew dim.

Seeing no prospect of ever finding the habitations of friends,
our companions, Clark and Sprague, like the lepers of old,
"said one to another, Why sit we here until we die?" If we
say we will pursue our journey, "we shall die; and if we sit
still here, we die also." They therefore resolved to return to
the lake if they could get there, and deliver themselves up
into the hands of the British.

They were both possessed of true courage, and a noble,

generous spirit. But they were wholly ignorant of the country east of Lake Champlain, and consequently had less to encourage them than Belknap and myself. They were "unwilling," said they, " that we should either return or remain with them, if we could ever reach inhabitants. But to go forward was apparent death, even if inhabitants might be found by two or three days' travel; as we are so weak we can hardly go, and still growing weaker." They requested us to leave them to be food for wild beasts or a prey to an exasperated foe. But the tender feelings of human sensibility forbade us to leave them; and Belknap and myself persuaded them to persevere and remain with us to the end by dealing out to them an extra allowance of provision, on condition that I should take the lead and be their pilot; to which I consented.

It being nearly night, we encamped till morning, when we concluded to change our course and steer nearly a south-south-westerly direction. We travelled on moderately, fearful of the event, till about noon, when, being some rods forward of my companions, I was so fortunate as to come to a road. Of this I notified my languishing companions, famishing with hunger and groaning under the weight of their wretchedness, which occasioned transports of joy, gladdened their hearts, and invigorated their bodies; yea, it " shed happiness around us and banished misery before us." For we could say with David, that we had " wandered in the wilderness, in a solitary way, and found no city to dwell in. Hungry and thirsty, our souls fainted within us. Then we cried unto the Lord in our trouble, and he delivered us out of our distresses; and he led us forth by the right way, that we might go to a city of habitation."

Animated with the prospect of soon finding inhabitants, we travelled on the road with joy and delight. Our hopes of again seeing our friends became brightened, and our expectations greatly strengthened our weak and trembling limbs. We soon came in sight of an old horse, and an old mare with a sucking colt by her side. As they were in a valley some distance from the road, we concluded not to go after them, hoping soon to find inhabitants, where we should be enabled also to find friends, who would lend the hand of charity. We therefore travelled on, and soon came to a stream, but could not determine whether it was Otter Creek or only a branch of it. If it were a branch, we knew we ought to follow the current till we came to the creek. But to follow the current of the creek itself would lead us directly to the lake, where we should be exposed to the British.

We however thought it most prudent to follow down the stream, and soon came to its mouth, and still were left in doubt whether the stream into which the first we discovered emptied itself was Otter Creek or some other branch.

As it began to draw near sunset, and seeing no prospect of finding inhabitants that night, we resolved to return to the place where we came to the first stream, having there found the walls of an old log house. Clark and myself went and procured the horses and colt; while Belknap and Sprague struck up a fire and built a camp.

Having returned with the horses and confined them in the old log house, we killed and dressed the colt and roasted some of the meat upon sticks by the fire and ate it; and surely " it was pleasant to the taste." Indeed, I never ate any meat of so delicious a flavor, although without bread, salt,* or sauce of any kind.

The next morning we started with our old horse and coltless mare, and travelled till after the middle of the day, when we came to the place we passed about noon the day preceding. We were confident it was the same place, by finding some spikenard roots which we had thrown away soon after we found the road.

---

* We brought a small quantity of salt from Prison Island, but lost the principal part of it in passing down the rapids. The remainder we gave to the heifer we killed, and took her gammon in exchange.

Being lost, and knowing not whether to turn to the right hand or to the left, having obtained a new supply of meat, by which we had been much refreshed, and as the sun had been invisible to us for several days, we concluded to tarry there through the day and encamp for the night, hoping the sun would rise clear the next morning, which would enable us the better to determine what course to take.

While we were patrolling about the fields, which appeared to have been unoccupied and but partially cultivated during the long war, we found a large yard of turnips.

We then prepared our camp, built a fire, and, having procured some turnips, kept continually roasting them successively during the night, first sleeping a little and then eating; thus alternately refreshing ourselves by sleep and eating cold meat with roasted turnips till the approach of day. As we had long lived upon the spontaneous growth of the wilderness, and had not only been almost entirely destitute of bread and meat, but wholly deprived of every cultivated vegetable, we were conscious that it would be injurious, and even dangerous, to eat immediately all we might crave for the night.

We therefore chose to satiate our hunger in a measure by piecemeals, while we truly feasted upon that kind of fare which was undoubtedly, of all kinds of food, the best adapted to our wretched condition and craving appetites. In the morning the sky was clear, and the sun rose, to every one of us, directly in the *west*. We now discovered the cause of becoming lost; and, feeling much refreshed and strengthened, we took our horses and directed our course according to the sun, diametrically against our own ideas of the true point of compass. We had not proceeded far when we came to three other horses, which we took, leaving the old mare for the benefit of the owner.

After travelling till about noon we came to a man chopping in the woods. Seeing us all on horseback, with bark bridles and no saddles, having on coats made of Indian blan-

kets, which were all in rags, with beards an inch long, and
each one of us armed with a cudgel, the trembling wood-
cutter stood in dreadful awe, with his axe raised above his
shoulder, dreading our approach, but fearing to try his success in an attempt to escape; while we drew near, rejoicing
that we had once more arrived where we could behold the
face of one whose hand should not be against us, and against
whom we were not compelled for our safety to put our own
hands.

We were not much surprised, though very sorry, to find our
friend so grievously alarmed while we only desired his friendship. We informed him of our wretched condition, and be-
sought him to be our friend, with tears of joy and tenderness
trickling down our emaciated cheeks. Finding we were not
his enemies, but the subjects of his pity and tender compassion, bursting into tears of sympathy at the short relation we
gave him of our sufferings, he invited us to go with him and
he would lead us to Pittsford Fort, which was only about one
mile distant, where we should be made welcome to every thing
necessary for our comfort.

We soon arrived at the fort. It was now about one o'clock
in the afternoon. We were received with the greatest marks
of sympathy and commiseration and treated with every
respect due to our wretchedness and want. And though
justice demands that I should acknowledge the generous display of philanthropic zeal, as well as selfish curiosity, common on such occasions, yet I could not forbear to notice
with pain that cold indifference for the miseries of others,
commonly observable in those who have long been familiar
with scenes of wretchedness and woe, which was manifested
by some, and especially by the commander of the fort, on our
arrival at that place.

Not long after we arrived at the fort the owners of the horses
came up, carrying their saddles upon their backs. They
had been out for the purpose of surveying land, and had turned

out their horses to feed. After hearing a short account of our sufferings and being made acquainted with our deplorable condition, they readily replied, with seeming compassion, that they were only sorry we had not been so fortunate as to find their saddles likewise.

After wandering in the wilderness twenty-two days, we arrived at the fort on the 2d day of October, 1782, having forded rivers of water up to our shoulders; traversing through dismal swamps, the habitations of beasts of prey; and climbing mountains of rocks, where no human eye could pity or friends console us; making the earth our bed of repose for the night, and extreme anxiety our constant companion through the day; nearly starved, and almost naked; little expecting ever again to see the faces of our friends or to behold those habitations which witnessed our juvenile years, where we enjoyed the kind embraces of tender and affectionate mothers and the paternal care of indulgent fathers; expecting every day to see the approach of that hour when our spirits should be called to leave our bodies in a howling wilderness to become food for wild beasts, and our friends to lament our absence, ignorant of our end. After enduring all this, yea, more than pen can describe or language express, who can tell our joy and gratitude when we came to behold a "city of habitation" and the abodes of plenty? What heart would not palpitate for exceeding great joy at such an event? Who could forbear to speak forth praise to the great Preserver of men on such an occasion? Would not every heart, susceptible of the least impression, acknowledge the hand of the Almighty in so great a deliverance?

Instead of making our bed upon the cold ground, with our clothes wet and our bodies benumbed, we could now enjoy sweet repose by the fireside, sheltered from storms and surrounded with friends. Instead of feeding upon frogs and the spontaneous growth of uncultivated nature, subsisting on roots, twigs, and bark, we could now taste the fruits of labor and industry, and feast upon the bounties of Heaven. Instead of wandering through a lonely wilderness, with our cheeks wet with tears of sorrow, almost overwhelmed with despair, we could now travel through a country of civilization free from enemies, and receive support from the hand of charity.

After sharing in the benevolence of many individuals, and receiving every token of friendship from the garrison at the fort, as they were expecting soon to be attacked by the British, we were advised to travel on still farther that night, that we might be the more safe from the grasp of the enemy.

We therefore proceeded on towards Rutland several miles, when we obtained lodgings in the house of a "poor widow," who furnished us with the best food her house afforded, of which we ate heartily. Having long been without bread of any kind, and being now furnished with a full supply of good wheat bread, it seemed as if we should die with the effect of eating it. It lay like lead in our stomachs, and caused us the most agonizing distress for some hours, while we rolled upon the floor with bitter groanings, although we had denied ourselves the satisfaction of eating the half of what our appetites craved. But our extreme hunger prevented the exercise of prudence and economy in the choice of that kind of food which was best adapted to our wretched condition. Nor did we wait long to consult about the propriety or impropriety of eating any thing we found within our reach. Our avidity for food, however, soon abated, when we found no injury to result from eating all we desired.

We made our escape on the night of the 10th of September, arrived at Lake Champlain in about ten days, and came to the fort on the night of the 2d of October following; having been in the wilderness twenty-two days, without speaking to any other person except our own company.* It is true,

* When the sun was invisible, having lost our compass, we directed our course by the moss upon trees, which is found only upon the

we had seen some of our species at a distance from us, though with terror and dismay, fearing their approach as we should have done that of a voracious animal ready to devour us.

In a few days we arrived at Bennington, in Bennington county, Vermont, where we were employed till we had acquired, by our own labor and the benevolence of others, some money sufficient to enable us to prosecute our journey to Connecticut.

Having travelled many days through the woods almost destitute of any covering for our feet, they had become very sore, which prevented our going far in a day.

Assisted by the hand of charity and by means of occasional labor on the way, we were enabled to reach our friends. Being destined to different places, our companions, Clark and Sprague, separated from us at Bennington. By a mutual participation of sufferings, we had acquired that affection for each other which will remain, I trust, till death. Having suffered many hardships and endured many trials together, having been rescued from many dangers and delivered out of many troubles, sharing equally in hunger, pains, and distress, as well as in the joys resulting from our deliverance, we now reluctantly parted, affectionately taking our leave, perhaps never again to see each other till we shall meet in that world where "the weary be at rest. There the prisoners rest together; they hear not the voice of the oppressor. The small and great are there; and the servant is free from his master."

And may it not be the unspeakable infelicity of either of us to fail of "entering into that rest because of unbelief."

Belknap and I continued our course together to Ellington, in Connecticut, where our friends resided. We arrived there on the 17th of October, 1782, being just two years from the day I was taken by the Indians at Randolph. What pen

---

north side. In passing over land timbered with cedar, which has no moss upon it, we were compelled to lie still and wait the appearance of the sun, which protracted our journey many days.

can describe the mutual joy which was felt by parents and children on our arrival? Truly our fathers, "seeing us while yet a great way off, ran and fell upon our necks and kissed us." Behold now the affection of a father. See him shed the tear of compassion. Hear him say, "This my son was dead, and is alive again; he was lost, and is found." See him "begin to be merry;" nor think it strange that the fatted calf should be killed.

Behold a kind father in tears of joy, and a tender step-mother * kindly embracing the subject of her husband's former grief, but present delight. See "the best robe" cast around him, with "the ring upon his hand and the shoes upon his feet." See brothers and sisters surrounding the returned brother. Hear their acclamations of joy and gladness, embracing their once lost but now living brother. What heart would not melt at the sight of such a joyful scene? And what can I say to express my own feelings on this delightful interview? Having endured the hardships of an Indian captivity and the pains of the prison, the gnawings of hunger, the tortures of the rack, and the still more dreadful distress of twenty-two days' wandering in the wilderness; filled with despair, anxiety, and fear; almost starved, and nearly naked; full of wounds, and constantly chilled with the cold; imagine, kind reader, the feelings of my heart when I came to behold the face of affectionate parents and receive the tender embraces of beloved brothers and a loving sister. Think of the festivities of that evening, when I could again enjoy a seat in a social circle of friends and acquaintance around the fireside in my father's house.

Vain is the attempt to describe my own feelings on that joyful occasion. Fruitless indeed must be all my endeavors to express the mutual congratulations manifested by all on my return.

---

* My own mother died while I was quite young, and my father had married again to a woman possessing the kindest affections and the most endearing love.

My long absence from my friends, together with a sense of the numerous and awful dangers through which I had been preserved, increased our gratitude, and caused wonder and astonishment to dwell in every breast. We could now heartily unite in ascribing praise and adoration to Him who granted me protection while exposed to the shafts of hatred and revenge. I was treated with all that friendship which pity could excite or sympathy dictate, and saluted by every person I met, whether old or young, with a hearty welcome. Every one seemed to be in a good degree conscious of the extreme sufferings I had undergone. In short, my return afforded me an opportunity to witness a display of all the tender passions of the soul.

Knowing the deplorable wretchedness of those who had the misfortune to become prisoners to the British, and consequently expecting every day to hear of my death, my friends were little less astonished at my return than they would have been had they witnessed the resurrection of one from the dead.

The extreme hunger and distress I had felt were clearly manifested to those who beheld my emaciated countenance and mangled feet; and no one was disposed to doubt the truth of my words who heard me relate the affecting tale of my sore afflictions. For, " by reason of the voice of my groanings, my bones," it might verily be said, did " cleave to my skin." I however had the satisfaction to find my deep anxiety to be delivered from bondage and escape from the enemy, my ardent wishes to see my friends, and my hungry, craving appetite, wholly satisfied in the full fruition of all my toils. The munificence of the wealthy was offered for my relief, and the poor approached me with looks of tenderness and pity. All things around me wore a propitious smile. From morning till night, instead of being guarded by a company of refugees and tories, or wandering in a lonesome wilderness, hungry and destitute, I could now behold the face of friends,

and at the approach of night repose my head upon a downy
pillow, under the hospitable covert of my father's roof. Instead of being made a companion of the wretched, I could
now enjoy the sweet conversation of a beloved sister and
affectionate brothers.

Having for more than two years been deprived of hearing
the gospel sound, surely " I was glad when they said unto me,
Let us go into the house of the Lord." For unto God I could
say, " Thou art my hiding-place ; thou shalt preserve me from
trouble ; thou shalt compass me about with songs of deliverance. I will be glad and rejoice in thy name ; for thou hast
considered my trouble ; thou hast known my soul in adversity."
This I hoped would be the language of every one who made
their escape with me. For myself, I trust it was the sincere
language of my heart.

Notwithstanding the prisoners whom we left on the island
were set at liberty shortly after our escape, and although our
sufferings in the wilderness were exceedingly great, yet I
never found cause to lament that I improved the opportunity
to free myself from the hands of those cruel tormentors and
oppressors of the afflicted. For " the spirit of a man will
sustain his infirmity." And under this consideration we chose
rather to hazard the consequences of an escape, though it
might prove our death, than to become the menial servants,
and thus gratify the infernal desires, of a petty tyrant.

> " Now I feel, by proof,
> That fellowship in pain divides not smart,
> Nor lightens aught each man's peculiar load."

I have never had the satisfaction to hear from either of my
friends and fellow-sufferers, Clark and Sprague, since I parted
with them at Bennington.

Mr. Belknap now lives in Randolph, Vermont, and, from
the sad experience of the like sufferings himself and his participation in my own, can witness to the truth of my statement.

Let not the preservation of my life through such a train of dangers be attributed to mere chance; but let the praise be given to " God our Rock, and the high God our Redeemer."

In September, previous to my escape, a treaty of peace was concluded between Great Britain and the United States at Paris, the glad news of which reached America not long after my return, which occasioned the release of the remainder of the prisoners who were confined upon Prison Island.

As the war had now terminated, my return to Randolph would not be attended with the danger of being again made captive by the Indians; which induced me, the spring following, to go to that place and resume my settlement.

On my arrival there I found my house was demolished, which recalled to mind the confusion and horror of that dreadful morning when the savage tribe approached, with awful aspect, my lonely dwelling. I went to work and erected a house upon the same spot, into which my father shortly after moved his family. The grass seed which the Indians had scattered for some distance from the house, as before observed, had taken root, stocked the ground, and remained entire for many years a fresh memento of that woful event, which proved but a faint prelude of all my direful sufferings.

Here my father lived by cultivating that soil which had borne the brutal band to my unwelcome door till April, 1812, when he died at the good old age of seventy-six. Here he has spent many a winter's evening in rehearsing the mournful tale of my " captivity and sufferings " to his friends and acquaintance.

Generous and hospitable by nature, and having been taught by my sufferings to feel for the needy, he was ever ready to extend the hand of charity to relieve their distresses. His house, always the abode of plenty, was an asylum for the naked and forlorn, an acceptable home to the poor and the wretched.

Always exhibiting a sense of what sufferings I had undergone for want of food, he seemed in nothing to be more delighted than "to feed the hungry and clothe the naked." My loving and aged step-mother, with one of her sons, (a half-brother of mine,) now lives on the same farm.

In the winter of 1785 I was married to Hannah Shurtliff, of Tolland, Connecticut, and settled at Randolph not far from my father's house, where I resided eight years, when I purchased a farm and removed to Brookfield, a town adjoining.

Here I have resided until the present time, (1816,) and obtained my own subsistence and that of my numerous family by means of cultivating the soil. By a steady course of industry and economy I have been enabled, under the divine blessing, to acquire a comfortable support, and enjoy the fruits of my labors in quietude and peace. As my occupation was that of a farmer, my opportunities for information, like those of many others of my class, have been limited.

My family, not unlike Job's, consists of seven sons and three daughters; nor have I reason to think my afflictions much inferior to his. Although death has never been permitted to enter my dwelling and take any of my family, yet my substance has once been destroyed by worse than Chaldean hands, and that, too, at the very outset of my adventures in life. Not only were my house and effects destroyed, but myself, at a most unpropitious hour, when far removed from all my friends, compelled to leave my employment, relinquish all those objects of enterprise peculiar to the juvenile age, and forced to enter the ranks of a savage band and travel into an enemy's country. Thus were all my expectations cut off. My hopes were blasted and my youthful prospects darkened. "I was not in safety, neither had I rest, neither was I quiet; yet trouble came. O that my grief were thoroughly weighed, and my calamity laid in the balances together!"

Notwithstanding that inhumanity and cruelty which characterized the conduct of the savages, yet I think that the barbarous treatment which we received from the impious commanders of the British fort, in whose charge we were kept, might put to the blush the rudest savage who traverses the western wild.  Their conduct illy comported with what might be expected from men who are favored with the light of revelation.

The savage, when he does a deed of charity towards his prisoner, is no doubt less liable to be actuated by a selfish principle, and influenced by the hope of reward or by a fear of losing his reputation, than he is who has been made acquainted with the gracious reward offered to those who " do unto others as they would that others should do unto them," and knows the bitter consequences of the contrary practice.

And I think the destruction of Royalton and all its evil consequences may with less propriety be attributed to the brutal malevolence of the savage tribe than to the ignoble treachery and despicable fanaticism of certain individuals of our own nation.

Scarce can that man be found in this enlightened country who would treat his enemy with as much tenderness and compassion as I was treated by the savage tribe ; though I had abundant cause to say that the " tender mercies of the wicked are cruel."

Who would not shudder at the idea of being compelled to take up their abode with a herd of tawny savages?  Yet, alas ! when I contrasted the sufferings I endured while with the Indians with those afflictions that were laid upon me by men who had been from their youth favored with the advantages of civilization, clothed with authority, and distinguished with a badge of honor, I could truly say the former chastised me with whips, but the latter with scorpions.

An Indian captivity will hardly admit of a comparison with

my wretched condition while in the hands of the British and under the domineering power of a company of refugees and tories.

While with the Indians my food was unsavory and unwholesome; my clothing, like their own, was scant and covered with filthy vermin; and my life was always exposed to the danger of their implacable hatred and revenge. This was a most perilous condition indeed for any one to be placed in. But my confinement with the British multiplied my complaints, added to my afflictions, rendered me more exposed to the danger of losing my life, increased my sorrows, and apparently brought me near the grave. My food was less filthy; but I was not allowed the half of what my appetite craved and my nature required to render me comfortable.

By these and my subsequent afflictions I have been taught a lesson that has made an impression upon my mind which I trust will remain as long as life shall last.

I have been taught, by ocular demonstration and sad experience, the depravity of man, and the fallacy of looking for durable happiness in terrestrial things.

My own sufferings have implanted within my breast that sympathy for the distressed which is better felt than described. Nakedness and poverty have once been my companions; and I shall not readily forget to lend a listening ear to the cries of the needy.

And I would exhort myself and all my fellow-men, by the extreme sufferings I have endured, to be ready at all times to "feed the hungry and clothe the naked," nor ever fail to extend the hand of charity for the assistance of the unfortunate.

*Names of a Part of the Persons killed and taken at the Burning of Royalton.*

Zadock Steele, taken at Randolph.
Experience Davis.
Elias Curtis.
J. Parks.
Moses Parsons.
Simeon Belknap, now living in Randolph.
Samuel Pember.
Thomas Pember, killed at Royalton.
Gardner Rix, now living at Royalton.
Daniel Downer.
Joseph Kneeland, killed at the encampment at Randolph.
Jonathan Brown, now residing in Williamstown.
Adan Durkee, died at Montreal.
Joseph Havens.
Peter Hutchinson.
John Hutchinson, now living in Bethel.
———— Avery.
John Kent.
Peter Mason.
Giles Gibbs, killed at Randolph.
Elias Button, killed at Royalton.
Nathaniel Gilbert.

———————

*The following Persons were released by the Intercession of Mrs. Hendee.*

Daniel Downer, Jr.
Andrew Durkee.
Michael Hendee.

Roswell Parkhurst.
Shelden Durkee.
Joseph Rix.
Rufus Fish.
—————— Fish.
Nathaniel Evans.

# EVENTS ON THE NORTH-WESTERN FRONTIER FROM 1794 TO 1811.

THIS was a period of comparative tranquillity; but the British still continued their intrigues, with the Indians, on the northern and western frontiers.

On the 17th of September, 1802, Governor Harrison, at Indiana Territory, entered into an agreement with various chiefs of the Pottawatomie, Eel River, Piankeshaw, Wea, Kaskaskia, and Kickapoo tribes, by which were settled the bounds of a tract of land near that place, said to have been given by the Indians to its founder; and certain chiefs were named who were to conclude the matter at Fort Wayne. This was the first step taken by Harrison in those negotiations which continued through so many years, and added so much to the dominions of the Confederation. He found the natives jealous and out of temper, owing partly to American injustice, but also in a great degree, it was thought, to the acts of the British traders and agents.

Governor Harrison, on the 18th of August, 1804, purchased from the Delawares their claim to a large tract between the Wabash and Ohio; from the Piankeshaws their claims to the same, and also to the lands granted by the Kaskaskias in 1803, from the Sacs and Foxes their title to most of the immense district between the Mississippi, Illinois, Fox river emptying into the Illinois, and Wisconsin rivers; comprehending, it is said, more than fifty-one millions of acres. This latter treaty was made at St. Louis.

On the 21st of August, 1805, Governor Harrison, at Vincennes, received from the Miamies a region containing two
million acres within what is now Indiana; and on the 30th of
December, at the same place, purchased of the Piankeshaws a
tract of eighty or ninety miles wide, extending from the Wabash
west to the cession by the Kaskaskias in 1803. At this time,
although some murders by the Indians had taken place in the
far west, the body of the natives seemed bent on peace. But
mischief was gathering. Tecumthe, his brother the Prophet,
and other leading men, had formed at Greenville, the germ of
that union of tribes by which the whites were to be restrained
in their invasions. We are by no means satisfied that Tecumthe
used any concealment, or meditated any treachery towards the
United States, for many years after this time. The efforts of
himself and his brother were directed to two points: first, the
reformation of the savages, whose habits unfitted them for con-
tinuous and heroic effort; and second, such a union as would
make the purchase of land by the United States impossible, and
give to the aborigines a strength that might be dreaded. Both
these objects were avowed, and both were pursued with wonderful energy, perseverance, and success; in the whole country
bordering upon the lakes, the power of the Prophet was felt, and
the work of reformation went on rapidly.

During 1808, Tecumthe and the Prophet still continued
quietly to extend their influence, professing no other end than
a reformation of the Indians. Before the end of June, they
had removed from Greenville to the banks of the Tippecanoe, a
tributary to the Upper Wabash, where a tract of land had been
granted them by the Pottawatomies and Kickapoos. In July,
the Prophet sent to General Harrison a messenger begging him
not to believe the tales told by his enemies, and promising a
visit; in August, accordingly, he spent two weeks at Vincennes,
and by his words and promises led the governor to think him

other than a fool and impostor, and to believe that his influence might be beneficial rather than mischievous.

Through the year 1809, we again find Tecumthe and his brother strengthening themselves both openly and secretly. Harrison, however, had been once more led to suspect their ultimate designs, and was preparing to meet any emergency that might arise. The probability of its being at hand was very greatly increased by the news received from the Upper Mississippi of hostile movements there among the savages. In reference to these movements and the position of the Shawanese brothers, Harrison wrote to the secretary of war on the 5th of July, as follows:

The Shawanese Prophet and about forty followers arrived here about a week ago. He denies most strenuously any participation in the late combination to attack our settlements, which he says was entirely confined to the tribes of the Mississippi and Illinois rivers; and he claims the merit of having prevailed upon them to relinquish their intentions.

I must confess that my suspicions of his guilt have been rather strengthened than diminished at every interview I have had with him since his arrival. He acknowledges that he received an invitation to war against us, from the British, last fall, and that he was apprised of the intention of the Sacs and Foxes, &c. early in the spring, and warmly solicited to join in their league. But he could give no satisfactory explanation of his neglecting to communicate to me circumstances so extremely interesting to us, and towards which, I had a few months before, directed his attention, and received a solemn assurance of his cheerful compliance with the injunctions I had impressed upon him.

The result of all my inquiries on the subject, is, that the late combination was produced by British intrigue and influence, in anticipation of war between them and the United States. It was, however, premature and ill judged, and the event sufficiently manifests a great decline in their influence, or in the talents and address, with which they have been accustomed to manage their Indian relations.

The warlike and well armed tribes of the Pottawatomies, Ottawas, Chippewas, Delawares, and Miamies, I believe neither had, nor would have joined in the combination : and, although the Kickapoos, whose warriors are better than those of any other tribe, the remnant of the Wyandottes excepted, are much under the influence of the Prophet. I am persuaded that they were never made acquainted with his intentions, if these were really hostile to the United States.

During the year 1810, the hostile intentions of Tecumthe and his followers towards the United States, were placed beyond a doubt. The exciting causes were—the purchase at Fort Wayne, in 1809, which the Shawanese denounced as illegal and unjust; and British influence. And here, as in 1790 to 1795, it is impossible to learn what really was the amount of British influence, and whence it proceeded; whether from the agents merely, or from higher authority.*

But however we may think the evil influence originated, certain it is that the determination was taken by " the successor of Pontiac," to unite all the western tribes in hostility to the United States, in case that power would not give up the lands bought at Fort Wayne, and undertake to recognize the principle, that no purchases should thereafter be made unless from a Council representing all the tribes united as one nation. By various acts the feelings of Tecumthe became more and more evident, but in August, he having visited Vincennes to see the governor, a Council was held, at which, and at a subsequent interview, the real position of affairs was clearly ascertained—

* Perkins.

of that Council we give the account contained in Mr. Drake's life of the Great Chieftain.

Governor Harrison had made arrangements for holding the Council on the portico of his own house, which had been fitted up with seats for the occasion. Here, on the morning of the 15th, he awaited the arrival of the chief, being attended by the judges of the supreme court, some officers of the army, a sergeant and twelve men, from Fort Knox, and a large number of citizens. At the appointed hour, Tecumthe supported by forty of his principal warriors, made his appearance; the remainder of his followers being encamped in the village and its environs. When the chief had approached within thirty or forty yards of the house, he suddenly stopped, as if awaiting some advances from the governor. An interpreter was sent requesting him and his followers to take seats on the portico. To this Tecumthe objected—he did not think the place a suitable one for holding the conference, but preferred that it should take place in a grove of trees—to which he pointed—standing a short distance from the house. The governor said he had no objection to the grove, except that there were no seats in it for their accommodation. Tecumthe replied, that constituted no objection to the grove, the earth being the most suitable place for the Indians, who loved to repose upon the bosom of their mother. The governor yielded the point, and the benches and chairs having been removed to the spot, the conference was begun, the Indians being seated on the grass.

Tecumthe opened the meeting by stating, at length, his objections to the Treaty of Fort Wayne, made by General Harrison in the previous year; and in the course of his speech, boldly avowed the principle of his party to be, that of resistance to every cession of land, unless made by all the tribes, who, he contended, formed but one nation. He admitted that he had threatened to kill the chiefs who signed the Treaty of Fort

Wayne; and that it was his fixed determination not to permit
the village chiefs, in future, to manage their affairs, but to place
the power with which they had been heretofore invested, in the
hands of the war chiefs.  The Americans, he said, had driven
the Indians from the sea coast, and would soon push them into
the lakes; and, while he disclaimed all intention of making war
upon the United States, he declared it to be his unalterable
resolution to take a stand, and resolutely oppose the further
intrusion of the whites upon the Indian lands.  He concluded,
by making a brief but impassioned recital of the various wrongs
and aggressions inflicted by the white men upon the Indians,
from the commencement of the revolutionary war down to the
period of that council; all of which was calculated to arouse
and inflame the minds of such of his followers as were present.

To him the governor replied, and having taken his seat, the
interpreter commenced explaining the speech to Tecumthe, who,
after listening to a portion of it, sprung to his feet and began
to speak with great vehemence of manner.

The governor was surprised at his violent gestures, but, as he
did not understand him, thought that he was making some
explanation, and suffered his attention to be drawn towards
Winnemac, a friendly Indian lying on the grass before him,
who was renewing the priming of his pistol, which he had kept
concealed from the other Indians, but in full view of the governor.  His attention, however, was again directed towards Tecumthe, by hearing General Gibson, who was intimately
acquainted with the Shawanese language, say to Lieutenant
Jennings, "those fellows intend to do mischief; you had better
bring up the guard."  At that moment, the followers of Tecumthe seized their tomahawks and war-clubs, and sprung upon
their feet, their eyes turned upon the governor.  As soon as he
could disengage himself from the arm-chair in which he sat, he
rose, drew a small sword which he had by his side, and stood

on the defensive. Captain G. R. Floyd, of the army, who stood near him, drew a dirk, and the chief Winnemac cocked his pistol. The citizens present were more numerous than the Indians, but were unarmed; some of them procured clubs and brickbats, and also stood on the defensive. The Rev. Mr. Winans, of the Methodist church, ran to the governor's house, got a gun, and posted himself at the door to defend the family. During this singular scene, no one spoke, until the guard came running up, and appearing to be in the act of firing, the governor ordered them not to do so. He then demanded of the interpreter, an explanation of what had happened, who replied that Tecumthe had interrupted him, declaring that all the governor had said was false; and that he and the Seventeen Fires had cheated and imposed on the Indians.

The governor then told Tecumthe that he was a bad man, and that he would hold no further communication with him; that as he had come to Vincennes under the protection of a council-fire, he might return in safety, but that he must immediately leave the village. Here the council terminated.

The now undoubted purposes of the brothers being of a character necessarily leading to war, General Harrison proceeded to strengthen himself for the contest by preparing the militia, and posting the regular troops that were under him, under Captains Posey and Cross at Vincennes.

# TIPPECANOE WAR.

THE difficulties with England seemed to increase, and during the early part of the year 1811, nothing was looked for but the breaking out of hostilities between England and the United States. But little was accomplished as far as concerned the Indians, during the first part of this year; yet a spirit of enmity was still rife among them, and the prospect of a contest was not improbable. Harrison sent a message to the Shawanese cautioning them to beware of hostilities. A visit from Tecumthe with about three hundred of his warriors followed, but nothing was done; the chief going south, for the purpose of enlisting the Creeks in his cause.

Harrison, in the meanwhile, received reinforcements, and after warning the Indians to respect the treaty of Greenville, he resolved if necessary to break up the Prophet's Town on the Tippecanoe. For this purpose, he marched to a point on the Wabash, some sixty miles above Vincennes, where he built Fort Harrison. One of his sentinels being fired upon, he entertained no doubt that the intentions of the Prophet were hostile.

Harrison reached the mouth of Vermilion creek on the 31st of October, where he built a block-house, as a depot for his lüggage, and the protection of his boats. He then proceeded to the vicinity of the Prophet's Town, where he was met by a party of Indians, who were assured that the Governor's intentions were peaceful, should they continue true to their treaties. One of the chiefs pointed out a place for an encampment, which

(284)

Harrison did not like, as it offered too great facilities for the approach of the savages. We give Harrison's own account of the order of encampment and battle

"For a night attack the order of encampment was the order of battle, and each man slept immediately opposite to his post in the line. In the formation of my troops I used a single rank, or what is called Indian file—because in Indian warfare, where there is no shock to resist, one rank is nearly as good as two, and in that kind of warfare the extension of line is of the first importance. Raw troops also manœuvre with much more facility, in single than in double ranks. It was my constant custom to assemble all the field officers at my tent every evening by signal, to give them the watchword and their instructions for the night; those given for the night of the 6th were, that each corps which formed a part of the exterior line of the encampment, should hold its own ground until relieved. The dragoons were directed to parade dismounted in case of a night attack, with their pistols in their belts, and to act as a corps of reserve. The camp was defended by two captains' guards, consisting each of four non-commissioned officers and forty-two privates; and two subalterns' guards of twenty non-commissioned officers and privates. The whole under the command of a field officer of the day. The troops were regularly called up an hour before day, and made to continue under arms until it was quite light. On the morning of the 7th, I had risen at a quarter after four o'clock, and the signal for calling out the men would have been given in two minutes, when the attack commenced. It began on our left flank—but a signal gun was fired by the sentinels or by the guards in that direction, which made not the least resistance, but abandoned their officer and fled into the camp, and the first notice which the troops of that flank had of the danger, was from the yells of the savages within a short distance of the line— but even under those circumstances the men were not wanting to themselves or to the occasion. Such of them as were awake, or were easily awakened, seized their arms and took their stations; others, who were more tardy, had to contend with the enemy in the doors of their tents. The storm first fell upon Captain Barton's company of the 4th United States regiment, and Captain Geiger's company of mounted riflemen, which formed the left angle of the rear line. The fire upon these was exceedingly severe, and they suffered considerably before relief could be brought to them. Some few Indians passed into the encampment near the angle, and one or two penetrated to some distance before they were killed. I believe all the other companies were under arms and tolerably formed before they were fired on. The morning was dark and cloudy; our fires afforded a partial light, which if it gave us some opportunity of taking our positions, was still more advantageous to the enemy, affording them the means of taking a surer aim; they were therefore extinguished as soon as possible. Under all these discouraging circumstances the troops (nineteen-twentieths of whom had never been in action before) behaved in a manner that can never be too much applauded. They took their places without noise and with less confusion that could have been expected from veterans placed in a similar situation. As soon as I could mount my horse, I rode to the angle that was attacked—I found that Barton's company had suffered severely, and the left of Geiger's entirely broken. I immediately ordered Cook's company and the late Captain Wentworth's, under Lieutenant Peters, to be brought up from the centre of the rear line, where the ground was much more defensible, and formed across the angle in support of Barton's and Geiger's. My attention was then engaged by a heavy firing upon the left of the front line, where were stationed the small company of United States riflemen (then, however, armed with muskets) and the companies of Baen, Snelling, and Prescott of the 4th regiment. I found Major

Davies forming the dragoons in the rear of those companies, and understanding that the heaviest part of the enemy's fire proceeded from some trees about fifteen or twenty paces in front of those companies, I directed the major to dislodge them with a part of the dragoons. Unfortunately the major's gallantry determined him to execute the order with a smaller force than was sufficient, which enabled the enemy to avoid him in front, and attack his flanks. The major was mortally wounded, and his party driven back. The Indians were, however, immediately and gallantly dislodged from their advantageous position, by Captain Snelling, at the head of his company. In the course of a few minutes after the commencement of the attack, the fire extended along the left flank, the whole of the front, the right flank, and part of the rear line. Upon Spencer's mounted riflemen, and the right of Warwick's company, which was posted on the right of the rear line, it was excessively severe; Captain Spencer, and his first and second lieutenants, were killed, and Captain Warwick was mortally wounded—those companies however still bravely maintained their posts, but Spencer had suffered so severely, and having originally too much ground to occupy, I reinforced them with Robb's company of riflemen, which had been driven, or by mistake ordered from the position on the left flank, towards the centre of the camp, and filled the vacancy occupied by Robb with Prescott's company of the 4th United States regiment. My great object was to keep the lines entire, to prevent the enemy from breaking into the camp until daylight, which should enable me to make a general and effectual charge. With this view, I had reinforced every part of the line that had suffered much; and as soon as the approach of morning discovered itself, I withdrew from the front line, Snelling's, Posey's, (under Lieutenant Albright,) and Scott's, and from the rear line, Wilson's companies, and drew them up upon the left flank, and at the same time I ordered Cook's and

Baen's companies, the former from the rear, and the latter from the front lines, to reinforce the right flank; foreseeing that at these points the enemy would make their last efforts. Major Wells, who commanded on the left flank, not knowing my intentions precisely, had taken the command of these·companies, had charged the enemy before I had formed the body of dragoons with which I had meant to support the infantry; a small detachment of these were, however, ready, and proved amply sufficient for the purpose. The Indians were driven by the infantry, at the point of the bayonet, and the dragoons pursued and forced them into a marsh, where they could not be followed. Captain Cook and Lieutenant Larrabee had, agreeably to my order, marched their companies to the right flank, had formed them under the fire of the enemy, and being then joined by the riflemen of that flank, had charged the Indians, killed a number, and put the rest to a precipitate flight. A favorable opportunity was here offered to pursue the enemy with dragoons, but being engaged at that time on the other flank, I did not observe it until it was too late."

There were near seven hundred Americans engaged in this battle, of whom thirty-seven were killed, and one hundred and fifty-two wounded: twenty-six mortally. On the part of the Indiana, forty were killed; the number of wounded not being known. Their numbers amounted to between eight hundred and a thousand warriors.

The Indians fought with unusual fury and courage. The Prophet did not engage in the battle, but sat on a rock, out of the reach of all danger, singing his songs, and going through with his absurd ceremonies. The cause of the obstinacy of his followers is ascribed to his assurance that the bullets of their enemies would do them no harm, and that victory would crown their efforts. Their defeat was the disgrace of the Prophet; and from that period his influence was almost entirely destroyed..

The battle of Tippecanoe was fought on the 7th of November, and on the 4th of December, Harrison asserted that the frontiers never enjoyed more perfect tranquillity.

Tecumthe upbraided his brother, for rendering his plans fruitless, by risking a battle at that time. The declaration of war by the United States against Great Britain, before he could mature new schemes, forced him to become an ally, when he aimed to be a principal.

25

# SURRENDER OF DETROIT.

At the commencement of the war with Great Britain, in 1812, preparations were made for an invasion of Canada. The command of the expedition was given to General Hull, who with about two thousand men was soon upon the north-western frontier. He took possession of the beautiful little town of Sandwich, some two miles below Detroit. The British and Indians, were posted at Malden; and amounted to about eleven hundred men, under the command of General Brock and Tecumthe.

Upon entering Canada, Hull issued a proclamation, offering them security if they submitted to the American arms, and destruction if they opposed them.

In the meantime the British and Indians at St. Joseph's, prepared to attack Fort Michilimackinac, on an island of the same name. The force of the enemy was some three hundred British and seven hundred Indians, under the command of Captain Roberts. That of the Americans amounted to only fifty-seven men. The inhabitants knowing this force to be inadequate to cope with the enemy, and being informed by Roberts, that unless they surrendered, the whole garrison would be delivered into the hands of the Indians, and subjected to their merciless treatment, fled in great numbers.

Lieutenant Porter Hanks, who commanded the garrison, resolved to offer as gallant a resistance as was in his power. The Indians were posted in an adjoining wood, while the British were stationed on an eminence, that commanded the weakest point of the little garrison.

(290)

A flag was now sent by Roberts for a surrender of the fort, and Hanks being for the first time informed of the state of affairs between the United States and England, and knowing that if he resisted, an indiscriminate slaughter would follow, prudently resolved to surrender the place. He entered into terms of capitulation, in which the right of private property was acknowledged, though he placed the enemy in possession of a fortress, capable of being rendered the strongest in America.

Meantime, on the 29th of July, Colonel Proctor had reached Malden, and seeing at once the power which the position of that post gave him over the supplies of the army of the United States, he commenced a series of operations, the object of which was to cut off the communications of Hull with Ohio, and thus not merely neutralize all active operations on his part, but starve him into surrender.

Hull dispatched Major Vanhorne to escort a company of volunteers, on their way from Ohio, with provisions for the army. They had arrived as far as the Raisin, a distance of thirty-six miles from Detroit. Vanhorne had nearly reached Browns-town, when he was attacked by a large force of British and Indians. The Americans stood their ground nobly, but were forced to retreat. This was performed in a masterly manner; Vanhorne only losing nineteen men killed, and nine wounded.

General Hull, contrary to the wishes and entreaties of his officers, abandoned the enterprise against Malden, and proclaimed his intention of evacuating Canada, and posting himself at Fort Detroit. Here they received the intelligence of the late skirmish. The communication between the Raisin and their present post, was entirely destroyed, and the way blocked up by savages. It was necessary that this should be opened, or the army would be in want of provisions very shortly.

For this purpose Colonel James Miller was dispatched with a force of five hundred men. The British and Indians anticipating a return of the detachment they had driven back, reinforced, increased their numbers sufficiently, as they supposed, to drive them off again.  They took possession of, and fortified a place called Maguaga, four miles from Brownstown.  They erected breastworks by felling trees, from behind which they might shower forth death and destruction.  Tecumthe commanded the Indians; the united force of British and Indians was commanded by Major Muir.

On the 9th, the American troops, though they proceeded with great caution, reached the ground on which the enemy desired to see them before they discovered their ambuscade.  Captain Snelling, commanding the advance, was attacked from it, and sustained a combat until the main body came up, when the British and Indians sprang suddenly from behind the works, formed a line of battle with great celerity, and commenced a brisk fire, accompanied with all the demonstrations of savage war.  Sudden and unexpected as was the attack, the intrepid commander of the American force was not the least dismayed; his troops received the shock without shrinking, and with a coolness and sagacity which are commonly looked for in soldiers of long experience, he as suddenly drew up his men, and after very a rapid fire, charged upon the enemy with such unlooked for firmness, as to throw them into complete disorder.  The obstinacy of the Indians, however, would not admit of flight; they might not act in concert with the British, and resorting to their own kind of combat, they were resolved not to abandon the contest.  But the British had now recovered from their confusion, and a scene of indescribable horror ensued.  Five hundred Indians, led on and encouraged by the regulars, (many of whom were like themselves, almost naked,) frightfully painted, and sending forth such dreadful whooping and yelling as might have appalled almost any other troops, were fighting on every side of the American detachment; but on every side they were gallantly repulsed.  No such means could induce these brave men to forsake their standard, or to disgrace their nation.  They saw danger strengthening around them, they knew what kind of destiny awaited their defeat, and they were resolutely determined to repel the foe, or to yield only with their lives.

Athough Colonel Miller was contending against a force greatly superior, he succeeding in driving them back into Brownstown, and would have totally conquered them, had not boats been in waiting to receive them.  The loss of the British was seven killed and wounded; while that of the Indians was about one hundred.  The Americans had fifteen of their number killed and between thirty and forty wounded.

The force at the Raisin still continued there, waiting an escort, when Captain Brush, who commanded the party, received instructions from General Hull, dated the 11th of August, to remain there, and in conjunction with the regiment, Le Croix's corps, and his own, protect the provisions until further orders. Hull added a postscript, in which he stated that Captain Brush on consulting Colonel Anderson, the bearer of the letter, might use his own discretion, about proceeding on an upper road, crossing the river Huron; but notice was to be given at Detroit, if this was determined on.  Hull sent Colonels Cass and M'Arthur, on the 14th, with some three hundred men, to assist in the transportation of provisions.

Captain Heald, who commanded at Fort Chicago, received orders on the same day that the battle of Maguaga was fought, to repair at once to Detroit.  After giving the friendly Indians all the goods in the factory, and the provisions that they could not take with them, he hastened to obey orders.  The inhabitants, principally women and children, accompanied them, fearing to be left·behind, as the place would be almost defenceless.

They had not proceeded far, when they suddenly discovered

that they were about to be attacked by a party of hostile Indians. Heald was forced to surrender, after nearly two-thirds of his army were slain. Heald stipulated for the safety of the women and children, but forgot to mention the wounded, whom, with the exception of Mrs. Heald, Mrs. Helm, Captain Heald, and Lieutenant Helm, who were saved by some friendly Indians, they massacred on the spot.

The other prisoners were distributed among the chiefs, and carried in different directions into the country of the Pottawatomies. Captain Heald and his heroic wife, who endured wounds and scenes of horror with wondrous fortitude, after many adventures and hair-breadth escapes, arrived safely at Detroit.

Meanwhile the British occupied a point opposite Detroit, and any attempt to accelerate the transportation of the provisions would be useless. Three days were occupied by the British in throwing up breastworks, without the slightest opposition from the Americans.

General Brock, on the 15th, sent Hull a flag, with a demand to surrender, stating that if they did not, that it would be utterly out of his power to control the numerous body of Indians, the moment the contest commenced; and that if he did not surrender, a war of extermination must ensue, as the character of the Indians was well known, and that nothing but blood would satisfy their savage natures.

Hull answered this summons by stating that the "town and fort would be defended to the last extremity."

An officer rode round Detroit, warning the inhabitants to seek a place of safety, as the batteries of the British, at Sandwich, would most probably soon open upon the town. The utmost panic and confusion ensued. Women were busy packing up their valuables; men running about, here and there, seeking a place for those dear to them by all the ties of blood;

THE FUGITIVES AT THE RAVINE ON THE CASS FARM.          Page 295.

infants crying and clinging to their agonized mothers; every thing in short conspired to render the town a second Babel.

The inhabitants commenced leaving the town about noon; but, alas! there seemed to be no place of safety. The enemy on one side; the woods swarming with Indians—professing friendship—but what dependence could be placed upon savage integrity, should the enemy gain the upper hand. A deep ravine on the "Cass farm," owned at that time by General Mc-Donald, seemed to offer the best security, and there assembled the mass of helplessness, with a few men for protectors.

The enemy then opened their fire from their batteries upon the town, which was returned with precision and effect. At daylight, on the 16th, the cannonade was renewed; and their whole force soon afterwards crossed the river and landed at Springwells, about three miles west of Detroit. Here the British general, learning the absence of Colonel Miller with his detachment, resolved at once upon forcing the American camp.

The American army appears to have waited the approach of the enemy with coolness and good order. Two twenty-four-pounders, loaded with grape, were planted in a favorable position for their annoyance. The regular troops were placed in the fort, and the militia and volunteers behind pickets, when, to the astonishment of every one, the whole force was ordered to retire into the fort, where their arms were stacked, and the artillerymen forbidden to fire. Here, crowded as they were, into a narrow compass, every ball from the enemy's batteries took effect, and the general soon ordered the white flag to be hung out in token of surrender. In a short time the terms of capitulation were agreed upon; and the whole army, including the detachments of Colonels Miller and M'Arthur, which returned in the evening of the same day, and the force under Captain Brush, at the river Raisin, were surrendered prisoners of war. The enemy found in the fort an ample supply of ammunition and provisions. They must have been greatly astonished at obtaining such a capital prize, with so little effort.

The indignation of the Americans at this cowardly and disgraceful transaction knew no bounds. Expectation had been raised to such a height by the confident language of previous dispatches from General Hull, that nothing less than the capture of all Upper Canada was expected. The surrender, therefore, of an American army to an inferior force, together with the cession of a large extent of territory, as it had never entered into the calculations of the people, was almost too much for them to bear. General Hull was openly accused of imbecility and cowardice.

As soon as he was exchanged, he was, of course, brought before a court-martial, tried on the charges of treason, cowardice, and un-officerlike conduct, found guilty of the two last, and sentenced to be shot. The President, however, in consequence of his age and former services, remitted the capital punishment, but directed his name to be stricken from the rolls of the army; a disgrace, which, to a lofty and honorable spirit, is worse than death.

# DEFENCE OF FORT HARRISON.

THE surrender of Detroit was not the only misfortune, although the leading one of this unfortunate summer. Fort Michilimackinac, the key of the northern lakes, was in the possession of the British and Indians; whilst the garrison at Fort Dearborne, under Captain Heald, had nearly all been massacred.

Thus by the middle of August, the whole north-west, with the exception of Forts Wayne and Harrison, was again in possession of the British and their red allies. These forts were attacked early in September, and had the latter not been stoutly defended, it would have shared a similar fate to the others. The following account is from its commander, then Captain Taylor, and will be perused with additional interest when it is remembered that he occupied so conspicuous a place in the recent war with Mexico.

*Fort Harrison, Sept.* 10.

"DEAR SIR—On Thursday evening, the 3d instant, after retreat beating, four guns were heard to fire in the direction where two young men (citizens who resided here) were making hay, about four hundred yards distance from the fort. I was immediately impressed with the idea that they were killed by the Indians, as the Prophet's party would soon be here for the purpose of commencing hostilities, and that they had been directed to leave this place, as we were about to do. I did not think it prudent to send out at that late hour of the night to see what had become of them; and their not coming in convinced me that I was right in my conjecture. I waited until eight o'clock next morning, when I sent out a corporal with a small party to find them, if it could be done without running too much risk of being drawn into an ambuscade. He soon sent back to inform me that he had found them both killed, and wished to know my further orders; I sent the cart and oxen, had them brought in and buried; they had been shot with two balls, scalped, and cut in the most shocking manner. Late in evening of the 4th instant, old Joseph Lenar and between thirty and forty Indians arrived from the Prophet's town, with a white flag; among whom were about ten women, and the men were composed of chiefs of the different tribes that compose the Prophet's party. A Shawanese man, that spoke good English, informed me that old Lenar intended to speak to me the next morning, and try to get something to eat.

At retreat beating I examined the men's arms, and found them all in good order, and completed their cartridges to fifteen rounds per man. As I had not been able to mount a guard of more than six privates and two non-commissioned officers for some time past, and sometimes part of them every other day, from the unhealthiness of the company; I had not conceived my force adequate to the defence of this post should it be vigorously attacked, for some time past.

As I had just recovered from a severe attack of the fever, I was not able to be up much through the night. After tattoo, I cautioned the guard to be vigilant, and ordered one of the non-commissioned officers, as the sentinels could not see every part of the garrison, to walk round on the inside during the whole night, to prevent the Indians taking any advantage of attacking us. About eleven o'clock, I was awakened by the firing of one of the sentinels; I sprang up, ran out, and ordered the men to their posts; when my orderly sergeant, who had charge of the upper block-house, called out that the Indians had fired the lower block-house, (which contained the property of the contractor, which was deposited in the lower part, the upper having been assigned to a corporal and ten privates as an alarm-post.) The guns had began to fire pretty smartly from both sides. I directed the buckets to be got ready and water brought from the well, and the fire extinguished immediately, as it was perceivable at that time: but from debility or some other cause, the men were very slow in executing my orders—the word fire appeared to throw the whole of them into confusion; and by the time they had got the water and broken open the door, the fire had unfortunately communicated to a quantity of whiskey (the stock having licked several holes through the lower part of the building, after the salt that was stored there, through which they had introduced the fire without being discovered, as the night was very dark,) and in spite of every exertion we could make use of, in less than a moment it ascended to the roof and baffled every effort we could make to extinguish it. As that block-house adjoined the barracks that made part of the fortifications most of the men immediately gave themselves up for lost, and I had the greatest difficulty in getting my orders executed—and, sir, what from the raging of the fire—the yelling and howling of several hundred Indians—the cries of nine women and children (a part soldiers' and a part citizens' wives, who had taken shelter in the fort) and the desponding of so many of the men, which was worse than all---I can assure you that my feelings were unpleasant—and indeed there were not more than ten or fifteen men able to do a great deal, the others being sick or convalescent—and to add to our misfortunes, two of the strongest men in the fort, and that I had every confidence in, jumped the picket and left us. But my presence of mind did not for a moment forsake me. I saw, by throwing off a part of the roof that joined the block-house that was on fire, and keeping the end perfectly wet, the whole row of buildings might be saved, and leave only a space of eighteen or twenty feet for the entrance of the Indians after the house was consumed; and that a temporary breastwork might be executed to prevent their even entering there—I convinced the men that this might be accomplished and it appeared to inspire them with more firmness and desperation. Those that were able (while the others kept up a constant fire from the other block-house and the two bastions) mounted the roofs of the houses, with Dr. Clarke at their head, who acted with the greatest firmness and presence of mind the whole time the attack lasted, which was seven hours, under a shower of bullets, and in less than a moment threw off as much of the roof as was necessary. This was done with the loss of only one man and two wounded, and I am in hopes neither of them dangerously; the man that was killed was a little deranged, and did not get off the house as soon as directed, or he would not have been hurt—and although the barracks were several times in a blaze, and an immense quantity of fire against them, the men used such exertions that they kept it under, and before day raised a temporary breastwork as high as a man's head, although the Indians continued to pour in a heavy fire of ball and an innumerable quantity of arrows during the whole time the attack lasted, in every part of the parade. I had but one other man killed, nor any other wounded inside the fort, and he lost his life by being too anxious—he got into one of the gallies in the bastions, and fired over the pickets, and called out to his comrades that he had killed an Indian, and neglecting to stoop down in an instant he was shot dead. One of the men that jumped the pickets, returned an hour before day, and running up toward the gate, begged for God's sake for it to be opened. I suspected it to be a stratagem of the Indians to get in, as I did not recollect the voice. I directed the men in the bastion, where I happened to be, to shoot him let him be who he would, and one of them fired at him, but fortunately he ran up to the other bastion, where they knew his voice, and Dr. Clarke directed him to lie down close to the pickets behind an empty barrel that happened to be there, and at daylight I had let him in. His arm was broken in a most shocking manner; which he says was done by the Indians—which, I suppose, was the cause of his returning —I think it probable that he will never recover. The other they caught about one hundred and thirty yards from the garrison, and cut him all to pieces. After keeping up a constant fire until six o'clock the next morning, which we began to return with some effect after daylight, they removed out of reach of our guns. A party of them drove up the horses that belonged to the citizens here, as they could not catch them very readily, shot the whole of them in our sight, as well as a number of their hogs. They drove off the whole of the cattle, which amounted to sixty-five head, as well as the public oxen. I had the vacancy filled before night, (which was made by the burning of the block-house) with a strong row of pickets, which I got by pulling down the guard-house. We lost the whole of our provisions, but must make out to live upon green corn until we can get a supply, which I am in hopes will not be long. I believe the whole of the Miamies or Weas, were among the Prophet's party, as one chief gave his orders in that language, which resembled Stone Eater's voice, and I believe Negro Legs was there likewise. A Frenchman here understands their different languages, and several of the Miamies or Weas, that have been frequently here, were recognized by the Frenchman and soldiers, the next morning. The Indians suffered smartly, but were so numerous as to take off all that were shot. They continued with us until the next morning, but made no further attempt upon the fort, nor have we seen any thing more of them since.

"I have delayed informing you of my situation, as I did not like to weaken the garrison, and I looked for some person from

26

Vincennes, and none of my men were acquainted with the woods, and therefore I would either have to take the road or the river, which I was fearful was guarded by small parties of Indians, that would not dare attack a company of rangers that was on a scout; but being disappointed, I have at length determined to send a couple of my men by water, and am in hopes they will arrive safe.    I think it would be best to send the provisions under a pretty strong escort, as the Indians may attempt to prevent their coming. If you carry on an expedition against the Prophet this fall, you ought to be well provided with every thing, as you may calculate on having every inch of ground disputed between this and there that they can defend with advantage.                         Z. TAYLOR.

His Excellency Gov. HARRISON.

# EVENTS ON THE NORTH-WESTERN FRONTIER DURING 1813.

But little of any importance was done on the north-western frontier during the latter part of the year of 1812, after the defence of Fort Harrison; although the Indians were as hostile as ever, and gave some trouble to the settlers of that portion of the country. General Harrison was appointed to the command of the army in the west. His main objects were, first to drive the Indians from the western side of Detroit river; second to take Malden; and third, having thus secured his communications, to recapture the Michigan Territory and its dependencies. But his plans were of no avail. A portion of his troops, under General Winchester, worn out and starved, were on the verge of mutiny. Under these circumstances, Harrison deemed it best to wait until the winter had bridged the streams and morasses with ice, and even when that had taken place, he was doubtful as to the wisdom of an attempt to conquer without vessels on Lake Erie.

On the 10th of January, 1813, Winchester with his troops reached the Rapids, General Harrison with the right wing of the army being still at Upper Sandusky, and Tupper with the centre at Fort McArthur. From the 13th to the 16th, messengers arrived at Winchester's camp, from the inhabitants of Frenchtown on the river Raisin, representing the danger to which that place was exposed from the hostility of the British and Indians, and begging for protection. These representations and petitions excited the feelings of the Americans, and led them, forgetful of the main objects of the campaign, and of military caution, to determine upon the step of sending a strong party to the aid of the sufferers. On the 17th, accordingly, Colonel Lewis was dispatched with five hundred and fifty men to the river Raisin, and soon after Colonol Allen followed with one hundred and ten more. Marching along the frozen Bay and Lake, on the afternoon of the 18th the Americans reached and attacked the enemy who were posted in the village, and after a severe contest defeated them. Having gained possession of the town, Colonel Lewis wrote for reinforcements, and prepared himself to defend the position he had gained. And it was evident that all his means of defence would be needed, as the place was but eighteen miles from Malden, where the whole British force was collected under Proctor. Winchester, on the 19th, having heard of the action on the previous day, marched with two hundred and fifty men, which was the most he dared detach from the Rapids, to the aid of the captor of Frenchtown, which place he reached on the next evening. But instead of placing his men in a secure position, and taking measures to prevent the secret approach of the enemy, Winchester suffered the troops he had brought with him to remain in the open ground, and took no efficient measures to protect himself from surprise, although informed that an attack might be expected at any moment. The consequence was that during the night of the 21st the whole British force approached undiscovered, and erected a battery within three hundred yards of the American camp. From this, before the troops were fairly under arms in the morning, a discharge of bombs, balls, and grape-shot, informed the devoted soldiers of Winchester of the folly of their commander, and in a moment more the dreaded Indian yell sounded on every side. The troops under Lewis were protected by the garden pickets behind which their commander, who alone seems to have been upon his guard, had stationed them; those last arrived were, as we have said, in the open field, and against them the main effort of the enemy was directed. Nor was it long so directed without terrible results; the troops yielded, broke, and fled, but fled under a fire which mowed them down like grass: Winchester and Lewis, (who had left his pickets to aid his superior officer,) were taken prisoners. Upon the party who fought from behind their slight defences, however, no impression could be made, and it was not till Winchester was induced to send them what was deemed an order to surrender that they dreamed of doing so. This Proctor persuaded him to do by the old story of an Indian massacre in case of continued resistance, to which he added a promise of help and protection for the wounded, and of a removal at the earliest moment; without which last promise the troops of Lewis refused to yield even when required by their general. But the promise, even if given in good faith, was not redeemed, and the horrors of the succeeding night and day will long be remembered by the inhabitants of the frontier. Of a portion of the horrors we give a description in the words of an eye-witness.*

*Nicholasville, Kentucky, April* 24, 1813.

" Sir :—Yours of the 5th instant, requesting me to give you a statement respecting the late disaster at Frenchtown, was duly received. Rest assured, sir, that it is with sensations the most unpleasant that I undertake to recount the infamous and barbarous conduct of the British and Indians after the battle of the 22d of January. The blood runs cold in my veins when I think of it.

" On the morning of the 23d, shortly after light, six or eight Indians came to the house of Jean Baptiste Jereaume, where I was, in company with Major Graves, Captains Hart and Hick-

* Perkins.

26*

man, Dr. Todd, and fifteen or twenty volunteers, belonging to
different corps. They did not molest any person or thing on
their first approach, but kept sauntering about until there was
a large number collected, (say one or two hundred) at which
time they commenced plundering the houses of the inhabitants,
and the massacre of the wounded prisoners. I was one amongst
the first that was taken prisoner, and was taken to a place about
twenty paces from the house, after being divested of part of my
clothing, and commanded by signs there to remain for further
orders. Shortly after being there, I saw them knock down
Captain Hickman at the door, together with several others with
whom I was not acquainted. Supposing a general massacre
had commenced, I made an effort to get to a house about one
hundred yards distant, which contained a number of wounded,
but on my reaching the house, to my great mortification, found
it surrounded by Indians, which precluded the possibility of my
giving notice to the unfortunate victims of savage barbarity.
An Indian chief of the Tawa tribe, of the name of M'Carty,
gave me possession of his horse and blanket, telling me by signs,
to lead the horse to the house which I had just before left. The
Indian that first took me, by this time came up and manifested
a hostile disposition towards me, by raising a tomahawk as if
to give me the fatal blow, which was prevented by my very
good friend M'Carty. On my reaching the house which I had
just started from, I saw the Indians take off several prisoners,
which I afterwards saw in the road, in a most mangled condition, and entirely stripped of their clothing.

" Messrs. Bradford, Searls, Turner, and Blythe, were collected round a carryall, which contained articles taken by the
Indians from the citizens. We had all been placed there, by
our respective captors, except Blythe, who came where we were
entreating an Indian to convey him to Malden, promising to
give him forty or fifty dollars, and whilst in the act of pleading

MASSACRE OF PRISONERS AFTER THE BATTLE OF FRENCHTOWN. Page 306.

for mercy, an Indian, more savage than the other, stepped up behind, tomahawked, stripped, and scalped him. The next that attracted my attention, was the houses on fire that contained several wounded, who I knew were unable to get out. After the houses were nearly consumed, we received marching orders, and after arriving at Sandy Creek, the Indians called a halt and commenced cooking; after preparing and eating a little sweetened gruel, Messrs. Bradford, Searls, Turner and myself, received some, and were eating, when an Indian came up and proposed exchanging his moccasins for Mr. Searls's shoes, which he readily complied with. They then exchanged hats, after which the Indian inquired how many men Harrison had with him, and at the same time, calling Searls a Washington or Madison, then raised his tomahawk and struck him on the shoulder, which cut into the cavity of the body. Searls then caught hold of the tomahawk, and appeared to resist, and upon my telling him his fate was inevitable, he closed his eyes and received the savage blow which terminated his existence. I was near enough to him to receive the brains and blood, after the fatal blow, on my blanket. A short time after the death of Searls, I saw three others share a similar fate. We then set out for Brownstown, which place we reached about twelve or one o'clock at night. After being exposed to several hours incessant rain in reaching that place, we were put into the council-house, the floor of which was partly covered with water, at which place we remained until next morning, when we again received marching orders for their village on the river Rouge, which place we made that day, where I was kept six days, then taken to Detroit and sold. For a more detailed account of the proceedings, I take the liberty of referring you to a publication which appeared in the public prints, signed by Ensign J. L. Baker, and to the publication of Judge Woodward, both of which I have particularly examined, and find them to be literally correct, so far as came under my notice.

I am, sir, with due regard, your fellow-citizen,

GUSTAVUS M. BOWER.

General Harrison was at Upper Sandusky when Winchester reached the Rapids. He received some word of a meditated movement, and hurried with all speed to Winchester's assistance, but all was in vain. He met the few survivors long before he reached the ground. Harrison with his troops retired to the Rapids; here a consultation was held, when it was determined to retreat yet farther in order to prevent the possibility of being cut off from the convoys of stores and artillery upon their way from Sandusky. The next morning the troops retired to Portage river, eighteen miles in the rear of Winchester's position, there to await the guns and reinforcements, which were daily expected.

General Harrison now found his army to be seventeen hundred strong, and on the 1st of February, again advanced to the Rapids, where he took up a new and stronger position, at which point he ordered all the troops to gather as rapidly as possible. This was done in the hope of advancing upon Malden before the middle of the month; but the warm weather had placed the roads in such a condition that his troops were unable to join him; so the winter campaign was of necessity abandoned, as the autumnal one had been before.

Thus far the operations in the north-west had certainly been discouraging. Nothing had been gained, and of what had been lost, nothing had been retaken; the slight advantages gained by a few officers over the Indians, had not shaken the power or confidence of Tecumthe and his allies, while the unsuccessful efforts of Harrison through five months, to gather troops enough at the mouth of the Maumee river, to attempt the reconquest of Michigan, which had been taken in a week, depressed the spirits of the Americans, and gave new life and hope to their foes.

Among the defensive operations of the spring and summer of 1813, that at Fort or Camp Meigs, the new post occupied by Harrison at the Rapids, and that at Lower Sandusky, deserve notice. It was supposed that in the beginning of spring, that the British would attempt the reconquest of the position upon the Maumee. As had been expected on the 28th of April, the English forces began the investment of Harrison's camp, and by the 1st of May, had completed their batteries. In the meantime, the Americans had thrown up a bank of earth twelve feet high, behind which they withdrew, the moment the enemy commenced operations.

Up to the 5th, nothing had been done of importance. On that day, General Clay, with twelve hundred additional troops, came down the Maumee in flat-boats, and according to orders received from General Harrison, detached eight hundred men under Colonel Dudley, to attack the batteries on the left bank of the river, while, with the remainder, he landed upon the southern shore, and fought his way into camp. Dudley succeeded in capturing the batteries, but he neglected spiking the cannon, and then returning to the boats, he suffered his men to dally with the Indians, until Proctor cut off their only chance of retreat, and only one hundred and fifty men out of the eight hundred escaped captivity or death. Colonel Miller, however, captured and made useless the batteries, that had been erected south of the Maumee.

The result of these proceedings was sad enough for the Americans, still the British general saw in it nothing to encourage him; and as news was received that the Americans were about to receive reinforcements from Ohio and Kentucky, Proctor deemed it best to retreat, and on the 9th of May, returned to Malden.

The principal stores of Harrison were at Sandusky, and
thither Proctor moved with immense bands of Indians.  Harrison himself was at Seneca, and Major Croghan at Fort Ste-
phenson, or Lower Sandusky.  It was deemed advisable to
abandon the fort, as it was indefencible against heavy cannon,
which it was thought the British general would bring against
it; but before this could be accomplished, the appearance of the
enemy on the 31st of July, rendered it impossible to carry out
their determination.

The garrison of this little fort was composed of one hundred
and fifty men, under a commander just past his 21st year, and
with a single piece of cannon, while the investing force, including Tecumthe's Indians, was, it is said, three thousand three
hundred strong, and with six pieces of artillery, all of them,
fortunately, light ones.  Proctor demanded a surrender, and told
the unvarying story of the danger of provoking a general massacre by the savages, unless the fort was yielded: to all which
the representative of young Croghan replied by saying that the
Indians would have none left to massacre, if the British conquered, for every man of the garrison would have died at his
post.  Proctor, upon this, opened his fire, which being concentrated upon the north-west angle of the fort, led the commander
to think that it was meant to make a breach there, and carry
the works by assault: he therefore proceeded to strengthen that
point by bags of sand and flour, while under cover of night he
placed his six pounder in a position to rake the angle threatened,
and then, having charged his infant battery with slugs, and
hidden it from the enemy, he waited the event.  During the
night of the 1st of August, and till late in the evening of the
2d, the firing continued upon the devoted north-west corner;
then, under cover of the smoke and gathering darkness, a
column of three hundred and fifty men approached unseen to
within twenty paces of the walls.  The musketry opened upon

them, but with little effect,—the ditch was gained, and in a moment filled with men; at that instant, the masked cannon, only thirty feet distant, and so directed as to sweep the ditch,—was unmasked and fired,—killing at once twenty-seven of the assailants; the effect was decisive, the columns recoiled, and the little fort was saved with the loss of one man;—on the next morning the British and their allies, having the fear of Harrison before his eyes, were gone, leaving behind them in their haste, guns, stores, and clothing.

Meanwhile Perry had gained his famous victory on the lakes, and the American army having been reinforced, set sail for Canada on the 27th of September, and in a few hours stood around the ruins or the deserted and wasted Malden, from which place Proctor had retreated to Sandwich, intending to make his way into Canada, by the valley of the Thames.

General Harrison started in pursuit, and he found Proctor posted on the Thames; his left flanked by the river, and his right by a swamp. Between this and another swamp, and still further to the right, was Tecumthe and his Indians. Proctor had formed his men in open order, that is, with intervals of three or four feet between the files. Colonel Johnson was ordered by Harrison to dash through the enemy's line in a column. This was done, and the broken line of the Indians assailed. The British threw down their arms, and begged for quarter.

Some fighting took place on the American left, with the Indians. Tecumthe rushed on Colonel Johnson with his tomahawk raised, and was in the act of striking him, when Johnson drew a pistol, and shot him dead. The Indians no longer hearing the cry of their chief, animating them to renewed exertions, gave way, and fled in great confusion. We give Harrison's account of the battle.

"The troops at my disposal consisted of about one hundred and twenty regulars of the 27th regiment, five brigades of Kentucky volunteer militia infantry, under his excellency Governor Shelby, averaging less than five hundred men, and Colonel Johnson's regiment of mounted infantry, making in the whole an aggregate of something above three thousand. No disposition of an army, opposed to an Indian force, can be safe unless it is secured on the flanks and in the rear. I had, therefore, no difficulty in arranging the infantry conformably to my general order of battle. General Trotter's brigade of five hundred men, formed the front line, his right upon the road and his left upon the swamp. General King's brigade as a second line, one hundred and fifty yards in the rear of Trotter's and Chiles's brigade as a corps of reserve in the rear of it. These three brigades formed the command of Major-General Henry; the whole of General Desha's division, consisting of two brigades, were formed *en potence* upon the left of Trotter.

" Whilst I was engaged in forming the infantry, I had directed Colonel Johnson's regiment, which was still in front, to be formed in two lines opposite to the enemy, and upon the advance of the infantry, to take ground to the left and forming upon that flank to endeavor to turn the right of the Indians. A moment's reflection, however, convinced me that from the thickness of the woods and swampiness of the ground, they would be unable to do any thing on horseback, and there was no time to dismount them and place their horses in security; I, therefore determined to refuse my left to the Indians, and to break the British lines at once, by a charge of the mounted infantry; the measure was not sanctioned by any thing that I had seen or heard of, but I was fully convinced that it would succeed. The American backwoodsmen ride better in the woods than any other people. A musket or rifle is no impediment to them, being accustomed to carry them on horseback from their earliest youth. I was persuaded, too, that the enemy would be quite unprepared for the shock, and that they could not resist it.

Conformably to this idea, I directed the regiment to be drawn up in close column, with its right at the distance of fifty yards from the road, (that it might be in some measure protected by the trees from the artillery) its left upon the swamp, and to charge at full speed as soon as the enemy delivered their fire. The few regular troops of the 27th regiment under their Colonel (Paull) occupied, in columns of sections of four, the small space between the road and the river, for the purpose of seizing the enemy's artillery, and some ten or twelve friendly Indians were directed to move under the bank. The crotchet formed by the front line, and General Desha's division was an important point. At that place, the venerable governor of Kentucky was posted, who at the age of sixty-six preserves all the vigor of youth, the ardent zeal which distinguished him in the revolutionary war, and the undaunted bravery which he manifested at King's Mountain. With my aids-de-camp, the acting assistant adjutant-general, Captain Butler, my gallant friend, Commodore Perry, who did me the honor to serve as my volunteer aid-de-camp, and Brigadier-General Cass, who, having no command, tendered me his assistance, I placed myself at the head of the front line of infantry, to direct the movements of the cavalry, and give them the necessary support. The army had moved on in this order but a short distance, when the mounted men received the fire of the British line, and were ordered to charge; the horses in the front of the column recoiled from the fire; another was given by the enemy, and our column at length getting in motion, broke through the enemy with irresistible force. In one minute the contest in front was over; the British officer seeing no hopes of reducing their disordered ranks to order, and our mounted men wheeling upon them and pouring in a destructive fire, immediately surrendered. It is certain that three only of our troops were wounded in this charge. Upon the left, however, the contest was more severe with the Indians. Colonel

Johnson, who commanded on that flank of his regiment, received a most galling fire from them, which was returned with great effect. The Indians still further to the right advanced and fell in with our front line of infantry, near its junction with Desha's division, and for a moment made an impression upon it. His excellency, Governor Shelby, however, brought up a regiment to its support, and the enemy receiving a severe fire in front, and a part of Johnson's regiment having gained their rear, retreated with precipitation. Their loss was very considerable in the action, and many were killed in their retreat.

# THE CREEK WAR.

In the spring of 1812, the southern Indians were visited by Tecumthe, the celebrated Shawanese chief, who attended their councils, and used every persuasion, to induce them to league with their brethren of the north, and with the aid of the British to extirpate the whites. He told them that the Great Spirit had ordered the destruction of the whites, and the re-possession of the country by the red men. The Creeks received these doctrines as gospel, and with other tribes were induced to commence hostilities against the United States.

Several murders and robberies were committed, and the perpetrators refused to be given up; evident appearances of hostilities were now every where visible. Alarm and consternation prevailed among the white inhabitants; those of the Tensaw district, a considerable settlement on the Alabama, fled for safety to Fort Mimms, on that river, sixteen miles above Fort Stoddard. The place was garrisoned by one hundred and fifty volunteers of the Mississippi Territory, under Major Beasly. The inhabitants collected at the fort amounted to about three hundred.

At eleven o'clock in the forenoon of August, a body of Indians to the amount of six or seven hundred warriors issued from the adjoining wood, and approached the fort; they advanced within a few rods of it before the alarm was given. As the sentinel cried out, "Indians," they immediately gave the war-whoop, and rushed in at the gate before the garrison had time to shut it. This decided their fate. Major Beasly was mortally wounded at the commencement of the assault; he ordered his men to secure the ammunition, and retreat into the house; he was himself carried into the kitchen, and afterwards consumed in the flames. The fort was originally square, but Major Beasly had enlarged it by extending the lines upon two sides about fifty feet, and putting up a new side, into which the gate was removed; the old line of pickets were standing, and the Indians on rushing in at the gate, obtained possession of the outer part, and through the port-holes of the old line of pickets, fired on the people who held the interior. On the opposite side of the fort was an off-set or bastion made round the back gate, which being open on the outside, was occupied by the Indians, who, with the axes that lay scattered about, cut down the gate. The people in the fort kept possession of the port-holes on the other lines, and fired on the Indians who remained on the outside. Some of the Indians ascended the block-house at one of the corners, and fired on the garrison below, but were soon dislodged; they succeeded, however, in setting fire to a house near the pickets, which communicated to the kitchen, and thence to the main dwelling-house. When the people in the fort saw the Indians in full possession of the outer court, the gate open, the men fast falling, and their houses in flames, they gave up all for lost, and a scene of the most distressing horror ensued. The women and children sought refuge in the upper story of the dwelling-house, and were consumed in the flames, the Indians dancing and yelling round them with the most savage delight. Those who were without the buildings were murdered and scalped without distinction of age or sex; seventeen only escaped. The battle and massacre lasted from eleven in the forenoon until six in the afternoon, by which time the work of destruction was fully completed, the fort and buildings entirely demolished, and upwards of four hundred men, women, and children massacred.

This event spread consternation and dismay through all the neighboring settlements; the inhabitants fled with the utmost precipitation, without taking any means of subsistance, to Fort Stoddard, Mobile, and other places, where they deemed themselves safe from the fury of the savages. Their dwellings and property were left a prey to the Indians, who plundered and laid waste the adjacent country to a great extent, without opposition.

These calamitous events, excited the liveliest feelings of anxiety in Tennessee and Georgia, and three thousand five hundred men were immediately raised in Tennesee, and placed under the command of General Jackson and General Cocke. Georgia organized and equipped eighteen hundred men, who were placed under the command of General Floyd, and marched into the southern section of the Creek nation.

The infatuated Creeks were now doomed to atone in the most exemplary manner for the massacre at Fort Mimms, and their subsequent ravages. The first object to which the troops under General Jackson were directed, was their encampments at the Tallushatches towns, on the Coosa river, a northern branch of the Alabama. On the 2d of November, General Coffee was detached with a part of his brigade of cavalry, and a corps of mounted riflemen, amounting to nine hundred, against this assemblage. He arrived on the morning of the 3d, and encircled the encampment with his cavalry; when he had approached within half a mile, the Creeks sounded the war-whoop, and prepared for action. Captain Hammond's and Lieutenant Patterson's companies advanced within the circle and gave a few shots for the purpose of drawing out the enemy. The Creeks formed and made a violent charge. Captain Hammond, according to his orders, gave way, and was pursued by the Indians, until they met the right column, which gave them a general fire, and then charged. The Indians immediately retreated within and

27*

behind their buildings, and fought with desperation ; but their destruction was soon accomplished. The soldiers rushed up to the doors of their houses, broke them open, and in a few minutes killed the last warrior of them : not one escaped to carry the news. None asked for quarters, but fought as long as they could stand or sit, and met death in various shapes without a groan. Two hundred warriors were killed, eighty-four women and children taken prisoners and discharged ; of General Coffee's troops five only were killed, and forty-one wounded.

General Jackson's head-quarter's were established at a place called the Ten Islands, on the Coosa river, and after fortifying it, he called it Fort Strother. Jackson received information from some friendly Indians, that the hostile Creeks were assembling in great numbers at Fort Talladega, thirty miles below, on the same river. He determined to commence his march the same night, and dispatched a messenger to General White, informing him of his movement, and wishing him to hasten his march, in order to protect Fort Strother. He had previously ordered General White to join him as speedily as possible, and had received his assurances that he would be with him on the 7th. General Jackson crossed the river at Ten Islands immediately, leaving his baggage wagons, and whatever else might hinder his progress, behind. He was within six miles of Talladega, about midnight, when he was overtaken by a runner, with a note from General White, informing him that he had altered his course, and was on his march back to join General Cocke, at the mouth of the Chataga.

It was then too late for the general to change his plan of operations, or make any new arrangements. He renewed his march at three o'clock, and at sunrise, came within half a mile of his enemy, whom he found encamped a quarter of a mile in advance of the fort. He immediately formed the line of battle ; the militia on the left, the volunteers on the right, and the cavalry on the wings; and advanced in a curve, keeping his rear connected with the advance of the infantry line, so as to inclose the enemy in a circle. The advance guard met the attack of the Indians with intrepidity, and having poured upon them four or five rounds, fell back to the main body. The enemy pursued, and were met by the front line. This line was broken, and several companies of militia retreated. At this moment a corps of cavalry, under Lieutenant-Colonel Dyer, which was kept as a reserve, was ordered to dismount and fill the vacancy. The order was promptly executed, the militia soon rallied, and returned to the charge. The fire now became general along the first line and the contiguous wings. The Indians fled, and were met and pursued in every direction. The right wing followed them with a destructive fire to the mountians, three miles distant. Two hundred and ninety of their warriors were found dead, and a large number killed in the pursuit, who were not found. General Jackson lost fifteen men killed, and eighteen wounded. In consequence of the failure of General White to proceed to camp Strother, General Jackson was obliged to give up further pursuit, and immediately return to his camp to protect his sick, wounded, and baggage.

In the meantime, General White, with a party of Tennessee militia, acting under orders from General Cocke, who considered that he held a command entirely separate from General Jackson, attacked the chief town of the Hillabee tribe of Indians, killed sixty warriors, and returned to Fort Armstrong with two hundred and fifty prisoners, without the loss of a man killed or wounded.

On the 29th of November, General Floyd, with a body of Georgia militia, attacked a number of hostile Indians, at the Autosee towns, on the southern bank of the Tallapoosa river. His line of battle was formed at half-past six in the morning, in front of the principal town. The Indians presented themselves at every point, and fought with desperate fury.  But the fire of the artillery forced them to take refuge in the copses, thickets, and out-houses, in the rear of the town.  At nine o'clock, the Indians were completely driven from the plain; the contest lasted about three hours.  Their loss was estimated at about two hundred killed, among whom were the Autosee and Tallisee kings.  The number of wounded could not be ascertained, as they were dragged from the field by their friends, yet they must have been considerable.

After resting a few days, General Floyd proceeded to camp Defiance, some fifty miles further west, into the enemy's country. Here he was attacked, about five o'clock in the morning on the 3d of January, 1814, and after a sharp contest, the enemy were driven from the field at the point of the bayonet, leaving thirty-seven dead, and from the numerous war-clubs, head-dresses, and trails of blood found in various directions their loss must have been much greater.  General Floyd lost seventeen killed, and one hundred and thirty wounded: of the friendly Indians five were killed, and fifteen wounded.

On the 13th of December, 1813, General Claiborne, marched a detachment of volunteers, from Fort Claiborne, on the east Alabama, eighty-five miles above Fort Stoddard, with a view of destroying some towns of the Creeks above the mouth of the Cahawba.  He proceeded up the river one hundred and ten miles, when he arrived at a newly erected town, called Eccanachaca, or Holy Ground, occupied by a large body of Indians, under the command of the noted chief Weatherford, who commanded at the massacre of Fort Mimms.  On the 23d at noon, the right wing, commanded by Colonel Carson, commenced the attack on the enemy, who had been apprised of Colonel Claiborne's approach, and judiciously chosen the ground.  Before the centre arrived so as to join in the action, the Indians fled in all directions, leaving thirty dead on the field.  A pursuit was immediately ordered, but owing to the nature of the country, nothing was effected. The town was nearly surrounded by swamps and deep ravines, which rendered the approach difficult, and facilitated the escape of the enemy. A large quantity of provisions, and property of various kinds was found, which, together with the town, were destroyed. The next day was employed in destroying another town, eight miles further up the river, and in taking and destroying the enemy's boats. Eccanachaca was built after the commencement of hostilities, as a place of safety for the inhabitants of several villages; and was the residence of their principal prophets, Weatherford, Francis, and Singuister. Three of the Shawanese, or Tecumthe's tribe from the north, were among the slain. General Claiborne had one killed and six wounded. At this town was found a letter from the governor of Pensacola, directed to Weatherford and the other chiefs, congratulating them on their success at Fort Mimms, encouraging them to continue the war, and promising them presents, arms, and munitions from Havana.

About this time a mutiny commenced among the Tennessee volunteers, which threatened to end in their total abandonment of the campaign. It arose from a want of provisions, and although occasional supplies were forwarded by the contractors, the army was in a state bordering on starvation. While General Jackson remained wholly unmoved by his own privations, he was filled with the deepest concern for his army. His utmost exertions unceasingly applied, were insufficient to remove the sufferings to which he saw them exposed; and although they were by no means so great as they themselves represented, yet were undoubtedly such as to be severely felt. Discontents and a desire to return home arose, and presently spread throughout the camp; and these were still further embittered and augmented by the arts of a few designing officers, who believing that the campaign would now break up, hoped to make themselves popular, on the return, by encouraging and taking part in the complaints of the soldiery.

At length revolt began to show itself openly. The officers and soldiers of the militia, collecting in their tents, and talking over their grievances, determined to abandon the camp. Jackson on being apprized of their determination to abandon him, resolved to oppose it. In the morning, when they were to carry their intentions into execution, he drew up the volunteers in front of them, with positive commands to prevent their progress, and compel them to return to their former position in the camp. The militia, seeing this, and fearing the consequences of persisting in their purpose, at once abandoned it, and returned to their quarters, without further murmuring; extolling, in the highest terms, the unalterable firmness of the general.

The next day, however, presented a singular scene. The volunteers, who, the day before, had been the instrument for compelling the militia to return to their duty, seeing the destruction of those hopes on which they had lately built, in turn began to mutiny themselves. Their opposition to the departure of the militia was but a mere pretence to escape suspicion; for they silently wished them success. They now determined to move off in a body, believing, from the known disaffection in the camp, that the general could find no means to prevent it. What was their surprise, however, when, on attempting to effectuate their resolves, they found the same men whom they so lately opposed, occupying the very position which they had done the day previous, for a similar purpose, and manifesting a fixed determination to obey the orders of their general! All they ventured to do, was to take the example through, and, like them, move back in peace and quietness to their quarters.

About this time Jackson received letters from the contractors, and principal wagon-master, stating that supplies were on the road and would shortly reach his camp. He hastened to lay

them before the division, and invited the field and platoon
officers to his quarters that evening, to consult on measures
proper to be pursued.   He addressed them in an animated
speech, in which he extolled their patriotism and achievements,
and lamented the privations to which they had been exposed.
He spoke of the great importance of the conquests they had
already made, and that if abandoned, dreadful consequences
must ensue.

"What," continued he, " is the present situation of our camp?
a number of our fellow soldiers are wounded, and unable to help
themselves.   Shall it be said that we are so lost to humanity,
as to leave them in this condition?   Can any one, under these
circumstances, and under these prospects, consent to an abandonment of the camp; of all that we have acquired in the midst
of so many difficulties, privations, and dangers; of what it will
cost us so much to regain; of what we never can regain,—our
brave wounded companions, who will be murdered by our un-
thinking, unfeeling inhumanity?   Surely there can be none
such!   No, we will take with us, when we go, our wounded
and sick.   They must not, shall not perish by our cold-blooded
indifference.   But why should you despond?   I do not, and
yet your wants are not greater than mine. To be sure, we do not
live sumptuously: but no one has died of hunger, or is likely
to die; and then how animating are our prospects! Large supplies are at Deposit, and already are officers dispatched to hasten
them on.   Wagons are on the way! a large number of beeves
are in the neighborhood; and detachments are out to bring
them in.   All these resources surely cannot fail.   I have no
wish to starve you—none to deceive you.   Stay contentedly;
and if supplies do not arrive in two days, we will all march back
together, and throw the blame of our failure where it should
properly lie; until then, we certainly have the means of subsisting; and if we are compelled to bear privations, let us

remember that they are borne for our country, and are not greater than many—perhaps most armies have been compelled to endure. I have called you together to tell you my feelings and my wishes; this evening, think on them seriously; and let me know yours in the morning."

They then retired to their tents, when the officers of the volunteer brigade came to this conclusion, that "nothing short of marching the army immediately back to the settlements, could prevent that disgrace which must attend a forcible desertion of the camp, by the soldiers." The officers of the militia concluded differently, and determined to remain a few days longer. Jackson ordered General Hull to march his brigade to Fort Deposit, and after satisfying their wants to return, and act as escort to the provisions. The second regiment, however, unwilling to be outdone by the militia consented to remain; and the first proceeded alone. Two days elapsed, and the militia demanded to be sent back to the settlements as agreed upon. There was no help for it, and Jackson had to comply with their demand. One hundred and nine men expressed their willingness to remain with him, and protect Fort Strother, the place at which they were then encamped. Rejoiced that he would not have to entirely abandon his position, he set out with the remainder of his army for Deposit. Before starting they were made distinctly to understand that in the event of their meeting supplies they were to return and prosecute the campaign. This soon took place, for scarcely had they proceeded more than ten miles, when they met one hundred and fifty beeves; but this was to them an unwelcome sight.

Their faces being now turned toward home, no spectacle could be more hateful, than one which was to change their destination. They were halted, and having satisfied their hungry appetites, the troops, with the exception of such as were necessary to proceed with the sick and wounded, were ordered to return to the encampment,—he himself intending to see the contractors, and establish more effectual arrangements for the future. So great was their aversion to returning, that they preferred a violation of their duty, and their pledged honor. Low murmuring ran along the lines, and presently broke out into open mutiny. In spite of the order they had received, they began to revolt, and one company was already moving off, in a direction towards home. They had proceeded some distance, before information of their departure was known to Jackson. Irritated at their conduct, in attempting to violate the promises they had given, and knowing that the success of future operations depended on the result; the general pursued, until he came near a part of his staff, and a few soldiers, who, with General Coffee, had halted about a quarter of a mile ahead. He ordered them to form immediately across the road, and to fire on the mutineers, if they attempted to proceed. Snatching up their arms, these faithful adherents presented a front which threw the deserters into affright, and caused them to retreat precipitately to the main body. Here, it was hoped, the matter would end, and that no further opposition would be made to returning. This expectation was not realized; a mutinous temper began presently to display itself throughout the whole brigade. Jackson having left his aid-de-camp, Major Reid, engaged in making up some dispatches, had gone out alone amongst his troops, who were at some little distance; on his arrival he found a much more extensive mutiny, than that which had just been quelled. Almost the whole brigade had put itself into an attitude for moving forcibly off. A crisis had arrived; and feeling its importance, he determined to take no middle ground, but to triumph or perish. He was still without the use of his left arm; but, seizing a musket, and resting it on the neck of his horse, he threw himself in front of the column, and threatened to shoot the first man who should attempt to advance. In this situation

28

he was found by Major Reid and General Coffee, who, fearing from the length of his absence, that some disturbance had arisen, hastened where he was, and placing themselves by his side, awaited the result in anxious expectation. For many minutes the column preserved a sullen, yet hesitating attitude, fearing to proceed in their purpose, and disliking to abandon it. In the mean time, those who remained faithful to their duty, amounting to about two companies, were collected and formed at a short distance in advance of the troops, and in rear of the general, with positive directions to imitate his example in firing, if they attempted to proceed. At length, finding no one bold enough to advance, and overtaken by those fears that in the hour of peril always beset persons engaged in what they know to be a bad cause, they abandoned their purpose, and turning quietly round, agreed to return to their posts.

He restored quiet at Deposit, where there was signs of mutiny and set out on his return to Fort Strother. Here another difficulty arose, the volunteers claimed that the period for which they had undertaken to act would end on the 10th of December. Jackson replied that he could not undertake to discharge them unless specially authorized. But he resolved in case of contingency to provide other means for the continuance of the campaign. He accordingly ordered General Roberts to return, and fill up the deficiencies in his brigade, and dispatched Colonel Carroll and Major Searcy into Tennessee to raise volunteers for six months, or during the campaign; writing at the same time, to many respectable characters, he exhorted them to contribute all their assistance to the accomplishment of this object. He received a letter from the Rev. Gideon Blackburn, assuring him that volunteers from Tennessee would eagerly hasten to his relief, if they knew their services were wanted.

Jackson was anxious to employ his troops actively, and to prosecute the campaign. He thought that by this method he might dispel their discontents. He wrote to General Cocke, desiring him to join him immediately at Ten Islands, with fifteen hundred men, as he desired to commence operations immediately. Notwithstanding his utmost efforts, the spirit of disaffection was still rife, and the volunteers through Colonel Martin, who addressed Jackson a letter, stating that their terms of service would expire on the 10th of December. He stated that he deplored the state of affairs, and that the company looked to their general for an honorable discharge. To this the general replied, that he had written to the governor of Tennessee on the subject, and the moment it was signified to him by any competent authority, that the volunteers might be exonerated from further service, that moment would he pronounce it with the utmost satisfaction. " I have only the power of pronouncing a discharge,—not of giving it, in any case ;—a distinction which I would wish should be borne in mind. Already I have sent to raise volunteers, on my own responsibility, to complete a campaign which has been so happily begun, and thus far, so fortunately prosecuted. The moment they arrive, and I am assured, that, fired by our exploits, on the first intimation that we need their services, they will be substituted in the place of those who are discontented here; the latter will then be permitted to return to their homes, with all the honor, which, under such circumstances, they can carry along with them. But I still cherish the hope, that their dissatisfaction and complaints have been greatly exaggerated. I can not, must not believe, that the ' Volunteers of Tennessee,' a name ever dear to fame, will disgrace themselves, and a country which they have honored, by abandoning her standard, as mutineers and deserters; but should I be disappointed, and compelled to resign this pleasing hope, one thing I will not resign—my duty. Mutiny and sedition, so long as I possess the power of quelling them, shall be put down; and when left destitute of this, I will still be found, in the last extremity, endeavoring to discharge the duty I own my country and myself."

He replied to the platoon officers, who had addressed him upon the same subject, in much the same manner. On the evening of the 9th, he was informed by General Hull, that his whole brigade was in a state of mutiny. He immediately issued the following general order:

"The commanding general being informed that an actual mutiny exists in the camp, all officers and soldiers are commanded to put it down.

"The officers and soldiers of the first brigade will, without delay, parade on the west side of the fort, and await further orders." The artillery company, with two small field-pieces, being posted in the front and rear; and the militia, under the command of Colonel Wynne, on the eminences, in advance, were ordered to prevent any forcible departure of the volunteers.

The general rode along the line, which had been formed agreeably to his orders, and addressed them by companies, in a strain of impassioned eloquence. He fully expatiated on their former good conduct, and the esteem and applause it had secured them; and pointed to the disgrace which they must heap upon themselves, their families, and their country, by persisting, even if they could succeed, in their present mutiny. But he told them they should not succeed, but by passing over his body; that even in opposing their mutinous spirit, he should perish honorably,—by perishing at his post, and in the discharge of his duty. "Reinforcements," he continued, "are preparing to hasten to my assistance; it cannot be long before they will arrive. I am, too, in daily expectation of receiving information, whether you may be discharged or not—until then, you must not, and shall not retire. I have done with entreaty,—it has been used long enough. I will attempt it no more. You must now determine whether you will go, or peaceably remain; if you still perist in your determination to move forcibly off, the point between us shall soon be decided." At first they hesitated; he demanded an explicit and positive answer. They still hesitated, and he commanded the artillerists to prepare the match; he himself remaining in front of the volunteers, and within the line of fire, which he intended soon to order. Alarmed at his apparent determination, and dreading the consequences involved in such a contest; "Let us return," was presently lisped along the line, and was soon after determined upon. The officers now came forward, and pledged themselves for their men, who either nodded assent, or openly expressed a willingness to retire to their quarters, and remain without further tumult, until information were had, or the expected aid should arrive. Thus passed away a moment of the greatest peril,—pregnant with the most important consequences.

But their purpose was not wholly abandoned, and Jackson determined to rid himself of men whose presence answered no other purpose than to keep discontent alive in the camp. He therefore ordered General Hull to march them to Nashville, and do with them as the governor of Tennessee should direct. He determined to make one more appeal to their honor and patriotism, however, and on the 13th, directed his aid-de-camp to read to them the following address:

"On the 10th of December, 1812, you assembled at the call of your country. Your profession of patriotism, and ability to endure fatigue, were at once tested by the inclemency of the weather. Breaking your way through sheets of ice, you descended the Mississippi, and reached the point at which you were ordered to be halted and dismissed. All this you bore without murmuring. Finding that your services were not needed, the means of marching you back were procured; every difficulty was surmounted, and, as soon as the point from which you embarked was regained, the order for your dismissal was carried into effect. The promptness with which you assembled, the regularity of your conduct, your attention to your duties, the determination manifested, on every occasion, to carry into effect the wishes and will of your government, placed you on elevated ground. You not only distinguished yourselves, but gave to your state a distinguished rank with her sisters; and led your government to believe that the honor of the nation would never be tarnished, when entrusted to the holy keeping of the 'Volunteers of Tennessee.'

"In the progress of a war, which the implacable and eternal enemy of our independence induced to be waged, we found that, without cause on our part, a portion of the Creek nation was added to the number of our foes. To put it down, the first glance of the administration fell on you: and you were again summoned to the field of honor. In full possession of your former feelings, that summons was cheerfully obeyed. Before your enemy thought you in motion, you were at Tallushatchee and Talladega. The thunder of your arms was a signal to them, that the slaughter of your countrymen was about to be avenged. You fought, you conquered! barely enough of the foe escaped, to recount to their savage associates, your deeds of valor. You returned to this place, loaded with honors, and the applauses of your country.

"Can it be, that these brave men are about to become the tarnishers of their own reputation! the destroyers of a name, which does them so much honor? Yes, it is truth too well disclosed, that cheerfulness has been exchanged for complaints: murmurings and discontents alone prevail. Men who a little while since were offering up prayers, for permission to chastise the merciless savage,—who burned with impatience to teach them how much they had hitherto been indebted to our forbearance; are now, when they could so easily attain their wishes, seeking to be discharged. The heart of your general has been

pierced. The first object of his military affections, and the first
glory of his life, were the volunteers of Tennessee! The very
name recalls to him a thousand endearing recollections. But
these men,—these volunteers have become mutineers. The
feelings he would have indulged, your general has been compelled to suppress—he has been compelled by a regard to that
subordination, so necessary to the support of every army, and
which he is bound to have observed, to check the disorder which
would have destroyed you. He has interposed his authority
for your safety; to prevent you from disgracing yourselves and
your country. Tranquillity has been restored in our camp,—
contentment shall also be restored; this can be done only by
permitting those to retire, whose dissatisfaction proceeds from
causes that cannot be controlled. This permission will now be
given. Your country will dispense with your services, if you
have no longer a regard for that fame, which you have so nobly
earned for yourselves and her. Yes, soldiers, you who were
once so brave, and to whom honor was so dear, shall be permitted to return to your homes, if you still desire it. But in
what language, when you arrive, will you address your families
and friends? Will you tell them that you abandoned your
general, and your late associates in arms, within fifty miles of a
savage enemy; who equally delights in shedding the blood of
the innocent female and her sleeping babe, as that of the warrior
contending in battle? Lamentable, disgraceful tale! If your
dispositions are really changed; if you fear an enemy you so
lately conquered; this day will prove it. I now put it to yourselves; determine upon the part you will act, influenced only
by the suggestions of your own hearts, and your own under-
standings. All who prefer an inglorious retirement, shall be
ordered to Nashville, to be discharged, as the president or the
governor may direct. Who choose to remain, and unite with their
general in the further prosecution of the campaign, can do so,

and will thereby furnish a proof, that they have been greatly traduced; and that although disaffection and cowardice has reached the hearts of some, it has not reached theirs. To such my assurance is given, that former irregularities will not be attributed to them. They shall be immediately organized into a separate corps, under officers of their own choice; and in a little while, it is confidently believed, an opportunity will be afforded of adding to the laurels you have already won."

This appeal failed of the desired effect. Captain Williamson alone agreed to remain. Finding that their determination to abandon the service could not be changed, and that every principle of patriotism was forgotten, the general communicated his order to General Hull, directing him to march his brigade to Nashville, and await such instructions of he might receive from the president, or the governor of Tennessee.

General Cocke with fifteen hundred men arrived on the 12th; but it was found that no part as his troops were brought into the field under the requisition of the president of the United States; and that the term of service of a greater part of them would expire in a few days; and of the whole in a few weeks. In consequence of this he was ordered into his district to comply with that requisition, and to carry with him and discharge near their homes, those of his troops, the period of whose service was within a short time of being ended.

Meantime the cavalry and mounted riflemen, who under an express stipulation to return and complete the campaign, had been permitted to retire into the settlements, to recruit their horses and procure winter clothing, had, at the time appointed, reassembled in the neighborhood of Huntsville. But, catching the infection of discontent from the infantry, on their return march, they began now to clamour with equal earnestness for a discharge. The cavalry insisted that they were as well entitled to it as the infantry; and the riflemen, that they could not be held in service after the 24th, that being three months from the time they had been mustered; and as that day was so near at hand, it was wholly useless to advance any farther.

General Coffee, who was confined at Huntsville by severe indisposition, employed all the means which his debilitated strength would allow him, to remove the dangerous impressions they had so readily imbibed, and to reclaim them to a sense of honor and duty; but all his efforts proved unavailing. He immediately ordered his brigade to head-quarters; they had proceeded as far as Ditto's Ferry, when the greater part of them refusing to cross the river, returned in a tumultuous manner, committing on the route many irregularities, which there was not sufficient force to restrain. Not more than seven hundred of the brigade could be gotten over; who, having marched to Deposit, were directed to be halted, until further orders could be obtained from General Jackson. At this place they committed the wildest extravagancies; profusely wasting the public grain, which, with much difficulty and labor, had been collected there, for the purpose of the campaign; and indulging in every species of excess. Whilst thus rioting, they continued to clamour most vociferously, for their discharge. General Coffee finding his utmost efforts ineffectual, to restrain or to quiet them, wrote to Jackson, acquainting him with their conduct and demands, and inclosing a petition that had been addressed to him by the rifle regiment. In his letter, he says, "I am 'of opinion, the sooner they can be gotten clear of the better; they are consuming the forage that will be necessary for others, and I am satisfied they will do no more good. I have told them, their petition would be submitted to you, who would decide upon it in the shortest possible time." This was truly disagreeable news to the general. Already sufficiently harassed by the discontents and opposition of his troops; now that they had retired, he looked anxiously forward, in hopes that the tranquillity of his camp would be no more assailed. On the brigade of Coffee, he had placed great reliance, and, from the pledges it had given him, entertained no fears but that it would return and act with him, as soon as he should be ready to proceed. He replied to General Coffee, and taking a view of the grounds and causes of their complaints, endeavored to reconcile their objections, and persuade them to a discharge of the duties they had undertaken, and covenanted to perform.

The signers of that address, observes the general, commence by saying, " that jealousy is prevailing in our camp, with respect to the understanding between themselves and the government, relative to the service required of them ; and believing it to be its policy to act fairly, are of opinion that a full explanation of their case will have a good effect, in promoting the cause in which they are engaged."

Jackson addressed them in the most pointed manner; he reminded them of the pledge they had given ; he appealed to their honor, believing that if this were unsuccessful, there was "nothing by which he could hope to hold them." Meantime Jackson received a letter from the governor of Tennessee. It recommended him to dismiss, not discharge them, because the latter was out of their power. To induce them to remain, the governor had suggested but one argument, which as yet had not been tried; " that it was very doubtful if the government would pay them for the services they had already rendered, if abandoned without her authority." The letter was enclosed for their inspection, accompanied with these remarks :

" I have just received a letter from Governor Blount, which I hasten to transmit to you, that you may avail yourselves of whatever benefits and privileges it holds out. You will perceive, that he does not consider he has any power to discharge you— neither have I :—but you have my permission to retire from the service, if you are still desirous of doing so, and are prepared to risk the consequences."

These letters, so far from answering the desired end, had a directly contrary effect. The governor's was no sooner read than they eagerly laid hold of it to support the resolution they had already formed; and without further ceremony or delay, abandoned the campaign, with their colonel, Allcorn, at their head, who, so far from having endeavored to reconcile them, is believed by secret artifices to have fomented their discontents.

So general was the dissatisfaction of this brigade, and with such longing anxiety did they indulge the hope of a speedy return to their homes, that their impatience did not permit them to wait the return of the messenger from head-quarters. Before an answer could reach General Coffee, they had broken up their encampment at Deposit, re-crossed the river, and proceeded four miles beyond Huntsville. On receiving it, Coffee had the brigade drawn up in solid column, and the letters, together with the pledge they had given, read to them; after which, the Rev. Mr. Blackburn endeavored, in an eloquent speech, in which he pointed out the ruinous consequences that were to be apprehended, if they persisted in their present purpose, to recall them to a sense of duty and honor; but they had formed their resolution too steadfastly, and had gone too extravagant lengths, to be influenced by the letter, the pledge, or the speech. As to the pledge, a few said they had not authorised it to be made; others, that as the general had not returned an immediate acceptance, they did not consider themselves bound by it; but the greater part candidly acknowledged, that they stood committed, and were without any justification for their present conduct. Nevertheless, except a few officers, and three or four privates, the whole persisted in the determination to abandon the service. Thus, in a tumultuous manner, they broke up, and committing innumerable extravagancies regardless alike of law and decency, continued their route to their respective homes.

Whilst these unfortunate events were transpiring in the rear,

matters were far from wearing a very encouraging aspect at
head-quarters.   General Robert's brigade of West Tennessee
militia, consisting in consequence of numerous desertions of
about six hundred men, imitating the example set them, began
on the day they thought themselves entitled to discharge to set
about returning home.   General Jackson, however, did not put
the same construction upon it that they did.   It was true the
act did not determine the time of their engagements; but it had
specified the object for which they had been called out; viz.:
the subjugation of the Indians; and as that object was not yet
attained, it was thought that they were not entitled to a discharge.   He again solicited the governor of Tennessee in the
most pressing manner to take the earliest measures for supplying by draft, or voluntary enlistment, the deficiencies, as well
as that which was so soon to be expected.

The governor replied that he had ordered General Cocke to
bring into the field fifteen hundred men of the detached militia,
as the secretary of war had required, together with a thousand
volunteers under the act of the assembly of Tennessee, and he
did not feel authorized to grant a new order.   He remarked
that he looked upon the further prosecution of the campaign as
fruitless, and concluded by advising him to withdraw the troops
into the settlements, and suspend all active operations, until the
general government should provide more effectual means, for
conducting it to a favorable issue.  Jackson determined to oppose
this advice, and in his letter remarks as follows:

"Had your wish, that I should discharge a part of my force,
and retire, with the residue, into the settlements, assumed the
form of a positive order, it might have furnished me some
apology for pursuing such a course; but by no means a full
justification.   As you would have no power to give such an
order, I could not be inculpable in obeying, with my eyes
open to the fatal consequences that would attend it.   But a bare

recommendation, founded, as I am satisfied it must be, on the artful suggestions of those fireside patriots, who seek, in a failure of the expedition, an excuse for their supineness; and upon the misrepresentations of the discontented from the army, who wish it to be believed, that the difficulties which overcame their patriotism are wholly insurmountable, would afford me but a feeble shield, against the reproaches of my country, or my conscience. Believe me, my respected friend, the remarks I make proceed from the purest personal regard. If you would preserve your reputation, or that of the state over which you preside, you must take a straight-forward, determined course; regardless of the applause or censure of the populace, and of the forebodings of that dastardly and designing crew, who, at a time like this, may be expected to clamour continually in your ears. The very wretches who now beset you with evil council, will be the first, should the measures which they recommend eventuate in disaster, to call down imprecations on your head, and load you with reproaches. Your country is in danger; apply its resources to its defence! Can any course be more plain? Do you, my friend, at such a moment as the present, sit with your arms folded, and your heart at ease, waiting a solution of your doubts, and a definition of your powers? Do you wait for special instructions from the secretary of war, which it is impossible for you to receive in time for the danger that threatens? How did the venerable Shelby act, under similar circumstances; or rather, under circumstances by no means as critical? Did he wait for orders, to do what every man of sense knew—what every patriot felt—to be right? He did not; and yet how highly and justly did the government extol his manly and energetic conduct! and how dear has his name become to all the friends of their country!

" You say, that, having given an order to General Cooke, to bring his quota of men into the field, your power ceases; and

29

that, although you are made sensible that he has wholly neglected that order, you can take no measure to remedy the omission. Widely different, indeed, is my opinion. I consider it your imperious duty, when the men, called for by your order, founded upon that of the government, are known not to be in the field, to see that they be brought there; and to take immediate measures with the officer, who, charged with the execution of your order, omits or neglects to do it. As the executive of the state, it is your duty to see that the full quota of troops be constantly kept in the field, for the time they have been required. For you are responsible to the government; your officer to you. Of what avail is it, to give an order, if it be never executed, and may be disobeyed with impunity? Is it by empty orders, that we can hope to conquer our enemies, and save our defenceless frontiers from butchery and devastation? Believe me, my valued friend, there are times, when it is highly criminal to shrink from responsibility, or scruple about the exercise of our powers. There are times, when we must disregard punctilious etiquette, and think only of serving our country. What is really our present situation? The enemy we have been sent to subdue, may be said, if we stop at this, to be only exasperated. The commander-in-chief, General Pinckney, who supposes me, by this time, prepared for renewed operations, has ordered me to advance, and form a junction with the Georgia army; and upon the expectation that I will do so, are all his arrangements formed, for the prosecution of the campaign. Will it do to defeat his plans, and jeopardize the safety of the Georgia army? The general government, too, believe, that we have now not less than five thousand in the heart of the enemy's country; and on this opinion are all their calculations bottomed; and must they all be frustrated, and I become the instrument by which it is done? God forbid!

"You advise me, too, to discharge, or dismiss from service,

until the will of the president can be known, such portion of
the militia, as have rendered three months' service. This advice
astonishes me, even more than the former. I have no such dis-
cretionary power; and it would be impolitic and ruinous to exercise it, if I had. I believed the militia, who were not specially
received for a shorter period, were engaged for six months,
unless the objects of the expedition should be sooner attained;
and in this opinion I was greatly strengthened, by your letter
of the 15th, in which you say, when answering my inquiry upon
this subject, ' the militia are detached for six months' service;'
nor did I know, or suppose, you had a different opinion, until
the arrival of your last letter. This opinion must, I suppose,
agreeably to your request, be made known to General Roberts'
brigade, and then the consequences are not difficult to be foreseen.
Every man belonging to it will abandon me on the 4th of next
month; nor shall I have the means of preventing it, but by the
application of force, which, under such circumstances, I shall
not be at liberty to use. I have labored hard, to reconcile these
men, to a continuance in service, until they could be honorably
discharged, and had hoped I had, in a great measure, succeeded;
but your opinion, operating with their own prejudices, will give
a sanction to their own conduct, and render useless any further
attempts. They will go; but I can neither discharge nor dismiss them. Shall I be told, that, as they will go, it may as
well be permitted; can that be any good reason why I should
do an unauthorized act? Is it a good reason why I should
violate the order of my superior officer, and evince a willingness
to defeat the government? And wherein does the ' sound policy'
of the measures that have been recommended consist? or in
what way are they ' likely to promote the public good?' Is it
sound policy to abandon a conquest thus far made, and deliver
up to havoc, or add to the number of our enemies, those friendly
Creeks and Cherokees, who, relying on our protection, have

espoused our cause, and aided us with their arms? Is it good policy to turn loose upon our defenceless frontiers, five thousand exasperated savages, to reek their hands once more in the blood of our citizens? What! retrograde under such circumstances! I will perish first. No, I will do my duty: I will hold the posts I have established, until ordered to abandon them by the commanding general, or die in the struggle:—long since have I determined, not to seek the preservation of life, at the sacrifice of reputation.

"But our frontiers, it seems, are to be defended, and by whom? By the very force that is now recommended to be dismissed; for I am first told to retire into the settlements, and protect the frontiers; next, to discharge my troops; and then, that no measures can be taken for raising others. No, my friend, if troops be given me, it is not by loitering on the frontiers that I will seek to give protection;—they are to be defended, if defended at all, in a very different manner;—by carrying the war into the heart of the enemy's country. All other hopes of defence are more visionary than dreams. What then is to be done? I'll tell you what. You have only to act with the energy and decision the crisis demands, and all will be well. Send me a force engaged for six months, and I will answer for the result,— but withhold it, and all is lost,—the reputation of the state, and your's, and mine along with it."

The governor immediately ordered twenty-five hundred militia, for a tour of three months, to rendezvous at Fayetteville, on the 28th of January. The command was given to Colonel Johnson, with orders to proceed without delay, by detachments or otherwise, to Fort Strother.

A difficulty now occurred with General Roberts' brigade. He had been ordered back to supply deficiencies, and returned on 27th with one hundred and ninety men, mustered for three months. He halted within a short distance of the camp, and proceeded to ascertain whether the general would receive them for the term they had stipulated. Jackson replied that he would prefer to engage them for six months, or during the campaign; but would gladly receive them for the period they had mustered; at the expiration of which time he would discharge them. Notwithstanding this assurance, however, they determined for some unknown cause to abandon their engagements, and return home. This was attributed to the conduct of General Roberts. He reported to his men, that he had been unsuccessful, and remarked that he had exonerated them from all obligations that they were under to him. They instantly set about returning. Jackson, on learning this, dispatched General Roberts after them, but he failed to induce them to return, when he was again ordered to bring them back at all hazards. Those who should willingly return to duty, except those officers, who had been reported as the instigators should be pardoned. Many of the men, upon understanding the nature of affairs, returned of their own accord, and laid the charge upon their general. He was afterwards arrested, and upon this and other charges exhibited against him, sentenced, by a court-martial, to be cashiered.

The day had arrived, when that portion of Roberts' brigade, which had continued in service, claimed to be discharged; and that whether this were given to them or not, they would abandon the campaign and return home. Jackson believed them not entitled to it, and hence, that he had no right to give it; but as Governor Blount had said differently, and his opinion, as he had required, had been promulgated, he felt it was improper that he should attempt the exercise of force to detain them. Nevertheless, believing it to be his duty to keep them, he issued a general order, commanding all persons, in the service of the United States, under his command, not to leave the encampment, without his written permission, under the penalties annexed, by the rules and articles of war, to the crime of desertion.

This was accompanied by an address, in which they were ex
horted, by all those motives which he supposed would be most
likely to have any influence, to remain at their posts, until they
could be legally discharged.   Neither the order nor the address
availed any thing.   On the morning of the 4th of January, the
officer of the day, Major Bradley, reported, that, on visiting his
guard, half after ten o'clock, he found neither the officer, Lieutenant Kearley, nor any of the sentinels at their posts.   Upon
this information, General Jackson ordered the arrest of Kearley,
who refused to surrender his sword, alleging it should protect
him to Tennessee; that he was a freeman, and not subject to
the orders of General Jackson, or any body else.   This being
made known to the general, he issued, immediately, this order
to the adjutant general; "You will forthwith cause the guards
to parade, with Captain Gordon's company of spies, and arrest
Lieutenant Kearley; and, in case you shall be opposed, in the
execution of this order, you are commanded to oppose force to
force, and arrest him at all hazards. Spare the effusion of blood,
if possible; but mutiny must, and shall be put down." Colonel
Sitler, with the guards and Gordon's company, immediately
proceeded in search, and found him at the head of his company,
on the lines, which were all formed, and about to march off.
He was ordered to halt, but refused.   The adjutant-general,
finding it necessary, directed the guards to stop him;  and
again demanded his sword, which he again refused to deliver.
The guards were commanded to fire on him, if he did not immediately deliver it, and had already cocked their guns.   At this
order, the lieutenant cocked his, and his men followed his example.   General Jackson, informed of what was passing, had
hastened to the scene, and arriving at this moment, personally
demanded of Kearley his sword, which he still obstinately refused to deliver.   Incensed at the outrage, and viewing the example as too dangerous to pass, he snatched a pistol from his

holster, and was already levelling it at the breast of Kearley, when Colonel Sitler, interposing between them, urged him to surrender his sword. At this moment, Dr. Taylor, the friend of the lieutenant, drew it from the scabbard, and handed it to the adjutant-general, who refused to receive it. It was then returned to Kearley, who now delivered it, and was placed under guard. During this crisis, both parties remained with their arms ready, and prepared for firing; and a scene of bloodshed was narrowly escaped.

Kearley being confined, and placed under guard, soon became exceedingly penitent, and earnestly supplicated the general for a pardon. He stated, that the absence of the guards and sentinels from their posts, was owing to the recommendation and advice of the brigade-major, Myers; that his not delivering his sword, when it was first demanded, was owing to the influence and arguments of others, who persuaded him that it was not his duty; that he had afterwards come to the determination to surrender himself, but was dissuaded by Captains Metcalf and Dooley, who assured him it would be a sacrifice of character, and that they would protect him in the hour of danger; why he resisted, in the presence of the general, was, that being then at the head of his company, and having undertaken to carry them home, he was restrained, at the moment, by a false idea of honor. This application was aided by the certificate of several of the most respectable officers of the camp, attesting his uniformly good behaviour heretofore, and expressing a belief that his late misconduct was wholly attributed to the interference of others. Influenced by these reasons, but particularly by the seductions which he believed had been practised upon him, by older and more experienced officers in his regiment, the general thought proper to order his liberation from arrest, and his sword to be restored to him. Never was a man more sensitive of the favor he had received, or more devoted to his benefactor, than he afterwards became.

As the term for which the East Tennessee troops had been engaged would expire on the 14th, and as Colonel Lillard's regiment had professed a desire to be led against the enemy before they quitted the service, Jackson issued the following address, hoping that they would willingly remain in the field, for a few days longer.

" Major-General Cocke having reported that your term of service will expire on the 14th, I assume no claim on you beyond that period. But, although I cannot demand as a right, the continuance of your services, I do not despair of being able to obtain them through your patriotism. For what purpose was it that you quitted your homes, and penetrated the heart of the enemy's country? Was it to avenge the blood of your fellow-citizens, inhumanly slain by that enemy;—to give security in future to our extended and unprotected frontier, and to signalize the valor by which you were animated? Will any of these objects be attained if you abandon the campaign at the time you contemplate? Not one! Yet an opportunity shall be afforded you, if you desire it. If you have been really actuated by the feelings, and governed by the motives, which, your commanding general supposes, influenced you to take up arms, and enter the field in defence of your rights, none of you will resist the appeal he now makes, or hesitates to embrace the eagerness, the opportunity he is to afford you.

The enemy, more than half conquered, but deriving encouragement and hope from the tardiness of our operations, and the distractions, which have unhappily prevailed in our camp, are again assembling below us. Another lesson of admonition must be furnished them. They must again be made to feel the weight of that power, which they have, without cause, provoked to war; and to know, that although we have been slow to take up arms, we will never again lay them from our hands, until we have secured the objects that impel us to the resort. In less than eight days I shall leave the encampment, to meet and fight them. Will any of you accompany me ? Are there any amongst you, who, at a moment like this, will not think it an outrage upon honor, for his feelings to be tested by a computation of time ? What if the period for which you tendered your services to your country has expired,—is that a consideration with the valiant, the patriotic, and the brave, who have appeared to redress the injured rights of that country, and to acquire for themselves a name of glory ? Is it a consideration with them, when those objects are still unattained, and an opportunity of acquiring them is so near at hand ? Did such men enter the field like hirelings,—to serve for pay alone ? Does all regard for their country, their families, and themselves, expire with the time, for which their services were engaged ? Will it be a sufficient gratification to their feelings, that they served out three months, without seeing the enemy, and then abandoned the campaign, when the enemy was in the neighborhood, and could be seen and conquered in ten days ? Any retrospect they can make, of the sacrifices they have encountered, and the privations they have endured, can afford but little satisfaction under such circumstances ;—the very mention of the Creek war, must cover them with the blushes of shame, and self-abasement. Having engaged for only three months, and that period having expired, you are not bound to serve any longer :—but are you bound by nothing else ? Surely, as honorable and high-minded men, you must, at such a moment as the present, feel other obligations than the law imposes. A fear of the punishment of the law, did not bring you into camp; that its demands are satisfied, will not take you from it. You had higher objects in view,—some greater good to attain. This, pour general believes,—nor can he believe otherwise, without doing you great injustice.

"Your services are not asked for longer than twenty days; and who will hesitate making such a sacrifice, when the good of his country, and his own fame are at stake? Who, under the present aspect of affairs, will even reckon it a sacrifice? When we set out to meet the enemy, this post must be retained and defended; if any of you will remain, and render this service, it will be no less important, than if you had marched to the battle; nor will your general less thankfully acknowledge it. Tuesday next, the line of march will be taken up; and in a few days thereafter, the objects of the excursion will be effected. As patriotic men, then, I ask you for your services; and thus long, I have no doubt you will cheerfully render them. I am well aware, that you are all anxious to return to your families and homes, and that you are entitled to do so; yet stay a little longer, —go with me, and meet the enemy, and you can then return, not only with the consciousness of having performed your duty, but with the glorious exultation, of having done even more than duty required."

But this address failed to move them, and on the 10th, four days before their term expired, they returned home. Jackson, however, by this time received reinforcements, and on the 17th of January, 1814, finding himself in a condition to commence active offensive operations, marched from Fort Strother with nine hundred volunteers, who were soon afterwards joined by three hundred friendly Indians, against an assemblage of Creeks at the Great Bend of the Tallapoosa. On the evening of the 21st, he fell upon a large trail, which indicated the neighborhood of a strong force. At eleven o'clock at night, he was informed by his spies that there was a large encampment of Indians, about three miles distant, who, from their actions, they judged to be apprised of his approach, and would either commence a night attack upon him, or make their escape. On receiving this intelligence, Jackson put himself in readiness for a

MASSACRE AT FORT MIMMS. Page 246.

night attack, or pursue them as soon as daylight would give him
an opportunity.

At six o'clock in the morning a vigorous attack was made
upon his left flank, which sustained it with bravery; the action
continued to rage at that point, and on the left of the rear, for
half an hour. As soon as it became light enough to pursue, the
left wing was reinforced by Captain Ferrill's company of infantry,
and led on to the charge by General Coffee. The enemy were
completely routed at every point; and the friendly Indians
joined in the pursuit, they were chased about two miles with
great slaughter. The chase being over, General Coffee was
detached to burn their encampment, but finding it fortified, he
returned to the main body for artillery. Half an hour after his
return, a large force appeared and commenced an attack upon
the right flank. General Coffee was permitted, at his own request,
to take two hundred men and turn the enemy's left, but by
some mistake only fifty-four followed him; with these he commenced an attack on their left; two hundred of the friendly Indians were ordered to fall upon the enemy's right, and co-operate with the general. The Creeks intended this attack upon
Jackson's right as a feint, and expecting to find his left weakened, directed their main force against that quarter; but General Jackson, perceiving the object of the enemy, had directed
that flank to remain firm in its position, and at the first moment
of attack they were supported by the reserve under Captain
Ferrill. The whole line met the approach of the enemy with
vigour, and after a few fires, made a bold and decisive charge.
The Creeks fled with precipitation, and were pursued a considerable distance with a destructive fire. In the meantime General
Coffee was contending on the right with a superior force; the
friendly Indians who had been ordered to his support, seeing
the enemy routed on the left, quit their post and joined in the
chase. That being over, Jim Fife, with the friendly Indians,

was again ordered to support General Coffee; as soon as he
reached him, they made a decisive charge, routed the enemy,
and pursued him three miles.  Forty-five of the enemy's slain
were found.  General Coffee was wounded in the body, and his
aid, Colonel Donaldson, and three others slain.  The next day,
General Jackson commenced his return march to Fort Strother.
His men and horses were exhausted, and he was not furnished
with either provisions or forage for a longer stay.  The enemy,
supposing they had defeated the general, hung on his rear; and
in the morning of the 24th, as he was on the point of crossing
Enotachopeo creek, the front guard having crossed with part of
the flank columns and the wounded, and the artillery just entering the water, an attack commenced on the rear.  The main
part of the rear guard precipitately gave way, leaving only
twenty-five men under Colonel Carrol, who held their ground
as long as possible.  There then remained on the left of the
creek to meet the enemy, the remnant of the rear guard, the
artillery company, and Captain Russell's company of spies.
Lieutenant Armstrong, of the artillery, immediately ordered
them to form and advance to the top of the hill, while he and
a few of his men dragged up a six-pounder, amidst a most galling fire from more than ten times their numbers.  Arrived at
the top they formed, and poured in upon their assailants a fire
of grape, and at length made a charge and repelled them.  Lieutenant Armstrong, Captains Hamilton, Bradford, and M'Govock,
fell in this rencontre.  By this time a considerable number had
re-crossed the creek and joined the chase; Captain Gordon, of
the spies, rushed from the front and partially succeeded in
turning the enemy's left flank.  The Creeks now fled in the
greatest consternation, throwing off their packs, and every thing
that retarded their flight, and were pursued for more than two
miles.  Twenty-six of their warriors were left dead on the field.
General Jackson's loss in the several engagements of the 22d

and 24th, was twenty-four killed, and seventy wounded. Judge Cocke, one of General Jackson's volunteers, entered the service at the age of sixty-five, was foremost in this engagement, continued the pursuit with youthful ardor, and saved the life of one of his fellow-soldiers by slaying his antagonist. In all the rencontres, one hundred and eighty-nine of the Creek warriors were found slain. A very seasonable diversion had been made in favor of the operations of General Floyd on the eastern boundary of the enemy. After the battle of the 24th, General Jackson was enabled to return to Fort Strother without further molestation.

The Creeks, encouraged by what they considered a victory over General Jackson's forces in the battles of the 22d and and 24th of January, continued to concentrate their forces, and fortify themselves at the Great Bend of the Tallapoosa. This river forms the north-eastern branch of the Alabama. Several miles above its junction with the Coosa, is a curve in the river in the form of a horse-shoe, called by the whites the Great Bend, and by the Indians Emucsau. The peninsula formed by the bend, contains about one hundred acres, and the isthmus leading to it, is about forty rods across; at the bottom of the peninsula is the village of Tohopisca, containing about two hundred houses. On this peninsula, the Indians from the adjoining districts had concentrated their forces, to the amount of one thousand warriors, with ample stores of provisions and ammunition, and had fortified themselves with great skill; having thrown up a breastwork, consisting of eight tiers of logs, with double port-holes across the isthmus, so that an assailing enemy might be opposed by a double and cross fire by the garrison, who could lie in perfect safety behind their works.

On the 16th of March, General Jackson, having received considerable reinforcements of volunteers from Tennessee, and friendly Indians, left Fort Strother with his whole disposable force, amounting to about three thousand of every description, on an expedition against this assemblage of Indians. He proceeded down the Coosa sixty miles to the mouth of Cedar creek, where he established a post called Fort Williams, and proceeded on the 24th across the ridge of land dividing the waters of the Coosa from the Tallapoosa; and arrived at the Great Bend on the morning of the 27th, having the three preceding days opened a passage through the wilderness of fifty-two miles. On the 26th he passed the battle-ground of the 22d of January, and left it three miles in his rear. General Coffee was detached with seven hundred cavalry and mounted gunmen, and six hundred friendly Indians, to cross the river below the bend, secure the opposite banks, and prevent escape. Having crossed at the Little Island ford, three miles below the bend, his Indians were ordered silently to approach and line the bank of the river; while the mounted men occupied the adjoining heights, to guard against reinforcements, which might be expected from the Oakfusky towns, eight miles below. Lieutenant Bean at the same time was ordered to occupy Little Island, at the fording-place, to secure any that might attempt to escape in that direction. In the meantime, General Jackson, with the artillery and infantry, moved on in slow and regular order to the isthmus, and planted his guns on an eminence one hundred and fifty yards in front of the breastwork. On perceiving that General Coffee had completed his arrangements below, he opened a fire upon the fortification, but found he could make no other impression with his artillery than boring shot-holes through the logs. General Coffee's Indians on the bank, hearing the roaring of the cannon in front, and observing considerable confusion on the peninsula, supposing the battle to be nearly won, crossed over and set fire to the village, and attacked the Creeks in the rear. At this moment General Jackson ordered an assault upon the works in front. The regular troops, led by Colonel Williams, accompanied by a part of the militia of General Dougherty's brigade, led on by Colonel Russell, presently got possession of a part of the works amid a tremendous fire from behind them. The advance guard was led by Colonel Sisler, and the left extremity of the line by Captain Gordon of the spies, and Captain M'Marry of General Johnson's brigade of West Tennessee militia. The battle for a short time was obstinate, and fought musket to musket through the port-holes; when the assailants succeeded in getting possession of the opposite side of the works, and the contest ended. The Creeks were entirely routed, and the whole margin of the river strewed with the slain. The troops under General Jackson, and General Coffee's Indians, who had crossed over into the peninsula, continued the work of destruction as long as there was a Creek to be found. General Coffee, on seeing his Indians crossing over, had ordered their places to be supplied on the bank by his riflemen; and every Indian that attempted to escape by swimming the river, or crossing the Little Island below, was met and slain by General Coffee's troops. The battle, as long as any appearance of resistance remained, lasted five hours; the slaughter continued until dark, and was renewed the next morning, when sixteen more of the unfortunate savages were hunted out of their hiding-places and slain. Five hundred and fifty-seven warriors were found dead on the peninsula; among whom was their famous prophet, Manahell, and two others, the principal instigators of the war; two hundred and fifty more were estimated to have been killed in crossing the river, and at other places, which were not found. General Jackson's loss was twenty-six white men, and twenty-three Indians, killed; and one hundred and seven white men, and forty-seven Indians, wounded

This decisive victory put an end to the Creek war. In the short period of five months from the 1st of November to the 1st of April, two thousand of their warriors, among whom were their principal prophets and kings, had been slain, most of their towns and villages burned, and the strong places in their territory occupied by the United States troops. After this battle, the miserable remnant of the hostile tribes submitted. Weatherford, the principal surviving chief and prophet, who led the Indians at Fort Mimms, accompanied his surrender with this address to General Jackson.

"I fought at Fort Mimms—I fought the Georgia army—I did you all the injury I could. Had I been supported as I was promised, I would have done you more. But my warriors are all killed. I can fight no longer. I look back with sorrow that I have brought destruction upon my nation, I am now in your power. Do with me as you please. I am a soldier."

A war with savages is necessarily attended with many circumstances distressing to the feelings of humanity. The Indian, having no means of supporting or confining his prisoner, knows no other mode of ridding himself of the burden, but by plunging the tomahawk into his head; and the Americans can no otherwise effectually prevent the savages from repeating their massacres, than by laying waste their villages, destroying their provisions, and compelling their surviving warriors to flee with their women and children into the wilderness beyond the reach of the whites.

The brilliant success with which this war was conducted and terminated, cast a mantle over its tragic scenes. The slaughter of unresisting warriors, and the burning of defenceless villages, marked much of its progress. To the enemy indeed no apology is necessary; the massacre at Fort Mimms, and the subsequent ravages of the surrounding country, would justify a war of extermination; and the unhappy victims can alone condemn the British and Spanish authorities by whose intrigues they were induced to engage in this fatal contest. The plea of necessity goes far toward justifying the mode in which this war was con ducted in the view of all. The savage warrior, who is suffered to escape, lives only to renew his ravages. The bold and decisive measures of General Jackson, in the conduct of this war, have probably prevented its ever being renewed by the same tribes, and struck a general dread among the surrounding nations. Though these considerations may justify the general mode in which the war was conducted, yet it is impossible to find a sufficient apology for hunting out and butchering sixteen warriors, on the day after the battle.

Soon after this victory, the Georgia forces, under General Floyd, formed a junction with those of Tennessee, and on the 20th of April, General Pinckney arrived at Fort Jackson, where the Tallapoosa and Coosa rivers uniting, form the Alabama, and assumed the command of all the forces in the Mississippi territory. New detachments of militia were ordered in to garrison the fortresses established in the Creek nation, and General Jackson and the Tennessee volunteers returned to Fayetteville and were discharged.

General Jackson and Colonel Hawkins were soon afterwards appointed commissioners to settle a peace with the Creeks; and on the 10th of August, concluded a treaty, dictated altogether by the United States commissioners. The Creeks yielded up a valuable portion of their territory to defray the expenses of the war; they conceded the privilege of opening roads through their country, and navigating their rivers, and stipulated to hold no further intercourse with the British or Spanish posts, and to deliver up all the property or persons of the whites, or friendly Indians, in their possession. On the part of the United States, the companies agreed to guarantee their remaining territory, to restore all their prisoners, and in consideration of their destitute situation, to furnish them gratuitously with the necessaries of life until they could provide for themselves.

# THE SEMINOLE WAR.

THE Creek war happily terminating in the spring of 1814, and a treaty of peace having been mutually concluded between the surviving chiefs of that nation, and the commissioners appointed on the part of the United States, but little opposition was apprehended from those Indians, who dissatisfied with the American government, had fled towards Pensacola. But it was found that they had united themselves with the different savage tribes, living within and on the borders of the Floridas, called Seminoles. In the fall of 1812, a settlement, located on the St. John's, was attacked, and eight persons were wounded; a party of twenty-one men, acting as an escort, were attacked, and two of them killed, and six wounded. Outrages of a similar character were continually occurring, and several of the Southern States, were kept in a continued state of alarm.

Colonel Nicholls, who had been expelled by General Jackson, went immediately to Florida, and organized a band, composed principally of negroes and Indians. In company with Francis Hillishago, a celebrated Seminole chief and prophet, he visited England, and entered into a treaty of peace with that nation. Arbuthnot and Ambrister succeeded him in the government.

Affairs continued in this unfortunate condition until 1817. In that year, the depredations of a party of smugglers in the Gulf of Mexico, was the first matter of importance that awakened the attention of the government. The smugglers, under the

(854)

command of one Aury, seized upon Amelia Island, which was made their rendezvous. Their conduct becoming outrageous, the executive resolved to employ force to suppress them. The ship-of-war John Adams, with a battalion of artillery, was ordered to expel the intruders from the island. On the 23d of December, the forces came into quiet possession of it; Aury and his party left in February.

Sometime before this Colonel Clinch, with an army composed of five hundred Indians, and some United States troops, was sent to attack a fort, which had been erected by the savages on the Appalachicola river. This fort was garrisoned by four hundred savages and negroes, who had twelve pieces of artillery. Clinch's force sailed up the river in schooners and gun-boats, each of which contained but one twelve-pounder, and twenty-five men; and although advised of the force of the enemy, the colonel determined to attack them. Scarcely had he commenced firing, when the principal magazine was struck by a hot shot, and the fort and two hundred and seventy-three of the garrison blown up. This event put an end to the war in that district.

Many horrid barbarities were practised by the Seminole Indians, some of which it may not be improper to mention. In the fall of 1817, the house of a Mr. Garrett, residing near the boundary of Wayne county, in East Florida, was attacked, during his absence, by a party of Indians, who murdered Mrs. Garrett and two of her children. They then set fire to the house, after they had plundered it of every article of value. Soon after, a man named McKrimmon, while on a fishing excursion, and having lost his way was espied and captured, by a party of Indians, headed by Hillishago. McKrimmon was bound to a stake, and the ruthless savages having stripped him and shaved his head, commenced dancing around him, yelling most horribly. Milly, the youngest daughter of Hillishago, when the burning torches were about to be applied, and the tomahawk raised to do its murderous work, placed herself between it and death, bidding the astonished executioner, if he thirsted for blood, to shed hers. A pause was produced by this unexpected occurrence, of which she took advantage by casting herself at her father's feet, and implored for his mercy. He yielded to her wishes, and McKrimmon was saved. He was ransomed some time afterwards, and married his deliverer.

In the frequent outrages committed upon the frontiers, it was somewhat difficult to determine who were the first aggressors. General Gaines, commander in Florida, demanded a surrender of those Indians, who had committed depredations on the frontier of Georgia. They refused, however, to comply with this demand, alleging that the first and greatest aggressions had been made by the white men. In consequence of this refusal, General Gaines received instructions from the secretary of war, to negotiate with the Creek Indians, in order that they might be transported to the country ceded by the United States government. General Gaines then summoned their chief Hornetlimed to appear at the fort. He answered by a haughty defiance. On the next day, Major David E. Twiggs, with about two hundred and fifty men, was sent against the fort. On the road he was attacked by a party of Indians, whom, after killing a number, he dispersed. He found the town deserted.

After this affair, Major Muhlenburg was dispatched with three vessels to Mobile, to obtain a supply of provisions. He had on board a number of volunteers and their families, beside the crew. He was obliged to halt on the Appalachicola, from sickness, where he was joined by forty men, under Lieutenant Scott. He detained half of his crew for his own use, and placed the balance, seven women and four children and the sick, on board the lieutenant's boat, and sent him back to Fort Scott. When near Flint river, the party was attacked by the Indians, and all killed with the exception of six men and one woman, who were carried into captivity, to undergo all the tortures inflicted upon the prisoners taken in battle.

The war now became serious. The Indians were assembled in considerable numbers, and made an open attack upon Fort Scott. General Gaines, with about six hundred regular soldiers, was confined to the garrison. In this state of things, General Jackson was ordered by the secretary of war to take the field. He was placed in command of eight hundred men, and directed that if he should consider that number insufficient, to call on the governors of the different states, for such numbers of the militia as he might think requisite. On receiving this communication, he immediately issued a proclamation to the West Tennesseeans, who had served under him in the last war, to join him in the coming struggle. Numbers obeyed his call, and were soon on their way to join him at Fort Scott. Jackson arrived there on the 9th of March, 1818; having mustered about one thousand men, principally Georgia militia, on his route. He found the garrison badly off for provisions, and determined to obtain supplies from the enemy; and for this purpose he pushed towards the Appalachicola on the 10th. General Gaines joined him on his march, and he built Fort Gadsden on the site of the Indian fort blown up by Colonel Clinch. He continued his march, and was joined by the Tennessee volunteers on the 1st of April. On the same day he drove back a party of Indians, and took possession of their town.

The grand army marched upon St. Marks, a Spanish garrison. Jackson learned that it was surrounded by a party of five hundred Indians and negroes, who had commanded its surrender. The place was one of great importance, being strongly built, and had once served as the main depot of the Indians, and was the scene of all their councils. As the garrison was feeble, Jackson determined to be before the enemy; and accordingly hastened on, and took possession of it, without encountering any opposition, sending the Spanish garrison to Pensacola. Here he captured Alexander Arbuthnot, and the two Indian chiefs Hornetlimed and Hillishago; the latter he hung.

Having garrisoned St. Marks with American troops, the army pursued its march eastward to Suwanee river, on which they found a large Indian town, which they destroyed, dispersing the Indians and negroes, after killing eleven of their number, and securing some provisions. On their return to St. Marks, bringing with them Robert C. Ambrister, who had been taken prisoner two days after the burning of the Suwanee towns. While at St. Marks, a court-martial was called, who found Arbuthnot and Ambrister guilty of inciting the Indians to aggression. Arbuthnot was sentenced to be hung, and Ambrister to be shot. The sentence was carried into effect on the 29th of April, and Jackson returned to Fort Gadsden on the same day.

Jackson received intelligence shortly after that the Seminoles were collecting near Pensacola, and that they were countenanced by the Spaniards at that place. Although Spain was then at peace with the United States, Jackson resolved to capture the garrison at Pensacola. On the 22d of May, he arrived near Pensacola, at the head of twelve hundred men. He was ordered by the Spanish governor to quit the country. He paid no attention to this, and entered the city on the 24th. He immediately commenced preparations for assaulting Fort Barrancas, to which place the governor with his small force had retired. After bombarding the place for three days, it surrendered, and the Spanish authorities were sent to Havana. The whole country was soon in the military possession of the United States, and General Jackson retired to the Hermitage, in Tennessee, leaving General Gaines in command, who acting under orders, captured St. Augustine. A treaty was concluded with Spain, in 1819, by which Florida was ceded to the United States.

# THE BLACK HAWK WAR.

In the year 1832, difficulties with the savages again broke out. These grew out of a treaty made with the Indians at Prairie-du-Chien, in 1823. An article in this treaty provided that any of the five nations concerned in it visiting the United States, should be protected from all insults by the garrison. Notwithstanding this, in the summer of 1827, a party of twenty-four Chippeways, on a visit to Fort Snelling, were fallen upon by a band of Sioux, who killed and wounded eight of them. The commandant of the fort captured four of the Sioux, and delivered them into the hands of the Chippeways, who immediately shot them. Red Bird, the Sioux chief, repaired to Prairie-du-Chien, with three companions, desperate as himself, about the 1st of July, and there killed two persons, wounded a third, and without taking plunder, retired to Bad-axe river. Here, soon after, he waylaid two keel-boats, that had been conveying some missionaries to Fort Snelling, in one of which, two persons were killed, the others escaped with little injury. Not long after, General Atkinson marched into the Winnebago country, and captured some hostile Winnebagoes and Red Bird, who died soon afterwards in prison. The Indians who were imprisoned for the murder at Prairie-du-Chien, were discharged, and Black Hawk and two others, who had been imprisoned for the attack on the boat, were also liberated.

It had been determined by the American government to sell

the land occupied by the Sacs and Foxes, and they were advised to remove. A majority of the nation, with their chief, Keokuk, determined to accept this advice; but Black Hawk, and a party who favored his cause, resolved at all hazards to remain. Outrages upon the Indians now became quite frequent. They were at last obliged to take up arms in self-defence, and a war would certainly have ensued, had not General Gaines, commander of the western division of the army, hastened to the scene of action. A council of chiefs was called, in which it was agreed that the Indians should instantly remove. They did so, crossing the river, and settling upon its western bank.

Black Hawk, however, determined to return to Illinois with his band, giving out that he had been invited by the Pottawatomies, residing on Rock river, "to spend the summer with them and plant corn on their lands." They recrossed the river, and marched towards the above named Indians, but without attempting to harm any one upon the road. The traveller passed by them without receiving any injury, and the inmates of the lowly hut experienced no outrage. There is little doubt but this amicable disposition would have continued had not the whites been the first to shed blood. Five or six Indians, in advance of the main party, were captured, and excepting one who escaped, put to death by a battalion of mounted militia. That one brought the news to Black Hawk, who immediately determined on revenge. He accordingly planned an ambuscade, into which the militia were enticed, fired upon, and fourteen of their number killed. The remainder fled in disorder.

As war had now begun, the Indians seemed resolved to all the mischief in their power. Accordingly they divided into parties, proceeded in different directions, and fell upon the settlements which were at that time thinly scattered over the greater part of Illinois. By this means they committed such outrages that the whole state was in the greatest excitement. Governor

Reynolds ordered out two thousand additional militia, who, on the 10th of June, assembled at Hennepin, on the Illinois river, and were soon engaged in pursuit of the Indians.

A party of savages attacked a small settlement on the 20th of May, 1832, and killed fifteen persons, and took considerable plunder. Five persons were also killed near Galena, shortly afterwards. General Dodge who happened to be in the neighborhood, with some mounted men, immediately started in pursuit. He came upon a party of twelve Indians, whom he supposed to be among those who had committed these murders. He drove them into a swamp, into which his mounted men pushed, and cut them off to a man; the whites then scalped the slain, that they might not be outdone in these or any other barbarities, by their savage foes.

In the meantime, the main body of Indians, under Black Hawk, were pursued by General Atkinson. They were encamped near the Four Lakes. Instead of making his escape by crossing the Mississippi, as was expected, Black Hawk descended the Wisconsin, by which means General Dodge came upon his track, and commenced a vigorous pursuit. He was overtaken by the general, about forty miles from Fort Winnebago, on the 21st of July. The Indians were in the act of crossing the Wisconsin. A short engagement followed, in which the Indians were beaten. It being dark, Dodge could not pursue them with any advantage. It is supposed that Black Hawk lost about forty men.

The Indians were now in a truly deplorable condition; several of them were greatly emaciated for want of food, and some even starved to death. In the pursuit previous to the battle, the soldiers found several lying dead on the road. Yet so far from being subdued they resolved to continue hostilities as long as they were able.

Meanwhile an army under General Scott, destined for the subjugation of Black Hawk, and the removal of all the north-western Indians to lands beyond the Mississippi, had been attacked by an enemy far more fatal than the Indians. With about one thousand regular troops, Scott sailed from Buffalo in a fleet of steamboats, across Lake Erie for Chicago. This was early in July. On the 8th of that month, the Asiatic cholera appeared on board the vessel in which were General Scott, his staff, and two hundred and twenty soldiers. In six days fifty-two men died, and soon after eighty were put on shore sick at Chicago.

In the summer, Scott left Chicago with but four hundred effective men, and hurrying on to the Mississippi, joined General Atkinson at Prairie-du-Chien, immediately after the battle, near the Badare river, which resulted in the defeat of Black Hawk.

Previous to this affair, a captured squaw had informed the whites that Black Hawk intended to proceed to the west side of the Mississippi, above Prairie-du-Chien—the horsemen striking across the country, whilst the others proceeded by the Wisconsin. A number of the latter were made prisoners on the road.

The steamboat Warrior was soon after sent up the Mississippi, with a small force on board, in hopes they might somewhere discover the savages. Upon the arrival of the boat at Prairie-du-Chien, the last of July, she was dispatched to Wapashaw village, one hundred and twenty miles higher up the river, to inform the inhabitants of the approach of the Sacs, and to order all the friendly Indians down to Prairie-du-Chien. On the return of the steamboat, they met one of the Sioux bands, who told them their enemies were encamped on Bad-axe river to the number of four hundred. The Warrior here stopped to take in some wood and prepare for action. They discovered the enemy about four o'clock on the afternoon of the 1st of August, who, as they approached, raised a white flag, which being looked upon as a decoy, no attention was paid to it. They declined sending a boat on board when ordered. After giving them a few minutes to remove their women and children, (a piece of courtesy somewhat rare in our border wars,) the boat fired a six-pounder, loaded with cannister, and followed by a severe fire of musketry. The battle continued for about an hour, when she weighed anchor and proceeded to Prairie-du-Chien. Twenty-three of the Indians were killed and many wounded. The Americans lost none.

Before the steamboat could return to the battle-field, next morning, General Atkinson and his army had engaged the Indians. The Warrior joined the contest; the army this day lost eight or nine killed, and seventeen wounded, whom the Warrior took to Prairie-du-Chien at night, and also captives to the number of thirty-six, women and children. The spot where this battle took place was about forty miles above Prairie-du-Chien, on the north side of the Mississippi, opposite the mouth of the Iowa. It was very fortunate for the whites, that they were able to co-operate on land and water at the same time.

After a toilsome and weary march, General Gaines overtook Black Hawk. The Indians were discovered in a deep ravine at the foot of a precipice, over which the army had to pass. Notwithstanding the misery of their condition, nothing but the bayonet's point routed them. Old logs, high grass, and large trees covered them until the charge was made, and as they were driven from one covert, they readily found another, and thus protracted the contest. At length, General Atkinson disposed his forces so as to come upon them from above, below, and in the centre. No chance now remained for the Indians but to swim the Mississippi, or elude the vigilance of their enemy by land, who had nearly encompassed them. Many, therefore, ventured to cross the river; but as the slaughter was greatest there, few escaped. However, a considerable number succeeded in escaping by land. One hundred and fifty were supposed to have been killed in this battle. Black Hawk was among those who escaped. His men deserted him continually, and came over to the whites. He was hunted like the wild deer of the forest, from place to place, until after many wanderings and much suffering, he was at last captured, and delivered up to General Street at Prairie-du-Chien. Here the war terminated. In his speech to General Street, he regretted his being obliged to close the war so soon, without having given the whites much more trouble. He asserted that he had done nothing of which he was ashamed, but that an Indian who was as bad as the white men would not be allowed to live in his community. He concluded as follows: "Farewell, my nation! Black Hawk tried to save you, and revenge your wrongs. He drank the blood of some of the whites. He has been taken prisoner, and his plans are stopped. He can do no more. He is near his end. His sun is setting, and he will rise no more. Farewell to Black Hawk."

Negotiations were commenced in September, by General Scott, with the Sacs and Foxes, by which five millions of acres of land were ceded to the United States on terms satisfactory to both parties.

On the return of peace, Black Hawk and his son were taken to Washington to visit the President. At different places on his route, he received many valuable presents, and was looked upon with great curiosity and interest. They returned by way of Detroit, and arrived at Fort Armstrong, in August, 1838. Black Hawk died at his village, on the Des Moines river, on the 3d of October, 1838.

# THE FLORIDA WAR.

As a Spanish province, Florida seemed to be a refuge for those savages, who still cherished a bitter feeling against the United States. In a treaty concluded between the Seminole Indians and the American government, they agreed to relinquish all claim to the land for a stipulated sum, and to retire beyond the Mississippi. It was further agreed that a number of them should visit the country in question, and give their opinion of it. Their report was very favorable, and every thing seemed to prosper precisely in accordance with the wishes of the American government. At this important moment, John Hert, who was one of the chief men of the tribe, died. The opportunity was too good to be lost, and it was seized by Osceola, or Powell, a celebrated chief, who quickly rose to the same importance as Hert himself; but it was wielded with far different purposes. Hert had always been in favor of the emigration of the Indians, but Osceola was opposed to it, and he used every means in his power to inflame the minds of his people against the whites, and against the execution of this measure. So violent did his conduct become, that he was arrested by the Indian agent, and put in irons; but subsequently professing to renounce his opposition he was released.

On the 19th of July, a party of Seminole Indians crossed their bounds, near the Hogstown settlement, for the purpose of hunting. They separated, and agreed to meet on a certain day. On

that day five of them were met together, when a party of white
men came by and commenced flogging them with their whips.
Two other Indians came up, and fired upon the whites, who
returned their fire. Three whites were wounded, and one Indian
killed and one wounded. On the 6th of August, Dalbon, the
mail-carrier, from Camp King to Tampa Bay, was murdered,
and although General Thompson, the Indian agent, demanded
the offenders, and the chiefs promised to deliver them up, they
were never brought to justice. In September, a party of Micka-
sukies, led by Osceola, waylaid and shot Charley Amatha, a
powerful friendly chief.

Other outrages of a similar character, increased so fast, that
the interior settlements had to be abandoned, and many families fled to other states, and General Clinch, who commanded in
that region, was obliged to call on the government for larger
forces to resist the Indians. His force amounted to but two
hundred and fifty men; and not receiving any assistance from
President Jackson, he obtained six hundred and fifty militia
from the governor of Florida. With this number, he commenced
active operations, and marched against the station on the Ouithlacoochee river.

The companies of Captains Gardiner and Frazer marched
from Tampa Bay to Fort King, on the 23d of December, 1835,
under the command of Major Dade. A six-pounder had to be
left behind, in consequence of the team that had been engaged
to transport failing. Major Dade wrote to Major Belton urging
him to forward it at once. Three horses and the necessary harness were purchased, and it joined the column that night.
Nothing was heard from the detachment until the 29th of December, when one of the soldiers, named Thomas, returned, and
another named Ransom Clarke, on the 31st. The latter gave
the following account of the fate of his comrades:

"It was eight o'clock. Suddenly I heard a rifle-shot in the

direction of the advanced guard, and this was immediately followed by a musket shot from that quarter. Captain Frazer had ridden by me a moment before, in that direction. I never saw him afterwards. I had not time to think of the meaning of these shots before a volley, as if from a thousand rifles, was poured in upon us from the front, and all along our left flank. I looked around me, and it seemed as if I was the only one left standing in the right wing. Neither could I, until several other volleys had been fired at us, see an enemy—and when I did I could only see their heads and arms peering out from the long grass, far and near, and from behind the pine trees. The ground seemed to me an open pine barren, entirely destitute of any hammock. On our right and a little to our rear was a large pond of water some distance off. All around us were heavy pine trees, very open, particularly towards the left, and abounding with long high grass. The first fire of the Indians was the most destructive, seemingly killing or disabling one half our men.

"We promptly threw ourselves behind trees, and opened a sharp fire of musketry. I, for one, never fired without seeing my man, that is, his head and shoulders. The Indians chiefly fired lying or squatting in the grass. Lieutenant Bassinger fired five or six pounds of cannister from the cannon. This appeared to frighten the Indians, and they retreated over a little hill to our left, one-half or three-quarters of a mile off, after having fired not more than twelve or fifteen rounds. We immediately then began to fell trees, and erect a little triangular breastwork. Some of us went forward to gather the cartridge boxes from the dead, and to assist the wounded. I had seen Major Dade fall to the ground by the first volley, and his horse dashed into the midst of the enemy. Whilst gathering the cartridges, I saw Lieutenant Mudge sitting with his back reclining against a tree, his head fallen, and evidently dying. I spoke to him, but he did not answer. The interpreter, Louis, it is said, fell by the first fire.*

"We had barely raised our breastwork knee high, when we again saw the Indians advancing in great numbers over the hill to our left. They came on boldly till within a long musket-shot, when they spread themselves from tree to tree to surround us. We immediately extended as light infantry, covering ourselves by the trees, and opening a brisk fire from cannon and musketry. The former I don't think could have done much mischief, the Indians were so scattered.

"Captain Gardiner, Lieutenant Bassinger, and Dr. Gatlen, were the only officers left unhurt by the volley which killed Major Dade. Lieutenant Henderson had his left arm broken, but he continued to load his musket and to fire it, resting it on the stump, until he was finally shot down; towards the close of the second attack, and during the day, he kept up his spirits and cheered the men. Lieutenant Keyes had both his arms broken in the first attack; they were bound up and slung in a handkerchief, and he sat for the remainder of the day, until he was killed, reclining against the breastwork, his head often reposing upon it, regardless of every thing that was passing around him.

"Our men were by degrees all cut down. We had maintained a steady fight from eight o'clock until two P.M., or thereabouts, and allowing three quarters of an hour interval between the first and second attack, had been pretty busily engaged for more than five hours. Lieutenant Bassinger was the only officer left alive, and he severely wounded. He told me as the Indians approached to lie down and feign myself dead. I looked through the logs, and saw the savages approaching in great numbers. A heavy-

---

* It has since been learned that this person only feigned death, and that he was spared, and read all the dispatches and letters that were found upon the dead to the victors.—*Cohen.*

made Indian of middle stature painted down to the waist, and whom I suppose to have been Micanope, seemed to be the chief. He made them a speech, frequently pointing to the breastwork. At length, they charged into the work; there was none to offer resistance, and they did not seem to suspect the wounded being alive — offering no indignity, but stepping about carefully, quietly stripping off our accoutrements, and carrying away our arms. They then retired in a body in the direction whence they came.

"Immediately upon their retreat, forty or fifty negroes on horseback, galloped up and alighted, tied their beasts, and commenced with horrid shouts and yells the butchering of the wounded, together with an indiscriminate plunder, stripping the bodies of the dead of clothing, watches, and money, and splitting open the heads of all who showed the least signs of life with their axes and knives; and accompanying their bloody work with obscene and taunting derision, and with frequent cries of 'what have you got to sell?'

"Lieutenant Bassinger heard all the negroes butchering the wounded, at length sprang up, and asked them to spare his life. They met him with the blows of their axes, and their fiendish laughter. Having been wounded in five different places myself, I was pretty well covered with blood, and two scratches that I had received on my head, gave me the appearance of having been shot through the brain, for the negroes, after catching me up by the heels, threw me down, saying, 'damn him, he's dead enough!' They then stripped me of my clothes, shoes, and hat, and left me. After stripping all the dead in this manner, they trundled off the cannon in the direction the Indians had gone, and went away. I saw them first shoot down the oxen in their gear, and burn the wagon.

"One of the soldiers who escaped, says they threw the cannon in the pond, and burned its carriage also. Shortly after the negroes went away, one Wilson, of Captain Gardiner's company, crept from under some of the dead bodies, and hardly seemed to be hurt at all. He asked me to go back with him to the fort, and I was going to follow him, when, as he jumped over the breastwork, an Indian sprang from behind a tree and shot him down. I then lay quiet until nine o'clock that night when D. Long, the only living soul beside myself, and I started upon our journey. We knew it was nearest to go to Fort King, but we did not know the way, and we had seen the enemies retreat in that direction. As I came out, I saw Dr. Gatlen stripped among the dead. The last I saw of him whilst living, was kneeling behind the breastwork, with two double-barrelled guns by him, and he said, 'Well, I have got four barrels for them !' Captain Gardiner, after being severely wounded, cried out, 'I can give you no more orders, my lads, do your best !' I last saw a negro spurn his body, saying, with an oath, 'that's one of their officers.'

"My comrades and myself got along quite well, until the next day, when we met an Indian on horseback, and with a rifle, coming up the road. Our only chance was to separate—we did so. I took the right, and he the left of the road. The Indian pursued him. Shortly afterwards I heard a rifle shot, and a little after another. I concealed myself among some scrub and saw-palmetto, and after awhile saw the Indian pass, looking for me. Suddenly, however, he put spurs to his horse, and went off in a gallop towards the road.

"I made something of a circuit before I struck the beaten track again. That night I was a good deal annoyed by the wolves, who had scented my blood, and came very close to me; the next day, the 30th, I reached the fort."

Thus perished one hundred and six men, under circumstances of hopelessness and misery, rarely equalled in modern warfare. Intelligence of this tragic event spread a degree of horror throughout the country, lasting and powerful; and even at the present day, the name of the gallant, ill-fated Dade, is a spell-word to conjure up the feelings of sorrow. Three of the whole command escaped.

On the 31st of December, General Clinch, had a severe engagement with the Indians, near the Ouithlacoochee river. He started from Fort King on the 28th, with a large force, and on the 31st, after many difficulties, attacked Osceola in a camp, and after a sharp battle of an hour's duration, succeeded in driving the enemy from their position.

But independent of these conflicts, the ravages of the Indians over the whole country are stated to have been fearful. Women and children were murdered, and the hearth made desolate in every portion of the country. In the more settled parts, near San Augustin, the sugar-cane plantations, with the expensive works attached to them were destroyed. The slaves were in many cases either carried off or they voluntarily joined the Indians.

In this state of affairs, General Gaines, was actively employed in endeavoring to raise a body of troops sufficient to suppress all opposition. He moved from Fort King, down the Ouithlacoochee, on the 22d of February, and on the 27th he had a slight skirmish with the enemy, at Clinch's crossing-place, where he lost eight killed and one wounded. On the 28th, when again fording the river, the Indians made another attack, in which Lieutenant Izard was killed, and two other officers wounded. This system of warfare was carried on until the 5th of March, when a number of Indians with Osceola at their head, appeared before General Gaines's camp, and expressed a willingness to terminate hostilities. General Gaines replied that he was not authorized to make a treaty with them; that on condition of their retiring to the other side of the river, and attending a council when called on by the American government, they should not be molested. To this they assented; but, unfortunately, General Clinch, who had been summoned by express from Fort Drane, encountered their main body; and supposing themselves surrounded by stratagem, they fled. Thus negotiations were ended for a time.

General Gaines was superseded by General Scott, and transferred his command to General Clinch, who retired to Fort Drane. Scott was succeeded by General Jessup. The summer and fall of 1837 passed away, without any thing worthy of note occurring, and the prospect of a reconciliation with the Indians was as remote as ever. In December, however, Colonel Z. Taylor, with a regiment of troops, came upon a trail of Indians, and commenced a vigorous pursuit. On the 25th, at the head of three hundred men, he came upon a body of seven hundred Indians, on Okee-cho-bee lake, under the celebrated chiefs, Alligator, Sam Jones, and Coacoochee. The Indians occupied a thick swamp, in front of which was a stream, rendered almost impassable, from the quicksands. The Americans waded through it, and the Indians were forced from their position, and driven some distance beyond the lake. We give Colonel Taylor's description of the battle-field, and his subsequent operations.

"Here I trust I may be permitted to say, that I experienced one of the most trying scenes of my life, and he who could have looked on it with indifference, his nerves must have been differently organized from my own. Besides the killed, (twenty-six in number,) there lay one hundred and twelve wounded officers and soldiers, who had accompanied me one hundred and forty-five miles, most of the way through an unexplored wilderness, without guides, who had so gallantly beaten the enemy under my orders, in his strongest position, and who had to be conveyed back through swamps and hammocks, from whence we set out without any apparent means of doing so. This service, however, was encountered and overcome, and they have been conveyed thus far, (Fort Gardiner,) and proceeded on to Tampa Bay, on rude litters, constructed with the axe and knife alone, with poles and dry hides—the latter being found in great abundance at the encampment of the hostiles.   The litters were carried on the backs of our weak and tottering horses, aided by the residue of the command, with more ease and comfort to the sufferer than I could have supposed possible, and with as much as they could have been in ambulances of the most improved and modern construction.    *    *    *    *    *

" We left our encampment on the morning of the 27th, for the Kissamee, where I had left my heavy baggage, which place we reached about noon on the 28th.   After leaving two companies and a few Indians to garrison the stockade, which I found nearly completed on my return, by that active and vigilant officer, Colonel Monroe, 4th artillery.   I left the next morning for this place, where I arrived on the 31st, and sent forward the wounded next day to Tampa Bay, with the 4th and 6th infantry, the former to halt at Fort Frazer, remaining here myself with the 1st, in order to make preparations to take the field again as soon as my horses can be recruited, most of which have been sent to Tampa, and my supplies in a sufficient state of forwardness to justify the measure."

Colonel Taylor was enabled by this battle to advance farther into the Indian country than any commander had previously done.   Shortly after this affair, Taylor was made a brigadier-general, and in 1838 was appointed to the command of the forces in Florida.   Although he had several minor skirmishes with the Indians, he could never bring them to a general battle. Bloodhounds were employed to drive the enemy from their hiding-places, but they were found to be of no avail.

Many heart-rending barbarities were committed by the Indians about this time.  The details of some are horrible.  Whole families, helpless old men and women, innocent children, and tender infants, were alike the subject of the tomahawk and scalping-knife. One instance will serve to give an idea of the attrocities practised at this period.

"It becomes again our mournful duty to record the successful effusion of blood in this all-fated territory, and the triumphant accomplishment on the part of the Indians of an adventure bordering on romance. Indian Key, a small spot of not over seven acres in extent, about thirty miles from our main land, on our southern Atlantic coast, was invested with seventeen boats, containing Indians, seven of its inhabitants murdered, the island plundered, and its buildings burned.

"About two o'clock on the morning of the 7th instant, a Mr. Glass, in the employ of Mr. Houseman, happening to be up, saw boats approaching, and informed a person in the same employ, when they passed into Mr. Houseman's garden, and were satisfied that the boats contained Indians. The Indians now commenced firing upon the house of Mr. Houseman, and Dr. Perrine; the former of whom with his family, and Mr. Charles Howe and his family succeeded in escaping to boats and crossed over to Tea-table Key. The family of Dr. Perrine passed through a trap-door into their bathing-room, from whence they got into a turtle-crawl, and by great efforts removed the logs, and escaped to the front of Houseman's store. They then went to a boat at the wharf, which six Indians had partly filled, and were in the store after a further supply. They then pushed off, and pulled with an oar, a paddle, and poles, towards the schooner Medium. When they had rowed a mile, they were met by a boat and taken to the schooner.

"Mr. Motte and wife, and Mrs. Johnson, a lady of seventy years of age, fled into an outhouse, from whence Mrs. Motte was dragged by an Indian, and while in the act of calling on her husband, 'John, save me!' she was killed. Mr. Motte shared the same fate, and was scalped; but the old lady, as she was dragged forth, suddenly jerking from the Indians broke his hold and escaped under a house. Her grandchild, a daughter of Mrs. Motte, aged four years, was then killed with a club, and the infant strangled and thrown into the water. This was seen by Mrs. Johnson from her hiding-place; but the Indians fired the building, she was again forced to flee, and after secreting herself under Malony's wharf, was finally rescued. James Sturdy, a boy about eleven years of age, hid himself in the cistern, under Mr. Houseman's house, and was scalded to death by the burning building heating the water. The remains of an adult skeleton were found among the ruins of Dr. Perrine's house, supposed to be the doctor, as well as that of a child, thought to have been a slave of Mr. Houseman.

"The Indians were what is known as Spanish Indians, and were headed by Chekekia, the same chief who led the party that massacred the men at Calooshatchee. They obtained a great amount of plunder from the houses and stores; and whilst engaged in obtaining these article, Mrs. Perrine, with her two daughters and a little son, reached a boat partially loaded, and put off to the schooner Medium, lying at some distance. They were promptly rescued by a boat coming to their assistance, and were taken to the schooner.

On Mr. Houseman reaching Tea-table Bay, Midshipman Murray, of the United States Navy, started with his only available force of fifteen men and two swivels. Ten of the men were in the hospital, so sick as to be certainly unfit for duty; but on urging their claims were permitted to accompany the others, hoping to cut off the boats, and thus prevent the escape of the Indians. On the second fire of his guns, they recoiled overboard, and the Indians then commenced a fire upon his boat, from a six-pounder belonging to Mr. Houseman, charged with musket-balls, and drove back this active officer.

"Communication was immediately dispatched to Lieutenant

McLaughlin, who was at Key Biscayne, with the United States schooners, Flirt and Ostego, and they proceeded down. The Indians, however, escaped, after maintaining possession of the island twelve hours, carrying off large quantities of powder and other articles, and laying the little settlement in ashes. All escaped save the unfortunates named above.

"Among all the bold and lawless feats which have characterized the enemy during the war, there is nothing that will bear comparison with this. We have seen the murdered remains of the citizen and soldier almost within sight of the garrison, when the white flag of overture was waving to these inhuman rascals in the act of kindness. We have seen the armed rider stricken by the bullet from the covert of the hammock, and the carriage of the traveller made to receive the last life-blood of its occupant. We have seen the faithlessness of the tribe, even when the humanity of the white man was devising every means for its comfort, planning their accursed schemes of murder, and Caloosahatchee, the ground of confidence and good will, red with the blood of our troops and citizens. But an island we had thought safe. As little would we have looked for an avalanche amid the sands of Arabia, or the glowing warmth of the equator amid Greenland's icy mountains, as an attack from Indians on an island. A force too, of seventeen canoes, averaging five men each, make a voyage of at least thirty miles from the main land, ransack, pillage, and destroy, and return in safety!"

General Taylor retired from Florida, in 1840, and in April, General Armistead was appointed to succeed him. His operations were of the same tedious and unsatisfactory character, and he was in turn succeeded by Colonel Worth, in May, 1841. The campaign, under this officer, was commenced under circumstances the most unfortunate, he having not less than twelve hundred men sick.

Wild Cat, the famous chief, surrendered his whole tribe, inclnding Ceacoochee and his family, at Tampa Bay in August. Many other chiefs and tribes followed his example. On the 19th of April, 1842, the enemy were found in great force, near Okeehumphee swamp. Colonel Worth commenced an immediate attack, and totally defeated the Indians, who were pursued some twenty or thirty miles. The big hammock of Palaklaklaha was the scene of this battle. On the 4th of May, Hallush-Tustenugge, with eighty of his band surrendered, and on the 12th of August, Colonel Worth announced, in general order, that the Florida war was ended. This, however, proved to be premature, for hostilities again commenced, and Worth received the submission of a large body of Creeks at Tampa.

Thus ended the war in Florida, the most unsatisfactory, and least glorious one in which our country has ever been engaged. All the Florida Indians are now transported to the Indian territory, and the possibility of another "Florida War," obviated.

# INCIDENTS IN THE BORDER WARS OF THE MEXICAN INDIANS.

THE Indians on the border, between Mexico and the United States, have been for years in a state of almost perpetual hostility, not only with the Mexicans, but with our own people. Their object generally is the plundering of villages and the stealing of horses and cattle; but in accomplishing this object they frequently commit murders and carry off prisoners. In this system of warfare, the Apaches, Eutaws, and especially the Camanches, are very active. A detailed history of their atrocities would fill volumes.

A gentleman, writing from Santa Fee, under date December 25, 1853, gives a narrative, which we copy, as exhibiting in one thrilling view the whole horrors of these border wars. We think this detail of the sufferings of an individual may be regarded as comprising a perfect specimen of the war; and is, therefore, preferable to a dry chronicle of many of their savage inroads into the country of the white people. The writer in his letter says, I send you a copy of the "Narrative of Mrs. Wilson," whose wonderful escape from the Camanche Indians, and terrible sufferings while with them, cannot but excite the sympathies of the whole reading community of our common country. Mrs. Wilson is now with the family of Mr. Spencer, and is suffering much from the pains of premature labor, induced by

(378)

the savage barbarities which have been inflicted upon her. How long will our government submit to such a state of things? After reading this narrative can any one be found to say, "Oh, the poor Indian!"

I saw, and two months since conversed with this young girl, who had made her escape from the same Indians, and was sent by Governor Merriwether to her parents in Chihuahua. Her family is respectable; I know her father well. She was made a captive near Chihuahua, last summer, and now returns to her family. She told me that there were more captives among the Camanche Indians than Indians themselves. This may readily be believed when we know the fact, that in their forays into Mexico and Western Texas, they murder the men and take the women and children captives. Imagination can hardly conceive what these poor women endure; and the children are reared up to become more savage and barbarous than their captors. This administration could well immortalize itself by "wiping out" this tribe; but I am sick of the theme, and will write no more.

## A NARRATIVE

OF THE SUFFERINGS OF MRS. JANE ADELINE WILSON, DURING HER CAP-
TIVITY AMONG THE CAMANCHE INDIANS.

I was born in Alton, Illinois, on the 12th day of June, 1837, and am, therefore, in the seventeenth year of my age. My father's name was William Smith; my mother's maiden name was Jane Cox. I had five brothers and four sisters. I think it was in 1846 that we moved to Missouri, and settled at a boat-landing or ferry, called Jamestown, on the North Grand river. My father kept the ferry.

About eight years ago we moved from this place to Texas, and settled near Paris, in Lamar county. Here my father and mother died within one day of each other, leaving six orphan

children behind them. Three of my brothers had died before
the death of my parents. My eldest brother, who was in a
ranging company, now came to settle my father's affairs and
make provision for our support. He secured homes for us with
different neighbors, but took the youngest sister, our pet, with
him to place her with one of our aunts.

One day's journey from the place where he left, he was
attacked by the winter fever, and died in one week. I have
three sisters older than myself. Their names are Elizabeth,
Cynthia, and Caroline. My brother James and sister Ellen are
younger than myself. Ellen was four years old when my parents died. Caroline is a dwarf, and the neighbors thought that
the medicine the doctors gave her stopped her growth. She
was a dear child, and we all loved her because of her misfortune. [Here Jane was unable to restrain her feelings, and
burst into tears.] I lived with several neighbors until the 1st
of last February, when I was married to Mr. James Wilson, a
young farmer, just beginning life, with a little property, consisting of horses and cattle. He was but nineteen years of age
when we were married. We knew but little of life, for I was
not sixteen. I fear we were crazy in getting married while we
were so young. [Poor girl! when her thoughts went back to
this period of her life, she wept as if her heart would break]

We had heard that people became rich very fast in California,
so we concluded to move and commence life in that distant
country. We gathered together the little property we possessed
and joined a party of emigrants, consisting of fifty-two men,
twelve women, and several children. The father and brothers
of my husband were among the number. There were in all
twenty-two wagons, and the whole company was placed under
the command of Mr. Henry Hickman. We started from Hunt
county, on the 6th of April last, and took the route for El Paso.
We arrived at the Guadalupe Mountains about the 1st of June.

Here the Mescalero Apaches stole from us nineteen head of cattle; six men started in pursuit, but were driven back by the Indians. We then went to El Paso. My husband not being able to travel well with Mr. Hickman's train, he determined to remain at El Paso till the arrival of another party of California emigrants. Five of Mr. Hickman's men staid with us. While here, the Mexicans stole nearly all the property we had, and left us unable to proceed on our journey. We could do nothing now except make our way back to Texas.

About the last of July, we started on our return, with the fragments of our property, which the thieves had spared. On the 1st day of August, my husband and his father left us, and fell into the hands of the Indians. I saw them no more after this. I was told that they had been murdered. You may, perhaps, be able to imagine my feelings when I found myself thus bereaved and destitute, in a land of strangers. My misfortunes seemed greater than I could bear, but I knew not that heavier trials were in store for me.

Unable to continue my journey, I returned to El Paso, where I remained till the 8th of September, when I started once more for Texas, with my three brothers-in-law, in company with a small party, consisting of five Americans and one Mexican. Mr. Hart, who owned and commanded this train, having some business in Texas, which required his immediate attention, travelled very rapidly, and I hoped in a few days more to be in the midst of my friends.

As we had seen only one Indian on the route, we flattered ourselves that we should not be molested by any of the tribes which infest this route. When near the borders of Texas, some of our party stole three animals from Mr. Hart, and ran off. Mr. Hart, anxious to overtake the thieves, started in pursuit, taking with him my eldest brother-in-law, a lad some fourteen years of age, leaving myself, a Mexican, and the two boys to follow as rapidly as we could.  We were at this time within three days' journey of a military post at Phantom Hill, and were considered out of danger.  A discharged soldier being unable to keep up with us was some distance behind, but I saw nothing of him after this.  The day after Mr. Hart left us, as we were travelling, about noon, we saw two Camanche Indians charging upon us in front, and at the same time two others were seen driving up behind.  We were all very much frightened, and the Mexican jumped out of the wagon and went towards the Indians, in order, if possible, to gain their friendship.

The mules of our wagon, four in number, becoming frightened by the war-whoop of the savages, turned out of the road, and commenced running as fast as they could.  One of them fell down before we had gone far, and the others were then obliged to stop.  The Indians now came upon us, and ordered the Mexican to take the mules out of the harness.  While this was going on, I got out of the wagon, and looked on in breathless suspense.  After the mules were unharnessed, the Mexican was stripped of his clothing, his hands tied behind his back, and ordered to sit down upon the ground.  One of them went behind him and shot him with a gun, while another stabbed him several times with a large butcher-knife.  His scalp was cut off before he was dead, and put into his own hat; the hat was then worn by one of his murderers.  I was stupified with horror as I gazed on this spectacle, and supposed that my turn would come next.  But the Indians having secured the plunder of the wagon, mounted us on the mules and ordered us to go with them.

As I left, I looked back and saw the poor Mexican weltering in his blood, and still breathing.

We took the north-east direction, and travelled slowly till sunset, when we encamped.  Here the plunder, consisting of blankets, bedding, clothing, bridles, and some money which I

had in my pocket, was divided among the Indians. Some articles considered useless were thrown into the fire. My clothing
was taken away, except barely enough to cover my person. In
the distribution of the captives, the eldest boy, about twelve
years of age, was claimed by the chief; I became the property
of one of the others. I should have mentioned that one of our
captors was a Mexican, who had been stolen from Chihuahua
when an infant. He was now as savage as the Indians, and
claimed the youngest boy as his prize. The scalp of the Mexican was stretched on a stick and dried by the fire.

After giving us some meat for our supper, the Indians began
to secure us for the night. The boys, with their arms tied
tightly behind them, were taken under guard by two of the
savages. My feet were tied together, and I was obliged to lie
between the other two. I did not sleep any during the night,
for I was afraid of being killed.

The next day we resumed our journey, and travelled in the
same direction. The boys were mounted on good animals, and
had bows and arrows. Their faces were painted Indian fashion,
and they looked like young savages. They appeared to enjoy
this new mode of life, and were never treated with excessive
cruelty. I was mounted on a good horse, but being obliged to
sit astride the animal, the journey was exceedingly painful.

I had a fine head of hair, which I valued very much, but the
chief ordered it to be cut off; I was not a little mortified in seeing it decorating the heads of the heartless savages. My head
was thus left entirely unprotected from the intensely hot rays
of the sun.

Nothing of interest occurred except repeated acts of inhumanity towards me, until the twelfth day of my capture. At
this time we were joined by two Indian men and a squaw. These
were all the Indians I saw till after my escape. Up to this
time my suffering had been so severe as to take from me all desire

to live, but now they were greatly increased.  The squaw, from whom I might have expected some compassion, was evidently the cause of the new cruelties which I now began to experience.

My horse was taken from me, and I was mounted on an un-broken mule without a bridle.  I had a saddle, but it was worn out and good for nothing except to torture me.  This animal would frequently top me over its head of its own accord; but not being wild enough to gratify the malice of the Indians, the chief would sometimes shake the Mexican's scalp before its eyes. The beast would then rear and plunge in the utmost fright, and I would be thrown upon the ground with great violence.  I have been tossed from the mule's back as many as half a dozen times a day, and once I was so stunned that I lay a considerable time before my senses returned.  My repeated falls greatly amused the Indians, whose horrid peals of laughter might have been heard at a great distance.

I never saw them exhibit the first signs of pity towards me. It made no difference how badly I was hurt, if I did not rise immediately and mount the animal which had just thrown me, they would apply their riding-whips, or gun-sticks, or the end of a lariat, to my unprotected body with the greatest violence. The squaw would also help me to rise by wounding me with the point of a spear which she carried.  You may understand one object the Indians had in view in putting me upon this wild animal and causing me to be thrown so often, when I tell you I expected to become a mother in a few weeks.  They under-stood my situation, but instead of softening their hearts it only made them more inhuman, and subjected me to far greater sufferings.

I was obliged to work like a slave while in camp; while there was any service to perform I was not allowed a moment's rest. I was compelled to carry large loads of wood on my back, which being destitute of sufficient clothing, was mangled till the blood ran down to my feet. I had to chase the animals through briars and bushes, till what little clothing I had was torn into ribbons. I brought the animals to camp in the morning, and had to watch them till they were ready to start, and if one more wild than the rest ran off, I must chase and bring him back, and be knocked down by the savage chief for my want of skill. When we were ready to start, I had to catch and saddle my own mule without assistance. If the party did not start immediately, I was compelled to pull at the lariat which the Indians would fasten to a bush. They seemed to study every method of putting me to death by piecemeal.

Exhausted by incessant toil and suffering, and extreme anguish from my wounds, I could not work as fast as the Indians desired, and often when scarcely able to stand, and hardly knowing what I was doing, I have been required to do the work of the strongest man. And because of my inability to accomplish my task satisfactorily, I have been whipped till my flesh was raw. Large stones were thrown at me. I was knocked down and stamped upon by the ferocious chief, who seemed anxious to crush me like a worm beneath his feet. My head sometimes fell under the horses' feet, and then the Indians would try to make the beasts kick me. After all was ready for the day's journey, I was obliged to travel as fast as the others, riding sometimes over rocks and through bushes, aching and sore from head to foot, and exposed alike to cold and heat, sunshine and storm.

I have gone two days at a time without tasting food. The Indians depended on hunting for their subsistence, and sometimes had nothing to eat themselves—unless there was an abundance of food, I received little or nothing—when any game was killed, the Indians would tear out the heart, liver, and entrails, and eat them raw. I suffered exceedingly from thirst; I was not allowed to drink, except while in camp. We frequently crossed beautiful streams through the day, and I would beg the privilege of dismounting to quench my thirst. But the Indians would always deny my request with contempt. It was in vain I pointed to my parched tongue and head blistered by the rays of the sun. Nothing could soften them into pity, and I ardently desired death that my torments might come to an end.

Every indignity was offered to my person which the imagination can conceive. And I am at a loss to know how I have lived through the barbarous treatment which was inflicted upon me. Frequently my feelings were so outraged that I was tempted to kill my inhuman masters. My indignation burned particularly against the chief, and I thought if I could only cut him to pieces I could die content.

We travelled every day—we usually started about ten o'clock in the morning, and halted about four in the afternoon. The Indians were accustomed to go to the tops of the highest hills, and stand there gazing in every direction. We always spent the night on a hill, and were thus exposed to the cold autumn winds; we slept on the ground, generally without covering. When it rained the Indians made a tent of the blankets and wagon-sheets they had stolen from us, but I was not allowed to take shelter in it—I preferred sleeping outside in the storm.

After my mule had become so gentle that I could ride it without being thrown, it was taken from me and I was obliged to travel on foot. The road over which we passed was often very rough and stony, and full of thorns. My feet were wounded and bruised till they were covered with blood and greatly swollen. But still I was obliged to keep up with the rest of the party, and if I fell behind I was beaten till I was nearly senseless. The Indians often urged me on by attempting to ride their horses over me; many a mile of that road is marked with my blood, and many a hill there has echoed to my useless cries.

I travelled thus on foot some five or six days. After the

party were ready to start in the morning, the direction of the route was pointed out to me, and I was required to go before the others, in order not to hinder them. They usually overtook me before I travelled far. I had always intended to make my escape as soon as I found an opportunity. I never expected to reach any friendly settlement, but I did not wish to give the Indians the pleasure of seeing me die. On the morning off the twenty-fifth day after my capture, I was sent on in advance as usual. I had eaten no breakfast, and was very weak, but the hope of escape now supported me. I hastened on as fast as I could, and finding a suitable hiding-place, I turned aside and concealed myself in the bushes. After this I saw nothing more of my captors. I found afterwards by the tracks of the animals, that they had searched for me; they probably thought I would die, and therefore took less trouble to find me. I have no doubt the next time they pass that way they will look for my bones.

My situation was now distressing beyond all description; I was alone in an Indian country, some hundreds of miles from the nearest friendly settlements. I was without food, without shelter, and almost without clothing. My body was full of wounds and bruises, and my feet were so swollen that I could hardly stand. Wild beasts were around me, and savages more wild than beasts, roamed on every hand. Winter was coming on, and death in its most terrible forms stared me in the face— I sat down and thought of my lonely and exposed situation. But I could not weep; my heart was too full of woe. I remembered the events of the few preceding weeks. The husband of my choice had been murdered, and I was not allowed the melancholy privilege of closing his eyes, and seeing his remains decently interred. My little property had been stolen, and when within a few days' march of sympathizing friends, I was captured by savages, and after three weeks of indescribable sufferings, found myself wandering solitary and destitute in the midst of the wild prairies—my cup was filled to overflowing, but I resolved to live in hope, if I died in despair.

After remaining three days in the place where I first concealed myself from the Indians, I went to a grove about half a mile distant and built a little house of bushes and grass. Here I lived nine days. My only food was the blackberries which grew on the bushes around. I quenched my thirst at a spring near by. My wounds pained me exceedingly, and I was wasted to a mere skeleton for want of proper nourishment. It rained upon me seven nights in succession, and my little house was unable to protect me from the cold storms. More than once I spent a sleepless night, perfectly drenched in rain; while the wolves, sometimes coming within five steps of me, would make the woods ring with their frightful howlings. They would also follow close behind me when I went to the spring during the day; I expected some time to be devoured by them; but they are great cowards, and I could easily frighten them away.

When I slept I would dream of seeing tables spread with an abundance of every kind of food, but when I stretched forth my hand to satisfy my hunger, the effort would awaken me, and I would find myself weeping bitterly.

When absent from my house, on the twelfth day after my escape, some New Mexican traders passed by on their way to the Camanche settlements. While standing on a small hill, looking after them in order to be sure they were not Indians, I was discovered by some three or four of the party, who happened to be some distance behind. They immediately came towards me, and soon understood my situation. They kindly offered to take me with them, and I gladly bade farewell to my house in the woods. The Mexican put me upon a *burro*, and gave me a blanket and some men's clothing, in which I dressed myself very comfortably.

Two or three days after this we came in sight of a band of

Camanches, and as it was not safe for me to be seen by them, I was left behind in a ravine, with the promise that the Mexicans would return for me at night. As they did not fulfil their promise, I started towards their camp; about midnight, while wandering among the bushes, a Camanche Indian passed within twenty steps. I thought I was a captive once more, but fortunately the savage did not see me. I threw myself on the ground and waited for day. In the morning I started again for the camp of the Mexicans, but before I reached it, I was discovered by one of the trading party who was herding the animals. This man is a Puebla Indian, of San Idlefonso, and is named Juan Jose. To him more than to any other man in the party, I owe my present freedom.

He told me the camp was full of Camanches, and if they saw me it would be impossible for the party to save me. He made me lie down on the ground while he covered me with dried grass. I lay here all day, and at night crept forth to quench my burning thirst. Juan came and brought me some bread, and told me not by any means to leave my hiding-place the next day. That day lagged slowly along, and I could hear the dreaded Camanches passing and repassing and shouting to each other. At night Juan returned, bringing another blanket and several loaves of bread, and told me that I must remain here for several days longer, as the party were obliged to go further on, and could not take me unless I was willing to become a captive once more. I saw the party disappear the next day, and it seemed as if my hopes of rescue disappeared with them. But I resolved to wait till the appointed time was up.

In a ravine near by I found a large log which had been left burning; this fire I kept alive day and night, till the Mexicans returned, and without it I should probably have been frozen to death, as the weather had become very cold. I covered a hollow cotton-wood stump with bark and leaves to keep out the cold wind. This stump was my house during my stay here. When I could endure the cold no longer, I would leave my house and run to the fire, but was afraid to stay there long lest the Indians should see me. The wolves soon found out my place of retreat, and frequently, while I was in the stump, they would come and scratch around and on its top. The blackberries were very scarce here, and had it not been for the bread Juan Jose gave me, I do not see how I could have been kept from starving to death.

The eight days passed slowly by, and I knew not whether to give way to hope or despair. But on the eighth I heard several persons calling to each other. I feared they were Indians, but they belonged to the trading party, and were on their return to New Mexico. They had lost the place where I was concealed, and were shouting to each other to attract my attention. I was so overjoyed that I rushed towards them unmindful of briars and sore feet.

Juan gave me a fine horse to ride, and the whole party treated me with the utmost civility and kindness. On the thirty-fourth day of our return towards New Mexico, we reached the town Pecos. Here I met Major Carleton and Mrs. Adams of the United States army, who took the deepest interest in my comfort. Here I laid aside men's apparel, and was furnished with a supply from Mrs. Adams's wardrobe. After remaining at of Pecos a few days, I was conducted to Santa Fe, by the son of Governor Merriwether.

To Governor Merriwether, and also to the American ladies of this place, I cannot be too thankful for their friendly sympathies and uniform kindness.

The past seems like a horrid dream. I have related nothing but the facts, and no language that I can use can fully express the sufferings of mind and body which I have endured. My two brothers-in-law are still captives, and unless reclaimed they will become as savage as the Indians. The Mexicans saw them with the Camanches, but were unable to procure their freedom. One is twelve years old, the other ten, and unless the strong arm of government is lifted up for their redemption there is no hope for them.

# RECENT INCIDENTS IN THE TEXAS AND MEXICAN BORDER WARS.

SINCE the Florida, or Second Seminole War, the Indians generally have been under subjection, and no outbreak of a very serious character has taken place, until the last few years, during which, the savages, perhaps, apprehensive of further incursions upon their territories, have carried on what might be called a skirmishing warfare, and to such an extent has this reached, that another Indian war, with all its horrors and barbarities, threatens our extreme western possessions. The native Indians upon our western boundaries, when the tide of emigration set that way, frequently attacked the wagon-trains of the settlers and miners, who crossed the plains, and many a scene of bloodshed, attended with all the peculiarities incidenta. to savage warfare took place. Lately the murders, and the incursions of these denizens of the forest became so frequent, that it was deemed necessary, in order to check their advances, to send a body of troops against them. This was accordingly done, and a respectable force has recently been ordered into the disturbed district.

In the autumn of 1852, accounts were received that several powerful bands of Camanches and Mescaleros had removed to the country between the Rio Grande and Bolson de Mapimi, and that they occasionally sent out war parties. If some of the

(392)

statements are to be believed, these Indians could then muster upwards of two thousand warriors. They have destroyed several flourishing settlements, and in some instances ventured directly into the streets of large towns, and carried away property of immense value.

On the 3d of October, 1853, a party of soldiers under the command of Lieutenant Able George, who had been dispatched by General Lane, from Jacksonville, for the purpose of protecting the emigrants, had a skirmish with some Indians, and succeeded in dispersing them. Several actions of minor importance occurred between the whites and the Indians, although it was not until 1854, that the Indians began to be troublesome, and to render the presence of any large body of troops necessary for the preservation of the lives and property of the settlers among the western wilds.

In April, a fight took place between the Indians and the United States dragoons, under General Garland, whose official account we give.

After the fight between Lieutenant Bell and Lobo's party, the Indians crossed the mountains and showed themselves on the road between Taos and Santa Fe. On the evening of the 20th ult. Major Blake, commanding at Cantonment Burgwine, ordered Lieutenant John W. Davidson, with sixty men of companies " F" and " I," first regiment of United States dragoons, to make a scout in search of the enemy. He left the cantonment the same evening, accompanied by Assistant-Surgeon D. L. Magruder. The next morning, Lieutenant Davidson, with his command, came upon a party of Apaches, supposed to number two hundred warriors, at the foot of the north slope of the mountains, and not far from the small Mexican village of Cieneguilla. When the troops appeared in sight, the Indians immediately raised their war-whoop, and manifested a disposition to make an attack.

The camp of the Apaches was situated upon a mountain ridge, and in a position naturally strong and difficult of access. Lieutenant Davidson saw that an action could not be avoided, and therefore made the necessary preparations for battle. He dismounted his men, and with a small guard to protect and hold them, placed his horses a little ways in the rear. With the balance of his command, not more than fifty strong, he made an attack upon the camp of the Indians. The soldiers charged bravely up the ridge and carried the position of the Apaches, who were forced to retreat. They rallied, however, almost immediately, and attacked the troops at close quarters with great desperation; they were several times repulsed, and upon each occasion—seven in number—rallied again to the charge, in every instance exhibiting the utmost determination and bravery. The troops maintained this unequal contest for nearly three hours, when they were forced to give way and retreat, which they succeeded in doing, and reached Taos the same afternoon with their wounded.

The loss on the part of the troops was very severe. The official report shows twenty-two killed upon the field, twenty-three wounded, several of them badly; and upwards of forty-five horses killed and lost in the action. Of the Indians it is not known how many were killed; but Lieutenant Davidson judges they must have lost at least fifty or sixty. On the arrival of the troops at Taos, Major Blake immediately started for the scene of action, to bring in the dead bodies, and took with him twenty soldiers, all he could mount, a few Mexicans and Americans, and a small party of Puebla Indians. They succeeded in recovering the bodies of those killed, which they took to Taos, and had them interred.

This is one of the severest battles that ever took place between the American troops and the Apaches, and our loss much greater in proportion to the numbers engaged. The Apaches fought with a bravery almost unprecedented, and we are well convinced that nothing but the stubborn valor of Lieutenant Davidson and his men saved the command from entire destruction. The troops had greatly the disadvantage. The Indians selected their own position, on a rugged mountain ridge, and the dragoons had to charge up a steep slope to reach them. The latter were encumbered with their horses, which it required nearly a fourth part of the command to take care of, and the valley in which the troops were at the time of the attack was so filled with large boulders as to render the movement of the horses almost impossible. Lieutenant Davidson and Dr. Magruder were both slightly wounded.

Since the fight at Cieneguilla, the Indians have retreated to the west side of the Rio del Norte, and are now hotly pursued by Colonel Cooke, with nearly two hundred dragoons and a spy company of citizens and Puebla Indians, under the command of Mr. James Quinn, of Taos. The troops are on their trail, which leads among the mountains to the north; and as the Indians are encumbered with their women and children, and are reported in low spirits, we think there is some chance of their being overtaken.

General Garland has taken prompt and vigorous means to bring the war to a speedy and successful termination. A large number of troops, under the command of gallant and experienced officers, have been ordered to the north, and are now in rapid pursuit of the enemy. We cannot conclude this article without signifying our approbation of the gallant conduct of Lieutenant Davidson and Dr. Magruder, and to whose bravery and good conduct is justly attributed the safe retreat of the survivors of the command. If brevets were ever earned, they were upon this occasion.

On the 8th of May, Colonel Cooke, with about two hundred men, came upon a party of Apaches, at a place called Agua Caliente Creek. The Indians took post in a strong and almost inaccessible mountain position; but the troops bravely charged them, drove them from it, and pursued them a mile and a half, fording a difficult stream, passing over a broken country, and keeping up a running fight. A good deal of plunder fell into the hands of the Americans. The Indians left six of their number upon the field, while the loss of the whites was one man killed and one wounded. Colonel Cooke pursued the Indians for some distance, and so hard were they pressed, that they were often obliged to separate into small parties in order to save themselves.

Many were the stories of the murders and other depredations of the Indians, circulated about this time, and although doubtless somewhat exaggerated, they were of a character to render the inhabitants of the thinly populated district of New Mexico, careful and watchful, not knowing whether they would not be the next subjects for the tomahawk and scalping-knife. The mail-coaches were stopped, the bags rifled of their contents, the horses stolen, and the drivers in many instances murdered. An amusing incident is related in a letter from Santa Fe, to this effect: the May mail, going east, was attacked by the Indians, and all their animals stolen. They afterwards promised to return them upon condition that the mail men would cook them a good dinner, which was complied with and the animals were returned. Fancy the Red Men sitting around, and the Americans cooking dinner for them. The Indians, no doubt, enjoyed it finely.

We extract from a paper of that period, an account of the last fight and death of Lieutenant Maxwell, a very promising and gallant young officer.

For the last few months a severe and deadly war has been waged between the troops in this territory and a warlike though diminished tribe of Indians, called the Tarcarella Apaches. In one battle we lost two killed and four wounded; in another twenty-two killed and twenty-three wounded. But, however severe those battles were, (St. Belles and Danson's) no officer had fallen. And now to speak of the last fight, which occurred on the 30th June, 1854, and in which our little army has lost a young and promising officer—namely, J. E. Maxwell, son of Mrs. Maxwell, of Athens, Georgia.

Lieutenant Maxwell graduated from the Military Academy in 1850, and has served honorably and faithfully as a brevet and second lieutenant in the third regiment of infantry, ever since in this country. In the fight which Lieutenant Bell had with the Apaches, Lieutenant Maxwell, although it was the first time he had been under fire, conducted himself most gallantly, as a man and a Georgian. In another skirmish with the same Indians, being adjutant of the commanding officer, he ran the gauntlet with the coolness of a veteran; yet he was to the last' degree unassuming.

On the morning of the 29th of June, Brevet Captain Sykes and Lieutenant Maxwell, with about sixty dragoons, (there being no dragoon officers on duty at the post,) started in pursuit of the party of Apaches, whose trail had been seen the day before, a short distance from the post. After a hard and vigorous trail, the command came in sight of the savages, early on the morning of the 30th. Captain Sykes sent Lieutenant Maxwell, with twenty dragoons, up a precipitate "mesa," or small mountain, to cut off the retreat of a band of about twenty Indians, who were attempting to gain difficult and almost impregnable passes of the mountains. Lieutenant Maxwell being well mounted, charged at the head of his men, to cut off the enemy ere they could pass a certain point above him. Unfortunately, possibly from being better mounted, himself, one sergeant, and two men arrived at the summit of the mesa, some few moments ere the rest of his troops had closed up. As soon as Lieutenant

Maxwell, who was ahead, with the three men, arrived at the above place, the Indians showed themselves above, and commenced a deadly discharge of arrows.

Lieutenant Maxwell, with revolver in hand, emptied it with deadly effect; but ere he had done so, he had received an arrow completely through his body. He drew his sabre, and in doing so his bridle arm received another arrow, which passed through and glanced against his left breast. He still used his sabre, and when he received his last shot, he was in the act of sabring an Indian; but in that act, while his head was bowed to his horse's mane, he fell—and fell like a knight of old, in his harness—his sword grasped in his hand, and a smile upon his face. The Indians fled. Then came the troops thundering up the hill—but too late, alas! for poor young Maxwell had fallen! And as Captain Sykes saw him, with upturned face, lying stark dead, whom but a moment since he viewed in the prime and bloom of manhood, he bowed his head and wept, as none but a warrior can.

Lieutenant Maxwell was buried at his post, with military honors; and around his lonely grave were heard sobs and were seen tears adown weather-beaten visages, where tears were strangers. He died without an enemy. He died as a soldier should, and lies wrapped in his martial shroud, as a soldier's due.

During the remainder of the year, 1854, nothing of any great importance transpired; and hopes were entertained that the war had closed, and that there would be a disposition on the part of the savages to listen to terms. These hopes, however, were not realized. Some idea may be formed of the position of affairs at the beginning of the year 1855, from the following account taken from the leading paper published in New Mexico.

With the opening of the new year, a strong current of success set in in our favor, and in all our encounters with the Indians the troops have been successful. In the first instance, the gallant affair of Lieutenant Sturgis, in pursuit of the party who committed depredations at Galisteo, had a very beneficial effect upon these Indians, and taught them a severe lesson. They lost several men, and had taken from them all the animals which they had stolen at Galisteo. In the same month, General Garland sent an expedition under Captain Ewell, into the Mescalero country, which penetrated into the very heart of the tribe, and surprised them in their stronghold. The Indians turned out in force, and fought the troops, but they were practically whipped, with the loss of some twenty warriors, two of whom were chiefs. The result of the expedition was highly successful, and every thing was accomplished that could have been expected. The third check and severe lesson they received was upon the grazing camp of Captain Ewell. Fifteen Indians, in the middle of the night, fell upon three dragoons, asleep in their tents, and the latter, after a severe fight, succeeding in defeating and driving them off, with the loss of four or five wounded, three of whom, we learn have since died.

Immediately after this affair, the Indians came in and begged for peace. In these and all other encounters with the savages, the officers and men of our army have behaved themselves in the handsomest manner. The commanding general has conducted his military operations with great energy, and deserves credit for the efforts he has made to afford protection to all our frontiers. If the Superintendant of Indian Affairs had the requisite instructions, he would immediately proceed to hold a treaty with the Mescaleros, and thus have them secured from further trouble; but at present his hands are tied, and he can do nothing.

The condition of the other Indians has not changed. The Navajoes are at peace, and are quietly awaiting the proposed treaty with them. The Utahs and Jicarillas are still hostile, and seem not disposed to make terms until they are well chastised. An expedition of nearly six hundred men is now in their country, and we may shortly expect to hear of active hostilities between them and our troops. We have not heard of the Gila Apaches committing any depredations, since they were guilty of the ungenerous act of stealing the horse of their own agent. At present such is our relation with the Indians of the territory.

On the 19th of March, 1855, Colonel Fauntleroy, with two companies, met a number of Apaches and Utahs, well armed and mounted in the Chow-atch pass; and in the running engagement which followed, killed five Utahs. They came up with the Apaches on the next day, who retreated, leaving seven of their number dead. The Americans did not lose a single man, either in killed or wounded.

Captain Ewell, and Lieutenants Moore and H. B. Davidson, left Los Lunas in command of eighty dragoons, the latter end of December, for a scout into the south-eastern section of the territory, where these Indians have their range. The troops were accompanied by Dr. Kennon, a citizen, as surgeon, and were joined at Antonchico by Mr. Gleason, as guide. They struck the Pecos, down which stream they marched nearly three hundred miles, and on the 17th of January, they encamped on the Penasco, a fine stream running east from the Sacramento mount. Here they were joined by eighty dragoons and infantry under command of Captain Stanton, and Lieutenants Daniel and Walker, from Fort Fillmore. Thus far no Indians had been seen, but in the night they set fire to the grass around the camp, and opened a brisk fire of balls and arrows, apparently aiming at the only two tents there were in the command.

The next morning, the Indians appeared in considerable numbers on the surrounding hills, and commenced an attack. The column moved on, fighting as they went, and hastened to reach the Indian camp in time to find their families "at home." The ground was rolling and much cut up by the deep ravines,

which enabled the Indians to approach within a few yards of
the column and fire upon them, and the trail was narrow and
difficult to follow. The front and flank were kept clear by
skirmishers, and officers and men used every exertion to get at
the enemy, it being required to check the men, and keep them
from unnecessary exposure. Mr. Gleason was always conspicuous and among the foremost in the fight. These skirmishers
were at different times under Lieutenants Daniel and Moore;
the latter charging at the head of some mounted men, but the
horses were too much worn out to accomplish a great deal. Sometimes the Indians came within arrow-range of the column; and
at one time a large fellow stopped alone on the trail, until the
troops approached within range, when he deliberately fired, but
was instantly picked off by a skirmisher, a sergeant. About the
time this man fell, the Indians, on a hill near by, raised a terrible wailing, and it is supposed he was a chief. A Mexican,
from Mr. Beck's ranche, named Jose Martinez, claims to have
killed Santa Anna, the Big Chief, and recent reports from the
Mescaleros confirms his death. The fight was continued until
three o'clock in the afternoon, when the Indians retreated, having suffered considerable loss.

This afternoon, the column found the Indian camp, of three
hundred lodges, on the banks of the Penasco, where they had
collected in large numbers to have a grand feast on stolen cattle.
A few oxen and some ponies were found; the rest had been
eaten. During the fight, Captain Stanton, of the 1st dragoons,
and two men were killed. He charged a body of Indians, and,
led away by the ardor of pursuit, became separated from his
men, and, on his return, was attacked by large numbers from
behind trees and rocks, and unfortunately killed. He fought
with desperation, as two ponies were left dead, and one ran into
camp without a rider. The Indians were pursued one day beyond the sources of the Sacramento mountains, when they scat-

tered and fled in different directions, and the guides could no longer trail them. The troops started back the 20th of January, and Captain Ewell reached Los Lunas in eighteen days, the horses being so completely broken down that the men had to march on foot. The loss of the Indians was from fifteen to twenty. The country in which the fight took place was entirely new, never having been visited before, and is represented as a pleasant and well-watered region.

In September, 1855, General Harney gained a complete victory, over the Sioux Indians. It struck terror into the whole of the savage tribes occupying that extended section of the country.

In the early part of August, General Harney's command left Fort Leavensworth, and arrived at Ash Hollow on the 2d of September, at which point the general ascertained that a band of forty or fifty Brule lodges were encamped on the Blue Water Creek, a fine tributary of the North Platte, about six miles from Ash Hollow.

The general at once determined to attack the camp early on the morning of the 3d, and in order to be more sure of his game, he dispatched the principal portion of his mounted force at three o'clock in the afternoon, to gain a position in the rear of the Indians—a movement which had to be made in the dark of course, and over an exceedingly rugged country. It was, however, eminently successful, being effected without rousing the suspicion of the Indians.

General Harney left his camp about four or five o'clock in the morning, with the infantry portion of his command, merely leaving a sufficient force to guard the train, which remained at Ash Hollow during the operations. He moved directly upon the first Indian village, (for it afterwards turned out that there were two,) but before he could reach it, the lodges were all struck and their occupants in rapid retreat up the valley of the

Blue Water. This, however, was just what was expected and desired, for if the cavalry gained the position designed it, the Indians would be brought to a stand and be compelled to fight.

They finally halted and took up a position on the bluffs, which skirted the banks of the stream, within a few hundred yards of our cavalry, which had concealed themselves so adroitly, that the general himself doubted very much whether they had succeeded in gaining the point assigned them. It was for this reason that in a parley which here ensued between General Harney and the Brule chief, "Little Thunder," the general's principal object was to amuse the Indians until he became satisfied of the presence of the cavalry.

At last it became pretty obvious, from the commotion among the Indians, that something had been observed by them that made them very uneasy; so the general at once cut short the parley, and opened the ball to the music of the Minie rifle from the skirmishers of the sixth infantry. The bluffs were scaled by these in an incredibly short space of time and cleared of the Indians, who had scarcely left their stronghold before they found themselves intercepted by the cavalry and placed between two fires.

The affair had by this time become exceedingly lively. The Indians plunged down the bluffs with their light, sure-footed ponies, and darted off through the only avenue not closed against them, being pursued in most gallant style by the mounted troops, who followed four or five miles, sabring and shooting a large number of them on the way.

It is quite impossible, owing to the extent and nature of the country covered by the two parties, to ascertain precisely the loss of the Indians in killed and wounded; but from observations subsequently made on the ground of principal combat, the number killed cannot fall very short of sixty or seventy. About fifty women and children were captured, and some sixty ponies and mules taken.    As for lodges, buffalo meat, robes, camp furniture of various descriptions, the end has not been seen yet, although a number of wagons have been employed in bringing this booty into the camp.

The entire loss sustained by the command was four men killed, three dangerously wounded, one slightly, and one missing, supposed to have been killed or captured.

On the 1st of September, news was received that Major Neighbors, the supervising Indian agent for Texas, had concluded a treaty with the Anadahka, Waco, Toncahua, Camanche, Tahwaccaro, and Caddo Indians, which was intended as supplemental to the treaty of May 15th, 1846.   The Indians agreed to abandon their roving or hunting life, and to settle on the reservations set apart by the Texas legislature; to adopt laws and police regulations; not to leave the reservation without the consent of the agent, under penalty of forfeiting all rights as settlers under the treaty; to break off all communication with bands of Indians outside the reservation, who refuse to settle down, unless by consent of the agent.   The United States government to protect them, feed them, furnish them with farmers, and to take all the steps necessary to aid them in adopting a civilized life.

The Lipans, a band of roving Indians, were not included in this treaty.   They are west of the Rio Grande, and regularly enrolled as Indians of Mexico.   Three companies of mounted riflemen, have been ordered to this part of the frontiers, under the command of General Smith.

In the meantime, Captain Calaban, had been authorized by Governor Pease, to cross the Rio Grande, and hunt these Lipans, in Mexico, and put a stop to their devastations if possible.  The captain, with one hundred and eleven men, encountered the enemy at Eagle Pass, on the 2d of October, 1855, and we give his own account of the battle.

At noon we encamped on a small stream ten miles west of the Rio Grande, where we refreshed ourselves and horses. Up to this time the Mexican authorities and citizens had shown us much kindness, and evinced their good wishes as to the success of the expedition, and many even volunteered to enlist under me, but none were received.

After resting an hour or two, we marched off towards San Fernando, beyond which were the Indian camps. Having proceeded some ten miles along the highway to the city, over a widely extended prairie, about three o'clock in the afternoon, while marching leisurely along, we descried three horsemen approaching us from a mot of timber, about a mile to the northward. At first these men were not noticed; we supposed them to be Mexican herdmen—but on their approaching within two hundred yards of us, we discovered them to be Indian chiefs, ready dressed and painted for battle; and they were trying to decoy us from our position.

Forming my men in a line along the road, I waited for the enemy to begin the battle; for by this time large numbers had emerged from the timber, seemingly with the intention of attacking us; they soon spread out in front of us, and to our right and left, to the amount of several hundred horsemen, and commenced to fire on us. About this time one of our men fired on a chief, about two hundred yards distant, and broke a leg of his horse. Perceiving that the enemy, composed of both Indians and Mexicans, were trying to outflank us, I ordered my men to charge, which was executed in fine style, and thirty of the enemy were slain.

While making our charge the left flank of the enemy, which extended for nearly half a mile, came in our rear and opened on us a very severe fire, during which four of our gallant men were killed. The front and right flank, on which we charged, after a gallant fire, fled before us, leaving us in possession of the position which it was our object and determination to gain.    Then we discovered that our enemy numbered some six or seven hundred, as all their footmen were concealed in the timber, and had not advanced in view on the prairie.

My men formed in a strong position beneath the bank of a small creek, on which the enemy had been encamped, and their whole force coming up against us, we continued the battle for about three hours, when they fled in the direction of San Fernando, leaving some eighty-five killed, and with the loss of one hundred wounded.    This we learned from some Mexicans, who were engaged in the battle, and from other sources, since my report to his excellency, the Hon. E. M. Pease.

The same Mexicans have also informed me that the actual number of our enemy was seven hundred and fifty men.    After the retreat of the enemy, which was about dark, we, supposing that they would come on us again before day with large reinforcements, fell back to the Rio Grande, where we would be safe from any number of men and any quantity of artillery they might bring against us.

Approaching the town of Piedras Negras about sunrise, we took possession of it, and now occupy a position opposite Eagle Pass, on the west bank of the Rio Grande.

Captain Calahan, in this engagement, lost five men killed and two wounded.

The Indian War in Oregon, in the meantime is assuming a threatening aspect.    All the Indian tribes in that region, with but few exceptions, are in arms against the United States, and murders are very frequent.    But a small force has as yet been sent against them, yet active preparations are in progress by which we hope to see the savages submissive to the rule of the whites, and engaging quietly in the pursuits common to civilized life.    In October, 1855, information was received that an Indian war was in progress, in Rogue River Valley, caused by the murder of several packers, teamsters, &c., on the different routes near the Oregon boundary line. The military, at Fort Lane, seemed powerless to restrain or punish the marauders, and the population forced to rise for their own protection. A company of volunteers, consisting of one hundred and twenty-five men, was formed, and started on the 7th, for the scene of hostilities, under the command of Major Lupton, and Captain Williams. They encountered the Indians near the Rancherias, and an engagement ensued, which ended in the total defeat of the Indians, who left forty of their number dead upon the ground. Of the volunteers, twelve were wounded, one of whom, Major Lupton, died the same night. The Indians committed many depredations, in their flight. They burnt the house of a Mr. Jones, killing him, and mortally wounding his wife.

An account received about the same time, stated that Major Haller, with a body of troops under his command, had been completely surrounded by the Indians, at a point about twenty-five miles from the Dalles. He occupied a position upon a hill, with ravines and brush around him, from which the Indians were constantly firing upon his devoted band. They were in a complete state of siege, and had been for forty-eight hours without water. Major Haller, managed to send a messenger to Dalles in the night, who arrived safely, and reported the condition of affairs, and that at least one thousand men would be necessary to dislodge the enemy. Lieutenant Day with one hundred and fifty men immediately marched to his relief, and measures were taken to raise the required number of soldiers.

There still remains much doubt about the extent of the hostile feeling among the Indians. In a letter from General Palmer, it is stated that the chief of the Wacos reports that proposals have been made to all the tribes east of the Cascades to unite in a general war for exterminating the whites, but that many refuse to enter an alliance to fight the Americans. And yet among nearly all the tribes are found some restless spirits ready to join in a general war. The Yakimas seem well united in a feeling of hostility. The Clikitats are divided. All sorts of Indian tales of wrongs are reported to induce a war spirit, and threats of hostility made against such tribes as will not join the Yakimas. Those best acquainted with the Indian character are disposed to think that disaffection has been so widely diffused that one flush of victory on the part of the Indians in a contest with the United States troops would induce nearly all the tribes to unite in a general war. Hence much anxiety is now felt in the result of Haller's expedition against them. We are satisfied that unless the Indians have greatly the advantage in position, his troops will be enabled to route the Yakimas. We regret, however, that his command had not been increased to about two hundred and fifty men, half of whom should have been mounted. He then would have been able to make a demonstration so formidable as to have appalled the Indians in the first attack, and followed them so closely and effectually that they would gladly have yielded all hopes of success against the whites.

THE END.